ATIŚA'S STAGES OF THE PATH TO AWAKENING

Atiśa's Stages of the Path to Awakening

Together with Commentaries and Ritual Texts

James B. Apple

Wisdom

Wisdom Publications, Inc.
132 Perry Street
New York, NY 10014 USA
wisdom.org

Library of Congress Cataloging-in-Publication Data
Names: Apple, James B., author. | Atīśa, 982–1054. Bodhipathapradīpa. English.
Title: Atiśa's stages of the path to awakening: together with commentaries and ritual texts / James B. Apple.
Description: New York, NY, USA: Wisdom, [2025] | Includes bibliographical references and index.
Identifiers: LCCN 2024029773 (print) | LCCN 2024029774 (ebook) | ISBN 9781614298441 (hardcover) | ISBN 9781614298663 (ebook)
Subjects: LCSH: Atīśa, 982–1054. Bodhipathapradīpa. | Bka'-gdams-pa (Sect)—Doctrines—Early works to 1800. | Buddhism—Doctrines—Early works to 1800.
Classification: LCC BQ7950.A877 A643 2025 (print) | LCC BQ7950.A877 (ebook) | DDC 294.3/444—dc23/eng/20241209
LC record available at https://lccn.loc.gov/2024029773
LC ebook record available at https://lccn.loc.gov/2024029774

ISBN 978-1-61429-844-1 ebook ISBN 978-1-61429-866-3

29 28 27 26 25
5 4 3 2 1

Cover and interior design by Gopa & Ted2, Inc.

Printed on acid-free paper that meets the guidelines for permanence and durability of the Production Guidelines for Book Longevity of the Council on Library Resources.

Printed in the United States of America.

Dedicated to the memory of my parents,
Carol Jeanne Shafer Apple Bedwell (1944–2024)
and
James Boyd Apple, Sr. (1942–2024),
who taught me the stages of life.

Publisher's Acknowledgment

The publisher gratefully acknowledges the generous help of the Hershey Family Foundation in sponsoring the production of this book.

Contents

Preface ix

Introduction 1

Part 1. The Hidden Wellspring of Tibetan Path Literature

1. Stages of the Path to Awakening (by Atiśa) 29

Part 2. Commentaries and Exegesis

2. A Summary and Structural Analysis 87

3. General Meaning of the Stages of the Path 101

4. Instructions for Select Disciples (by Atiśa) 137

5. Pointing-Out Instructions in Sets of Five (Attributed to Atiśa) 183

Part 3. Performance and Ritual Texts

6. Enhancing Practice and Removing Obstacles on the Path 225

7. A Ritual for Generating the Awakening Mind 259

8. Essence of the Bodhisattva Vows (by Atiśa) 291

Appendix 1. Table of Texts 305

Appendix 2. Table of Tibetan Transliteration 309

Notes 313

Bibliography 345

Index 367

About the Author 389

Preface

Geshé Lhundup Sopa (1923–2014) introduced me to stages of the path (*lam rim*) theory and practice in the summer of 1992 on a retreat at Deer Park Buddhist Center in Oregon, Wisconsin. During this time, I acquired a used copy of Phabongkha Rinpoché's *Liberation in the Palm of Your Hand* from an old bookstore on State Street in nearby Madison. After that summer, on returning to Indiana University to finish my undergraduate degree, I worked shelving books on the ninth floor of what is now the Herman B. Wells Library. The ninth floor has one of the largest collections of Tibetan books in North America, and I would often look at the books between shifts. One time I spotted a volume entitled *Writings of Lord Atiśa on the Theory and Practice of the Graduated Path.* I was excited to see a work by Atiśa after my experience at Deer Park, so I unwrapped the volume and began to flip through the folios. My initial excitement became disappointment, as the text was in handwritten cursive script (*dbu med*), which I was not yet able to read. I carefully put the volume away and explored other Tibetan works. Now, three decades later, the present book contains a full translation and study of Atiśa's *Stages of the Path to Awakening* and its accompanying works for the first time in a modern Western publication.

I went to live at Deer Park for a year before pursuing graduate studies at the University of Wisconsin–Madison beginning in the fall of 1994. I learned further about the stages of the path from Geshé Sherab Thabkye and his translator Sharpa Tulku, specifically on Tsongkhapa's *Three Principal Aspects of the Path* (*Lam gyi gtso bo rnam gsum*). Geshé Sopa also introduced me to the stages of the path in the thought of Tsongkhapa (1357–1419) through several summer seminars at Deer Park from 1995 to 1998, when he taught mind training (*blo sbyong*) and Tsongkhapa's *Great Treatise on the Stages of the Path to Enlightenment* (*Lam rim chen mo*).

As I have noted in a previous publication (Apple 2018), I began to acquire facsimiles of the *Collected Works of the Kadampas* (*Bka' gdams pa gsung 'bum*) using available grant funds when I landed a position at the University of Calgary in 2008. In August of 2016 I acquired the fourth and final set of thirty volumes, containing volumes 91 to 120, published the previous year. As always, I was excited to explore the collection and learn about the teachings it contained. When I opened volume 91 and saw that it read "folios for the *Stages of the Path to Awakening*" (*Byang chub lam gyi rim pa la ldeb*) by Atiśa in the table of contents, a new level of excitement spurred my interest. My fingers raced through the pages, and when I saw the beautiful Tibetan script, I had a flashback to that moment twenty-four years earlier on the ninth floor of the Indiana University library. The folios were apparently a reproduction of the very same manuscript, and the modern Tibetan editors at the Paltsek Institute, in the preface to the facsimile, attributed the work to Atiśa. I immediately began to study and translate the manuscript.

I photocopied the facsimile and began transcribing and translating the *Stages* and other texts in August 2016, and by May of 2017 I had finished transliterating the manuscript, writing out the romanization on the back pages of the photocopy. Having analyzed the manuscript line by line, I presented a paper at the Pacific Northwest Region of the American Academy of Religion in May 2017 entitled "The Stages of the Path to Awakening (*Byang chub lam gyi rim pa*; **Bodhipathakrama*) of the Indian master Atiśa Dīpaṃkaraśrījñāna (ca. 982–1054): Analysis of a Forgotten Manuscript." This initial analysis and conference paper resulted in table 1 below. I continued working on the manuscript and translation and input the transliteration onto a computer. In March 2018, at the meeting of the American Oriental Society in Pittsburgh, I presented "Atiśa's **Bodhipathakrama*: A Significant, Yet Forgotten, Manuscript in the History of Inner Asia Buddhist Path Literature." I finished the transliterations and translations in 2019 and 2020.

Atiśa's collected works typeset in *dbu can* script in two volumes became available on the Tibetan Buddhist Resource Center, now the Buddhist Digital Research Center (bdrc.io), in August 2020, and they included *Stages* and its accompanying texts. I proceeded to check my own transliteration against the modern book-format volume. That volume contained some errors, readings of the facsimile that did not agree with my own. Also, the published volume did not divide the manuscript into twenty-seven texts as I had based on my own analysis. While finalizing the manuscript for the present volume, I decided to add the page numbers from the typeset edition to my translation for scholars without access to the facsimile reprints of the source manuscript. The typeset-edition page numbers appear in the first appendix below.

At Wisdom Publications, I especially thank David Kittelstrom, whose incisive editorial insights significantly improved the book. I thank Patrick Lambelet, whose line editing contributed to the book as well.

I would like to take this opportunity to convey my sincere thanks my parents, Jeanne Bedwell and James Apple, whose support and advice has been invaluable. Foremost, I must express my profound thanks to Shinobu, my wife and companion, who supported me day in and day out throughout the writing of this book.

Organization and Structure of the Book

The book is organized in three parts and follows the sequence of texts in the *Stages of the Path* source manuscript. I have divided the major works into chapters and provided introductions for each. Minor texts have been appended as supplements to the chapters in which they occur. Part 1 introduces and is a translation of Atiśa's *Stages of the Path to Awakening*, an extensive teaching that he composed in Tibet and transmitted to his advanced Tibetan disciples. This is the earliest known Tibetan text on guiding meditators through the stages of the path (*lam gyi rim pa*).

Part 2, "Commentaries and Exegesis," introduces and translates the commentaries and guidance texts that accompany the root text of Atiśa's *Stages*. Chapter 2 contains two short works that analyze the content of the *Stages* in two different ways. The *Condensed Stages of the Path* provides a brief summary of the whole work in one page. *Structural Analysis of the Stages of the Path to Awakening* is a topical outline of the text. Chapter 3 is an anonymous early Kadam-school commentary entitled *General Meaning of the Stages of the Path*. Chapter 4 is a work attributed to Atiśa entitled *Instructions for Select Disciples* that gives detailed and practical guidance for meditators. Chapter 5 consists of a special oral teaching attributed to Atiśa called *Pointing-Out Instructions in Sets of Five* that lays out advanced meditation guidance for nondual union based on later portions of the *Stages*.

Part 3, "Performance and Ritual Texts," contains works on enhancing practice, cultivating the awakening mind (*bodhicitta*), and properly maintaining bodhisattva vows. Chapter 6 introduces and translates an early Kadam work entitled *Enhancing Practice and Removing Obstacles on the Path*. The text outlines the way to clear obstructions to meditation practice and enhance realization. Chapter 7, *A Ritual for Generating the Awakening Mind*, is an early Kadam ritual with commentary based on Atiśa's system. Chapter 8 furnishes an introduction and translation of Atiśa's *Essence of the Bodhisattva Vows* (*Bodhisattvasaṃvarahṛdaya*), a work of fifty stanzas of guidance on the bodhisattva vows. Together these chapters are the primary sources that Atiśa's early Kadam followers used to study and practice his *Stages of the Path*.

Technical Notes

Note that Tibetan names have been rendered in phonetic form, for which the transliterated equivalent can be found in the table in appendix 2.

Notes on the Chapters

Sections of chapter 1, from an earlier draft, were published in *Atiśa Dīpaṃkara: Illuminator of the Awakened Mind* (Boulder, CO: Shambhala Publications, 2019).

An earlier draft of chapter 5 was published as "Kadampa Pointing-Out Instructions," *Revue d'Études Tibétaines* 56 (October 2020): 170–262.

An earlier draft of chapter 8 was published as "Atiśa's *Essence of Bodhisattva Vows* (*Bodhisatvasaṃvarahṛdaya*)," in *Manuscripts for Life: Essays in Memory of Seishi Karashima*, edited by Noriyuki Kudo, 27–40 (Tokyo: International Research Institute for Advanced Buddhology, Soka University, 2023).

Introduction

OVER NINE and a half centuries ago, one of the greatest Indian Buddhist masters to ever set foot in Tibet wrote a guidebook for realizing all the stages to awakening at the repeated request of his closest and most faithful disciple. The work would entail guidance on the Buddhist path synthesizing all aspects of Indian Buddhist practice from the very beginning of the path, reflecting on the fortunate opportunity of human rebirth, through to attaining omniscient buddhahood by integrative techniques of nondual meditation. The Indian master's most devoted and faithful Tibetan disciple kept these teachings secret, and they were only transmitted to select disciples in a closely guarded sequence of transmission. Now, due to recently recovered manuscripts, this significant work of Buddhist path literature has become available. This book offers a study and complete translation of this hidden monument of guidance on the Buddhist path, the *Stages of the Path to Awakening* by Atiśa Dīpaṃkaraśrījñāna (982–1054), and its accompanying commentaries and ritual texts.

The Bengali Buddhist master Atiśa is famous for his journey to Tibet and teaching in the Land of Snows for thirteen years. An Indian Buddhist *mahāpaṇḍita* from the celebrated monastic university of Vikramaśīla, he is well known among both traditional Tibetan and modern scholars for his *Lamp for the Path to Awakening* (*Bodhipathapradīpa*; *Byang chub lam gyi sgron ma*; hereafter *Lamp*), composed in western Tibet for his royal Tibetan disciple Lhatsun Jangchup Ö. *Lamp*, a concise presentation in sixty-eight verses, is generally considered the prototype for all subsequent stages of the path (*lam rim*) literature in Tibetan scholastic history. Atiśa's *Lamp* became, according to the historian Ronald Davidson (1995, 293), "one of the most influential of Indian texts received by Tibetans" and was "the model for mainstream Tibetan monastic Buddhists for the next nine hundred years." *Lamp* has been translated into English at least seven times since the 1893 study of Sarat Chandra Das and is used by contemporary Tibetan teachers such as the Dalai Lama for teaching Buddhism to general audiences.[1]

Atiśa's *Stages of the Path to Awakening* (*Bodhipathakrama*; *Byang chub lam gyi rim pa*; hereafter *Stages*),[2] although it was just as influential as *Lamp* was earlier in Tibetan scholastic history, was virtually unknown to later traditional and modern scholars. Atiśa's *Stages* is not only the hidden wellspring for the stages of the path tradition in Tibet but also the cornerstone for other well-known Tibetan Buddhist teaching traditions. Prototypical instructions on the awakening mind (*bodhicitta*), the bodhisattva vows, pointing-out instructions (*ngo sprod*), and advanced innateist forms of nondual mindfulness (e.g., "coemergent union," *lhan cig skyes sbyor*) are found in the *Stages* and its commentaries.

Atiśa's *Stages* is located within a ninety-one-folio unique exemplar manuscript (*codex unicus*) in handwritten cursive (*dbu med*) Tibetan script. The treatise is found among the recently published manuscript facsimiles of the *Collected Works of the Kadampas* (2006–15) recovered from the Potala Palace and Drepung Monastery in Tibet in the early years of the twenty-first century.[3]

Stages consists of Buddhist prescriptive teachings on classical Mahāyāna Buddhist thought and practice indicating stages of cultivation to reach the state of buddhahood. The text outlines Atiśa's instructions for his close and advanced disciples, who were both lay and monastic. An annotation in the manuscript's colophon mentions that the text was composed at the request of Atiśa's Tibetan lay disciple Dromtön Gyalwai Jungné (1004–64). The 181 stanzas of Atiśa's *Stages*, although a single coherent text, are structured as a presentation of the stages of the path to awakening based on three types of persons: those of small capacity (*chung ba*), middling capacity (*'bring*), and supreme capacity (*chen po*). The small- and middling-capacity persons are not explained in *Lamp*, as previous scholarship has noted. However, it is emphatically not the case that later Kadampa teachers were the first ones to "flesh out" the details of the lower stages of the path (Roesler, Holmes, and Jackson 2015, 5). Atiśa's *Stages* thoroughly discusses the small-capacity individual in lines 13–507 (494 lines), the middling-capacity person in lines 508–846 (338 lines), and the supreme-capacity person for the remainder of the text (704 lines; see table 1). Atiśa's *Stages* therefore provides key details on the sequence of practices outlined for these individuals throughout Indian and Tibetan Buddhist path literature.

Atiśa's *Stages* is accompanied by twenty-six minor texts of related rituals and practices.[4] The accompanying texts, eighteen of which are no longer than a folio, include two commentaries to the main work. Others are summaries of the stages of the path and related special instructions. The minor works include verses from Mahāyāna sūtras for recitation, special mantras, and two drawings of protection wheels for clearing obstacles to practice (see appendix 1).

Stages and its accompanying texts were a hidden tradition upheld by Atiśa's close disciples known as the Kadampa. They furnish previously unknown foundations for renaissance-period (*gsar ma*) Tibetan scholastic exegesis, instructions in meditative practice, and rituals for lay and monastic communities. Although Atiśa's *Stages* discusses sequences of practice for three types of individuals like *Lamp*, it differs in its content from other known works on the stages of the path. For instance, Tsongkhapa's *Great Treatise on the Stages of the Path to Enlightenment* (*Lam rim chen mo*), a masterpiece composed in 1402 that is patterned after Atiśa's *Lamp*, ends with a brief discussion of the practice of esoteric Buddhism, succinctly mentioning the qualities of a spiritual teacher, the principles for receiving consecration, and prescriptions for maintaining the secret vows that have been promised. Atiśa's *Stages*, on the other hand, finishes with guidance for cultivating nondual realization based on meditative techniques found in esoteric Indian Buddhist literature. The elaborate meditation instructions found in later sections (stanzas 129–30 and 142–75) of *Stages* resemble, in terminology and structure, guidance found in later *mahāmudrā* meditation manuals among the diverse traditions of the Kagyü schools. *Stages* and its commentarial literature reveal the beginnings of meditative techniques related to not-specifically-tantric mahāmudrā practices that were later dominated by the Kagyü tradition after the time of the erstwhile Kadam monk, and subsequent Kagyü lineage founder, Gampopa Sönam Rinchen (ca. 1079–1153).

Atiśa's *Stages* also contains forgotten, or even previously unknown, Indian Buddhist lore, mythology, and doctrinal content. For example, it contains an unusual account of Buddhist cosmology in its description of hungry ghosts (*preta*) in sections 43–47 and a rare discussion of the immediate environmental effects of karmic actions in sections 59–62. The work also mentions Mahāsāṃghika Vinaya precepts, a distinctive account of dependent arising (section 98), a unique list of the root downfalls of a bodhisattva (section 125), and important prescriptions on the ultimate awakening mind (section 128). *Stages* is based on Indian Buddhist sūtras and tantras, synthesizing basic Buddhist doctrines with altruistic bodhisattva practices and culminating in advanced meditation techniques similar to what later Tibetan tradition calls "essence mahāmudrā."

Stages of the Path in the Life of Atiśa: Influences and Sources

As early transmission of *Stages* was kept to only select disciples, and as the text does not have any direct textual citations, the influences and sources for Atiśa's composition must be inferred from contextual evidence. This includes influences mentioned in his biographies and works that Atiśa is known to have written and translated.

Elements of *Stages* and its system of practice may be found in the biographical accounts of the teachings Atiśa received in his youth. According to these accounts, Atiśa took refuge and received lay vows from the lay teacher Jitāri. Atiśa received from the scholar-monk Bodhibhadra at Nālandā novice vows and teachings on the awakening mind. Vidyākokila, a hermit monk residing to the north of Nālandā, is said to have instructed Atiśa in his youth on the general features of the stages of the path. Atiśa was also thoroughly versed during his youth in the practices of the *Hevajratantra* under the masters Avadhūtipa and Rahulaguptavajra. After becoming a monk, Atiśa studied Vinaya and Abhidharma in various monasteries of Bodhgayā and in Vikramaśīla and Odantapuri. He also traveled to Sumatra in Indonesia and received guidance in the *Ornament for Clear Realization* (*Abhisamayālaṃkāra*) and the Mahāyāna stages of the path training from Dharmakīrtiśrī of Suvarṇadvīpa (a.k.a. Serlingpa) over a twelve-year period.[5]

We do not know if Atiśa formulated the stages of the path system or genre himself or if such a genre already existed at Nālandā and Vikramaśīla. The instructions he received on the stages of the path from Vidyākokila may have reflected a Nālandā tradition. At the same time, the *General Meaning of the Stages of the Path* (see chapter 3) comments on Atiśa's *Stages* according to the Vikramalaśīla tradition, as discussed in Tsongkhapa's *Great Treatise* (Tsong kha pa, *Lam rim chen mo*, 3; Cutler and Newland 2000, 34).

As mentioned, the *Stages* manuscript indicates that it was composed at the behest of Dromtönpa while Atiśa was residing at Nyethang. Even though *Stages* was composed late in Atiśa's life, he had begun formulating synthetic works on the Buddhist path earlier, both in India and in Tibet. Atiśa would often compose a text at the request of students, fashioning the work based on the audience's inclinations, capacities, and wishes. Based on what we know of Atiśa's earlier writings, we can chart those that most influenced his composition of *Stages*.

Among Atiśa's Indian writings, the earliest use of the term "stages of the path" (*lam gyi rim*) occurs in his *Analysis of Realization* (*Abhisamayavibhaṅga*) commentary on the esoteric tradition of Cakrasaṃvara. In this work Atiśa brings together points of the explanatory tantras of the *Cakrasaṃvaratantra*, such as the *Abhidānottara*, *Herukābhyudaya*, and *Vajraḍāka*, to outline the "stages of the path of the definitive meaning" (D 186a4, *nges don lam gyi rim*).

In India, Atiśa composed a set of three short synthetic texts on advanced practices of Cakrasaṃvara that was translated into Tibetan before he arrived in Tibet. These three works—the *Small Text on View and Meditation* (*Lta *sgom chung ngu*), the *Medium Text on View and Meditation* (*Lta sgom 'bring po*), and the *Great Text on View and Meditation* (*Lta sgom chen mo*)—appear to be brief lecture notes that overlap in content. The *Small Text on View and Meditation* praises Cakrasaṃvara and indicates that it is for those who wish to integrate the practice of clear light (*prabhāsvara*; *'od gsal*) with the completion stage of Cakrasaṃvara. The *Great Text on View and Meditation* has a colophon stating that Atiśa composed the teaching after repeated requests from the Tibetan translator Rinchen Sangpo (958–1055) and that it was later translated into Tibetan by Gya Tsöndrü Sengé. The *Great Text on View and Meditation* is longer than the other two works because it expands the exegesis from the Cakrasaṃvara cycle to "the condensed special instructions on the essence of all sūtras, tantras, and technical digests, like a wish-fulfilling jewel." These works demonstrate Atiśa's interest in synthesizing diverse strands of Buddhist thought and practice into a coherent system of gradual realizations.

Atiśa composed his *Open Basket of Jewels*[6] in the great temple of Vikramaśīla before leaving for Tibet circa 1040. He cites sūtras and tantras, and his discussion provides one of the most thorough overviews on the awakening mind in Indian Buddhist literature. The text contains guidance on meditation and the awakening mind and special instructions on the Madhyamaka lineage from Nāgārjuna, aspects of thought and practice that are also central to his *Stages*. Nevertheless, the work contains no detailed discussion of the stages of the path per se or the three types of individuals.

Other compositions by Atiśa in India that presage *Stages* include his *Delivering the Mind from Cyclic Existence*, *Explanation of the Ten Nonvirtuous Paths of Action*, and *Analysis of Actions*.[7] *Delivering the Mind from Cyclic Existence* provides instructions that correspond to guidance for practitioners of the small and middling capacities. This work presents a sequence of teachings on topics such as karma and mental afflictions, suffering in the realms of saṃsāra, impermanence, and the necessity of a spiritual friend. These are followed by instructions on how to meditate on dependent arising to counteract the three poisons of ignorance, hatred, and desire. However, although these topics are found in *Stages*' discussion of the small- and middling-capacity individuals, the sequence of topics is presented differently. *Explanation of the Ten Nonvirtuous Paths of Action* contains teachings corresponding to several stanzas in the guidance for small-capacity individuals. *Analysis of Actions* also contains guidance on the teachings of karma found in *Stages*, particularly on cause and effect as it relates to the lower realms.

Atiśa composed his *Lamp for the Summary of Conduct*[8] while he was in Nepal on his way to western Tibet. This work outlines general Mahāyāna practices but includes no instructions on esoteric Buddhism. The work was composed for a deaf monk who wished for instructions based on the bodhisattva perfections but who did not practice tantra. Alongside *Stages* and *Lamp*, *Lamp for the Summary of Conduct* is one of three texts mentioned in *Stages* (folio 22b3) for studying the practice of the path.

Atiśa certainly composed other precursors to *Stages* after arriving in Tibet. When Atiśa and his entourage arrived in Tholing, in the western Tibetan region of Ngari, in the year 1042, Atiśa was sixty years old. In Tholing, he and his entourage settled in the monastic temple of Jangchup Ling, where Atiśa began to teach, translate, and compose works under the patronage of Jangchup Ö.

Explanation of Going for Refuge[9] outlines in detail points concerning taking refuge in mainstream and Mahāyāna forms of Buddhism. This work specifies a number of refined points on refuge not mentioned in *Stages*. While in western Tibet, Atiśa also wrote his *Concise Method of Achieving the Great Vehicle Path*[10] and *Concisely Written Method of Achieving the Great Vehicle Path.*[11] Both works contain themes related to the gradual path for beings of the three capacities. For individuals of small and middling capacity, these themes include impermanence, faith and refuge in the Three Jewels, and the maintenance of vows. For individuals of supreme capacity, they include cultivation of the awakening mind, the four divine abidings (*brahmavihāra*), the six perfections, the bodhisattva vows, the importance of the spiritual friend, the unity of wisdom and method, serenity (*śamatha*; *zhi gnas*) and insight (*vipaśyanā*; *lhag mthong*), the ten bodhisattva grounds, and buddhahood. The sequence of themes in these texts is comparable to Atiśa's other works mentioned above. The topics correspond to what is found in *Stages* in that they present a complete gradual path for all three types of persons. What these works lack is an explicit division into the three types of persons, and they do not mention any teachings related to secret mantra as found in *Lamp* and alluded to in *Stages*. Both these texts mention the bodhisattva grounds culminating in buddhahood, a topic found in neither *Lamp* nor *Stages*.

In sum, Atiśa composed numerous works in India, Nepal, and Tibet at the request of his patrons and disciples. These works demonstrate aspects of his stages of the path teachings and share content with *Stages*, but the sequence or manner of presentation is different. Importantly, what these works are missing is an explicit description of a complete gradual-path system addressing three types of persons.

Lamp for the Path to Awakening

Atiśa's most well-known composition among both traditional Tibetan and modern scholars is, of course, his *Lamp for the Path to Awakening*. To understand how *Stages* complements, yet is distinct from, *Lamp* necessitates a brief overview of *Lamp*'s structure and content. The ruler of Ngari, Lhatsun Jangchup Ö, entreated Atiśa to give a formal teaching that would benefit the survival of the Buddha's Dharma as a whole. According to several sources, Lhatsun Jangchub Ö put seven questions to Atiśa concerning the practice of esoteric Buddhism.[12] In response to this request Atiśa composed *Lamp* for his Tibetan royal disciple. *Lamp* is widely considered the prototype for all subsequent works in the stages of the path genre. Notably, *Lamp* is a public document sanctioned by a king and translated with the assistance of translator monks under the auspices of the king's court.

Atisa's *Lamp* was composed during his initial stay in Tholing (Eimer 1986, 5). The original Indic version has not survived, and the Tibetan translation is included in Tengyur editions and in separate manuscripts and blockprints.[13] The text of *Lamp* consists of 276 lines comprising sixty-eight stanzas. The stanzas vary in length, with three stanzas of six lines, one stanza of ten lines, and one of twelve lines (Eimer 1986, 8). The stanzas in *Lamp* also vary in meter, with most stanzas having lines of seven syllables, three stanzas with nine-syllable lines, and two stanzas having eleven-syllable lines (Sherburne 1976, 18). *Lamp* integrates the vows of the pratimokṣa, bodhisattva, and mantra within an overarching Mahāyāna approach. *Lamp* references nine Buddhist works and directly quotes twelve stanzas from four different sources (Sherburne 1976, 32).[14]

As indicated in the left side of table 1 below, *Lamp* discusses topics related to the three types of spiritual persons and the vows of moral discipline, or *pratimokṣa*, in verses 1 to 21. Verses 22 to 59 outline the discipline for bodhisattvas (vv. 22–33), the cultivation of supersensory knowledge (vv. 34–37), serenity (vv. 38–40), and the perfection of wisdom, insight (vv. 41–59). Verses 60 to 68 outline the vehicle of secret mantra, or Buddhist tantra, and the disciplinary commitments for yogis of esoteric Buddhism. Although *Lamp* succinctly outlines a program of instructions for the three types of individuals, practices specific to the small and middling capacities are not discussed. Also, the guidance for bodhisattvas in *Lamp* differs from *Stages* in style and content (see below). In brief, *Lamp* and *Stages* are distinct teachings, composed at different times and places for different audiences.

Atiśa's Stages of the Path: An Overview

The following provides an overview of Atiśa's *Stages*, including a description of the manuscript, the format of the composition, the authenticity of the authorship, and a general outline of its structure and content.

The Manuscript

Stages takes up the first twenty-two folios of volume 91 in set 4 of the *Collected Works of the Kadampas* (*Bka' gdams pa gsung 'bum*). The facsimile in this collection closely resembles another facsimile of the manuscript published in the United States Library of Congress PL480 program in 1973 as *Byang chub lam gyi rim pa, Writings of Lord Atiśa on the Theory and Practice of the Graduated Path.*[15] Both facsimiles are reproduced from the same manuscript. Surprisingly, therefore, a copy of this manuscript has been sitting on the shelves of PL480 depositories in the United States for the past forty-six years with little notice until selections were published in 2019 (Apple 2019). Unlike *Lamp*, which has versions in canonical and paracanonical blockprints and manuscripts, the manuscript of *Stages* reproduced from Ladakh is a *codex unicus*—that is, the only extant manuscript volume bearing the text. The text is written in a legible cursive script that contains several ligatures difficult to parse at first glance. The manuscript also contains enough spelling mistakes to suggest the copyist did not always understand what was being copied.

The complete manuscript is ninety-one folios, as Atiśa's *Stages* is accompanied by twenty-six related minor texts, and the scribe, or the community that circulated these texts, has provided a topic outline of these texts. After the one-page *Condensed Stages of the Path to Awakening*, the manuscript reads, "The treatise has the following topical outline and various texts: three ritual texts, four texts of special instructions, secret instructions, pointing-out instructions, [wheels for] eliminating hindrances, rituals, and various other texts."[16] These accompanying texts also include instructions for conducting rituals for both monks and laypeople, such as taking refuge, producing the aspiration for awakening, and taking the lay precepts. Altogether, these texts accompanying *Stages* form a complete cycle of works for the thought and practice of Atiśa's stages of the path system. The cycle of texts was transmitted among early Kadam lineage figures and eventually written down by Kagyü monks (see below).

Format of the Composition

Atiśa's *Stages* is composed of 181 poetic stanzas with lines of nine syllables. The stanzas have varying numbers of lines, with a total of 1,557 lines. Some stanzas are only two lines long, whereas others have up to thirty-four lines. All told, *Stages* is five and a half times longer than Atiśa's *Lamp*. The only breaks to the continuous series of poetic lines are the division of stanzas indicated by the scribe with the punctuation mark known as the "precious-pile division stroke" (*rin chen spung shad*).[17] This may well replicate divisions that Atiśa himself intended, as each division presents a distinct topic. For example, as seen at the bottom of the table 1, stanza 139 in twenty-nine lines discusses the practice of perceiving one's teacher as a buddha.

Authenticity of Authorship

Unlike *Lamp*, whose authorship is authenticated by its known history in Tibetan sources and its inclusion in the Tibetan Tengyur, *Stages* is not in the Tengyur. The work is also unacknowledged by its specific title, as far as I am currently aware, in traditional Tibetan histories or Tibetan commentarial works. The title page and colophon state that the text was composed by "Śrī Dīpaṃkarajñāna (*dpal mar me mdzad ye shes kyis mdzad pa*, 1a1) and provides a Sanskrit title for the text as *Bodhipathakrama*. However, no Tibetan translator is mentioned. Atiśa conceivably could have translated or composed the work in Tibetan himself. In any event, internal textual evidence strongly suggests that this work was composed by Atiśa. For example, *Stages* provides an analogy of "the female servant of Śrāvastī" (section 9) in its discussion of karma, mentions the Indian deity Viṣṇu (section 28), and furnishes the example of the skillful cowherd (*gopālaka*; section 170). These illustrations drawn from Indian religious culture suggest an Indian author. Further, the fulcrum point of the text is its emphasis on karma, the principle of cause and effect in the perpetuation of cyclic existence or the causes and conditions leading to the highest awakening of buddhahood. Tibetan biographies of Atiśa note that when he first arrived in western Tibet, he was called the "teacher of cause and effect"[18] owing to the great attention he placed on karma in his initial teachings. The early sections of Atiśa's *Stages* may well be comprised of the notes on cause and effect that he had used for earlier teachings in Tibet. The text also briefly discusses Mahāsāṃghika monastic rules and emphasizes the practice of the one-day precepts (*upavāsa*), a ritual practice that eventually died out in Tibet.[19] These are details that only an Indian author would use in a composition. And most importantly, Atiśa is widely known to have been ordained in the Mahāsāṃghika lineage while all Tibetan monks in Tibet, since the late seventh century, have taken ordination in the Mūlasarvāstivāda lineage.[20] The fact that the manuscript mentions Mahāsāṃghika Vinaya rules not only points toward Atiśa's authorship but may also be a reason contributing to its later exclusion.

General Structure and Content of *Stages*

Atiśa's *Stages* is a prescriptive teaching on classical Mahāyāna Buddhist thought and practice indicating the stages of cultivation to reach buddhahood. The text outlines Atiśa's instructions for his close and advanced disciples who, as laypeople and monks, were dedicated to Buddhist meditation. An annotation in the colophon mentions that it was composed at the request of Geshé Tönpa Gyalwai Jungné.[21]

The 181 stanzas of *Stages* instruct on subject matter found in later Kadam texts and will be familiar to anyone with knowledge of Geluk stages of the path literature. Table 1 shows the contents of *Lamp* on the left side, while the right side illustrates that *Stages* includes such topics as the rarity of human rebirth, the sufferings of cyclic existence, and the principles of karma that are found in later stages of the path texts but absent from *Lamp*. *Stages* also concludes with instructions on the practice of serenity and insight rather than tantra, as in

Table 1. Structure and Content of Atiśa's *Lamp* and *Stages*

Lamp	Stanza
Dedication	1a
Reason for writing	1b
Three persons	2–5
Superior person	6
Triple refuge	7–9
Thought of awakening	10–19
Monastic life	20–21
Bodhisattva vows	22–33
Supersensory knowledge	34–37
Serenity	38–40
Insight	41–59
Tantra	60–67
Concluding verse	68
Colophon	

STAGES	STANZA	LINE	PERSON
Reason for writing	1–2	1–2	
Three types of person	3	3–12	
Lesser person	4–5	13–16	Small
Refuge	6–9	17–37	
Principles of conduct	10–12	38–52	
Fortunate opportunity of human rebirth	13–20	53–99	
Impermanence of conditioned existence	21–32	100–162	
Nature of nonvirtuous actions	33–36	163–93	
Lower realms of rebirth	37–51	194–326	
Sinful actions	52–55	327–70	
Ten wholesome courses of action	57	371–407	
Results of wrongdoing and virtue	63–76	408–507	
Moral discipline	77–79	508–56	Middling
Eliminating attachment	80–83	557–630	
Sufferings of birth, aging, sickness, and death	84–88	631–96	
Misfortune	89–96	697–759	
Eradicating afflictions	97–98	760–91	
Training in the three wisdoms	99–108	792–846	
Aspiration for awakening	109–24	847–938	Supreme
Downfalls for bodhicitta and bodhisattvas	125–27	939–1013	
Ultimate bodhicitta	128–31	1014–59	
Benefitting others	132–33	1060–79	
The falsity of appearances	134–38	1080–1131	
Perceiving the teacher as the Buddha	139	1132–61	
Meditation	140–44	1162–1219	
All things are one's own mind	145–50	1220–54	
Emptiness	151–54	1255–1304	
Mindfulness	155–57	1305–31	
Integration of the basis, path, and result	158–68	1332–1494	
Introspection	169–72	1495–1518	
Mindfulness	173–76	1519–38	
Integration of one's own mind	177–79	1539–51	
Buddhahood	180–81	1552–57	
Colophon			

Lamp. Moreover, the instructions on insight in *Stages* focus on a nonconceptual direct vision of the emptiness of one's own mind, a significant difference from the analytical insight using reasoning found in *Lamp*. In brief, Atiśa's *Stages* is a far more extensive teaching than *Lamp* and contains additional prescriptive practices and distinct instructions for advanced meditations.

Commentaries and Ritual Texts Accompanying *Stages of the Path to Awakening*

In this volume I have preserved the order of the ancillary texts as they appear in the Tibetan manuscript. The sequence reflects the final redaction of the manuscript, most likely in the thirteenth century (see below). All of the texts appear to be copied by one scribe, indicating that the complete manuscript is a copy from another source. Based on external evidence, some of the larger works attributed to Atiśa, such as *Pointing-Out Instructions in Sets of Five* (chapter 5), circulated independently from the other texts found in the manuscript. Some works in the manuscript are attributed to Atiśa, such as *Instructions for Select Disciples* (chapter 4) and *Essence of the Bodhisattva Vows* (chapter 8), while others are anonymous compositions as with *Enhancing Practice and Removing Obstacles on the Path* (chapter 6). The sequence of the texts accompanying Atiśa's *Stages* reflects pedagogical and ritual purposes of the Kadam (and Kagyü) lineage holders of this cycle of teachings. The commentaries and exegesis I have called part 2 and the performance and ritual texts part 3. Part 2 consists of the explanatory *General Meaning of the Stages of the Path* (chapter 3) and advanced instructions on meditation in chapters 4 and 5. The latter works build upon the meditation instructions in *Stages*.

The performance and ritual texts in part 3 offer guidance on practicing and implementing the teachings found in the *Stages*. Several of these works also ritually establish followers in a certain social status or practice. For instance, *A Ritual for Generating the Awakening Mind* (chapter 7) is also accompanied by several minor ritual texts for taking refuge, bestowing the one-day precepts, or establishing someone as a lay disciple. In content, the ritual texts are initially concerned with practices of basic Buddhism and are oriented toward laypeople. Part 3 centers around *Essence of the Bodhisattva Vows*, which outlines the vows of a bodhisattva and is aligned with four minor works that provide a summary of the vows, a way to counteract downfalls, and a citation from scripture.

The texts accompanying *Stages* were most likely compiled by Atiśa's early Kadam followers. They were assembled to provide guidance for Atiśa's system of gradual realizations. Several are attributed to Atiśa (chapters 4, 5, and 8) while others may have been based on his oral teachings (chapter 7). However, evidence for who exactly organized these teachings, where they were compiled, and how they were brought together is not currently available.

Stages of the Path among Atiśa's Early Tibetan Followers

Was this important text by Atiśa forgotten and not acknowledged by subsequent generations of Tibetan scholars? The very existence of the *Stages* manuscript belies this assumption. However, one may still ask, "Why is this work not as well known as Atiśa's *Lamp*?" To answer this question requires a complex response based on internal evidence, external evidence, and numerous cultural and historical conditions. First, the internal evidence is that found within Atiśa's *Stages* manuscript and its accompanying texts. The external evidence comes from other Kadam, as well as non-Kadam, Tibetan manuscripts and histories.

As mentioned, the colophon to *Stages* states that Atiśa composed the treatise at the behest of his disciple Dromtön. *General Meaning of the Stages of the Path*, chapter 3 below, provides the only lineage list in the manuscript. *General Meaning* lists three lineages that Atiśa united: a lineage of view beginning with Nāgārjuna, a lineage of extensive deeds beginning with Maitreya, and a lineage of blessing descending from Tilopa and Nāropa. After affirming that Atiśa was the crown jewel among five hundred scholars at Vikramaśīla, *General Meaning* lists individuals who received the *Stages* transmission. From Atiśa, the teachings went to Gönpawa Wangchuk Gyaltsen (1016–82), Gya Chakriwa (eleventh century), Gampopa (ca. 1079–1153), and then Phakmodrupa (1110–70).[22] Phakmodrupa, a great figure in Kagyü traditions, is the last figure mentioned by name. The lineage ends with the mention of three names that I examine below. This list indicates that the active transmission of this cycle of texts most likely halted in the early thirteenth century at the time of the manuscript's redaction.

The colophon and lineage list provides important clues about the transmission of *Stages* and its early circulation, and later Kadam historians provide additional clues for this transmission. The *Blue Annals* by Gö Lotsāwa Shönu Pal explains that Atiśa gave Dromtön personal guidance on the three types of individuals—that is, the stages of the path—during the later years of Atiśa's life at Nyethang.[23] Lechen Kunga Gyaltsen, a fifteenth-century historian, wrote in his *Lamp Illuminating the History of the Kadam Tradition*,

> The king of special instructions for unifying view and practice is renowned as "the stages of the path of the three types of

> individuals." The text of this is *Lamp for the Path to Awakening* (*Bodhipathapradīpa*), and it relies on the special instructions of the *Ornament for Clear Realization* (*Abhisamayālaṃkāra*). The Lord [Atiśa] secretly guided Geshé Tönpa in the practice of the stages of the path. Furthermore, Geshé Tönpa asked Lord [Atiśa] why, having bestowed secret mantra instructions to others, he bestowed this practice of the stages of the path to him personally. [The Lord] replied, "I could not find another recepient to entrust it to other than you." These guidance instructions were entrusted to Geshé Tönpa. He is the blessed master of these teachings. Therefore these [teachings] also exist thanks to the pervasiveness of Drom[tönpa]'s miraculous activity.[24]

A crucial phrase in this citation is that Atiśa guided Dromtön secretly, in a restricted manner (*lkog tu 'khrid pa*), in the practices of the stages of the path. Earlier in his history, Lechen states that the practices of "the stages of the path" (*lam gyi rim pa*) tradition has a number of synonyms such as "the stages of the doctrine" (*bstan pa'i rim pa*), "the entryway that reveals the teaching" (*bstan pa'i srol ka bstan pa'i 'jug ngogs*), "the Dharma tradition of beings of supreme capacity" (*skyes bu chen po'i chos lugs*), "the approach to the path of the great charioteers" (*shing rta chen po'i lam srol*), and "the stages of the path of the three types of individuals" (*skyes bu gsum gyi lam rim*).[25] In fifteenth-century Tibet, the tradition of the stages of the path had various names but was considered to be initially a restricted teaching given to Dromtön. In addition, this citation suggests that the practice of the stages of the path was differentiated from the publically known teaching in texts such as Atiśa's *Lamp* and the *Ornament for Clear Realization*. Related to this point, the Kadam master Sangyé Öntön (1138–1210) is cited by Lechen as stating, in part, "our Kadampa is the graded path (*lam rim*) explained in public teachings. As well, meditation and guidance in secret is only the practice of the stages of the path (*lam gyi rim pa*)."[26] An early history of Radreng Monastery written in 1299 by Drom Sherab Meché states that Atiśa wrote *Lamp* as an antidote to the extreme views of Tibetans and taught the stages of the path in secret.[27]

Another early Kadam history written in 1484 by the ecumenical master Sönam Lhai Wangpo (1423–96) quotes Chengawa as commenting on the subtle distinction between stages of the doctrine (*bstan rim*) and stages of the path (*lam rim*), saying, "when taught in public it is the stages of the doctrine, when distilled into practice it is the stages of the path, when written in a text it is *Lamp for the Path to Awakening* (*Bodhipathapradīpa*): it is like three names given to one meaning."[28]

These citations make clear a distinction between public teachings with audiences (*tshogs chos*) and restricted teachings (*lkog chos*) regarding meditation and guidance in practice (*nyams len*). These citations also suggest that Tibetan scholars made a slight distinction between public graded path teachings (*lam rim*) and more restricted guidance on the practice of the stages of the path (*lam gyi rim pa*). I think that these distinctions, although debated and discussed much later than the time of the *Stages* manuscript, may reflect why the manuscript is not better known. That is, the early Kadam followers of Atiśa, beginning with Dromtön, distinguished between public teachings on the graded path and restricted guidance on practicing and meditating on the stages of the path. This distinction also accords with a division between the public, royally sanctioned, and officially translated teachings of *Lamp for the Path to Awakening* and its autocommentary and the private, restricted, and noncanonical teachings of *Stages of the Path to Awakening* (*byang chub lam gyi rim pa*). The secrecy that Kadam followers of Atiśa kept regarding restricted private guidance on practice of the stages may well be a major factor in why *Stages* is not as well known today as *Lamp*.

The manuscript colophon and traditional sources agree that Dromtönpa was the recipient of Atiśa's stages of the path teachings. However, the lineage list in *General Meaning* differs from later Kadam and Geluk traditions. Present lineages of the stages of the path seem to have been established by the fifteenth century based on the works of Tsongkhapa (1357–1419), the great advocate of the stages of the path traditions.[29] Tsongkhapa's works on this genre have defined the Geluk understanding of the subject. The colophon of Tsongkhapa's *Great Treatise*, written in 1402, states that he received several lineages of the stages of the path. These include lineages passing from Atiśa to Gönpawa to Neusurpa, a lineage passed from Chengawa, and lineages passed from Potowa to Sharawa and from Potowa to Dölpa.[30] These lineages are also mentioned in Tsongkhapa's *Middle-Length Stages of the Path* and his *Record of Teachings Received*.[31]

Tibetan historians also record stages of the path transmissions and their affliated texts. Lechen outlines, in addition to his discussion of Dromtönpa, early transmissions through Naktso Lotsāwa and his disciples, through Ngok Lekpai Sherab, through Gönpawa, and others. Gönpawa's tradition, according to Lechen, came down through Neusurpa and Kamawa.[32] Another Tibetan historian, Tsalpa Kunga Dorjé, focuses his account (ca. 1346) of the Kadam stages of the path lineage (*bka' gdams lam rim pa'i brgyud*) upon Naktso's student Rongpa Chaksorpa (fl. eleventh century) and his four early followers (Jackson 1996, 239). Each of these four disciples took notes on these teachings and established their own lineages, but the transmissions of these traditions were eventually lost. These anecdotes demonstrate that individual early Kadam masters taught and transmitted their own lineages of the stages of the path. Yet they also demonstrate that Atiśa's disciples did not write and transmit stages of the path teachings based upon commentaries to Atiśa's *Lamp*, perhaps because Atiśa himself composed a long autocommentary to the work. Rather, early Kadam masters transmitted and composed stages of the path lineage teachings based upon the tradition and the points of emphasis that they received from their own Tibetan masters.

Until now, the earliest extant textual evidence among stages of the path traditions are found in fragments of Naktso Lotsāwa's teaching, Potowa's *Blue Compendium*[33] and *Dharma Exemplified: A Heap of Jewels*, Neusurpa's instructions, and a recently recovered manuscript of Sharawa Yönten Drak's (1070–1141) *Stages of the Path of the Three Types of Individuals*.[34] As discussed by Jinpa (2008, 8–10), Potowa Rinchen Sal (1027–1105) became entrusted with the Kadam lineage of authoritative treatises (*gzhung*), which approached Atiśa and Dromtönpa's teachings through the study and practice of Atiśa's *Lamp* along with "six treatises authoritative for Kadam" (*gzhung drug*). These six texts included the *Garland of Birth Stories*, *Collection of Purposeful Sayings*, *Bodhisattva Levels*, *Ornament of Mahāyāna Sūtras*, *Introduction to the Practice of Awakening*, and *Compendium of Training*.[35] The study of these treatises was complemented with further Indian Buddhist classics like Nāgārjuna's *Fundamental Verses on the Middle Way*, his *Seventy Stanzas on Emptiness*, and Atiśa's *Entry into the Two Truths* and *An Instruction on the Middle Way*.[36] Potowa's manner of teaching the stages of the path system through Atiśa's *Lamp* along with these six texts is exactly what is found in Sharawa's *Stages of the Path*.

Sharawa's text is one of the oldest extant Kadam path works after Atiśa's *Stages* and Potowa's *Blue Compendium*. Sharawa was a direct disciple of Potowa, studying with him for eight years, and after Potowa passed away, a great number of Potowa's disciples followed Sharawa. Sharawa established a following of three thousand monastics and is recorded as having composed two stages of the path texts, a smaller and a greater, as well as a biography of Potowa. The smaller stages of the path manuscript is eighty-five folios long and is the work that is newly accessible. This smaller manuscript cites Atiśa's *Lamp* and its autocommentary, sayings of Dromtönpa and Potowa, and the six treatises authoritative for the Kadam. However, Sharawa's *Stages of the Path* does not cite Atiśa's *Stages*, and neither is it similar in structure and content.

Nevertheless, Sharawa's *Stages* is a true *lam rim* text, as the work is structured into three parts correlated to practices for the three types of individuals: the small, the middling, and the supreme person, the bodhisattva. Interestingly, Sharawa cites the *Ratnagotravibhāgavyākhyā*, which he attributes to Asaṅga, as an authoritative source for the theory of the three types of persons in the "graded path" (*lam rim*).[37] Atiśa himself will cite the *Abhidharmakośabhāṣya* as a source in his commentary to the *Bodhipathapradīpa* (see the introduction to chapter 1). Sharawa emphasizes (Sha ra ba, *Lam rim*, 58) that all practices outlined in the text are directed toward, and integrated into, the single path of the bodhisattva. Sharawa refers to the cultivations of the inferior and middling person as common mental trainings (*thun mong gi blo sbyong*), while cultivations beginning with love and compassion are uncommon mental trainings (144, *thun mong ma yin pa'i blo sbyong*). Sharawa's work has a great number of divisions and subdivisions in the subject matter indicating that the graded path among the Kadam was already a complex and detailed Tibetan genre within sixty years of Atiśa's death. Sharawa's graded path also focuses on a controversy (161–68) regarding the Madhyamaka and Yogācāra rites for developing the awakening mind. Sharawa's approach tells us that the now well-known divisions of Madhyamaka into Prāsaṅgika and Svātantrika did not exist when he composed the text.[38] Sharawa refers to his view (69) as Great Madhyamaka (*dbu ma chen po*) and follows Atiśa's *Madhyamakopadeśa* and Kamalaśīla's *Bhāvanākrama* in his graded-path exegesis of insight. In brief, Sharawa's *Stages of the Path* represents the teaching tradition of Potowa that gained prominence in Tibet. The manuscript evidence conforms with the remarks in Lechen's history that the lineage of Potowa's *Blue Compendium* and Sharawa's *Stages of the Path* became very popular.[39]

As noted, *General Meaning* below mentions a lineage transmission sequence of Gönpawa, Gya Chakriwa, Gampopa, and then Phakmodrupa, a lineage of Atiśa's *Stages* that was neither transmitted nor recorded among later Kadam or Geluk historians. Is such a lineage transmission viable, looking back over Tibetan history? Yes, it is! Earlier and different historical sources indicate not only the possibility of such a transmission but also help explain its eventual fading away.

The lineage sequence first mentions Gönpawa (1016–82), an important early disciple of Atiśa and Dromtönpa. Gönpawa, whose given name was Wangchuk Gyaltsen, initially met Atiśa in Nyantso. He became known for his meditative abilities and insight and was among the younger generation of Atiśa's initial Tibetan disciples who were receptive to Madhyamaka teachings (Apple 2018). The colophon to Atiśa's mahāmudrā instructions on coemergent union (Apple 2019, 245–50) indicates that Gönpawa was the first Tibetan disciple to receive these advanced teachings. Gönpawa later became an important figure in the monastic community of Radreng. After the passing of Amé Jangchup Rinchen in 1078, Gönpawa became the third abbot of Radreng, roughly from 1078 to 1082. Geshé Gönpawa gave teachings on Madhyamaka instructions in private (Apple 2018, 21) and is recorded by Tsongkhapa as transmitting a stages of the path teaching.[40] The lineage is recorded as having been transmitted to Neusurpa Yeshé Bar (1042–1118), a known principal disciple of Gönpawa and also a disciple of Potowa. The manuscript's recorded transmission of Atiśa's *Stages* after Gönpawa, however, goes to the elusive, yet pivotal, figure of Chakriwa.

Chakriwa most likely refers to Gya Chakri Gongkawa Jangchup Pal, an eleventh-century Kadam master who was one of Gampopa's Kadam teachers (Apple 2018, 396n571). Nyangral Nyima Öser's (1124–92) *History of Dharma: Pure Honey Extracted from the Essence of a Flower* lists Gya Chakriwa as a contemporary of Khampa Lungpa (1023–1115), Langri Thangpa (1054–1123), Sharawa, Shawo Gangpa (twelfth century), and Neusurpa among others.[41] The early Kadam history of Sönam Lhai Wangpo mentions that Gya Chakriwa was a student of Atiśa's direct disciple Shenyen Balpo.[42] In a later section of his history, Lechen describes Gya Chakriwa as a student of Langri Thangpa, who healed Chakriwa from an attack by a demoness.[43]

Along these lines, preserved lineage lists, early Kadam manuscript evidence, and Kagyü histories present Gya Chakriwa as an important late eleventh-century figure who was a lineage holder of seminal works of Atiśa, a disciple of Gönpawa, and a mentor to Gampopa. In lineages related to teachings on the awakening mind, the *Seven Points of Mind Training*, and *Guidance on the Heart of Dependent Arising*, Gya Chakriwa is often listed third or fourth after Atiśa, following Dromtönpa, Gönpawa, and Potowa.[44]

The collected works of Gampopa record several dialogues with Chakriwa, and they describe Chakriwa's instructions from his two teachers, possibly Gönpawa and Langri Thangpa (Sherpa 2004, 197–200). Lechen's history, written in 1494, mentions in its discussion of the great translator Rinchen Sangpo that two young monk attendants repeatedly requested teachings on Cakrasaṃvara from Atiśa on behalf of Rinchen Sangpo. These monks, after the passing of Rinchen Sangpo, went to central Tibet and met Chakriwa, who was on pilgrimage in Lhasa at the time. The monks gave teachings to Chakriwa, possibly related to Cakrasaṃvara, as the history describes Chakriwa having a dream about a Cakrasaṃvara temple the night before meeting the monks. This episode concerning Chakriwa receiving teachings on Cakrasaṃvara matches the colophon of Atiśa's *Great Exposition of View and Meditation* (*Lta sgom chen mo*), which lists a Chakriwa as a primary lineage figure. The colophon also indicates that this Cakrasaṃvara-based work was translated into Tibetan after many requests from Rinchen Sangpo.[45]

These anecdotes indicate that Chakriwa traveled to central Tibet in Ü and received esoteric Buddhist as well as Madhyamaka teachings from two figures who had been associated with Rinchen Sangpo and/or Atiśa in their youth. *General Explanation*, an early Kadam Madhyamaka teaching attributed to Atiśa, mentions Chakriwa and directly cites him.[46] The work praises Chakriwa several times as "possessing incomparable knowledge" and being "unmistaken" with regard to Atiśa's advanced Madhyamaka teachings (Apple 2018, 174). *General Explanation*, after quoting Atiśa's *Lamp*, cites Chakriwa as stating: "If the means do not dependently arise—that is, the stairway of correct conventional reality—the three individuals who go along the stages of the path will not occur" (Apple 2018, 223). This statement demonstrates that Chakriwa not only knew advanced Madhyamaka teachings regarding correct conventional reality but that he also knew the stages of the path system of the three types of individuals.

In sum, Chakriwa, although not well represented in later Kadam histories, is described in other sources as receiving advanced teachings of Atiśa from Potowa or Gönpawa and transmitting these teachings in a lineage that went to Gampopa through to Phakmodrupa. In light of this evidence, the lineage list of Atiśa's *Stages* presented in *General Meaning of the Stages of the Path* becomes a viable possibility.

The lineage list in *General Meaning* states that Atiśa's *Stages* was transmitted from Chakriwa to the great master Gampopa Sönam Rinchen, also known as Dakpo Lhajé, "the doctor from Dakpo." Gampopa, well known as a Kagyü master, initially trained as a Kadam monk after the tragic death of his wife and child. Gampopa then became a student of the poet-siddha Milarepa (1052–1135), under whom he learned advanced esoteric practices such as inner-heat meditation and the great seal (mahāmudrā) for thirteen months in 1110–11. Gampopa is well known for combining the Kadam trainings he received with the esoteric Buddhist teachings of Milarepa into the "converged rivers of the Kadam and Great Seal teachings."[47]

Before receiving advanced instructions under Milarepa, Gampopa became fully ordained at the age of twenty-five (1104) and studied under various Kadam masters for up to five years. His Kadam masters include Jayulwa Shönu Ö (1075–1138), Gyayön Dak (eleventh century), Geshé Drepa (eleventh century), Nyukrumpa Tsöndrü Bar (1042–1109), and Chakriwa.[48] Gampopa received initial training in the stages of the path from Nyukrumpa and more advanced stages of the path instruction from Gyayön Dak, a student of Gönpawa. He is said to have received all of Atiśa's special instructions from Chakriwa.[49] As noted above based on the manuscript evidence, the special transmission from Chakriwa to Gampopa included esoteric practices, teachings on Madhyamaka, and Atiśa's *Stages*.

Even though Gampopa is famously remembered for joining the Kadam and mahāmudrā teachings, speaking to his creativity and ingenuity as a Buddhist scholar and meditation master, the transmission from Chakriwa to Gampopa is marked by tensions that may have contributed to Atiśa's *Stages* fading in popularity and being overlooked in later Tibetan histories. The foremost tension was between Gampopa's former Kadam teachers and Milarepa, as depicted in the histories and life stories preserved in both Kadam and Kagyü sources. Chakriwa never approved of Gampopa visiting Milarepa, and other Kadam teachers warned Gampopa not to visit a yogin who "wears dog skin" when he departed to train under Milarepa.[50] When Gampopa initially meets Milarepa, as famously depicted in the *Blue Annals*, Milarepa belittles the Kadam meditation training that Gampopa received as inferior and not conducive to buddhahood. Milarepa also disparages the Kadam understanding of esoteric practice.[51] These episodes suggest conflicts between monastic and yogic practice, differences in interpretation of sūtra and tantra, and distinct pedagogical styles, among other differences. A hypothesis that I have proposed elsewhere for other early Kadam manuscripts also applies to the transmission of Atiśa's *Stages*. Atiśa's *Stages* may not have been widely disseminated among Kadampas after Gampopa because Gampopa left his Kadam teachers when he became a student of Milarepa (Vetturini 2013, 139–40). Likewise, these teachings were not widely transmitted among Kagyü communities after Gampopa because the stages of the path had been characterized as a graduated, sūtra-based discourse that did not include tantric teachings from masters such as Nāropa or Milarepa. In this way, rather than evincing the active propagation of Atiśa's *Stages*, Gampopa's works demonstrate his creative adaption of the Kadam-based path training.

Gampopa's collected teachings contain works on the stages of the path and the stages of the teaching, and several of his other works allude to his training in the Kadam stages of the path. *Scriptural Sunshine* (*Bstan bcos lung gi nyi 'od*), a thematic scriptural compendium, discusses topics found in the stages of the path (Kragh 2015, 612–63). *Jewel Garland of the Supreme Path* (*Lam mchog rin chen 'phreng ba*) is a middle-length repository of oral instructions on the practice of the path (Jackson 1996, 233n3). Gampopa's collected works also contain small works with titles such as *Essence of the Stages of the Path* (*Lam rim snying po*) and *Condensed Stages of the Path* (*Lam rim mdor bsdus*), the latter sharing the same title as the text in chapter 2 below. Gampopa's miscellaneous sayings (*gsung thor bu*) also contain advice on the stages of the path. His most famous work on the bodhisattva path was his *Ornament of Precious Liberation* (*Thar pa rin po che'i rgyan*), highly regarded as a stages of the teaching meditator's manual of essential advice (Roesler, Holmes, and Jackson 2015). *Ornament of Precious Liberation* cites Atiśa's *Lamp* over fifteen times in its outlining of the practices and meditations of a bodhisattva. Does *Ornament of*

Precious Liberation demonstrate knowledge of Atiśa's *Stages*? Although the evidence is minimal, Gampopa does make an allusion to stages of the path teachings other than *Lamp* in chapter 17. After directly citing *Lamp*, Gampopa states, "[Atiśa] explains in the teachings on the gradual path that all substantial realities, or beliefs in substantiality, are included within the two kinds of self, and that both these entities are by their very nature emptiness."[52] The mention that "beliefs in substantiality" (*dngos po 'dzin*) are emptiness (*stong nyid*) is not directly addressed in Atiśa's *Lamp* or its autocommentary (Sherburne 2000), yet is alluded to in *Stages* (stanzas 151, 155, and 179). This may explain why Gampopa directly cites *Lamp* while separately referencing a graded path taught by Atiśa.

General Meaning specifies that these teachings went from Gampopa to Phakmodrupa.[53] Phakmodrupa Dorjé Gyalpo (1110–70), one of Gampopa's most prominent students, later became a founding figure for the Drigung, Taklung, and Drukpa Kagyü subsects. In his youth Phakmodrupa traveled from eastern to central Tibet, receiving full monastic ordination at age twenty-four. In central Tibet he studied under a number of Kadam masters and received several lineages of transmission. Notably, he received a transmission of Atiśa's *Lamp* descending from Kharak Gomchung (ca. eleventh century), Geshé Lhopa Könchok Pal, and Geshé Ar Jangchup Yeshé (ca. eleventh century).[54] Phakmodrupa would later study the path with the result (*lam 'bras*) teachings under Sachen Kunga Nyingpo (1092–1158) and receive further teachings under the Kadampa geshé Dölpa Sherab Gyatso (1059–1131), who compiled the *Blue Compendium* of Potowa's stages of the path instructions. Phakmodrupa studied under these teachers before meeting Gampopa at age forty-one. Phakmodrupa received a number of teachings from Gampopa, the most significant being Gampopa's teaching on mahāmudrā and coemergent union (*lhan cig skyes sbyor*).[55] After the death of Gampopa, Phakmodrupa taught for a couple of years at several locations and then resided in meditative seclusion in a thatched hut east of the city of Tsethang at a place called Phakmodru, or "Sow Crossing." This location would eventually become Densathil Monastery, an important religious and political center.[56]

Phakmodrupa composed several works related to the stages of the path and stages of the teaching. Works on the stages of the path include *Jeweled Stairway* (*Rin po che'i them skas*), *Stairway of Secret Mantra Stages of the Path* (*Gsang sngags lam rim them skas*), and *Jeweled Stairway Uniting the Meaning of Sūtra and Tantra* (*Mdo rgyud dgongs pa bsdebs pa lam rim rin po che'i them skas*). These works await further study but appear to be original compositions influenced by the teachings Phakmodrupa received from Kadam masters and Gampopa. Phakmodrupa's well-known stages of the teaching work is *How to*

Enter the Buddha's Doctrine by Stages. This early work of ten chapters outlines the stages of the path leading to the integration of wisdom and compassion, resulting in buddhahood. The treatise is a meditation-oriented work influenced by Gampopa with minimal citations from Atiśa.[57]

Phakmodrupa's works on the stages of the path and stages of the teaching do not appear to be explicitly influenced by Atiśa's *Stages*. However, several analogies in Phakmodrupa's mahāmudrā teachings on integrating thoughts into the path (*lam du 'khyer*) are found in Atiśa's *General Explanation*, *Great Exposition of View and Meditation*, and *Stages*. These analogies include (1) meeting and recognition of friends, (2) melting snow, and (3) the spread of forest fire.[58] This may indicate that Atiśa's *Stages* overlaps with advanced meditation instructions that circulated separately in distinct transmissions. A good example is *Pointing-Out Instructions in Sets of Five* attributed to Atiśa. This advanced meditation teaching was considered by twelfth-century yogin-meditators to be a teaching on mahāmudrā, yet it is closely related, if not derived from, Atiśa's *Stages* (see chapter 5).

After Phakmodrupa, the lineage list shifts from naming individuals and invokes place and clan names. *General Meaning* next specifies that the teachings of *Stages* went to "both the Drigung and Taklung," the "Khamkom," the Khön, and then a final anonymous recepient.[59] The mention of Drigung and Taklung may be refering to Drigung Jikten Gönpo (1143–1217) and Taklung Thangpa Tashi Pal (1142–1210), both well-known disciples of Phakmodrupa and founders of the respective Drigung and Taklung branches of the Kagyü.

Taklung Thangpa was twenty-three when he first met Phakmodrupa in 1165 and followed him for several years. It is certainly possible that Taklung Thangpa received transmission of the stages of the path from Phakmodrupa, but sources suggest that Taklung Thangpa also met and received teachings from the Kadampa master Chekawa Yeshé Dorjé (1101–75) in Maldro in 1170.[60] Chekawa is said to have given Taklung Thangpa the transmission of Kadam teachings.[61] Chekawa upheld lineages descending from Potowa and Sharawa.[62]

Jikten Gönpo, or Drigung Sumgön, founder of the influential Drigung branch of the Kagyü, is said to have received stages of the teaching and stages of the path from Radreng Gomchen in his youth (Sobisch 2002, 330). Later sources state that Jikten Gönpo received the Kadam teaching from Geshé Langlungpa (1123–93), who upheld an oral stages of the path transmission descending from Dromtönpa and Chengawa Tsultrim Bar (1038–1103).[63] Nevertheless, a transmission of the stages of the path from Taklung Thangpa to Jikten Gönpo is possible but not currently documentable beyond the suggestion here in *General Meaning*.

General Meaning's reference to "Khamkom" (*khams skom*) is not clear, even whether it is a person or a place. It might refer to a thirteenth-century monastic seat that upheld the stages of the path teaching transmission. From this place or person, *General Meaning* says that *Stages* went to Khön. The Khön family are traditionally the hierarchs of the Sakya lineage. The position of Sakya Throneholder continues to the present day as a hereditary position within the Khön family, rather than one based on incarnate teachers. The fact that our anonymous author of *General Meaning* refers to a clan name rather than Sakya Monastery may reflect an early thirteenth-century perspective, since the Sakya tradition had yet to gain hegemony in Tibet under Mongol support after 1240. For before the Sakya became a powerful religious sect, their teachings were known under the name of Khön.[64] A Khön, or Sakya, recipient that fits the time range of the manuscript lineage would be a young Sakya Paṇḍita Kunga Gyaltsen (1182–1251). Sakya Paṇḍita is recorded as receiving a number of teachings from Chiwo Lhepa Jangchup Ö (b. 1144), including Madhyamaka, mahāmudrā, and Kadam teachings in the domain of practice (*spyod phyogs*). The "domain of practice" is mentioned in numerous colophons within the *Stages* manuscript. Chiwo Lhepa held Kadam teachings in a lineage descended from Neusurpa.[65] Moreover, as van der Kuijp (1987, 58) suggests, not only did Sakya Paṇḍita receive various teachings on logic and epistemology (*tshad ma*) from Kadam masters, he also received teachings on a number of distinct Kadam stages of the path texts. It is conceivable that Sakya Paṇḍita may have received an oral or written transmission of Atiśa's *Stages* in addition to the other Kadam teachings he received from Chiwo Lhepa.

At this point the lineage figures named in *General Meaning* come to an end. This suggests that the active transmission of the cycle of texts in this manuscript ends in the early thirteenth century. The thirteenth century as a period when these teachings dissipate fits with the broader conditions in Tibet at that time (see table 2).

To briefly recapitulate the historical context, Potowa Rinchen Sal (1027–1105) served as the fourth abbot at Radreng Monastery, the founding institution of the Kadampas. After Potowa departed from Radreng, the monastic center underwent a period without leadership known as the "Dharma famine" (*chos kyi mu ge*, beginning ca. 1085–1115), that lasted sixty-five years.[66] The later appointed fifth abbot, Shang Ö Jowa (?–1150), cultivated a patron-monk relationship (*mchod yon*) with the kingdom of the Tangut that would last through the tenures of the sixth and seventh Radreng abbots, Geshé Gangthang Karwa (?–1173) and Gön Ö Jowa (?–1229). The Tangut kingdom, known in Chinese as Xixia and in Tibetan as Minyak (*mi nyag*), existed as an independent state from 1032 to 1227, and Kadam-based institutions flourished in central Tibet during this period. This flourishing, however, came to an end in the early thirteenth century. The Mongols began military excursions into Xixia in 1205, and by 1227 the Tanguts had been overthrown.[67] In 1240 the Mongolian ruler Göden sent his general Dorta and cavalry into Tibetan areas northeast of Lhasa. This military incursion resulted in the destruction of Radreng, Phenyul Gyal Lhakhang, and the hermitage of Drakgyab, all Kadam-based monastic institutions.[68] As recent scholarship has stated, "The Mongol conquest of Tibet in 1240 was a bloody one, creating much hardship, social upheaval, and resentment."[69] In the following turbulent period under Mongké Khan (r. 1251–59), various monastic seats (*gdan sa*) were patronized by different Mongolian rulers. The monastic seat of Sakya established relations with Göden, the Tsalpa Kagyü with Khubilai, the Taklung Kagyü with Arigh Böge, the Phakdru Kagyü with Hülegü, and the Drigung Kagyü with Mongké.[70] The monastic seat of Drigung Thil ruled over Central Tibet by proxy from 1240 to circa 1260.[71] The authority of the Drigung and Phakdru Kagyü was also officially recognized in western Tibet and empowered by the Mongols during this time.[72] Whether by happenstance or more nefarious historical conditions, Kadam monastic institutions were not supported during this fragmented and tumultuous era. Gradually, over the next hundred years, the Sakyapa would gain dominance over Tibet, ruling as regents until the 1350s, the declining years of the Mongol Yuan dynasty (1271–1367).[73] Within these turbulent conditions, active transmission of the *Stages* manuscript came to an end. Certainly other manuscripts of *Stages* and other lineages of the *Stages* oral transmission must have existed. However, the current manuscript is the only evidence extant.

After the fourteenth century, the dominant system of the stages of the path was that of Tsongkhapa. Did Tsongkhapa receive these teachings on Atiśa's *Stages*? The lineage outlined above, and the structure and content of the *Stages* manuscript, seem to indicate that Tsongkhapa did not receive them, and he, at very least, does not explicitly comment on them. However, Tsongkhapa's biography and writings indicate that he received several lineages of stages of the path teachings, both oral and written. The oral transmissions include those from Lhodrak Namkha Gyaltsen—a Kadam master of Chiwo Lhepa's monastery—and Khenchen Chökyab Sangpo. If Tsongkhapa did receive an oral transmission of the stages of the path teachings similar to those in the *Stages* manuscript, this might explain how he came to incorporate content of the small- and middling-capacity teachings in his *Great Treatise* that are not found in Atiśa's *Lamp*. In his writings on the stages of the path, Tsongkhapa ostensibly always follows Atiśa's *Lamp* and also explicitly follows Drolungpa's *Great Exposition of the Stages of the Doctrine*, as mentioned in both the colophon of the *Great Treatise* and episodes recorded in Tsongkhapa's biography.[74] Tsongkhapa also praises the works of Potowa and Sharawa as early exemplars in the stages of the path teachings.[75] The only stages of the path teaching of Tsongkhapa's that resembles Atiśa's *Stages* is Tsongkhapa's *Songs of Experience*, which is written in stanzas of nine-syllable lines, focused on meditative experience, and given as a sequence of stages of the path topics.[76] Nevertheless, the content of this work does not fully match Atiśa's *Stages*. *Stages* ends with advanced instructions that point out a direct nonconceptual experience of emptiness that is related to an innate, nondual, sudden recognition. This type of instruction is not found in Tsongkhapa's works, and he explicitly argues against similar understandings of meditation practice in his *Queries from a Sincere Heart*.[77] Moreover, the differences in content between *Stages* and *Lamp* also help to explain Gö Lotsāwa Shönu Pal's statement that Tsongkhapa's "analytical approach" does not properly comprehend the system of *Lamp* for the Gelukpas (Mathes 2008, 136 and 142). In other words, Tsongkhapa's analytical style of teaching the stages of the path in 1405 did not match the "direct realization" style that would have been familiar to audience members like Shönu Pal who had received Kadam-based meditative instructions derived from *Stages*.[78]

Be this as it may, in his record of teachings received, Tsongkhapa differentiates between a stages of the path lineage he receives in the tradition of Gönpawa and a lineage of Atiśa's *Lamp* that descends from Dromtönpa and Potowa. Notably, the stages of the path lineage begins with Atiśa and does not have any other Indian predecessors.[79] This lineage may be related to *Stages* and its accompanying works, which also begin with Atiśa. This suggests that even though Tsongkhapa may have received teachings on Atiśa's *Stages*, he did not formulate his own writings on the stages of the path according to *Stages* and instead creatively fashioned his own exegesis based on *Lamp* and works of Potowa, Sharawa, and Drolungpa. This is perhaps why Lechen remarks that Tsongkhapa relied on perfection path treatises and the oral teachings (*man ngag*) of the three types of individuals of the stages of the path in formulating his system.[80]

As previous scholarship has observed (Napper 2001), Tsongkhapa actually cites only three verses of Atiśa's *Lamp* in his *Great Treatise*. Tsongkhapa invokes Atiśa as an exemplary figure for Atiśa's ethical discipline and moral virtue. However, Tsongkhapa does not call upon Atiśa for his Madhyamaka view or his practice of esoteric Buddhism and, perhaps as well, does not appeal to Atiśa's advanced pointing-out instructions of nondual meditation found in the latter portions of *Stages*.

Table 2. Atiśa's Stages of the Path to Awakening Lineage

Atiśa (982–1054)

Dromtönpa (1005–64)

Gönpawa (1016–82)

Gya Chakriwa (late eleventh century)

Gampopa (1079–1153)

Phakmodrupa (1110–70)

Drigung (Jikten Gönpo) (1143–1217)

Taklung (Thangpa Tashi Pal) (1142–1210)

Khamkom

Khön (Sakya Paṇḍita) (1182–1251)

Final anonymous recipient

Conclusion

Atiśa's *Stages* is not as well known as *Lamp* due to a combination of historical and cultural conditions. As discussed, Atiśa's *Stages* mentions Mahāsāṃghika Vinaya rules that were never adapted or followed in Tibetan Buddhism. *Stages* also presents Atiśa's own approach to Madhyamaka that was not followed by later Tibetan traditions. As van der Kuijp (2018, 102 and 113) emphasizes regarding knowledge and manuscripts in Tibet, traditions were local. This is most likely the case with the *Stages* manuscript and its teachings. *Stages* was composed for Atiśa's close disciples within a context of teachings for individuals of highest capacity following the stages of the path approach. From this perspective it may have not been widely disseminated. Certainly the manuscript evidence suggests that this was the case.

Part 1
The Hidden Wellspring of Tibetan Path Literature

1. Stages of the Path to Awakening

THIS CHAPTER presents an analysis of Atiśa's *Stages* as a system of path realization and offers a complete translation of this seminal work. As mentioned, *Stages* is a long continuous series of poetic prescriptive instructions. The work was most likely memorized by early disciples and only later put into writing. The Tibetan copyist of the manuscript has provided vertical line punctuation marks (*shad*) indicating divisions within the sections or stanzas. I have sequentially numbered these sections 1 to 181 and placed references to them in brackets.[81]

After the initial reverence to buddhas and bodhisattvas, Atiśa pays homage to the spiritual master (*guru*) as well as the Three Jewels (*triratna*). The supreme refuge of the spiritual master will be an important theme throughout the work. Atiśa explains that the reason for composing the teaching is for his audience to realize (*rtogs*) the stages of the path to awakening [§1–2].

The main body of *Stages* opens with a classification of the three types of individuals. In his earlier *Lamp*, Atiśa gave a brief description of these individuals. *Lamp* states,

> A person of small capacity seeks only the pleasures of cyclic existence
> by whatever means possible and pursues his own benefit.
> The middling individual cares about his own peace, turning away from
> the pleasures of existence and reversing unwholesome deeds.
> The supreme individual, because of personal suffering, seeks the
> complete extinction of others' suffering.[82]

In his *Commentary on the Difficult Points of the Lamp for the Path to Awakening*,[83] Atiśa cites the great fourth-century Indian master Vasubandhu as a source for this threefold classification. The citation of Vasubandhu's *Treasury of Higher Knowledge Autocommentary* states,

> The inferior one seeks his own happiness through various means;
> the middling one seeks only to eliminate suffering, but does not

> seek happiness, because that is a source of suffering. The supreme person, through taking suffering upon himself, seeks the happiness of others and thereby totally eliminates suffering, because the suffering of others is his own suffering.[84]

In this commentary, Atiśa clarifies that he will not elaborate upon the individuals of small and middling capacity, since their definitions are easy to understand. He also explains that he composed *Lamp* for those who are good vessels of the Mahāyāna doctrine.[85] *Stages*, however, places emphasis on understanding the realizations of all three types of individuals [§3]. Moreover, *Stages* specifies that the small-capacity individual seeks a future heavenly rebirth, the middling one practices to achieve liberation—that is, nirvāṇa—and the supreme individual seeks buddhahood out of compassion for others. *Stages* and its commentaries state that each type of individual has (1) practices, (2) meditation objects, (3) a reversal of tendencies, and (4) a result. These four are not discussed in *Lamp* and its commentary. In addition to explicitly mentioning these four qualities, *Stages* demarcates differences in vows, orientations, processes of realization, and stages of indivisibility (*dbyer med pa*) that an individual upholds as they ascend through the stages of the path. Table 3 provides an overview of the qualities of the three types of individuals in *Stages*.

As table 3 indicates, different qualities are developed and enhanced at various stages of the path, based on the capacity and inclination of the individual. The *General Meaning* commentary (chapter 3) indicates, based on the *Ten Wheels of Kṣitigarbha Sūtra*, that the initial practices and meditation objects of the small and middling capacities are "built upon" (*thog tu brtsegs pa*), rather than shared in "common" (*thun mongs ba*), as is the case in other, later, stages of the path systems. This means that a person of supreme capacity must first gain the realizations of small and middling individuals. In terms of realization and practice, Atiśa has explained in *Entry to the Two Realities* and its commentaries that the lower-level practices lead toward superior attainments, culminating in the realization of ultimate reality. In this system, based on principles found in the *Ornament of Mahāyāna Scriptures* (*Mahāyānasūtrālaṃkāra*) and known among early Kadampas as the "system of inclination" (*gzhol lugs*), the sequence of subsequent practices and realizations arises based on previous ones.[86] The overall structure of *Stages* presumes that inferior practices are presented before superior ones and coarse realizations before subtler ones, subtle realizations being more difficult and requiring greater capacity.

Atiśa specifies in both his *Lamp* (verses 20–21) and *Stages* (stanza 122) that he accepts seven kinds of *pratimokṣa* vows.[87] Atiśa's *Commentary on the Difficult Points of the Lamp for the Path to Awakening* provides a detailed exegesis of these types of vows based on the works of his teachers Bodhibhadra and Serlingpa.[88] In his *Open Basket of Jewels*, where he discusses the conduct based on having accepted vows, Atiśa differentiates both pratimoḳsa and bodhisattva vows on the basis of the stages of progress along the path, a principle similar to his stages of the path system.[89] In general, Atiśa ranks the pratimokṣa vows according to the respective degrees of spiritual commitment and renunciation. The vows of a fully ordained monk rank the highest while vows of a lay person are lowest. For Atiśa, the seven kinds of pratimokṣa vows serve as the necessary foundation for bodhisattva vows. Atiśa does not regard another type of vow, the one-day precepts (*upavāsa, bsnyen gnas*), as a type of pratimokṣa vow because of its temporary nature.[90] While acknowledging that Vinaya and Abhidharma works classify the one-day precepts as an eighth type of pratimokṣa vow, Atiśa follows Bodhibhadra and the renowned Asaṅga (fourth century), scholars he admires as masters of bodhisattva discipline, in not ranking this vow as worthy of pratimokṣa status.[91] These distinctions have significance for *Stages* in that he presents the one-day precepts as the type of vow appropriate for individuals of small capacity, despite their not having pratimokṣa status. Along these lines, the seven kinds of pratimokṣa vows are to be upheld by individuals of middling capacity, and they are considered the foundation for the bodhisattva vows and for fulfilling the qualities of an individual of supreme capacity. *General Meaning* (see chapter 3; folio 34b) states that such a sequence follows the principle of "upwardly progressing good qualities." An apt analogy invoked by this principle is that of constructing a building. As Barron (2011, 15) describes this, "The foundation remains in place as upper levels are added, and the presence of higher and higher stories in no way obviates the need for that foundation." In this way, pratimokṣa vows are the foundation of all the practices and meditations in Atiśa's stages of the path system.

Sections 4 to 75 of *Stages* present the vows, practices, and meditations of individuals of small capacity. The orientation of the small-capacity individual is toward practices affecting future lifetimes. They uphold the initial lay precepts, practice virtuous actions, increase their stock of merit, refrain from negative actions, and take refuge in the Three Jewels: the Buddha, his teachings (Dharma), and the community of followers (Saṅgha) [§4–5]. Here, Atiśa emphasizes that the lay precepts must be taken through a ritual and that one takes refuge voluntarily. Initially, individuals of small capacity must also realize the differences between non-Buddhists and Buddhists, place their faith in the Buddha, and abandon devotion to non-Buddhist deities. The sections on refuge describe the eight great benefits of refuge and mention paying homage to the buddha of whichever direction one travels in [§6–9].

After refuge, the text addresses the basic principles of lay conduct based on the pratimokṣa code [§10–12]. The one-day precepts are initially emphasized for the lay community. The one-day precepts—literally "abstinence" or "fasting" in Pāli and Sanskrit—are vows taken by laypeople during the fortnightly confession ceremony traditionally observed at the times of the new and full moon.[92] The term for this practice has also been translated as "approximation" (Sobisch 2002, 38n85), in that laypeople temporarily emulate the discipline of ordained monastics by keeping the eight constituents outlined in *Stages* [§10] for one day. *Stages* next describes the basic principles of conduct according to the Mahāsāṃghika laws of monastic conduct (*phal chen tshangs spyod gtan gyi khrims*): avoiding the four root types of misconduct [§11]. The four root types of conduct are abandoning the taking of life, taking what is not given, lying, and having sexual intercourse.

The mention of Mahāsāṃghika regulations here is notable. Although Atiśa was fully ordained as a Mahāsāṃghika monk, the Mahāsāṃghika ordination lineage was never established in Tibet, and he was never allowed to ordain anyone in Tibet (Apple 2014 and Apple 2019). The brief mention of the Mahāsāṃghika supports the view that *Stages* was authored by Atiśa. Atiśa does not single out this ordination lineage in either *Lamp* or its commentary when discussing monastic discipline. In Indian Buddhism, the pratimokṣa vows were not to be heard or seen by non-monastics, and the Mahāsāṃghika had a prohibition against verbatim recitation of the rules to the laity (Clarke 2009). A Mahāsāṃghika monk could explain the *content* of the four rules but not its verbal formulation. This may be why the four root downfalls are only described in an oblique manner in stanza 11. As Clarke suggests, these four proscriptions are not exactly the five vows of the laity nor the rules of a monk. Rather, they are shared basic ethical prescriptions held in common by Buddhists before proceeding to take the full vows of the laity and later of ordination. In his *Commentary on the Difficult Points of the Lamp for the Path to Awakening*, Atiśa describes two types of lay devotees: those who abstain from illicit sexual activity and those who abstain from sexual activity with their own spouses. The training in common for both is abstaining from the four root downfalls and alcohol.[93] The mention of abandoning sexual intercourse (*mi tshangs spyod*) at this point in the *Stages* suggests that Atiśa considered the celibate layperson to be of higher capacity in the stages of the path.

Stages [§12] then explains increasing merit and making physical and mental offerings dedicated to oneself and others. One then contemplates the fortunate moments (*kṣaṇasampad*) afforded by the precious opportunity of human rebirth endowed with leisure and fortune [§13–20]. A precious human rebirth is free from the oppressive conditions of the lower realms of rebirth and has the fortune of riches acquired from others as well as personal endowments. Atiśa briefly outlines the conditions that define "abodes of bad rebirth" (*akṣaṇa*), including the traditional eight inopportune moments[94] along with rebirth in the realm of neither perception nor nonperception, one of the formless realms [§13]. Ten aspects of opportunity are then succintly described in terms of five riches that depend on others and five personal endowments [§14]. The rarity of leisure and fortune is indicated by the well-known analogy of the turtle swimming in the ocean [§17]. Based on these contemplations, *Stages* motivates its audience to take advantage of fortunate conditions and to vigorously cultivate merit and virtue.

Impermanence is the next major object of meditation for the person of small capacity [§21–32]. Impermanence, the transitory nature of conditioned existence, can be either external or internal. External impermanence for Atiśa refers to the observable changes of the worldly environment, such as the change in seasons and the growth and decay of plants and trees. Internal impermanence is the transitory nature of sentient beings, exemplified by aging, sickness, and death. Internal impermanence includes the varied human situations for death and the fragility of the human body. Death is inescapable and cannot be overturned. The meditation on impermanence overturns the fixation on permanence and encourages the practitioner to take advantage of the fortunate opportunity of human rebirth. The topic of impermanence is followed by an initial discussion of cause and effect, focusing on the nature of nonvirtuous actions in relation to keeping vows. *Stages* emphasizes the futility of committing nonvirtuous actions and the repercussions of the maturation of nonvirtuous actions [§33–35].

Stages then outlines the specific sufferings and anguishing conditions of the lower realms of rebirth (*durgati*) [§36–51], including the realms of hell denizens (*nāraka*) [§36–42], hungry ghosts (*preta*) [§43–47], and animals (*tīrañc*) along with nāgas [§48–51]. The names and general characteristics of the hell realms outlined by Atiśa conform to the well-known system of eight hot hells and eight cold hells found in Indian Buddhist works such as Vasubandhu's *Treasury of Higher Knowledge* and its autocommentary as well as later Tibetan path literature.[95] However, the specific area sizes and lengths of lifespan of the various hot hells mentioned by Atiśa differ from other currently known works. *Stages* [§41] also provides a unique description of individual, ephemeral hells (*pratyekanaraka*; *nyi tshe*) that are correlated to results of rebirth based on the ten paths of nonvirtuous actions.[96] For instance, *Stages* specifies that for lying, "the tongue is stretched out for five hundred yojanas and plowed by one thousand blazing plows . . ." Following Asaṅga's *Yogācārabhūmi*, *Stages* describes three types of hungry ghosts, differentiating them in terms of whether they have obstructions that are external, internal, or both external and internal.[97] The lifespans of hungry ghosts, animals, and nāgas are derived from Vasubhandhu's *Treasury of Higher Knowledge* and its autocommentary. Atiśa emphasizes that the sufferings of the three lower realms are uncontrollable, meaningless, and long-lasting. He encourages his audience to cultivate virtue after contemplating the fearful consequences of rebirth in any one of these lower realms.

The attainment of lower or higher states of rebirth is based on the principles of karma found in classical Buddhist descriptions of the effects of virtuous or nonvirtous actions. The negative effects of nonvirtuous actions are based upon mental afflictions and wrongdoing. Atiśa describes the concordant effects (*niṣyandaphala*) of the ten nonvirtuous actions [§52] as well as the causally concordant behavioral effects of past habituated actions. The general dominant result (*adhipatiphala*) of nonvirtuous actions manifests as negative effects in the immediate environment [§54].

At this point, Atiśa states that "afflictions and wrongdoing are self-manifestations of the mind" (*nyon mongs sdig sems rang snang shar ba*) [§55], indicating that the anguishing experiences in the lower realms of rebirth are not external conditions but appearances based on the state of one's own mind. Underlying this statement is Atiśa's understanding of the Middle Way (*madhyamaka*), based on the works of Nāgārjuna. Rather than positing that existence resides in external objects, like Vaibhāṣikas, or that it resides in consciousness, like Yogācārins, Atiśa posits "mere appearances" (*snang ba tsam*; *pratibhāsamātra*), meaning that all objects and cognitions are dependently designated and are therefore mere imputations (*btags pa tsam*; *prajñaptimātra*) by the mind. The dependent arising of conventional reality thus occurs in correlation with the impurity or purity of one's awareness. In another work, Atiśa refers to this process as "the mere appearance of appropriate manifestations" (*rang snang gi snang ba tsam*), where perspectives and awarenesses transform appearances, depending upon one's level of realization on the path. In this way, for Atiśa, self-manifestations of the mind are mere appearances.[98] The mentalism of mere appearances will also be discussed at more advanced levels in the stages of the path.[99]

At this point in the text, Atiśa prescribes countermeasures to the mental afflictions and encourages the achievement of virtue. He briefly mentions an interesting point regarding nonanalytical cessation [§56]. In general, nonanalytical cessation is one of the types of unconditioned factors found among the lists of various Buddhist Abhidharma traditions.[100] The factor signifies a type of cessation that occurs not due to analysis or insight but is rather a nonarisal due to the lack of sufficient conditions. This cessation is not regarded as a separation due to the application of an antidote against mental afflictions. Its specific characteristics were debated among different traditions of Abhidharma. Atiśa provides an ethically prescriptive approach to this concept by stating that one attains this type of cessation merely by applying restraint to nonvirtue.

Stages then outlines virtues and the wholesome courses of action as well as their immediate environmental effects [§57–58]. When one becomes habituated to virtuous actions, this leads to their increase due to the compatibility of cause [§60]. Atiśa then describes the immediate environmental effects as the correspondence between wholesome actions and the resulting agricultural conditions and productions of crops [§61]. One is then encouraged to be diligent in the practice of virtue based on this outline of cause and effect in relation to virtuous actions. The text then recapitulates negative actions and their results in order to encourage the elimination of subtle nonvirtue and the accomplishment of even the most subtle virtuous actions. Atiśa indicates how all experiences of happiness and suffering are due to the results of karma, as illustrated by the sufferings of the lower realms of hell denizens, hungry ghosts, and animals and the conditions of the upper realms of gods and humans [§63–66]. *Stages* briefly returns to the mentalism of mere appearance by instructing that all appearances of happiness and suffering are one's own mind manifesting as cause and effect [§67–68].

The text then succinctly summarizes the general principles of cause and effect [§69–73], outlining the results of projecting and completing virtuous or nonvirtuous actions [§69], the manner in which causes are accumulated based on underlying obstructions, afflictions, or wrongful actions [§70], and the way in which effects arise in relation to countermeasures, the potency of the deeds, and the underlying motivation [§71–72]. The person of small capacity is then given initial instructions on the relationship between cause and effect, emptiness, and their own mind. The nature of one's own mind is indivisible from emptiness and from the cause and effect of actions [§73]. Atiśa refers to the indivisibility of emptiness from cause and effect as the Great Middle Way (*mahāmadhyamaka*; *dbu ma chen po*), which avoids the extremes of nihilism and permanence. Realization of this first level of indivisibility (*dbyer med pa*) is said to heighten one's attention to eliminating the subtlest nonvirtuous actions and cultivating virtuous actions. It also contributes to more advanced realizations of union at the higher stages of the path.

The meditations on the stages of the small-capacity individual reverse the tendencies of laziness, wrongdoing, and attachment to the eight worldly concerns (*aṣṭalokadharma*). The eight worldly concerns encapsulate the fixation of ordinary individuals with loss (*alābha*) and gain (*lābha*), suffering (*duḥkha*) and pleasure (*sukha*), blame (*nindā*) and praise (*praśaṃsā*), and disrepute (*ayaśas*) and fame (*yaśas*). The meditations on death, impermanence, and karma overturn these tendencies [§74]. Implementation of the small-capacity stages leads to the casually concordant effect of eliminating nonvirtue and increasing virtue, the separation effect (*visaṃyoga*) of eliminating rebirth in lower states, and the maturation effect (*vipāka*) of gaining high states of rebirth among gods and humans [§75].

Stages next addressses the vows, practices, and meditations of middling-capacity individuals [§76–108]. The middling-capacity individual has an orientation toward achieving liberation, or nirvāṇa, from the rounds of rebirth. This type of individual upholds either the five major vows (*pañcaśīla*) of a layperson, the complete vows of a novice, or the more potent vows of a full monk (*bhikṣu*) [§76–77]. This section of the text emphasizes the importance of moral discipline, highlighting the faults of the householder life and the exponential benefits of taking monastic vows. *Stages* describes monastic moral discipline as the basis for the paths of all vehicles, a point shared with all the sūtras and tantras. As Atiśa underscores, the arhat buddhas of the past, present, and future all uphold monastic vows [§77–79].

Stages then describes the initial meditations of the middling-capacity individual on the faults of cyclic existence [§80–96]. The general faults of cyclic existence are initially described as the fact that cyclic existence is totally overridden with delusion, conditioned by uncertainty, and driven by unsatisfactory sense desires [§80–81]. Atiśa outlines the faults of cyclic existence in detail, focusing on the specific sufferings within each realm of rebirth. The text first illustrates the faults of the specific sufferings in the lower realms, those of the hell denizens, hungry ghosts, and animals [§82–84]. The dissatisfactory sufferings in the upper realms of humans, demigods, and gods are then explained. *Stages* initially describes the human sufferings of birth, aging, sickness, and death in strikingly insightful detail [§84–88]. The human sufferings within various situations include not finding what is sought [§89], the problems of maintaining wealth [§90], encountering enemies [§91], and being separated from beloved friends and relatives [92]. The section on the faults of cyclic existence concludes with a discussion of three types of suffering based on the five appropriated aggregates (*upādānaskandha*) [§93–95]. This section of the text concludes with summarized instructions for contemplating the faults of cyclic existence [§96].

After contemplating the faults of cyclic existence, the individual of middling capacity focuses on the cause of cyclic existence and the path that liberates from cyclic existence [§97–106]. The cause of cyclic existence is when the suchness of the mind (*sems kyi de nyid*)—later equated with emptiness—

grasps onto inner and outer things as pertaining to a self (*ātman*), due to ignorance (*avidyā*) and delusion (*mohā*). The text succinctly outlines the progressive order of the dependent arising of cyclic existence [§98] followed by the reversal of dependent arising in conjunction with the practices of learning, reflection, and meditation (*śrutacintābhāvanā*) [§99].

The next phase of cultivation for the person of middling capacity is meditation on the close placements of mindfulness (*smṛtyupasthāna*). Here, Atiśa provides a distinct meditation on each of the four types of mindfulness, including focus on the unclean physical body [§100], the momentary conceptual mind [§101], the impermanence of feelings [§102], and the internal and external dharmas that are clung to due to self-grasping [§103]. The attainment of the cessation of cyclic existence is concisely explained through the practices of serenity (*śamatha*) and special insight (*vipaśyanā*). At the middling-capacity level, serenity brings cessation to feelings and conceptual thoughts [§104–5], while special insight eliminates all mental afflictions (*kleśa*), resulting in arhatship [§106].

The meditations of the middling-capacity individual reverse the tendencies of taking rebirth among the six types of sentient beings within cyclic existence. By fulfilling this stage, the individual overcomes ignorance, self-grasping, and tendencies that arise due to mental afflictions [§107]. The middling-capacity individual achieves separation from all sufferings of cyclic existence. They attain the various degrees of sanctity included in the mainstream Buddhist stages of the path, beginning with the attainment of stream enterer (*srotaāpanna*) and culminating with the maturation effect (*vipākaphala*) of nirvāṇa, the state of arhatship.[101] Atiśa specifies that the casually concordant effect (*niṣyandaphala*) of the middling-capacity individual's attainment of arhatship is benefiting others through emanations (*rdzu 'phrul*; *ṛddhi*) [§108]. This point presumes the overall Mahāyāna orientation of *Stages*, as works such as the *Abhidharmakośabhāṣya* do not accept that arhats experience causally concordant effects.[102]

In Atiśa's other works, he advocates the single-vehicle (*ekayāna*) theory of the Madhyamaka.[103] This is a Mahāyāna theory in which the end results of other non-Mahāyāna paths are provisional goals while the result of perfectly complete omniscient buddhahood, the culmination of the bodhisattva path, is the final goal. In the single-vehicle system, although arhats have ceased their karmic propensities to take rebirth in the three spheres of existence, they take rebirth by means of uncontaminated karma (*zag med kyi las*) and abide with mental bodies in uncontaminated realms until entering the Mahāyāna path.[104]

After the stages of small and middling capacities, the remainder of *Stages* describes in detail the practices, vows, meditation objects, reversal of tendencies, and results for the supreme-capacity individual [§109–80]. It first provides a brief summary of the supreme-capacity individual, who cultivates the awakening mind (*bodhicitta*), integrates skillful means and wisdom, and seeks to attain omniscient buddhahood for the sake of others [§109]. This is followed by an extensive explanation of the practices [§110–30] and meditation objects [§131–78] of the supreme-capacity individual.

The aspiration for, and engagement with, the awakening mind are the initial practices for the supreme-capacity individual. *Stages* first discusses the meditations on limitless virtue and the four immeasureables of love (*maitrī*), compassion (*karuṇā*), joy (*muditā*), and equanimity (*upekṣā*) toward all sentient beings as causes to aspire for awakening [§110–12]. The beneficial qualities of buddhahood are discussed by way of an analogy, where the merit of the awakening mind is said to extend beyond the containment of space. This is an uncited allusion to the *Inquiry of Vīradatta* scripture, which Atiśa references in his *Lamp* [§113].[105] The text prescibes a brief ritual for taking the vows of aspiration for the awakening mind [§114–15] followed by guidelines to enhance its cultivation, including the exchange of oneself and others [§115–19].[106] The engagement of the awakening mind through practice of the six perfections is only briefly mentioned [§120]. *Stages* then emphasizes the importance of the application of counteragents to wrongdoing and the immediate confession of transgressions [§121].

The supreme-capacity individual takes whichever of the seven types of pratimokṣa vows is suitable as a foundation for the bodhisattva vows. The pratimokṣa vows are kept with compassion to develop the mental continuum in the Great Vehicle [§122–23]. Atiśa then explains the three types of bodhisattva moral discipline: the discipline of vows (*saṃvaraśīla*), the discipline of gathering virtuous qualities (*kuśaladharmasamgrāhakaśīla*), and the discipline of benefitting sentient beings (*sattvānugrāhakaśīla*) [§124]. The threefold bodhisattva moral discipline is based on the chapter on conduct in Asaṅga's *Bodhisattva Levels* (*Bodhisattvabhūmi*). Atiśa mentions this threefold discipline in his *Lamp* and then defines and describes each type of discipline in his *Commentary on the Difficult Points of the Lamp for the Path to Awakening*.[107] *Stages* then lists the eighteen root downfalls (*rtsa ltung*; *mūlāpatti*) [§125] and forty-six faulty actions (*nyes byas*; *duṣkṛta*) of bodhisattvas [§126]. The specific listing of these downfalls and faulty actions is not found in Atiśa's *Lamp* and its commentary. The listing of root downfalls is comparable to the listing found in Śāntideva's *Compendium of Training* (*Śikṣāsamuccaya*), although the wording is different.[108] Further prescriptions for confession of transgressions are discussed, along with a brief mention of the four opponent powers: the powers of support, antidote, regret, and turning away from future faults [§127].[109]

After outlining the practices and rituals for the aspirational and engaging awakening mind, *Stages* describes the procedure, principles of training, and meditation for the ultimate awakening mind (*paramārthabodhicitta*) [§128]. In general, the ultimate awakening mind is emptiness. Atiśa does not teach the ultimate awakening mind in the *Lamp* or its commentary, explicitly stating in *Commentary on the Difficult Points of the Lamp for the Path to Awakening* that guidance on this contemplation must be sought from the spiritual teacher.[110] Atiśa's *Open Basket of Jewels,* composed earlier in India, outlines bodhisattva practices to integrate the cultivation of insight (*prajñā*) and compassion (*karuṇā*) through developing the awakening mind at both ultimate and conventional levels. The ultimate mind of awakening—equated with emptiness and the birthless, luminuous, nonconceptual realm of reality (*dharmadhātu*)—is cultivated during meditation, and the conventional mind of awakening is practiced during the post-meditative state. In *Open Basket of Jewels*, the two levels of the awakening mind are integrated and stabilized, having the essence of emptiness and compassion (*śūnyatākaruṇāgarbha*).[111]

In relation to cultivating the ultimate awakening mind, *Stages* outlines a procedure in which one takes refuge and makes offerings to the spiritual teacher (*guru*). The spiritual teacher is visualized as the Dharma body (*dharmakāya*) and referred to as "great Vajradhara" (*rdo rje 'chang chen po*; *mahāvajradhara*). The mention of visualizing the guru as Vajradhara, a foundational esoteric Buddhist practice, is the first explicit reference to esoteric Buddhist practice in the *Stages*. According to esoteric Buddhist traditions, Vajradhara is a primordial buddha and the principal deity in many advanced tantras of the mahāyoga and anuttarayoga classes in Atiśa's classification of tantras.[112] Vajradhara plays an important role in the traditions of the *Guhyasamājatantra* and is the principal buddha-deity of mahāmudrā lineage traditions. Biographies of Atiśa describe him as the holder of the lineage of blessings descending from Vajradhara, Tilopa, and Nāropa (Apple 2019, 20). In *Open Basket of Jewels*, Atiśa cites a quotation that describes Vajradhara as the object of a special type of meditative concentration in the tradition of Guhyasamāja (Apple 2018, 109). Vajradhara also appears as the foundational lineage figure in Atiśa's mahāmudrā-based transmission of the *Special Instructions on Coemergent Union*, which come down from Tilopa and Nāropa (Apple 2019, 250). In his *Extensive Commentary on the Root Downfalls*, a work on esoteric Buddhist practices, Atiśa instructs the reader, "Do not consider the guru as different from Vajradhara."[113] The practice of visualizing the guru as Vajradhara, therefore, is an important esoteric Buddhist practice for Atiśa, and he integrates this practice into *Stages* as an important preliminary to more advanced stages of meditation later in the text. As a key point in this practice, *Stages* then describes the primordially unborn nature of phenomena as equivalent to the awakening mind, the guru as Buddha, and the Dharma body [§129]. These lines of guidance appear to paraphrase verses from the second chapter of the *Guhyasamājatantra.*[114] Based on these principles, Atiśa's instructions on the training of the ultimate awakening mind are given in highly innateist language. He states that "there is nothing anywhere to meditate upon" and teaches that one should remain in the "effortless, naturally perfected state" (*lhun grub rtsol bral ngang*) [§130].

The meditations on the awakening mind are followed by an explanation of meditation objects [§131–78] of the supreme-capacity individual: skillful means [§131–36] and wisdom [§137–78]. Here, *skillful means* comprises the practices of purifying love, compassion, and the engaging awakening mind. The engaging awakening mind benefits others, prevents wrongdoing, and accomplishes virtue [§131]. The prime directive for the implementation of skillful means is the altruistic benefit that brings happiness to others [§132–33]. While supreme-capacity individuals accrue merit and cultivate the qualities of altruism that enable them to benefit others, they also meditate on the illusory nature of appearances. This meditation leads to an understanding of the false, deceptive, and unreal nature of impermanent entities. Recognition of things as false leads this individual to eliminate aversion and attachment to appearances [§134]. The text briefly describes the faults of not cultivating this meditation [§135], followed by further instructions for bringing about the cessation of grasping to appearances as real [§136].

Stages then provides guidance on the cultivation of wisdom for the individual of supreme capacity [§137–78]. Atiśa first outlines the preliminaries [§137–40] to cultivating wisdom and then directly indicates the actual practices [§141–78] of serenity, insight, and union (*yuganaddha*). *Lamp* and its autocommentary use analysis and proofs of emptiness with reasoning to explain wisdom, or insight. In the autocommentary, Atiśa explains wisdom, asking, "What is insight? Either it is coemergent or it arises from learning, reflection, and meditation. . ."[115] In *Stages,* the guidance for cultivating wisdom culminates in the realization of the coemergence and indivisibility of appearance and emptiness. In this way, the supreme-capacity meditations on wisdom comprise one of the longest sections of *Stages.*

In the preliminaries to cultivating wisdom, Atiśa returns to the important role of the spiritual teacher, or master. The spiritual master should be ascertained to be a buddha in order to emulate the virtuous qualities embodied in that contemplation [§137]. Atiśa describes the faults of criticizing the spiritual teacher, comparing the consequences of such disparaging to the example of Sunakṣatra, a long-serving attendant to the Buddha who, due to his lack of respect and veneration to the Buddha, eventually left the Buddhist order, died, and took rebirth as a hungry ghost [§138].[116] The text explains the benefits of contemplating the spiritual teacher's virtuous qualities along with the way to properly follow a spiritual teacher [§139]. Following the preliminary exercise of properly contemplating the spiritual master, *Stages* recommends residing in seclusion to avoid distractions in activities and eliminate mental afflictions [§140].

Following these preliminary instructions, the actual meditation practices for cultivating wisdom are delineated in a series of instructions pointing out the cultivation of serenity [§141–44], insight [§145–57], and union [§158–78]. From this point forward, *Stages* differs from the teachings given in the *Lamp* as well as all other stages of the path works. The meditation practices described in this section of *Stages* contain archetypal features that serve as the prototype for later Kagyü meditation manuals on mahāmudrā. As Karmapa Mikyö Dorjé (1507–54) states, in part, "The system of guidance in serenity and insight taught these days that is shared with the causal Perfection Vehicle comes from the lineage of the protector Atiśa. It is the esoteric instruction of the *Lamp for the Path to Enlightenment* renowned as *coemergent union*."[117]

The instructions for serenity begin with guidance on how to cultivate meditative equipoise while remaining in effortless spontaneous presence (*rtsol med lhun grub*). The text then describes the qualities of nonconceptualization and clarity, advising the meditator to pay attention to the blissful nature of nonconceptuality [§141–43]. The instructions emphasize the qualities of one-pointedness and firm ascertainment while directly pointing out the condition of one's own mind as the inseparability of clarity and emptiness (*gsal stong dbyer med*). The text then gives advice for sustaining the practice and succinctly lists the characteristics of progress and the obstructions to concentration [§144].

Stages initiates the instructions on cultivating insight by pointing out that all things are one's own mind, like a reflection or mirror image, having the essence of luminosity and emptiness [§145]. Atiśa explains that the emptiness of one's own mind is pure, spontaneously present, unconditioned, free from extremes, and free from any views. From the beginning, the mind-as-such (*sems nyid*) is perfect gnosis (*yang dag ye shes*) that is equal to the Dharma body [§146]. The unconditioned mind-as-such is free from causal conditions and the eight extremes of elaboration: permanency, nihilism, arising, cessation, sameness, difference, coming, or going. Atiśa qualifies this as the naturally occuring awakening mind (*rang byung byang chub sems*) [§147–49]. *Stages* then gives instructions on equalizing cyclic existence and nirvāṇa with one's own mind [§150]. This is followed by instructions to abandon self-grasping and realize the empty nature of one's own mind—that is, to recognize that it is selfless and cannot be perceived with sense faculties. The guidance on the mind being without color or shape, and being unseen by the Buddha, complements the instructions in Atiśa's Middle Way–based works, where emptiness is realized in a nonconceptual manner through analytical meditations.[118]

Rather than giving instructions based on analytical methods or reasonings, *Stages* prescribes a direct approach to realizing that one's own mind is emptiness [§151]. These instructions are followed by advice for realizing the emptiness of conceptual thought. The meditator is guided to the recognition that the stream of thoughts, which is comprised of conceptual mental factors (*caitta*), flows and spontaneously subsides into the pure realm of reality (*dharmadhātu*) [§152]. The text then gives instructions for sustaining the direct vision of emptiness by applying this realization to the body and all appearances [§153]. The meditator should not be distracted by the faults and defects of discordant factors, such as afflictions and sufferings, whose nature is also emptiness [§154]. The realization of emptiness is likened to a weapon that can eliminate self-grasping and conceptual thought.

Stages then mentions purification through the application of union to the "four times." The four times are usually considered to be the past, present, future, and atemporality.[119] *Instructions for Select Disciples* (chapter 4 below), as well as a scribal note to the *Stages* manuscript, indicates that unifying the times of the flickering (*'gyus pa*) of thought, mindfulness (*dran pa*), emptiness, and dissolution (*grol ba*) synchronically purifies the four times. This purifying union is maintained by correct mindfulness (*yang dag dran pa*) [§155]. The text then advises that discordant factors can be transformed into virtuous qualities through the special instructions of the spiritual teacher [§156]. The stanzas on the cultivation of insight conclude by indicating the benefits of directly realizing emptiness [§157].

The final major section of *Stages* outlines the meditations on union (*zung 'jug, yuganaddha*) for the individual of supreme capacity [§157–78]. The initial terse stanzas of this section point out that the union of the ground (*gzhi*), the path (*lam*), and the result (*'bras bu*) is self-arisen, emptiness, and the pure realm of reality (*dharmadhātu*). The ground aspect of union has the inherent nature of emptiness. This essential nature is self-arisen coemergent clarity, which is unceasing, translucent radiance, like the sun in a cloudless sky. The ground aspect of this self-arisen coemergence is characterized by the indivisibility (*dbyer med pa*) of the unceasing appearance of lucidity and awareness (*gsal rig*) and emptiness (*snang stong dbyer med*), which is inseparable from one's own mind. The union of the abiding ground of indivisible coemergence appears like the pure light of crystal [§158]. The path aspect of union consists of the primordial pure mind itself. This is equal to the realm of apparent reality, pervading all inner, mental phenomena and outer, sensory perceived objects. The primordial pure mind pervades all appearances like sesame oil pervades sesame seeds. The essential nature of all appearances is nondually unified with one's own mind [§159]. The union of the result to be achieved is indicated by the pure Dharma body, which is inseparable from manifest self-cognizant wakefulness (*ye shes rang gsal mngon gyur*). All the buddha bodies, buddhafields, and buddha qualities are appearances of pure, space-like gnosis; they also have the character of indivisible appearance and emptiness. The pure appearances of awakened qualities are the appearances of one's own mind, resulting from the maturation of merit and virtue [§160].

Stages then outlines practices in the vision of union in which nonconceptual, empty mere appearances are seen as free from the extremes of nihilism and permanence. The beginner is instructed to cultivate virtue and gain a refined understanding of cause and effect, as initial levels of understanding union are merely intellectual. The vision of union is supported by understanding the indivisibility of cause and effect and emptiness. *Stages* explains that the mind has the nature of emptiness, which is the nature of all things, and that one should not fall into any philosophical positions. The nature of the mind and emptiness are inseparable, like the wings of a bird [§161]. More advanced yogis should also practice the indivisibility of cause and effect and emptiness, practicing virtue and abstaining from nonvirtue even while realizing their emptiness [§162].

The yoga of engaging emptiness as cause and effect is the understanding of one's own mind as free from extremes, what Atiśa calls the Great Middle Way. The realization of emptiness magnifies the effects of virtuous actions yet also quickly ripens nonvirtuous actions. Therefore the vision of the unmistaken coalescence of emptiness and cause and effect must be practiced in a subtle manner [§163]. The yoga of own's mind as emptiness must be unified with the practice of skillful means in order to reach buddhahood. *Stages* instructs the yogin to practice the skillful means of love, compassion, and the awakening mind as inseparable from the wisdom of emptiness. The virtue of integrating love, compassion, and the awakening mind should be dedicated to supreme awakening to fulfill the practicess of the union of skillful means and wisdom [§164].

The person of supreme capacity is then instructed in the practice of the indivisible union of one's own mind, appearances, and emptiness. All the sufferings and happiness that occur are the display of one's own perception (*rang snang*). These displays lack inherent existence and should not be apprehended as real. Discarding attachment and aversion, the yogin should practice the nonconceptual cognition of the indivisible union of unceasing appearance and emptiness, seeing things like a dream. *Stages* refers to this practice as the union of appearance and emptiness (*snang stong zung 'jug*) [§165]. These instructions are followed by brief instructions to accumulate merit and purify negativities while supporting the previous cultivations of serenity and insight [§166].

Atiśa then outlines further instructions for achieving meditative stabilization in the nondual union of one's own mind (*rang sems gnyis med zung 'jug*). *Stages* indicates that one's own mind is free from extremes (*rang sems mtha' bral*), embodying the Great Middle Way [§167]. In the condition of union, the yogin should stabilize the nongrasping of appearances without adopting or rejecting things. As all things are of equal nature in the primordially pure mind, they should recognize spontaneous presence (*lhun gyis grub*) while residing in the indivisibility of one's own mind [§168–69].

A series of stanzas then outlines guidance for sustaining (*bskyang pa*) unified meditative stabilization. Atiśa employs the analogy of a skillful cowherder (*mkhas pa ba glang skyong ba*) to indicate how mindfulness is used to rest naturally, without projecting or concentrating, in the union of one's own mind free from elaborations. Any internal or external appearances should be received as allies in emptiness, like snow melting in water. Along these lines, the conceptuality that appears should be seen to naturally dissipate, like the traceless tracks of birds flying across the sky. This conceptuality should continously be realized as emptiness, sustained by undistracted mindfulness and conscientiousness. This method of mindfulness eliminates the conceptuality that grasps at sensory objects [§170–73].

The special instructions for meditation on the indivisible union of serenity and insight conclude with advice on the method and technique. When a person of supreme capacity maintains uninterrupted mindfulness, that practice is considered to be residing in a state of meditative equipoise. Any activity without such mindfulness is known as post-meditative awareness (*rjes thob*; *pṛṣṭalabdha*). Mindfulness of emptiness should be supported with conscientiousness and attention [§174]. The sense faculties should be restrained and activities relinquished [§175]. Practitioners should engage in the purification of mental afflictions, confess downfalls, and accumulate merit while realizing that all appearances are emptiness. The person of supreme capacity should at all times reside in the unified state of their own mind with undistracted mindfulness and conscientiousness, all the while endeavoring for the welfare of others [§176–78].

The meditations on the stages of the supreme-capacity individual reverse the tendencies of the afflictions and of pursuing one's own benefit. They also reverse dualistic fixations (*gnyis su 'dzin pa*) that perceive sensory objects as externally existent and mental factors as internally existent, and they overturn extreme views, such as eternalism and nihilism [§179]. The supreme-capacity individual attains buddhahood along with its concomitant separation effects (*visaṃyogaphala*), maturation effects (*vipākaphala*), and outflowing correlative effects (*niṣyandaphala*) [§180]. The fruits of separation entirely eliminate the accumulations of obstructions (*āvaraṇa*). *Instructions for Select Disciples* (chapter 4 below) indicates that three types of obstructions are eradicated: karmic obstructions (*karmāvaraṇa*), afflictive obstructions (*kleśāvaraṇa*), and the obstructions to omniscience (*jñeyāvaraṇa*).

The supreme-capacity individual also attains the fruits of maturation, consisting of a buddhahood that has three bodies and five wisdoms. A fundamental doctrine of Mahāyāna Buddhism, the three bodies (*sku gsum*; *trikāya*) are the Dharma body (*dharmakāya*), enjoyment body (*saṃbhogakāya*), and emanation body (*nirmāṇakāya*).[120] The five wisdoms (*ye shes lnga*; *pañcajñāna*) are facets of perfect awakening and consist of (1) the wisdom of the realm of reality (*dharmadhātujñāna*), (2) the mirror-like wisdom (*ādarśajñāna*), (3) the wisdom of equality (*samatājñāna*), (4) the wisdom of specific knowledge (*pratyavekṣaṇajñāna*), and (5) the wisdom of accomplishing what was to be done (*kṛtyānuṣṭhānajñāna*).[121] *Stages* mentions that the result of buddhahood carries out various types of miraculous activities (*'phrin las*), but these are not specified. *Instructions for Select Disciples* mentions that the correlative effect of buddhahood results in guiding all sentient beings with five aspects of miraculous activity (*'phrin las rnam pa lnga*), although the five aspects are not listed. A scribal note to the *Stages* manuscript succinctly lists four apects of miraculous activity: pacifying (*zhi ba*), increasing (*rgyas pa*), magnetizing (*dbang ba*), and wrathful activity (*drag po*). A fifth aspect added to this list of four is spontaneous accomplishment (*lhun gyis grub pa*).[122]

Stages concludes with a dedication (*pariṇāmanā*) for all sentient beings to attain supreme awakening based on the roots of virtue (*kuśalamūla*), or cumulative wholesome deeds, that have arisen due to composing the text.

TABLE 3. *STAGES OF THE PATH* OVERVIEW

CAPACITY	VOWS	PRACTICES	MEDITATION OBJECTS
Superior	Bodhisattva Awakening mind	Ultimate awakening mind Engaging awakening mind Aspirational awakening mind	Union Wisdom Skillful means
Middling	Full monk Novice vows Layperson	Three trainings Moral discipline	Causes of cyclic existence Faults of cyclic existence
Small	One-day precepts	Virtuous actions Increasing merit Restraint Refuge	Cause and effect Impermanence The opportunity of leisure and fortune

Reversal of tendencies	Process	Indivisibility	Result
Holding extremes Dualistic fixations One's own benefit Afflictions	Instantaneous Gradual	Appearance and emptiness Means and wisdom	Omniscient buddhahood Correlative Fivefold awakened activities Maturation Major and minor marks Separation Karma, afflictions, knowledge obstrutions
Self-grasping Ignorance Wrongdoing	Gradual	Cause/effect and emptiness, continued	Arhatship ↑ Stream entry
Attachment to eight worldly concerns Laziness Wrongdoing	Gradual	Cause/effect and emptiness	Maturation High rebirth Separation Elimination of lower rebirth Causally concordant

Stages of the Path to Awakening

Śrī Dīpaṃkarajñāna

[**1b**] In the Indian language: *Bodhipathakrama*.
In the Tibetan language: *Byang chub lam gyi rim pa*.

Homage to all buddhas and bodhisattvas!

[§1] I pay homage to the supreme refuge, the spiritual master, and the Three Jewels. [§2] I will explain the realizations on the stages of the path to awakening.

[§3] In this regard, there are three types of individuals: those of small, middling, and supreme capacities. The individual of small capacity does not practice for this life and seeks blissful heavenly rebirth in the future. The middling individual does not seek to rest in the round of rebirth and always practices to achieve liberation. The supreme individual does not seek out their own purpose and has the awareness that wishes to attain buddhahood for the sake of others. You should understand each of the three individuals to possess four qualities: (1) practices, (2) meditation objects, (3) a reversal of tendencies, and (4) a result.

[Small-capacity stages]

[§4] As an individual of small capacity, you take refuge, observe the one-day precepts (*upavāsa*), maintain pure conduct, and protect the vows. You meditate on the fortunate rebirth, impermanence, positive and negative actions, and cause and effect. For this life, you reverse the tendency to cling to permanence, abandon transgressions, and practice virtue in order to eliminate evil states of rebirth and achieve leisure and fortune. [§5] Frightened by death and lower states of rebirth and certain with regard to cause and effect, with faith in refuge, you seek happiness.

[§6] You take the pledges through the ritual of the *ācārya*. [**2a**] [§7] You make the promise and take refuge voluntarily, not relying on another. Understand the distinctions between outsiders (non-Buddhists) and insiders (Buddhists). Then go for refuge and place trust by cognizing the good qualities of insiders.

[§8] Do not relinquish refuge, even for the sake of life and reward. Abandon both external non-Buddhists and mundane gods. Abandon other [deities] despite any difficulties. Dedicate yourself to the Buddha; do not pay homage to others. Abandon harm to sentient beings, wherever they are. Refrain from joining with non-Buddhists. Mindful of virtuous qualities, repeatedly go for refuge. Offer to the Three Jewels the first portion of whatever food you eat. Offer to a great king offerings for the auspicious occasions (the four periodic offerings). Pay homage to the buddha of whichever direction you are heading![123]

[§9] The eight great benefits [of taking refuge]: (1) you are included among Buddhists, (2) you become a support for all the vows, (3) the past sins that have been done are like the female servant of Śrāvastī,[124] (4) you are not thwarted by other human or nonhuman harms, (5) it brings joy like finding a treasure, (6) you avoid falling into the miserable realms and fulfill all needs and wishes, (7) you complete the accumulation of merit, and (8) you attain nirvāṇa and buddhahood.[125]

[§10] Abandon killing, taking what is not given, sexual misconduct, false speech, drinking beer, dancing, and so forth, [**2b**] sitting on high seats, and eating food at the inappropriate time.[126] Protect [against the circumstances for] these eight constituents, and attain the higher realms and liberation.

[§11] A few of the perpetual laws of good conduct of the Mahāsāṃghikas: the first [of these] is abandoning the taking of life and taking what is not given. The Mahāsāṃghikas have four root downfalls for the sake of abandoning lies, eliminating desire for sexual enjoyment, maintaining celibacy, and eliminating sexual misconduct.[127]

[§12] Extensively increase the merit of oneself and others. Make offerings daily, in as many imagined world systems as there are particles of dust. With generosity, offer leftovers to deities. For some laypersons, the supreme offering is cooked food. Common folk offer oil lamps. The supreme offering of a layperson is to mentally offer butter lamps as large as Mount Meru.

[§13] [Being born in] the three lower realms, as long-lived gods, in the realm of neither perception nor nonperception, in a primitive border tribe, with impaired faculties, and [holding] wrong views—these conditions, arising from a lack of good fortune and from not making the aspiration to be born at the time of a buddha, are conditions explained by the Victorious One as the "abodes of bad rebirth." When one abandons the eight places, it is called the "supreme of leisure."[128]

[§14] The presence of the Buddha, his teaching the Dharma, his teaching remaining, its subsequent practice, and receiving kindness to practice [from a Dharma teacher] are the five riches from others. A human body, with pure faculties, faith in the right place, a concordant lifestyle, and birth in a central land are the five personal endowments.

[§15] Among the immeasurable sentient beings of the three realms, very few obtain the precious opportunity of human life. [§16] Among the sentient beings in the six realms of cyclic existence, virtuous action as a cause for leisure and fortune is rare. [§17] For the neck of a turtle to enter the hole in a piece of wood floating on the great ocean is the analogy indicating the extreme difficulty of obtaining leisure and fortune.[129]

[§18] In this way, unknowing, confused beings—who have gained this jewel-like human body, free and well favored, who have agitated minds with many afflictions of attachment and hatred fixated on the meaningless distractions of this life—perform manifold unvirtuous sinful actions, senselessly and mistakenly [**3a**] falling into lower realms of rebirth. They deceive themselves, causing themselves great harm. When great suffering descends, you must have compassion for yourself. Though you see, hear, and know [the lower realms], still you cause evil, like a person crazed when falling into bad conditions. You suffer, but foolishly your wrongdoing increases.

[§19] In this way, desiring happiness and wishing to avoid suffering, do not return empty-handed from the island of jewels. Take up the precious jewel of virtuous holy Dharma as if it were a jewel that fulfills all needs and wishes. Making effort to abandon distractions and afflictions, like a master oarsman fording a river, cross the river of suffering with the supreme support of the human boat.[130] Sustain yourself with simple food and clothing and rely on virtue. Abandon laziness and practice vigorously.

[§20] You may be healthy and in balance and possess property, but aging, decline, and the Lord of Death will deprive you of life; because of impermanence, you must not be complacent. Do not achieve for this lifetime; aim for the hereafter. You may have attained mastery over wealth, but if you do not achieve your own purpose and instead fall into lower realms of rebirth under another power, what benefit will wealth be to you then?

[§21] Conditioned and impermanent, transient worlds are created and destroyed; years, months, days, and nights they are constantly changing. Even grass, trees, and leaves wax and wane. Moments of time are impermanent, like a torrent over a steep cliff; things change constantly, without pause.

[§22] Although many previous sentient beings born with a body have died, you say, "This I have not seen, nor have I heard." Again, you think, "This will not occur. Even now there is no death," stating that it does not exist; but death is certain. Seeing, hearing, and being mindful of death in the past, think about all the burial grounds, and overturn the fixation on permanence.

[§23] All sentient beings' bodies and other conditions without exception quickly and definitely disintegrate because they are conditioned. Do not let your mind stray even to good times or future means of livelihood; do not achieve for this life; think about the hereafter.

[§24] Time does not pause for even two moments. By days, months, and years, life diminishes. [**3b**] Since no increase whatsoever comes from elsewhere and death is definite, eliminate the perception that fixates on permanence.

[§25] Some possessed by ghosts cause chaos. Some die due to enemies, spirits, fire, water, or prosperity. Some without food and clothing die of cold and hunger. Some die from food that is poisoned, others from diseases of wind, bile, and so forth. As all is arisen through conditions, you can have no confidence; you do not know the time of death. Therefore eliminate distraction and contemplate impermanence.

[§26] Since lifespans in Jambudvīpa are not certain, some people die in good conditions when death comes at an advanced age, others die in the prime of life, and some in the womb. Therefore you cannot rely on youth and wealth [to overcome death].

[§27] The body of a sentient being is like a fragile reed. Not even a hair of an essence is established [for the body] at all. Like a feather, like dew on grass, unable to withstand even a trifle of adverse conditions, the body quickly dies.

[§28] There is no way to overturn the certainty of death, like a lamp running out of oil in the darkness of night. The courageous cannot turn back death; the strength and great power of Viṣṇu, tigers, lions, snakes, and so forth cannot subdue death. Even your own power and capability are unable to overturn death. You cannot escape death, like a person who has swallowed poison.

[§29] Protective deities, extraordinary spells, even skill in the method of dependent arising cannot repel death. The wealthy, with their wealth, cannot turn back death. Therefore there is no other way of averting the Lord of Death.

[§30] Friends, relatives, and others, lords of the land, and [§31] even sovereigns cannot repel the Lord of Death. You should contemplate, taking up the path, thinking, "Where do I go? Where do I disappear to?" [§32] Even knowing while not meditating is like talking about discarded food in order to protect it. Therefore attachment to children, relatives, wealth, fame, riches, and honor are enemies that arise. Foolishly fixated on permanence, you commit sinful acts, distracted by perception and afflictions oriented to this life. [**4a**] The fixation on permanence, which is like trying to renovate one's freedom when practicing for this life, is extremely foolish. Having left behind all enemies and friends, wealth, and fame, upon dying, you alone will carry the burden of sin. At that time, with no possibility of protection, you will experience suffering, anguish, and regret for prior sins, to no avail. Therefore contemplate impermanence, cast away the notions of this life, and achieve happiness for the future. Leisure and fortune benefits you only temporarily.

[§33] For this reason, you should eliminate and identify all sins, which are contradictory to revealing the fundamental nature.

[§34] Sentient beings under the influence of attachment, hatred, and delusion violently rob others of life and cunningly take the wealth of others. Householders protect themselves. With desire, they engage in sexual misconduct. The worldly act with pettiness and duplicity toward spiritual teachers. In fact blind to subtle realities, they speak divisively and falsely, and return abuse for good qualities. Idle talk, the opposite of truth and correct speech, destroys the substance of oneself, others, and both oneself and others. Giving gifts and seeking friends go in opposite directions. Correct worldly truths are perceived wrongly. These and others are the nature of nonvirtuous actions. For any individuals who would do as such, the particular effects that arise are suffering. A vow should be taken to block [nonvirtuous actions] from being born.

[§35] Vows are declared with a promise, and transgressions arise by the power of afflictions. Confess, refrain from doing, and abandon; moreover, what is the use of any nonvirtuous sinful actions? Since they cause you to fall into the lower realms of rebirth, with mindfulness and vigilance, along with conscientiousness, quickly eliminate all sinful transgressions, destroying the bad result as one would eliminate poisonous food.

[§36] Nonvirtuous actions ripen by themselves, like a shadow follows one's own body. The Reviving Hell (Saṃjīva; *yang gsos*) and the Hell of Blisters (Arbuda; *chu bur can*), which arise from these, are more than fifty thousand yojanas below Jambudvīpa. The rest of the hot hells are located in the next forty thousand yojanas, and the cold hells are located in the last ten thousand yojanas. Each hell is two hundred thousand yojanas wide.[131] [**4b**]

[§37] Generally, regarding the suffering of the eight hot hells, all eight have a base of burning iron covered with a net of blazing iron and are encircled by an iron fence. Each of the sixteen, the eight hot plus eight cold, has four special gates.[132]

[§38] In the Reviving Hell, fires burn sentient beings with iron to agitate the mind. Having taken up various weapons such as swords, beings there kill one another. Revived by the sound of thunder, they kill again. [In the Black Line Hell (Kālasūtra; *thig nag*)], each being is marked with a line, and their body is destroyed by being ripped by saws and scorched by iron. In the Hell of Crushing Pain (Saṃghāta; *bsdus 'joms*), they are crushed by mountains and then revived by wind, machines (*yantra*) push them into boxes, and then they are pressed down by mountains, with fire burning in all directions. In the Wailing [Hell] (Raurava; *ngu 'bod*), they run away screaming, scorched by burning forests. Further, they try to flee from an iron house without doors, which is scorched and blazing with fire. In a house of manure burning in the forest, they shout with great difficulty. In the Hot Hell (Tapana; *tsha ba*), having arisen from pits of burning heat, they are struck, pierced with tridents and so forth, and cooked. In the Exceedingly Hot Hell (Pratāpana; *rab tu tsha ba*), they are cast out from scorched pits, having been beaten, cut into pieces, and impaled on stakes. In Relentless Agony (Avīci; *mnar med pa*), they are cooked in iron cauldrons five hundred yojanas wide and cast upon five stakes on top of burning iron. Their extended tongues are staked, their skin is peeled off, and they are drawn up with nets. They are put in winnowing baskets, cooked, and brought to a mountain top, and the terrified retinue is eaten by birds.

The Cold [Hells] are the Cold Sore Hell, Burst Cold Hell, Chattering Teeth Hell, Sneezing Hell, "Alas!" Hell, [the Hell Where Frostbitten Skin Cracks in the Shape of an] Utpala, [the Hell with Cracks like a] Lotus, and [the Hell with Cracks like] Giant Lotuses.[133]

[§39] [From these hells] they flee in terror and are hung up on a hooks at the four doors and flattened. [The adjoining hells at the four gates of each hot hell are] Burning Embers (Kukūla; *me ma mur*), Swamp of Rotting Corpses (Kuṇapa; *ro myags 'dam*), Plain of Razor Blades (Kṣuramārga; *spu gri thang*), Forest with Sword Leaves (Asipattravana; *ral gri'i lo ma*), and Forest of Iron Thorns (Ayaḥśalmalīvana; *shal ma li'i nags*). Beings are then roasted while crossing over the salty river [known as River without Ford (Vaitaraṇī; *shu bo rab med*)]. Having escaped Relentless Agony Hell, [those entering the adjoining hells say,] "These hells are what we desire! We are hungry and thirsty!" [But they are only] scorched with blazing iron balls; likewise, burning copper is poured into their bodies.[134]

[§40] The occasional hells have the form of stone boulders and so forth and **[5a]** have intermittent suffering in solitary places and so forth.[135]

[§41] Killing causes you to be frightened and so forth and is an unharmonious deed. [While in the hells as a result of killing,] you must eat food from many various vessels with brims of hot iron, the directions become indivisible from fire, you are surrounded by enemies, falling into deep ravines and abysses many yojanas deep, you are scorched by iron, and your body descends into fire and is burned. You are born and eaten by beings who destroy your vital organs and dice you up with spinning blades, while you intensely experience these sufferings with acute sensations.

Taking what is not given brings mirage-like wealth. While you abide burning in fire, you deludedly view [an object], and in your desire you think, "It is mine." When you go to it, the Death Lord of Karma (*las kyi gshin rje*; Karmayama) pulverizes you with a weapon.

Due to sexual desire, you chase after previous lovers in your attachment. Having been embraced by that lover, [who is actually] blazing iron but offers you food and meat, saying, "Come here!" you then descend into the forest and are pulverized by leaves of swords and thorns while simultaneously being chopped up and burned with blazing iron. You are scorched by blazing iron nets coming from above.

As a result of telling lies, your tongue is stretched out for five hundred yojanas and tilled by a thousand blazing plows, and if profane demons enter the mouth, having taken hold, they destroy with blazing weapons.

Due to divisive speech, the tongue is spretched to the length of three yojanas, cleaved and cut into small pieces, and eaten as food.

Due to harsh words, your tongue is cut into pieces and fed to you as food. Your tongue is cleaved by the blades of a thousand plows.

Due to idle talk, molten iron burns the tongue from the throat, and the heart and internal organs are gradually scorched.

Covetousness perceives wealth like a magical creation. Having gone to that place, you are pulverized by the sword of the Lord of Death.

Due to harmfulness, although you flee fearfully from tigers, lions, and cobras, you cannot escape, and demonic spirits burn you from above and eat you.

Due to wrong view, diamond thunderbolts appear as weapons, and you are constantly stricken by the fires of hunger and thirst.

[§42] The length of one day and night in the Reviving Hell and so forth, and [**5b**] in the successive six hot hells, is as long as the lifespan of the six kinds of desire-realm gods.[136] The lifespan in the hot [hells] is half an eon, and in Relentless Agony it is one eon. A hundred years passes for each seed removed from a storage bin. The lifespan of Hell of Blisters lasts until a thousand of those bins have been emptied. The [lifespans in the] remaining hells will successively become twenty times that.[137]

In this way, this fierce suffering of hell is a cause for recollecting terror in the mind. You should totally cease committing transgressions out of the afflictions of hatred and so forth. As not cultivating patience for whatever harm comes from another's harsh words produces hatred, like sparks that lead to flames, you will burn for a long time in the unbearable fires of hell for moments of impatience in this life. Given this, what then is the purpose of this life? Refrain from wrongdoing; make effort in virtuous actions.

[§43] Three hundred yojanas beneath [the earth] is the realm of hungry ghosts. Dispersed, not definite, there are 360 million hungry ghosts.[138]

[§44] Due to the fierce maturation of stinginess and desirous attachment, there are those whose obstruction is external[139] and who have their own appearances of appropriate manifestations (*rang snang*). Food and drink is not perceived, and any river they would wish to consume is perceived as dried up. For some, a little bit [of food and drink appears]; for some, [food and drink] do not appear at all; some are protected [from hunger and thirst]. For some, [food and drink] appear as pus and blood (*rnag khrag*), and they are not able to eat it.[140]

[§45] Those whose obstruction is internal have ugly bodies. They have small mouths, thin necks, and large bellies, and although they eat and drink, [the food and drink] dries up in their throats; due to fierce feelings of hunger and thirst, their body and mind degenerate.

[§46] Some perceive food and drink, anything that can be consumed, but as all of it blazes like fire, their bodies are scorched. Their body is like a dead tree trunk and their hair is made of droplet particles. Their limbs are thin and their belly is stuck to their back. They obtain a little filthy food to live, and due to hunger they cut off their own flesh and are consumed.

[§47] One month for humans is one day for a hungry ghost. When thirty of those days comprise a month, twelve months like that are one year. That year is five hundred [human years], the lifespan of hungry ghosts.[141] If humans are overwhelmed by experiencing hunger and thirst for one day, who is able to endure the thirst of an old hungry ghost? In this way, right now and powerfully, [**6a**] eliminate the subtle wrongdoing that will cause you to become a hungry ghost.

[§48] The abode of animals is among the four outer continents, in the greater and lesser oceans, and in the depths of the sea. There are dispersed abodes, those that are not fixed, those that are elevated, and so forth. There are 360 million types [of animals].

[§49] Great clustered clouds of fish and so forth and other small waterborne beings are consumed as food. Smaller sentient beings are food for larger fish, who pierce [smaller fish] like bristles of hair and shake them, causing overwhelming pain. The oceans appear awash in blood as they eat one another. Those who are harvested are butchered horribly or suffer from being boiled by foolish hungry and thirsty beings.

[§50] The lifespan of nāgas and so forth does not extend beyond an eon. The lifespan of the remainder [of the animals] varies.[142]

[§51] In this way, the sufferings of the three lower realms of rebirth are chaotic, seemingly interminable, and without profit. Contemplating this inspires a great urgent purpose to engage in virtue. You should pursue virtue with concerted effort, suffering amid your challenges. The actions that have become afflictions, wrongdoings, and obscurations you should energetically eliminate.

[§52] Sinful rebirth or high heavenly states are attained through concordant effects: killing causes untimely death by generating conditions for a short lifespan. From taking what is not given, wealth becomes small. From committing adultery, companionship will elude you. From lying, you will be deceived by others. If you speak divisively, you will have no friends. From harsh speech, you will be targeted with blame. From idle talk, your words will not be heeded. Covetousness will destroy your hopes. Harmfulness will bring enemies, harm, and terror. And wrong view will induce a view that clings to a self.[143]

[§53] Action resembling its cause[144] is behavior you have become accustomed to, doing whatever action you do with delight and engaging with enthusiasm. Therefore you should strive to eliminate nonvirtue and cultivate virtue, for once you become accustomed, anything can become easy. Since all things arise from conditions, things occur through [**6b**] causally concordant conditions, whether for good or ill.

[§54] The general dominant result of negative actions is that one is born in a bad region. Killing degenerates the essence of the life force. Stealing results in drought, rain, frost, and harvest-destroying hail. With adultery, one stinks with defilement and is powerless to mitigate extremes of heat and cold. Telling lies leads to having bad food and no success in contemplation. Divisive speech leads to the treacherous river banks that create salty land. Harsh (*rtsub po*; *paruṣa*) speech leads to thorny deep ravines and abysses. Useless speech leads to hard times, where the vital seeds of the crops do not ripen. Covetousness leads to famine with poor harvests. Harmfulness leads to crops being poached by enemy hunters. Wrong view leads to crops not ripening and then disappearing. Therefore one should eliminate subtle nonvirtue.[145]

[§55] In this way, the sufferings of the lower realms of the hells and so forth do not exist from without. They are like a reflection or an echo, as afflictions and wrongdoings arise as manifestations of the mind. Therefore if you do not desire the sufferings of hell and so forth, protect the mind from afflictions and nonvirtue. When the mind eliminates afflictions and wrongdoing, the sufferings of the round of rebirth in the hells and so forth stop, like the leather soles of boots cover the ground.[146]

[§56] In this way, to destroy the enemy of the afflictions, marshal the forces of mental counteragents. Eliminate nonvirtue and achieve virtue. The mere nondoing of nonvirtuous actions is called *nonanalytical cessation*.[147] Having refrained from negative actions, rely on the counteragent virtue. [§57] Virtue is preserving life and giving material things to sentient beings, chastity, speaking truthfully, reconciling, speaking softly, being intent on what is beneficial, eliminating covetousness, cultivating love, and upholding correct views. [§58] By practicing the ten virtues along with their characteristics, you gain the excellent result: the happiness of gods and humans. When they are conjoined with emptiness and compassion, you attain awakening.

[§59] By preserving life, you become free from disease and have a long life. Due to giving material things, you obtain great wealth. Through pure conduct, you gain good friends. Through speaking truthfully, you are not deceived by another, [7a] and through reconciling, you have many relatives and friends. Through soft words, your own words are heard pleasantly. Through speaking thoughtfully on what is beneficial, you are respected. By abandoning attachment, your mind achieves contemplation. Cultivating love frees you from enemies, harm, and fear. Through correct view, you realize the good view free from extremes.

[§60] Make effort in virtuous actions with a wish to increase it, for virtue that you have become accustomed to has the effect compatibile with its cause. [§61] Preserving life, medicine, and food produces health. Giving material goods leads to a good harvest. Pure conduct levels out extreme temperatures and cleanses the environment. Speaking truthfully achieves goodness and contemplation. Reconciling leads to pleasurable conditions and diminishes anger. Speaking softly leads to rebirth in areas without deep ravines or abysses. Purposeful speech leads to crops ripening on time. Eliminating covetousness brings the bounty of good crops. Through cultivating love, your crops become free from harmful enemies. With correct view, you encounter uncultivated crops in natural settings.

[§62] Therefore make diligent effort in virtue. Practicing merely to procure food and clothing leads to actions marked by wrongdoing, exhaustion, and difficulty with cold and hunger. When you are tenacious for meat broth, how can you achieve the happiness of yourself and others, the higher realms and liberation, and the highest awakening?

Knowledge without meditation is like the recitation of a parrot. It is heedless of the great harm of suffering. Do not establish the three doors of body, speech, and mind in the ordinary; make effort in virtue.

[§63] The blazing fires of hell have a scorching iron foundation, and you are pierced with blazing weapons by the malevolent guardians of hell. You are boiled in the flaming hot springs of an iron house with no exit. Razors and so forth cover the ground. The searing and the frigidity of the hells bring so much tribulation. However much wrongdoing you have performed, the result is you become hated, harmed, and killed, struck down by enemies, evil spirits, and other maleficent beings.

[§64] Hungry ghosts' suffering is that they are stricken by agonizing over hunger and thirst, meeting with frost and hail, [**7b**] being bereft of material things due to poverty, lacking food and clothing, and being starving and parched at the time of death. These are the results of the varied forms of previous karma: desire, avarice, and theft.

[§65] Animals eat one another in their stupidity and dullness. Being deaf, mute, blind, insane, and so forth are karmic results of prior ignorance.

Therefore do not give way to afflictions for even an instant, and if you do, then eliminate them.

[§66] The happy fruits of higher rebirth as gods and humans such as possessing a wish-fulfilling gem and so forth, feasting on the food of the gods of ambrosia and so forth, and having abundant crops, a well-built house, servants, and a lineage of good qualities and prosperity are results of meritorious karma made manifest. Therefore accomplish even the most subtle virtues.

[§67] All such appearances of happiness and suffering are not established from the outside; they are not externally caused.[148] You cause virtuous and evil deeds yourself. Those appearances are the maturation of particular actions. Whatever appears, it is all like a reflection. All that appears is a natural reflection of what is within; whatever there is is the natural expression of that. Therefore mind does not really exist, and external appearances do not really exist; one's own karma does not really exist; whatever is experienced does not really exist. If you wish to achieve happiness, eliminate unfavorable conditions; it is not achieved otherwise, because whatever [karmic] seeds that are within your own ever-shifting mind sprout at the same time as increasing effects. Through understanding the seed and sprout in conjuction with the mental continuum, endeavor in actions to achieve the unmistaken elimination [of mental defilements].

[§68] Your own mind appears through cause and effect. The accumulation of actions involves three factors: the preparation, the actual action, and the conclusion.[149] [For actions to be accumulated, they must be] undiluted and undistracted, uninterrupted, and intentional. Unaccumulated actions are ones that are unintentional, done with a distracted mind, or performed with body or speech alone. Actions neither performed nor accumulated are associated by similar time period concordant with mind. Accumulated uncreated deeds are others' virtue and are to be rejoiced in with joy. [**8a**]

[§69] When nonvirtue is discarded and virtue completed, the result is like the minor happiness of an animal. When virtue is discarded and suffering is completed, the result is a taste of the suffering of gods and humans. The projection and completion (*'phen rdzogs*) of virtue results in the happiness of higher states of rebirth, and the projection and completion of nonvirtue results in the suffering of the lower realms of rebirth.[150]

[§70] When [actions are] an obstruction but not wrongdoing, latent afflictions become manifest. When [actions are] wrongdoing and not an obstruction, what makes an action nonvirtuous rather than virtuous is the intention. Actions that are both wrongdoing and an obstruction are created from nonvirtue that is animated by afflictions. Actions that are neither wrongdoing nor an obstruction are indeterminate and may become virtuous.

[§71] A single counteragent occurs for a single good or evil deed. Likewise a single action's intensity determines the strength of the deed. Whether you will experience the results of unaccumulated deeds is indefinite.

[§72] For deeds that are accumulated and have no counteragents, when the time is right, karma is definitely experienced. The effects of past deeds are consummated in the future; deeds projected in the past abide as potential future results. Great karma matures from a previous great amount, and small [karma] later matures from a limited amount. When assembled conditions ripen quickly, they do not assemble subsequently. Desire leads to hell, hatred leads to [birth as] an animal. Motivation is the most important component of all karma; it leads to completion and persists as an unripened result. An example of the karma that mixes consummated virtue with projected nonvirtue is a butcher with long life who is happy to live in poverty. The scriptures explain that the limited number of wealthy areas with hospitable climate and food are the result of giving and so forth.[151]

[§73] All dharmas are the mind; the mind itself is free from all extremes.[152] The multiple various causes and effects of virtue and wrongdoing are unceasing, definitely liberated from the extreme of nihilism. Since whatever appears of the cause and effect of the round of rebirth and nirvāṇa is the nature of one's own mind, it is not at all established, and it is definitely liberated from the extreme of permanence. Emptiness indivisible from cause and effect [**8b**] is the nature of one's own mind, free from the proliferations of extremes, the Great Middle Way.

[§74] The eight worldly perceptions of this lifetime,[153] laziness, future plans, wrongdoing, and afflictions are symptoms that are reversed and eliminated by the path of meditation. You should possess the signs of progress on the path, not merely words.

[§75] Eliminate evil states and so forth. With confidence in cause and effect, and through the practice of virtue, you will experience states such as those of Brahmā, Indra, a universal sovereign, a brahman, a member of the ruling class, or a prosperous householder.

[Middling-capacity stages]

[§76] Beyond the aforementioned stages, the middling path includes guarding the thoroughly complete novice vows and the more powerful vows of a fully ordained monk. The faults of the cycle of rebirth are what compel cultivation of the path of liberation. Reverse the factors that fuel the round of rebirth: ignorance, self-grasping, and wrongdoing. Accomplish any step toward nirvāṇa: peace, happiness, and others' welfare.

[§77] If you possess the five major vows, you are a complete layperson, and if you have the signs of a renunciate, you are a novice monk. The supreme monk guards against the five kinds of downfalls.[154] Holding pledges of discipline is the basis that supports the creation of all good qualities.

[§78] Without discipline, you cannot eliminate evil states. If even the path to higher realms is beyond your reach, why even try for liberation or omniscience? Just as the blind do not see phenomena, those without moral discipline do not see the Dharma. Just as one without legs cannot enter a path, one without moral discipline cannot be liberated. Therefore discipline is necessary for arhatship and the unmatched attainment of omniscience. Stricken by the fires of desire in the householder life, nonvirtuous karma occurs due to too much attachment and aversion on behalf of children, spouses, wealth, enemies, and friends. The demonic sense-faculties create a mass of wrongdoing, casting you to the lower realms with odious [qualities], scarcity, and various fraught conditions like poverty and so forth.

[§79] Some, deluded from not studying the scriptures, grasp onto the Lower Vehicle discipline of a monk. Deluded regarding cause and effect and lacking correct view, the afflictions are carelessly indulged: such are attributes of the desire realm. [**9a**] Pretending to be on the Great Vehicle and so forth, they stumble along the path. Monastic moral discipline on the path of all vehicles is taught by the Victorious One in all the sūtras and tantras. Why? Moral discipline is the support that increases merit. The virtue accumulated for a hundred years by a householder is a mere day's accumulation for a monk. Compared to one who resides in the teaching of the Buddha, the former [i.e., the householder] has an infinitesimal share of merit. With a mind not discouraged from entering into awakening for the sake of all sentient beings in the billionfold universes, you should forswear children and spouse for a full eon. More than that, if while being accustomed to a mind of renunciation you also generate the awakening mind, the merit is especially superior. The offering up of the possessions of a precious householder and so forth to as many buddhas as there are sands in the banks of the Ganges by one who has been a monk for a single day and night and who brings to mind impermanence, suffering, and selflessness is supreme. Why? The arhat buddhas of the three times have arisen through their possession of the moral discipline of monastic vows. Released from household affairs, bereft of the distractions that lead one astray, free from the attachments of children and mate, unattached to wealth, you attain the great wealth most pleasing of all: the performance of virtue unafflicted by distraction. You have the practice of virtue in solitude without attachment, and you attain the higher realms, liberation, and omniscience.

[§80] [The sentient beings of] the three realms—due to self-grasping through delusion, the ignorance that grasps inner and outer objects as real—experience multiple sufferings in the cycle of rebirth. Although their bodies and minds are repeatedly tormented, their fully ripened afflictions cause them to commit wrongs, compelled by desire to engage in the causes of suffering. People have attachment to friends and aversion for enemies; they are distracted, wasting their time with so many activities that increase the afflictions; and they commit a great deal of wrongdoings. Busy with farming and business, their bodies and minds finish life distracted. All their activities [**9b**] are in vain and become only a cause for more suffering. Having left behind friends, enemies, and wealth, they fall deluded into the lower states, weighted down with their misdeeds. Deluded about cause and effect, they do not understand how to abandon suffering.

Therefore, now, while you enjoy the freedom to seek happiness, invest in virtuous activities. In this cyclic existence marked by uncertainty, the elevated fall to the low, the low become elevated. Undergoing much happiness and suffering, they pass away and transmigrate. Friends becomes enemies, enemies becomes friends. With all the fluctuations between birth and death, nothing is certain. Although parents beget a child, the child may come to see the parents as the enemy. A onetime enemy may again become a friend. Given all these transferences back and forth between being a friend or an enemy, who should you long for and who should you hate? Therefore regard all beings equally and abandon attachment and aversion.

[§81] In this life, through delusion—apprehending things as real due to the view of permanence—you pursue your aims attached to the five objects of desire, continously relying on intention and yearning. Since sense desires do not bring satisfaction, like drinking salty water, sentient beings are ruined by these five desires, just as the deer is destroyed by sound, the jackal by smell, the fish by taste, and the elephant by touch. In this way, the deceitful and so forth produce all suffering. Beautiful forms and nice clothes should be relied on no more than a rainbow in the sky. The various hosts of enemies are like [the reverberation of] an echo. Smell and taste are [deceptive,] like salty water and a dream. [Acquiring] tangible objects is [endless,] like scratching an itch. Meditating on impermanence and emptiness is heroic. On account of the five objects of desire, so many wrongdoings are perfomed until, at the time of death, no virtue has been created. When objects of desire—both friends, and material things—are left behind, you must carry the great burden of wrongdoing and delusion by yourself. Driven by the winds of uncontrolled karma, you engage over and over in the causes to experience vile suffering. Now, at this time when you have self-control, eliminate wrongdoing!

[§82] The boiling hot springs with a foundation of scorching iron, a doorless iron house scorching within with blazing fire, the malevolent guardians of hell with blazing weapons, the Forest with Sword Leaves that cut one up, the Plain of Razor Blades and so forth, all the sufferings of the hot hells [**10a**]; proceeding through the various inexhaustible sufferings of the cold hells like Splitting Like a Lotus; suffering because of manifold hardships unbearable and fierce, for a long time—knowledge of that is connected with your own continuum. Contemplate again and again, and definitely become detached. Do not become complacent by understanding through mere words; settle your continuum into meditation without distraction. If you cannot withstand even a fragment of the suffering of humans, how will you withstand the fierce sufferings of hell? Therefore, for the sake of this life, commit no wrongdoing; eliminate even subtle afflictions.

Think about the many sufferings of thirst of a feeble hungry ghost. Retain this object of meditation in your mind; when just a little bit of human hunger and thirst is unbearable, who can endure the hunger and thirst of a feeble hungry ghost? Therefore what purpose are friends and material things? Eliminate attachment to unaccumulated wrongdoing and afflictions.

[§83] The countless animals eat one another in their delusion; they lose their lives through being killed. Their lives are shortened by multiple conditions of involuntary death, they cry due to hunger and thirst, they are made slaves, and so forth. Arouse the intention to engage in repeated contemplation: to approach the wise, to listen to the excellent Dharma, and to contemplate it.

[§84] From beginningless lifetimes until now, you have experienced countless sufferings in hells and so forth; you enter the causes of suffering again and again. Ignorance is the great fault of cyclic existence. Through understanding these faults of cyclic existence and becoming unsettled with grief, eliminate subtle wrongdoing. The suffering of humans, in brief, is of eight and three types.[155]

The first [the suffering of birth] is that you are rooted in the womb as a lump in darkness, tormented by heat; it is like being bound, and the smell is dreadful. Being born is like being pulled by the snout with your eyes closed. [Your body placed on your mother's lap feels] like a baby bird carried by a hawk and placed on thorns. [When you are born,] you undergo the painful turbulance in the Brahma cavity [in the crown of the head] that is experienced during the fierce sufferings of birth and death. Even wise ones who are called *paṇḍita* and so forth, [**10b**] to gain knowledge [in their new birth], must first train from scratch in the alphabet. Those are the faults of the suffering of birth.

[§85] Likewise, the immeasurable suffering of aging. Imperfections in your body's shape and complexion manifest while the skin diminishes. The radiance of your skin and the strength of your body degenerate. You are unable to work, becoming fatigued by even a little labor. Your body temperature degenerates, and you are subject to infections. Your diminished faculties are unable to experience objects. You turn away from the blundered ugliness of everyone. Others have sickness, and even one's own son has the pain of aging. No one listens to what you say, and people argue as if you're not there. Others are reluctant to spend time with you. Your taste also becomes salty. You are powerless to accumulate wealth yourself. You cannot hear good advice from others. Again, you are subject to unpleasing, abusive speech. If you think "we," it is only you, yourself, and it will be like this. Brooding and gloomy, there is nothing to say or praise [when one is aged].

[§86] When you get sick, sharp pain strikes your body, and the mind is overcome with harsh suffering. The mind, withdrawn, does not engage objects. Food stinks, and your complexion deteriorates. There is much pain from bloodletting, moxibustion, and other interventions. It is not good to be hungry, for you must ingest bitter medicine, and as delicious food is harmful, you are powerless to eat. Even in trying to keep your bedclothes unsoiled, you are thwarted. Even if you are offered pleasing food, it stinks. Gently spoken words fall harsh upon your ear. A great loss of food and wealth occurs and goes to demons and so forth. Fearing death, your mind is tormented. Day and night, suffering arises and nurses cannot alleviate your pain.

[§87] You may be surrounded by friends at the time of death, but you go alone like a hair pulled from butter. At that time, you have no ability to cling to life. Some cry out while in their desire clinging to wealth. Some die howling, suffering without friends. Some die with hatred as they are murdered. Some have the suffering of separation from friends, and some fasten the mind by attachment to wealth and friends. Some die obsessing about unfinished good works. [**11a**] This life ceases and the Lord of Death appears. Some, struck with intense pain, succumb to fear and terror. Some suffer gloominess with no means of relief. Uttering "Alas! Friends, what can I do?" and struck with fierce suffering, they see none who can protect them. In accordance with delusion, you will involuntarily die.

[§88] In this way, the four streams of birth, aging, sickness, and death are faults of cyclic existence. Contemplate just this again and again. Liberate yourself from the streams of suffering, eliminate wrongdoing, and achieve virtue.

[§89] [Encountering what is unpleasant is] suffering that occurs largely against your will: the aged are subject to the will of others. If you have chronic sickness and fatigue, you are exploited by others, and you may go long stretches without aid from others. You require coverings for your aged legs and arms. You may be given cooling astringents, wool, or iron. Due to the burden of a long convalescence, the putrid, fatigued body settles down. Tormented by heat and thirst, with age, you endure many hardships.

Some who are aged, due to the heat and cold of inner thirst, beg for soup and the wealth of others. Some kill in battle and so forth to feed their desires. Some break the law to steal the wealth of others. Foolishly not refraining from wrongdoing, some become hunters. Some, for their trading activity, must wander a long time. The thieves of fatigue gather, and there is much suffering and sickness. These are the immeasurable sufferings of the impoverished.

[§90] Even if you have wealth, robbers will carry it away, and enemies will plunder and destroy with fire and water. While keeping watch at night, you suffer from sleeplessness. You suffer from heat and cold for the sake of wealth. While fatigued and exhausted, you are powerless to help others. Engaging in too many activities causes you to suffer broken bones. Due to the many distractions of this life, through commiting many evil deeds, you fall to lower realms of rebirth.

[§91] Pride, debasement, and fear when meeting with enemies; destroying land and killing; being imprisoned, receiving injuries like losing an eye, [**11b**] plundering, and so forth—these are the sufferings that torment the body and mind due to hatred.

[§92] In the great suffering of the departure of kind and beloved friends, you memorialize their flaws as good qualities. Since you need to [remember their failings as positive attributes], that's how you commemorate them. Later, you are stuck, having been coerced into compassion by your attachment. Distressed with suffering, your mind tormented—these are the sufferings caused by reciting flattering words.

[§93] In dependence upon the five appropriated aggregates, you create much wrongdoing and nonvirtue, which produces the suffering of future aggregates; this is called the suffering of conditioned karmic action.

[§94] The suffering that arises due to happiness being impermanent is, for example, becoming sick when healthy or becoming poor when wealthy. When the lofty lose their advantages, impermanent happiness transforms into suffering.

[§95] The appropriated aggregates are suffering; disease strikes suddenly, enemies rise up before you, and you are separated from friends. One suffering after another afflicts you through myriad contrary conditions, such as diminishing wealth and so forth.

The sufferings of gods and demigods are fights and battles, separation, disintegration, intoxication with desire, a lack of time for virtue, the pain of falling to a lower rebirth, and so forth; these fierce sufferings can be seen with your own [supersensory] knowledge.

[§96] In this way, you should contemplate to register in your mind the many faults of cyclic existence, stating, "All the harm that occurs while wandering aimlessly in cyclic existence is unbearable when it enters my mental continuum." Having repeatedly considered the certainty of this—that which is created by all the suffering of cyclic existence, the perception of this life, the eight worldly concerns and so forth, the many activities driven by the afflictions—[you may ask] what you should you do [in this life] about the cause of pointless suffering. You should foremost eliminate all activities on behalf of this life, because the purpose of the human body is to achieve everlasting liberation. The fortunate should apply themselves to virtuous activity.

[§97] The suchness of the mind, under the sway of deluded ignorance, views a self taking up the cause and effect of grasping inner and external [things]. Strong attachment to desires, [**12a**] excessive clinging, and aspiration [for the future] will produce anger and hatred. Then, subtle and gross afflictions will expand unchecked. The great mass of karma and various nonvirtues produced by that accumulate, and in your attachment to nonvirtue, you create no virtue. All the sufferings of existence without exception will arise. Enduring and not repudiating that is senseless confusion, causing you great harm.

With what life you have left, you should attack the enemy that harms you, your afflictions. When taking up the battle diligently without concern for [your own] body, wealth, and life, it is right to destroy the enemy that creates the great harm of hells and so forth. Therefore marshall the various countering forces and destroy the great enemy, the afflictions, which creates everlasting suffering.

[§98] Ignorance, formations, consciousness, name-and-form, sense bases, contact, feeling, craving, grasping, becoming, birth, and aging and death. Among the twelve roots of existence, the first [ignorance], the eighth [craving], and the ninth [grasping] are afflictions. The second [formations] and tenth [becoming] are the links of karma. The seven remaining ones [consciousness and so forth] are the links of suffering. When the three that are afflictions exist, [links of karma] will occur. When the two kinds of karmic action exist, the seven [links] that are suffering arise. The cycle of existence that gives rise to the three afflictions from the seven spins continually, like a ceaseless waterwheel. Again and again, you are held without escaping. Generating [correct] conditions liberates you from the extremes of permanence and annihilation; small causes lead to a great effects, like a *nyagrodha* tree. Effects are congruent with their causes. Without [the intervention of] a creator, transient collections give rise to collections of effects, which cease when their capacities are exhausted.[156]

[§99] To overturn the stream of karma, you must follow the wise. If you make effort with analysis to produce wisdom, ignorance up through aging and death comes to cessation. With the permanent end to the suffering of saṃsāra, you attain nirvāṇa. Therefore make effort in learning, reflection, and meditation. To meditate with little study is like climbing a rock when you have no arms: you fall back into the chasm, never reaching the top. Study without meditation is like dying of thirst in a vast lake. Not eradicating the afflictions and transgressions, you fall into lower states of rebirth. [**12b**] Therefore first study, then reflect, and finally meditate in due order. Strive with effort in unmistakenly gaining all three factors because the unmistaken result occurs for those who follow the path of liberation.

[§100] The unclean material body is like the remains of a swollen corpse of the cremation grounds or a skeleton. As there is no entity that is clean and permanent, eliminate attachment to the external and internal body.

[§101] The conceptual mind is momentary and is distinguished throughout the three times as emptiness. By understanding that your mind is impermanent and emptiness, you eliminate mistaken cognitions apprehending entities as permanent.

[§102] Feelings of joy, because they are impermanent, are suffering. Other feelings as well have the nature of suffering. The intelligent should eliminate mistaken attachment that conceives things as pleasurable.

[§103] The term *dharma* refers to all entities, both internal and external forms and so forth. Since they are selfless, the five external elements have no self. Your body and mind also have no self. Since a self is not established, that which belongs to a self does not exist. Apprehension of a self and apprehension of something as a self is mistaken awareness. When you eliminate self-grasping, the disagreeable (*mi mthun*)—suffering—ceases.

[§104] With continuous, undistracted meditative stablization of insight on the meaning of selflessness, you attains the result of an arhat, having actualized cessation.

[§105] Through residing in serenity, all feelings cease. Residing on the single-session path of application,[157] you do not need enjoyments like food; you bring all subtle and coarse conceptual thoughts to cessation. For as long as conditions do not arise, even for an eon, you remain in the meditative stabilization of cessation. You rouse only due to the clamor of noise and so forth.

[§106] Special insight destroys all afflictions without exception. Liberated from the seminal aspects [of the afflictions], you attain the state of arhat. Gradually, once you are entirely free from suffering, you obtain the liberation from [the seminal] aspects [of the afflictions] to the result of arhat. Immediately upon eliminating the afflictions, you are liberated from both any remaining suffering of [afflictions and their seminal aspects].[158]

[§107] Reverse the tendencies for all of saṃsāra, with its six classes of beings. [13a] Reverse ignorance, self-grasping, and the tendencies toward afflictions, sense pleasures, and transgressions. They are like sorceress spirits on a demonic island.[159]

[§108] Entirely eliminate the sufferings of the threefold world and reach the attainments of stream enterer through the state of arhat.[160] Once you have attained happiness passing from saṃsāra, you can benefit others through emanations and so forth.

[Supreme-capacity stages]

[§109] Above the paths of the small and middling individuals are the practices of the supreme individual, who practices the aspiring and engaging mind of awakening and comprehends the instruction leading to the ultimate. You integrate means and wisdom in meditation. You reverse the tendencies that seek your own benefit, reification, and holding of extremes. Eliminating obstructions, you complete the benefit of others through your attainment of omniscience.

[§110] When you have virtue that is without hatred, nonviolent, and free from doubts, likes, and dislikes, [§111] with limitless vast objects and aims wholly filling the reaches of space, the results are immeasurable.

[§112] Having seen the suffering of the threefold world along with its causes, with knowledge of the meaning of the inescapable relation between karma and its results, with objectless insight that is free from extremes, you should meditate on the four immeasurables of loving kindness and so forth. Wishing migrating beings to have happiness, to be free from suffering, and to not be separated from happiness along with viewing them all equally: these are the four immeasurables. Sentient beings have created kindness for you many times as your father and mother in previous lifetimes. Therefore you should make all migrating beings equally happy, free from suffering, and undivorced from happiness.

[§113] With omniscient wisdom, the four immeasurables, compassion, and the various unobstructed activities of the three bodies of a buddha, protect beings from all the suffering of the three realms. Generate the aspiration that wishes to attain buddhahood due to seeing, hearing, and contemplating [the awakening mind]. If the merit of the awakening mind were to take material form, it could not be contained in the realm of space; it is perfect merit that exhausts transgressions. Attaining buddhahood establishes all wishes. For consummate merit, make prostrations, make offerings, confess transgressions, rejoice, [13b] exhort [Dharma teachers to teach], and offer aspirational prayers. Motivated by faith, take refuge for your own welfare; motivated by compassion, take refuge for others' welfare. Become a vessel for the common vows and path. Be a vessel and support for Mahāyāna vows and paths. Train and practice for your own aim, and train in the path for the sake of others. Take refuge for as long as you live traversing the path, until attaining unsurpassable awakening. The "supreme emanation body" (*mchog gi sprul*) is a śrāvaka, and the "peaceful Dharma body" is a bodhisattva.

[§114] Perceive the teacher as a buddha, offer your body without attachment, and supplicate the teacher to remove hindrances in relation to the teacher. The ritual for the [bodhisattva] vows to be upheld continuously is the promise made three times to rescue the unrescued and so on.[161]

[§115] You, with your body composed from effects, will immediately become a child in the lineage of buddhas. You should then proclaim the major and minor precepts.

[§116] Eliminate belligerent thoughts toward sentient beings, and pass beyond resentment.

Do not avoid regret for deceiving the praiseworthy with perverted views.
Do not wallow in points of doubt; do not avoid confessing.
Do not turn a blind eye to doubts or disparage the awakening mind.
Do not overlook regret for dishonesty toward others stemming from desire.
Moreover, eliminate cognizing the cause for pointless aspirations.

[§117] The antidote to these is meditating with thoughts of love and not uttering false words for the sake of body and life. Generate the Mahāyāna mind that establishes virtue for the sake of migrating beings. Respectfully praise whoever produces the awakening mind. Honestly, without deceit, contemplate the welfare of others.

[§118] Contemplate the extensive benefits of the awakening mind. The awakening mind is like a wish-fulfilling jewel giving rise to the strong desire for oneself and all others to finally be free from any suffering and have happiness. Worship this most precious object, the supreme benefit for sentient beings.

[§119] Eliminate temporary and ultimate suffering; bear the burden, holding in mind sentient beings' suffering along with its causes, and accomplish their happiness. For this purpose, [14a] contemplate equalizing and exchanging yourself and others. With the four immeasurables and the four ways of gathering disciples,[162] do as much as possible to fufill the welfare of others and dedicate that to awakening. Strive that all activities of your three doors [of body, speech, and mind] may become virtuous actions, produced with the supreme awakening mind.

[§120] Make every effort to achieve the six perfections[163] and so forth, with actions that are pure in their object and intent. Increase your resolve, and apply yourself to the awakening mind.

[§121] If root infractions should occur, applying the counteragent and feeling regret, confess and restore the former condition within a third of a day. If it goes beyond that, take the vow again. Confess your misdeeds, imagining the Three Precious Ones in your presence. If you confess three times a day and three times at night, you are undefiled. Undeteriorated, having exhausted wrongdoing, you obtain immeasurable merit and gain the conditions of happiness, culminating in buddhahood.

[§122] Take whichever of the seven types of pratimokṣa vows is suitable as a basis for the bodhisattva vows. Stabilize the wish for awakening and study the scriptures. With the capacity for faith and for protecting the scriptures, [§123] a skillful, capable one who keeps the vows with compassion should aspire with effort to attain a Mahāyāna mental continuum.

[§124] The discipline of vows, the discipline of gathering virtuous qualities, and the discipline of benefiting sentient beings are the three vows of [bodhisattva] moral discipline. The vows are promised through the ritual, and you should guard them, keeping them uncorrupted.[164]

[§125] The root downfalls of a bodhisattva are (1) [due to seeking] honor and gain, praising yourself and deprecating others; (2) causing suffering to the unprotected and not giving Dharma and wealth; (3) holding on to anger and not listening to apologies; (4) giving up the Great Vehicle while appearing to teach the excellent Dharma; (5) stealing the property of the Three Jewels; (6) completely abandoning the sacred Dharma; (7) causing harm to the life and so forth of a monk; (8) deliberately commiting the five heinous acts;[165] (9) holding wrong views, being ignorant of cause and effect, and so forth; (10) destroying cities and kingdoms; (11) proclaiming emptiness while not training in the Great Vehicle; (12) turning [anyone] away from engaging in highest awakening; (13) abandoning the pratimokṣa **[14b]** vows while practicing the Great Vehicle; (14) engaging in desire and so forth and not eliminating them through training; (15) falsely saying "I know the profound"; (16) discontinuing virtuous practices while donating to the Three Jewels; (17) giving up serenity and appropriating wealth; and (18) forsaking the awakening mind. These are the root downfalls.

[§126] The [secondary] faulty actions of bodhisattvas are (1) passing a day and night without offering to the Three Jewels; (2) following desires; (3) voluntarily accepting personal gain and honor; (4) not respecting elders out of vanity and so forth; (5) relishing in speech while evading questions; (6) not accepting an invitation to a feast and not accepting gold, wealth, and so forth; (7) not giving to those seeking the holy Dharma; (8) forsaking those with offensive qualities and so forth; (9) not instilling faith through training; (10) not protecting the mind; (11) not obtaining wealth for the benefit of others; (12) not committing a nonvirtuous action for others' welfare with compassion; (13) earning a living through wrong livelihood; (14) wasting time on frivolous actions, distracting others, and so forth; (15) not having joy for liberation; (16) not being fearful of afflictions and so forth; (17) not foresaking your stains that are disreputable; (18) not eliminating afflictions from a mind capable of doing so; (19) lashing out with abuse when your own faults are exposed; (20) neglecting those who are angry with you; (21) refusing to accept the apologies of others; (22) allowing anger to arise within your mental continuum; (23) gathering disciples out of desire for material gain and respect; (24) wasting time and not countering laziness; (25) relying on frivolous talk; (26) with conceit and so forth, not seeking concentration; (27) not abandoning desire, aspirations, and so forth when these become obstacles; (28) viewing the enjoyment of concentration as a virtuous quality; (29) abandoning the doctrines of the Śrāvaka Vehicle and identifying with the Great [Vehicle] and yet endeavoring in Śrāvaka Vehicle practices; (30) making effort in outsider practices while not making effort in Buddhist practices and making effort in outsider practices for their own sake; (31) abandoning the great, extensive vehicle; (32) praising yourself and belittling others with a turbulent mind; (33) not attending Dharma ceremonies or spreading the teachings; [**15a**] (34) disparaging a Dharma preacher and not relying on his words; (35) not assisting those who need help; (36) avoiding the duties of caring for the sick; (37) not working to relieve those who suffer; (38) not admonishing those who are careless; (39) not repaying the kindness of others; (40) not alleviating the distress of others; (41) not giving to those who desire food and resources; (42) not caring for your companions with Dharma and provisions; (43) not acting in accordance with others' wishes; (44) not praising those who have good qualities; (45) not preventing harmful acts as circumstances allow; (46) forgoing acting on others' behalf and so forth if you have miraculous powers.

[§127] Continuously having fetters (*kun tu sbyor ba*; *saṃyojana*) and having little shame and modesty while viewing [fetters] as joyful, pure, and good qualities and, despite admonishment, passing a day without overturning [fetters] is a great downfall. Furthermore, accepting to aspire to the Three Jewels and so forth while turning away from completely repudiating fetters is a middling downfall. Slight self-dissipating [fetters] are to be confessed one or three times and are not an affliction unless one defends the forgetfulness [to confess] and so forth. Afflictions such as attachment, hatred, and so forth should be confessed mentally with the four powers.

[§128] With a desire to produce the ultimate mind of supreme awakening, offer your body or possessions, viewing the guru as the Dharma body. Offer whatever you can afford and go for the highest refuge, serving the guru motivated by the wish to be established in buddhahood. In one million worlds, while traversing cycle existence, the object of observation is the guru, who is the great Vajradhara.[166] The path to train in is actually your own mind free from extremes. This is activity you carry out as a worthy recipient of that path. Practice going for the supreme refuge in this way.

[§129] The aggregates, elements, sensory spheres, subjects, and objects are primordially unborn, one with the awakening mind. Generating the awakening mind in the condition of being free from extremes is practicing to view the guru as the Buddha, the Dharma body.

[§130] As your own mind, primordially, is free from elaborations in the three times, [**15b**] there is nothing anywhere to meditate upon. Establish yourself within the effortless, naturally perfected state. Later on, one should meditate all day long without interruption.

[§131] Even if you realize concepts are empty, you should accomplish virtue and abandon wrongdoing. Even if you realize the equality of self and others, you should benefit others. Although you abide in the condition of equanimity, you should keep to secluded places. Even though you realize nonduality, you should abandon deprecating things. Although you are without hope or fear, you should abandon wrongdoing and achieve virtue. Although you attain the result—the three bodies—you should remain harmonious with others. At all times and on all occasions, eliminate wrong view. As the activity of a beginner bodhisattva cannot actually achieve great benefit for others, through contemplation, you should abandon your own concerns and achieve others' welfare. What use is generating the awakening mind if you do not achieve others' welfare? With your activities of body, speech, and mind set on achieving others' happiness and welfare, you should want beings to be freed from suffering and to have happiness. In this way, when equalizing yourself and others, accomplish the welfare of others as much as you can. With as many resources as possible, with body, speech, and mind, practice giving in small portions initially, even just a mouthful of food to animals and so forth. Then, later, you will even be able to offer your own body for the welfare of others without difficulty. When cultivating love, compassion, and the awakening mind, do not harm others such as enemies, evil spirits, and animals. Free yourself from fears of fire, water, precipices, and so forth. Trust in yourself, no matter what you perceive. If you have hateful or harmful thoughts, turn away from them. Whatever is within you is how the external world appears; on that basis, understand all external and internal things. Ascertain experiences to be nothing but karma and conditions, and purify any defilements you have collected quickly, with certainty.

[§132] The chief principle of happiness is benefitting others; benefitting and respecting others achieves happiness, because greatly benefitting others brings happiness to you as well. And, ultimately, benefitting others leads you to complete buddhahood. Acting for your own benefit is to become a slave or dog. It makes you stupid, ugly, and the object of others' disdain. In the end, [**16a**] you experience only the unbearable sufferings of the hells and so forth. In the past, you have experienced immeasurable sufferings in the six realms of saṃsāra; all of that is misfortune and calamity created by seeking your own benefit.

[§133] Therefore abandon your own benefit and achieve the welfare of others, doing as much as you can and always keeping them in mind, like your own child. Through that, you will complete the accumulations of merit and attain extensive happiness. Therefore always train in the awakening mind. Since the faulty nature of sentient beings is like fire, do not proclaim others' faults; refrain from belligerence; hearing or seeing the faults of others should be left unspoken. Listen and speak about others' good qualities, because it is the cause that produces happiness for you and others. Please the minds of others with whatever actions are suitable.

[§134] Parents, children, relatives, health, wealth, possessions, pleasure, comfort, enemies, disease, hunger and thirst, cold and hunger: all the various sufferings are due to unfavorable conditions. Since they are not established as real entities at all—like a lifeless dream, a delusion that produces joy and sadness—although water is a cool beverage when thirsty, [unreal entities] are unquenchable. Similarly, the hungry are not [long] satisfied with food. With respect to this, hunger and thirst do not really exist, and food and drink do not really exist. Likewise, all the various joys and sufferings are not actually real, like a dream. As they are not real, you should abandon attachment or aversion for appearances. As the impermanent is false, in that it is deceptive, impermanent entities should not be a focus of awareness.[167] Things that are not real, that are like an illusion, should not be apprehended as real; they are mere illusions. If you know they are false, the sufferings of attachment and aversion are cleared away. Therefore all joys and sufferings are mere mistaken appearances; they are not actually established.

[§135] When grasping and imagining joy and suffering about nothing whatsoever, suffering arises repeatedly and flourishes. In this way, even though you may understand [intellectually], suffering is not cleared away. You may hear many Dharma teachings, but if you do not clear away the afflictions, you are devoid of practice and merely proclaim words, like a starving person chattering on [about food].

[§136] When you have received the special instructions and take up practice, [**16b**] the suffering of grasping things as real diminishes. And when you continuously meditate on things to be like an illusion, discordant suffering experiences cease. In this way, practice what is indicated by the dream metaphor. See appearances as not being real things.

[§137] With great wisdom, realize the meaning of the Dharma; with great compassion, free from selfish desires, carry the burden of the welfare of others. The capacity to instill virtuous qualities in faithful disciples, benefitting others, is buddhahood. With the intention to benefit sentient beings, the Great Sage taught, "I take form as the teacher in the world to display the [means] for taming whomever is to be trained." By ascertaining that the spiritual master is the Buddha, contemplate the good qualities that come from seeing the spiritual master in that way. By pleasing the master, all your virtuous, wholesome qualities will increase.

[§138] When thinking about a fault, see whatever it is that you did as a fault. Denigrating the spiritual teacher greatly increases your faults and delusions, and arcane self-justifications only increase afflictions. Repeatedly contemplate the contours of these faults. These faults arise in you. Contemplation is cut short under the sway of demonic forces; the mind becomes powerless, and leprosy and so forth manifest; virtue degenerates, and you fall into wrong paths. The attendant Sunakṣatra (*legs pa'i skar ma*) served the Buddha for many years, but through a lack of trust, devotion, and veneration, he practiced wrongly and fell to the lower realms in his next birth.

[§139] Since all virtuous qualities arise from pleasing the spiritual teacher, the spiritual teacher is like a wish-fulfilling jewel. Whatever he does, do not regard it as a fault; see his virtuous qualities. If he becomes pleased, it is appropriate for your own mind, and afflictions are suppressed; the three trainings arise in your mental continuum. By increasing devotion and veneration, you give rise to other virtuous qualities, extinguish a great amount of moral wrongdoings, and complete an expansive amount of merit. Moreover, the blessings of specific instances of devotion and respect give rise to particular virtuous qualities. Therefore, when the faulty recognize the virtuous qualities that are objects of meditation, it is like applying medicine to a sick person. Generate the perception [of the teacher] as a buddha, and venerate him. Refrain from coming too close; with respect, listen to the holy Dharma. [**17a**] Listen to what is spoken; do not practice mistakenly. Without deceit, honestly please the spiritual teacher. Do not sidestep an occasion [to please the spiritual teacher]. If you make effort in requesting, listening, and practicing, the result, buddhahood, will quickly be attained. If you have much aversion and attachment, you become included among servants to the king, people, and townsmen who desire advantages and so forth by having a distracted body and mind. If you have desire for worldly abundance, you become distracted by craving for wealth and possessions. You might attain great wealth and such, but the suffering of protecting and losing the things that you have accumulated, mixed with evil deeds, distract you and increase craving due to aging and desire. When things are not acquired, your hungry and thirsty body is tormented by uncontrollable enslavement, and the body becomes tired. Your mind, distracted, is unable to contemplate. With your body distracted by many activities, meditative stabilization does not arise. Even if you have meditative stabilization, that gradually degenerates. Therefore abandon the desires for food and clothing and remain in seclusion.

[§140] When you are attached to sentient beings, grasping them as "mine," when an ego exists, your suffering is increased due to children, spouses, and friends. You become distracted by many aversions, attachments, and conceptual thoughts. You are not satisfied in the company of those things; your mental afflictions arise again and again, and you crave more and more. If you become separated from those people, suffering and sorrow arise. Harmed with respect to those [friends and so on], you suffer. Even for just a little while, it is possible that they become enemies. Beneficial speech falls on deaf ears, and once again there is belligerence. You may even resort to evil deeds and fall into lower realms of rebirth.

Friendly people make you happy, but since you are unable to accomplish the welfare of others, you should relinquish social activities and keep the childish at a distance. Meditative stabilization depends on physical isolation. In that solitary place, use antidotes to eliminate the crippling negative forces that arise. In that place, destroy the mental afflictions and guard moral conduct. Even in physical isolation, afflictions can arise when the mind is distracted. The mind does not settle in equipoise and elaborations increase. Therefore relinquish the worldly mind and eliminate afflictions; [**17b**] do not lose your awareness of other distracting mental afflictions, as regret and mental discomfort are unfit outflows of a distracted mind. Gradually, the body and speech engage in nonvirtuous karma, then karma increases, and various sufferings arise. Therefore you should eliminate mental afflictions and conceptual thought. The mind that is pliable and happy quickly attains meditative stabilization, and other virtuous qualities arise. These are the beneficial qualities of pure moral conduct. Therefore protect moral conduct without hypocrisy. By engendering a great amount of virtuous qualities, hindrances are cleanly cut off and cleared away. Separate from the causes and effects of savages, carnivorous beasts, and evil spirits and collect the necessities, the abundant conditions to be in solitude.

[§141] Your body on a comfortable seat and your mind in meditative stabilization, give rise to the mind for supreme awakening, relax the three doors [of body, speech, and mind], and sever the elaborations of conceptual thought related to the three times; uncontrived like pure, unmuddied water, freely relax the six aggregates of consciousness (*tshogs drug*)[168] and eliminate grasping thoughts. Free from activities, remain in effortless, spontaneous presence.

[§142] Having ceased all subtle and coarse external and internal concepts, remain in nonconceptual meditative stabilization. Then, at this time, clarity, without thoughts grasping at apparent objects, and your own mind, afterward objectless, appears as a mirage like pure space. [§143] Without the thorns of conceptuality, the body and mind are blissful. Listen to the serviceable contemplating body that is light.

[§144] With desires and so forth turned off, in unwavering meditative stabilization, maintain your mind in the condition of inseparable clarity and emptiness. Experiencing it by yourself, free from doubts, and with firm, ascertaining awareness, internalize the changeless. Forsake physical and mental activities, and restrain the sense doors. In seclusion, sustain the elimination of mental afflictions and concepts. With no attachment to desires, leveling out the eight worldly concerns, having conviction in cause and effect, strive to eliminate evil deeds and achieve virtue. Delighting in solitude and not forsaking the focal object, eliminate desires and aspirations, maliciousness, excitement and worry, sleepiness and lethargy, and doubt: [**18a**] the obstructions to concentration (*dhyāna*).

[§145] All things of saṃsāra and nirvāṇa are your own mind, like the examples of a mirror, a reflection, or an echo. All is unstained (*ma 'dres*; *anupakliṣṭa*); the unity of all transcends limited views. The essence [of your mind] is luminous and naturally empty. The characteristic of union is liberated from the extremes of elaborations. Whatever happiness or suffering appears is your own mind. There is no separate dharma not cognized by the mind. When [something] is construed as a distinct, established elaboration that is other than mind, that is mistaken.

[§146] The mind is from the beginning innately pure, unconditioned, free from extremes, sameness, and without acceptance or rejection of views. In this way, the mind itself is established as the way of things; mind as such is pure like the sky. Whether the victorious ones of the three times teach it or not, whether sentient beings realize it or not, perfect gnosis is from the beginning the Dharma body, unfabricated, not taken up; from the beginning, it is the awakening mind. From the beginning it is stainless and pure; the afflictions and sufferings of cyclic existence are not at all established.

[§147] Mind itself, spontaneously established from the beginning, cannot be realized by the many who deliberately seek out signs of it. Meditating without a view and free of activity, the result, not to be sought elsewhere, is established from the beginning. [§148] Whether through the condition of the spiritual teacher's teaching or not; whether a yogi meditates or not; [§149] whether wise ones realize or not; the unconditioned mind-as-such is free from causal conditions. It is not permanent, and it is free from the extremes of nihilism; it is without arising or cessation, sameness or difference, coming or going. Being pacified of these eight extremes of elaboration is the characteristic of the naturally occuring awakening mind.

[§150] Since saṃsāra is not established as other than a nonexistent mind, the sufferings of the lower realms and so forth do not exist to be eliminated. As the nonexistent mind will not be established as something else since it is not awakened, the sameness of saṃsāra and nirvāṇa, happiness and suffering, is equal to the sameness of your own mind.

[§151] Without exception, all who have a view of the perishable aggregates, who grasp extremes, [**18b**] who view things as real, and who think themselves supreme do not see their own mind. Not seeing anything at all is established as the nature of the mind itself. From the beginning, free from elaborations, the nature of the mind is unestablished, without shape and color, and free from signs. Without a mind underlying the sense faculties, there is not a sense object. There is not a mind other than that; it is emptiness. The empty mind does not have heavenly or lower rebirth; as it is selfless, it is free from suffering. The individual who apprehends the sense of "I" makes a mistake; because an individual is selfless, it is suitable to abandon self-grasping. The nonmind is emptiness. The Buddha does not see, has not seen, and will not see the mind.[169] Because a buddha, whose eyes are dust free, is without a mind, even a mind badly agitated neither is born nor dies. Likewise, mind itself—emptiness—is not burned even by the fire at the end of an eon. Because your mind from the beginning is emptiness, emptiness is not destroyed, subdued, purified, or cultivated. Naturally, from the beginning, it is emptiness; there is no object at all to be cultivated. For one who is not meditating, who is free from all views and practices, everything is unestablished; your mind is empty and everywhere, nonmeditation, undistracted, in the state of emptiness.

[§152] When in a meditative equipoise with nothing discarded or adopted, then subtle and coarse mental facets (*caitta*; *sems byung*) are ascertained as empty. While flowing down like water, appearing from themselves to themselves, appearances that lack intrinsic essence are directly identified as subtle or coarse flickers of thought. They spontaneously subside by themselves, vanishing into the fundamental nature of existence (*chos nyid dbyings*).

[§153] After that, imagine the body and all appearances without exception as emptiness. Mental facets, like the appearance of external objects, are not truly existent; perceive them as reflections, echoes, dreams, the objects of your perception (*yul snang*), mirages, hairs in your vision, or, like clouds in the sky, self-arising and dissolving. In this way, all appearances and conceptual thoughts are eradicated by the mind in emptiness, which abandons mental self-grasping. This should be applied as an antidote for all negative conditions.

[§154] [Even] the sufferings at the hands of the legions of wrathful guardians of hell [**19a**] and the lower realms of rebirth, such as the hungry ghosts and so forth: all sufferings, even though they emerge as your enemies, do not taint the mind. Likewise, [the mind in emptiness is] not tainted by the afflictions, conceptions, sufferings, and discordant obscurations. Just as the storms or fires at the end of an eon do not taint the sky, likewise the mind is insubstantial, free from the sufferings of birth and death. Therefore your own mind is emptiness from the beginning. Practice to definitely realize that. If you are not naturally disposed toward emptiness, train in undistracted mindfulness.

[§155] With the weapon of wisdom that realizes emptiness, eradicate the enemies of self and self-grasping that arise due to delusion. Moreover, unestablished free-flowing conceptual thought is purified by unifying the four times.[170] That will be established by correct mindfulness. Moreover, do not let go of the weapon of emptiness; eradicate all subtle and coarse conceptual thought.

[§156] If while realizing emptiness you do not cut off the discordant factors, since you lack the power and blessing of the spiritual teacher, your realization of emptiness will be a mere intellectual understanding of words, not effective for your mental continuum. All negative conditions become suitable concordant conditions when you are friends with the path of awakening. When practiced, the path produces all good qualities.

[§157] When you realize the meaning of emptiness, transgressions are consumed and great merit is completed; discordant conditions do not oppress the mind; all the sufferings of cyclic existence, the hells and so forth, are destroyed. Abide effortlessly in the meaning of union; if emptiness did not exist, union would be merely chasing words. When you have the realization of emptiness, all external things appear like reflections. Cut the totality of elaborations of the mind—all things that appear, the internal and external, causes and effects, the multiple dependent arisings. Mere words are utterly mundane when speaking about emptiness. When you are liberated from all of cyclic existence without exception, omniscient buddhahood [**19b**] is realized.

[§158] The union of the basis, the path, and the result is self-arisen, emptiness, the realm of reality, pure, unconditioned, naturally free from elaborations, with nothing at all established, like empty space. The traces of entities are not established in that. It is the coemergent way of things, the essence, the factor of clarity, without object, without conceptual thought, inherent translucent radiance, unceasing, appearing like the sun in a cloudless sky, the unity of the unelaborated character of coemergence, self-illuminating, the unceasing appearance of lucidity and awareness; it is indivisible appearance and emptiness, like a conch shell and the whiteness of the conch shell. There is nothing at all that is not indivisible from your own mind. Nonconceptual awareness is devoid of a grasping subject and grasped object, while the unceasing, agitated mind is like the wind. The appearance aspect (*snang cha*) of indivisible coemergence has its own form (*rang gi gzugs*), like the shining light of pure crystal without the five-colored lights within the sphere of sense objects. The mode of apprehension (*'dzin stang*) of saṃsāra and nirvāṇa will appear as dual due to realizing or not realizing the cognition of sense objects.

[§159] The mind itself, pure from the beginning, is the realm of reality; it pervades whatever entities that appear, even if it does not directly appear due to delusion; it is all-pervading, like sesame oil in sesame seeds. The grasping subject and grasped object of karma and appearance is like an illusion. Appearances, reflections, deluded appearances, emanations, nonconceptual appearances, and mirages are like space. All that appears is your own mind. The nature of all that appears is emptiness, and all various appearances, without exception, are nondually unified with your own mind. Cause and effect are indivisible and thus empty, like water and waves. Whatever appears is not other than the mind; it is like the variety of golden things, which do not change from their golden form. The formations of virtuous and nonvirtuous mental facets are diverse activities like reflections, the pure Dharma body free from passing stains, inseparable from manifest self-cognizant wakefulness, pure like a cloudless sky. Just as the buddha bodies and the buddhafields, along with the celestial mansions, are appearances of pure gnosis and not other, your own mind is a manifestation of merit. [**20a**]

[§160] Cognize the realm of reality with space-like gnosis. The body, fields, and so forth all appear pure; indivisible appearance and emptiness, the two collections, arise naturally and do not arise from another. They do not externally appear. The unstained powers, fearlessness, the buddha qualities of the minor and major marks, and other qualities—the streaming rain of sacred Dharma from the clouds of omniscient mercy, recollection of the cause of the harsh three realms, the fully ripened harvest of the three bodies—these are the ripened awakening activity (*'phrin las*; *samudācāra*) of virtuous qualities.

[§161] Put into practice the view free from extremes. A beginner practices the meaning of union based on intellectual understanding. Your practice should establish the nature of virtue and nonvirtue, of cause and effect, and of the subtle and coarse in terms of understanding the subtle emptiness of intrinsic nature. Everything that you practice does not pass beyond emptiness.

Therefore, because of being free from the elaboration of extremes, whatever conditions that occur are undeceiving cause and effect; your own mind is liberated from the extreme of nihilism. Since nonconceptual mere appearance is empty, it is free from the extreme of permanence. Your own mind is liberated from the extremes of permanence and nihilism. The indivisibility of causality and emptiness is the meaning of view. It is an error of yogic vision when you fall into limited views; therefore do not fall into an established philosophical position. The clear mind is inseparably pervaded with emptiness, the nature of all dharmas, like sesame is pervaded by sesame oil. What is the use of apprehending emptiness with the mind? Emptiness and the mind are inseparable, like the wings of a bird.

[§162] A yogi should not abandon cause and effect, even when realizing all things as empty, because from the mere appearance of virtue and sin arises various effects. For the happiness of yourself and others, subtly cultivate, like illusions, the causes and effects of virtue and sin. Because your empty mind is the inseparability of cause and effect, the meaning of dependent arising is free of limitations. When you apprehend entities and nonentities as permanent, it is the pitfall of lapsing from yogic vision. Therefore practice the indivisibility of emptiness and positive and negative actions. Even if you realize emptiness, it is possible to fall into nihilism; [**20b**] therefore, like having two legs for walking on the path, do not cast away cause and effect. With the weapon of wisdom, which realizes things as empty yet discerns unmistakable cause and effect, eliminate unfavorable conditions.

[§163] The yoga that engages emptiness as cause and effect is devoid of seeking out the undifferentiated. Your own mind being free from extremes, like space: this is the meaning of the Great Middle Way. Put it into practice continuously and do not get established in a theoretical understanding of what is actually the case in all its immediacy (*yin thog*). When nonvirtuous karma is mixed with emptiness, the force generated by that nonvirtue quickly ripens into a great result. When virtuous karma is mixed with emptiness, the force generated by that virtue quickly ripens into a supremely good result. Therefore, although you realize the equality [of emptiness], vigorously generate and achieve in practice even the most subtle aspects of virtue and sin. An emptiness that erases virtue and sin falls into nihilism. Therefore practice causality and emptiness as inseparable. Do not be established in the intellectual understanding of mere words, purify the mental continuum, and put into practice the vision of unmistaken union.

[§164] Even if the realization of your own mind as emptiness becomes stable, without the supreme method of the awakening mind and compassion, you will not find the path of omniscience. Even if you have love, compassion, and the awakening mind, if you do not comprehend things with emptiness, you will not be liberated from saṃsāra for a long time. But when you unify the supreme method of compassion with emptiness, putting into practice the exalted path that is correct and unmistaken, the excellent results of extraordinary rebirth as gods and humans and the supreme result of buddhahood will be attained. This is the great path of all buddhas. If means are separated from wisdom, you will not be able to proceed, like someone with broken legs trying to walk a path. Therefore means and wisdom are inseparable; the intelligent should put them into practice. Furthermore, when you engage in all activities while generating love, compassion, and the awakening mind, you should pursue all activities together with emptiness. Dedicate the virtues of integrating emptiness, compassion, and the awakening mind to supreme awakening. In this way, put the union of means and wisdom into practice.

[§165] All the sufferings of enemies, demons, maleficent beings, unharmonious appearances, hunger, thirst, and so forth—[**21a**] all that appears that is undesirable—is your own mind, emptiness, your own perception;[171] there is nothing from without. Therefore refrain from the suffering of attachment and aversion toward all unharmonious appearances; the appearance aspect (*snang cha*) of your own mind ceases, indistinguishable from emptiness. There is nothing other than the inseparability of your own mind, appearance, and emptiness. All excellent appearances—the happiness of friends, attendants, wealth, youth, and health—are emptiness; for this reason, eliminate haughtiness. In this way, do not apprehend any appearances of happiness and suffering as real; eliminate attachment and aversion. Since all happiness and suffering are the nature of emptiness, appearance and emptiness are indivisible, like an illusory dream. Likewise, all objects that appear to the six sense-faculties do not exist; the unreal appearance is a unity of indivisible, unceasing appearance and emptiness, like a dream. Therefore discard attachment, aversion, and suffering in relation to all happiness or pain. Put into practice nonconceptuality free from activity, in the condition of the indivisible unity of your own mind, appearance, and emptiness. The childish intellect that conceptualizes existence and nonexistence falls down in the end, adopting or abandoning the apprehension of existent or nonexistent signs. You will not be liberated from saṃsāric states (*'khor ba'i gnas*) if you hold onto extremes. Therefore the skilled, wise person who has heard the special instructions always puts into practice the unity of appearance and emptiness. Furthermore, you should view all that appears—your own body, which is illustrated by the example of a reflection, and so forth—as lacking inherent existence. Eliminate all suffering and mental afflictions with a mind that is untainted by suffering and afflictions in relation to nonexistent appearances.

[§166] Remaining with an undistracted mind and body in meditative equipoise, having previously engendered love, compassion, and the awakening mind, arouse the aspiration that desires realization, accumulation of merit, purification of evil deeds, and *guru yoga*. Nourish the previous serenity and insight.

[§167] With your own mind free from extremes—the Great Middle Way, free from conceptuality with and without signs—remain without the grasping thoughts of the extremes of permanence and nihilism. Not abiding in mere nonconceptuality, [§168] remain free from elaborations, in free relaxation from the unceasing appearances of the six aggregates of consciousness (*tshogs drug*). Since all apparent objects are the emptiness of your own mind, appearing [**21b**] yet lacking inherent existence, remain in the condition of not grasping to the appearances of objects of your own mind, which are like the moon's reflection in water. When all things within saṃsāra and nirvāṇa are one in the condition of being indivisible from your own mind, since saṃsāra is not abandoned and nirvāṇa is not achieved in the unified mind, remain in the condition that forgos taking up hopes and abandoning fears.

[§169] Since buddhas and sentient beings are, from the very beginning, of equal nature; since appearance and emptiness, cyclic existence and nirvāṇa, and conceptuality and nonconceptuality are likewise of equal nature in the mind, primordially pure; understand all appearances as empty, like knowing ice as water. There is no object of meditation and no one who meditates. There is spontaneous presence without being bound or liberated, without contemplation and subsequent realization. Since everything is indivisible, like water and waves, remain in the condition of the nondual wisdom of your own mind.

[§170] Continously sustain your own mind free from elaborations; mentally relax, without fixing on a single object of knowledge; stay with mindfulness, like a skillful cowherd (*mkhas pa ba glang skyong ba*); be free by resting naturally, without projecting, without concentrating.

[§171] All objects that appear—all external and internal conceptual thoughts—are taken in as a friend, emptiness, like snow falling on water. Through emptiness, wisdom increases, and attachments and aversions cease. Thoroughly know the appearance of all six sensory objects as emptiness. All conceptuality that appears (*snang rtog*) is emptiness, just as a bird flying through the hazy sky leaves no tracks, simultaneously liberated upon arising. Sustain the realization of your own mind with undistracted conscientiousness.

[§172] Remain in ungrasping cognition, carefree, unbound, relaxing naturally, like a bird flying up from a boat. Through awareness, sustain whichever path of activity you like; understand which experiences and realizations are increasing.

[§173] Accordingly, even though you have awareness, through meditative equipoise, increase serenity and insight in physical and mental solitude;

make effort in the activities of accumulation and purification with continuous mindfulness; with mindfulness, sustain the aim of realization, undistracted, like a mother tending to her dying son.

[§174] When there is uninterrupted mindfulness, there is meditative equipoise. Anything not embraced with mindfulness is postmeditative awareness. The method of undegenerated mindfulness eliminates grasping thoughts. With conscientiousness and attention, recollect emptiness.

[§175] Do not pursue or grasp as real the features (*mngon rtags*) for any appearance of the [**22a**] phenomenal marks (*mtshan ma*) of the six sense objects. With correct mindfulness, apprehend any appearance whatsoever as emptiness at the time of restraining the sense doors with your own mind. Without differentiating between distraction and quiet seclusion, between meditative equipoise and multiple activities, practice the indivisibility of serenity and insight, relinquishing activities and residing in meditative equipoise while in the hermitage.

[§176] Reflect upon nonvirtuous mental afflictions and confess downfalls related to vows you have pledged. Gather the accumulations of both merit and wisdom, untainted by natural evil deeds.

[§177] During any of the four daily activities,[172] with undistracted mindfulness and conscientiousness at all times, understand any appearances whatsoever as emptiness when you desire to reside in the unified state of your own mind.

[§178] Refrain from the subtlest nonvirtues and mental afflictions while understanding whatever appears to be false, and eliminate reification (*dngos 'dzin*; *bhāvagraha*). Endeavor to achieve trust in the occurrence of happiness and pain from virtuous and evil deeds, and level out the eight worldly concerns with equanimity. Without becoming disconnected from love and compassion, make effort for others' welfare.

The following are signs of progress on the path of unmistaken realization: [§179] reversing afflictions, reversing all intentions for your own benefit, turning back dualistic fixation on external and internal entities, reversing the tendency to hold extremes of permanency and nihilism, and so forth; and leveling out the eight worldly concerns, having compassion, and having faith in cause and effect.

[§180] When you have firmly and completely eliminated the accumulation of [karmic, afflictive, and knowledge] obscurations by attaining buddhahood endowed with the three bodies and the five wisdoms, you will with various awakening activities lead all those to be trained to the omniscience [of buddhahood], the perfected result, as well as other states [such as happiness and heavenly rebirths, until attaining buddhahood].

[§181] Due to whatever roots of virtue have arisen from writing this text, may sentient beings without exception achieve supreme awakening.

Stages of the Path to Awakening, composed by Śrī Dīpaṃkarajñāna (for the sake of Dromtönpa), is concluded.

Part 2
Commentaries and Exegesis

2. A Summary and Structural Analysis

THE INITIAL TWO works among the ancillaries to Atiśa's *Stages* are *Condensed Stages of the Path* (*Lam rim mdor bsdus pa*) and *Structural Analysis of Stages of the Path to Awakening* (*Byang chub lam rim bsdus don*). Both works are anonymous summaries of *Stages* and appear to be of Tibetan authorship, perhaps composed by an early Kadampa master who was influenced by Atiśa or who was among the early transmitters of Atiśa's lineage of teachings. The titles of each of the respective texts reflect the hermeneutical or commentarial technique of placing the contents into a summary (*bsdus pa*).

The Kadam tradition was formative for the development of Tibetan scholasticism, affecting Tibetan Buddhist scholarly endeavors to the present day. Until recently, the earliest available Kadam commentarial works that used the technique of summary were those of Ngok Loden Sherab (1059–1109; Kano 2008) and Chapa Chökyi Sengé (1109–69; Hugon 2009). These scholars were influenced by the scholastic traditions of Sangphu Neuthok Monastery, founded by Ngok Lekpai Sherab in 1073. The summary texts in this chapter appear to be some of the earliest known works of this genre and may have been influenced by Atiśa himself.

Condensed Stages of the Path presents a general summary of *Stages* as a whole work rather than enumerating a portion of *Stages* or focusing on individual topics within the text (Verhagen 2005, 194). In this sense, *Condensed Stages of the Path*, as a brief work summarizing the meaning of the entire treatise, is similar to the Indian Buddhist hermeneutical category of "summary meaning" (Skt. *piṇḍārtha*; Pali *piṇḍattha*; Edgerton 1953, 345a). As part of a technique for the exegesis of Buddhist works, "the term *piṇḍārtha* refers to a statement to be included at the beginning of a commentary, which summarizes the treatise and is easy to understand and memorize" (Hugon 2009, 58). This form of summary exegesis seeks to encourage "a quick and systematic understanding of the entire body of a root text, rather than to assist in memorising its main topics" (Kano 2008, 146). *Condensed Stages of the Path* therefore quickly summarizes all the content *Stages* by briefly enumerating the primary practices of the three types of individuals.

Structural Analysis of the Stages of the Path to Awakening is a detailed topical outline of *Stages*. The Tibetan title of the work reflects the ambiguous use of the term *bsdus don* in the eleventh and twelfth centuries. In the early phases of the Later Dissemination (*phyi dar*) of Buddhism in Tibet, *bsdus don* may refer to two quite distinct types of texts: a (1) synoptic table or (2) concise guide (Hugon 2009, 56; Kano 2016b, 233). *Structural Analysis* is a synoptic table, or what later Tibetan tradition calls *sa bcad*, "topical outline." This type of text is "an enumeration of topical outlines which expresses a hierarchical stratification superimposed onto an Indian treatise" (Hugon 2009, 56). The topical outline is widely used throughout Tibetan scholarly exegesis up to the present day. The historical beginnings of this form of analysis are unknown, but they may have started in China (Steinkellner 1989; Verhagen 2005; Hugon 2009). According to Tibetan anecdotes, "the paṇḍita Atiśa . . . is said to have noted with approval its [i.e., the topical outline's] existence among the Tibetans" (Jackson 1993, 5; Kano 2008, 136n33). The Tibetans were already refining the technique before Atiśa's arrival in Tibet.

As a synoptic table or topical outline, *Structural Analysis of the Stages of the Path to Awakening* is more than just a mere table of contents. The work functions as a tool for the guided, systematic understanding of *Stages*. With its refined and exhaustive stratifications of subdivisions, it serves as a type of commentary, superimposing a structure that is not immediately apparent in the root text (Hugon 2009). The synoptic table would be memorized by the Kadampa lineage-holder of these teachings, as the Tibetan text has no markers that enumerate the root text. What the sources are for the hierarchical stratification and how the subdivisions were created are frequent questions in relation to the analysis of Tibetan synoptic tables. However, the source for the topical outline of Atiśa's *Stages* is most likely Atiśa's *Instructions for Select Disciples*, which is translated in chapter 4. *Instructions for Select Disciples* indicates a stratification of the main points and divisions of the stages of the path system, and the work is attributed to Atiśa himself. In the English translation that follows, I have structured *Structural Analysis* into a formal outline. I have also placed section numbers of Atiśa's *Stages* in brackets to facilitate correspondence between the topical outline and the root text.

Condensed Stages of the Path

Homage to the spiritual teacher! With a foundation based on conduct, [the individual of small capacity] understands the difficulty of finding freedoms and favorable conditions, reflects upon death and impermanence, abandons laziness, eliminates wrongdoing, [**22b**] and enthusiastically practices virtue. [The middling-capacity individual] recollects the sufferings of cyclic existence, eliminates the causes of that—afflictions and wrongdoing—heeds subtle cause and effect in any activity, and focuses on the reality of selflessness. [The supreme-capacity individual] trains in love, compassion, and the awakening mind, reflects that things are like illusion, and is mindful in recognizing all entities as lacking inherent existence. When you practice the indivisibility of appearance and emptiness, marvelous and excellent results occur. Nourishing that aim, in solitude give up preoccupation with the notions of this life; when you practice while possessing four qualities,[173] you attain the result. This concludes the summarized stages of the path.

Structural Analysis of Stages of the Path to Awakening

This array of essential holy Dharma has three points: the essence of the visible conventional, the essence of the path to be achieved, and the essence of the three practices. This threefold essential array is the quintessence of the three scriptural collections.

Among these, first, this essence of the path to be achieved has four cycles of teachings: a cycle of root texts [*Stages of the Path*, *Lamp for the Path*, *Lamp for the Summary of Conduct*]; a cycle of ritual practices [taking refuge, the one-day precepts, lay vows, awakening-mind ritual]; a cycle of practical guidance and special instruction [*Instructions for Select Disciples* in chapter 4 and *Pointing-Out Instructions in Sets of Five* in chapter 5]; and a cycle of enhancing practice and removing obstacles [chapter 6].

This *Stages of the Path to Awakening* has three general points:

I. Preliminary introduction
II. That which is wished for, the main body of the text
III. The thoroughly completed conclusion

I. The first, preliminary introduction, has three topics.
- A. Showing the title of the text
- B. Paying homage [§1]
- C. The oath of composition [§2]

II. The main body of the text has two topics.
- A. A synopsis of the body of the text [§3]
- B. An extensive explanation of its elements
    - 1. The path of small capacity [§4–75]
        - a. Summary [§4]
        - b. Extensive explanation
            - 1) Practices
                - a) Refuge [§6–8]
                    - i) Cause
                    - ii) Condition
                    - iii) Measure
                    - iv) Training
                    - v) Benefit
                - b) One-day precepts [§9]

c) Lay vows [§10–12]
i) Training
ii) Benefit [**23a**]
2) Meditation objects [§13–20]
a) Leisure and fortune
i) Leisure [§13]
ii) Fortune [§14]
iii) Difficulty in finding [§15]
a' Difficulty by means of enumeration [§15]
b' Difficulty by means of cause [§16]
c' Difficulty by means of example [§17]
iv) Not wasting attainment [§18]
a' The fault of wasting what is found [§18]
b' Being endowed with that aim [§19]
c' The instruction for that aim [§20]
b) Impermanence [§21–32]
i) External impermanence [§21]
ii) Internal impermanence [§22]
a' Contemplating the certainty of death [§23]
1' One dies by being born as a sentient being [§24]
2' Because sentient beings are conditioned
3' The certainty of death as life draws to its end [§24]
b' Death strikes without warning
1' There are many conditions opposing [life] [§25]
2' Life is without certainty [§26]
3' The body is without essence [§27]
c' Death is not overturned in any case
1' You cannot overturn death [§28]
2' Protective deities and so forth cannot overturn death [§29]
3' Other individuals cannot overturn death [§30–31]
d' Final instructions [§32]
c) Cause and effect has three topics
i) Cause and effect of negative actions
a' Making the connection [§34]
b' Actual cause and effect
1' Cause [§35]
a'' Ordinary nonvirtue
b'' Evil deeds that are different from ordinary nonvirtue

2' Effect
a" Maturation
1" Hell [§36]
(a) [Located in] another place
(b) Suffering
(i) General suffering
(a') Hot hells [§37]
(1') General [§38]
(2') Specific
(b') Cold hells [§39]
(c') Neighboring hells [§40]
(d') Limited duration
(ii) Specific suffering [§41]
(c) Measure of life [§42]
(d) Final instruction
2" Hungry ghosts [§43]
(a) Place [§44]
(b) Suffering
(i) External obstructions [§44]
(ii) Internal obstructions [§45]
(iii) Tongues become wheels of flame [§46]
(c) Measure of life [§47]
(d) Instruction
3" Animals [§48]
(a) Place [§49]
(b) Suffering [**23b**]
(c) Measure of life [§50]
(d) Instruction [§51]
b" Harmonious cause [§52]
1" The experience similar to the cause
2" Effect of compatibility of cause [§53]
c" Dominant result [§54]
c' Concluding instructions [§55]
ii) Cause and effect of positive actions [§56]
a' The connection [§57]
b' Actual cause and effect [§58]
1' Cause
2' Effect
a" Maturation

b" Casually concordant [§60]
1" Experience
2" Effectivness
c" Dominant result [§61]
c' Instruction [§62]
iii) General instructions on positive and negative actions
a' Teaching all happiness and suffering as karmic experience
1' The appearance of lower realms of rebirth
a" Hell [§63]
b" Hungry ghosts [§64]
c" The appearance of animals [§65]
2' The appearance of heavenly realms [§66]
b' Teaching everything as the mind [§67–68]
c' Instructions on general cause and effect [§69–73]
1' The manner of accumulating causes
a" The four extremes in the manner of accumulation
b" The four extremes of impulsion and exhaustion
c" The four extremes of evil deeds and obscurations
2' The manner of the arising of effects
a" Indefinite experience [of virtuous and harmful actions]
b" Definite experience [having done virtuous and harmful actions]
c" Clearing away mixed-up doubt
d' Teaching the general characteristics of cause and effect
3) Reversal of tendencies [§74]
4) Results [§75]
2. The path of middling capacity [§76–108]
a. Summary
b. Extensive explanation of the factors
1) Practices
a) General teaching of three practices [§76–77]
b) The benefits of those practices [§78–79]
i) Faults of householder life
ii) Benefits of taking monastic vows
2) Meditation objects
a) The faults of saṃsāra [§80–96]
i) General presentation [§80]

a' Total delusion
b' Uncertainty
c' Dissatisfaction [§81]
ii) Detailed explanation
a' Instructions on the sufferings of the lower realms of rebirth [§82–84]
1' Hell
2' Hungry ghosts
3' Animals
4' General instructions on successive lifetimes
b' Instructions on the upper realms
1' The sufferings of humans [§84]
a" Sufferings of the four currents of results
1" Birth [§84]
2" Aging [§85]
3" Sickness [§86]
4" Death [§87] **[24a]**
5" General instruction [§88]
b" The suffering of what is unwished for
1" Not finding what is sought [§89]
2" Maintaining the wealth you have [§90]
3" Meeting with enemies [§91]
4" Being separate from beloved friends [§92]
c" The nature of suffering
1" Suffering of conditioned existence [§93]
2" Suffering of change [§94]
3" Suffering of suffering [§95]
2' The sufferings of gods and demigods [§95]
c' General instructions [§96]
b) The cause of saṃsāra [§97]
i) The actual cause
ii) Instructions on eliminating that
c) The path that liberates from saṃsāra
i) The path of dependent arising [§98]
a' The progressive order
b' The order of reversal
ii) Close placements of mindfulness
a' Body [§100]
b' Mind [§101]
c' Feeling [§102]

- d' Mindfulness of dharmas [§103]
- ii) Cessation [§104–6]
  - a' Brief teaching [§104]
  - b' Extensive explanation
    - 1' Cessation of sensations through serenity [§105]
    - 2' Cessation of mental afflictions through insight [§106]
- 3) Reversal of tendencies [§107]
- 4) Results [§108]

3. The supreme individual has two topics [§109–81]
   - a. Summary
   - b. Extensive explanation
     - 1) Practices
       - a) Aspiring for the awakening mind [§113]
         - i) The cause of arising
           - a' The cause of arising the aspect
             - 1' The nature
             - 2' The verbal definition
             - 3' The object of observation
             - 4' The means of cultivation
           - b' The cause of giving rise to the aspiration
             - 1' The beneficial qualities of omniscient buddhahood
             - 2' The beneficial qualities of awakening
         - ii) The ritual
           - a' The preliminaries
             - 1' Accumulating merit
             - 2' Taking extraordinary refuge
             - 3' Offering the body
           - b' The actual practice
           - c' Subsequent practices
         - iii) The training
           - a' Uncorrupted protection
             - 1' Eliminating fundamental downfalls [§125]
               - a" Actual fundamental downfalls
               - b" Their antidotes
             - 2' Eliminating [secondary] faulty actions [§126]
               - a" The beneficial qualities of the awakening mind
               - b" Purifying the awakening mind
               - c" Accumulating the two collections
           - b' Protecting if deteriorating

- c' Countermeasures
- b) Engaging in the awakening mind
  - i) Acquiring what has not been attained
    - a' The person who is the basis of the practice
      - 1' The student
      - 2' The preceptor
    - b' Purified vows
  - ii) Protecting undegenerated attainment
    - a' Fundamental downfalls
    - b' Infractions [**24b**]
  - iii) Countermeasures if deteriorating [§127]
- c) Ultimate awakening mind
  - i) Ritual [§128]
    - a' Preliminaries
    - b' Actual practices
    - c' Subsequent practices
  - ii) Training [§129–30]

2) Meditation objects
- a) Skillful means
  - i) Purifying love, compassion, and the awakening mind [§131]
    - a' The method of purifying
    - b' The causal characteristics of purifying
    - c' The beneficial qualities [§132]
    - d' The faults of your own purpose
    - e' Instruction in purifying [§133]
  - ii) Training in illusory appearances
    - a' Meditating on everything as unreal [§134]
    - b' The benefits of meditating
    - c' The faults of not meditating [§135]
    - d' Instruction on meditation [§136]
- b) Wisdom
  - i) Preliminaries
    - a' Following a spiritual teacher [§137]
      - 1' The characteristics of a spiritual teacher
      - 2' The fault of examining defects [§138]
      - 3' The benefits of contemplating the spiritual teacher's virtuous qualities
      - 4' The manner of following the spiritual teacher [§139]

b' Keeping to secluded places
1' Isolating the body and relinquishing activities [§140]
a" Eliminating attachment to external wealth
b" Eliminating attachment to the mind within
2' Mental isolation eliminating afflictions
ii) Actual practices [§141–44]
a' Cultivating serenity
1' Preliminaries
2' Actual practices
a" Meditative equipoise [§141]
b" Directly pointing out
1" Nonconceptual [§142]
2" Clarity
3" Bliss [§143]
4" One-pointedness
5" Firm ascertainment
3' Subsequent practices
a" Undegenerated
b" Unmistaken signs of progress
c" Eliminating obstructions
b' Cultivating insight [§145–57]
1' Pointing out the mind [§145]
a" All is mind
b" Settling that [all is mind]
1" Summary
2" Extensive explanation [§146]
(a) Purity
(b) Spontaneous presence
(c) Unconditioned [§147]
(d) Free from extremes [§148–49]
(e) Sameness [§150]
(f) Free from the wishful thinking of views
2' The practice of that
a" The stages of realization [§151]
1" Practicing the realization of emptiness
2" Practicing realizing conceptual thought as empty [§152]
b" Subsequent attainment [§153–56]
1" Training in bodily perception as empty

2" Being unpolluted by faults and defects
3" Destroying discordant factors
4" Cultivating skillful means
3' Indicating the benefits [§157]
c) Union [§158–60]
i) Pointing out
a' The union of the abiding ground
1' Abiding nature
a" The inherent nature that remains as emptiness
b" The essential nature that remains as clarity
c" The characteristic that remains as indivisible
2' Way of appearing [**25a**]
b' The union of the path indicated
1' Inherent nature
2' Essence
3' Characteristic
c' The union of the result to be achieved
1' Inherent nature
2' Essence
3' Characteristic
ii) Practice [§161]
a' Practicing the view [§161–65]
1' Practices of the beginner
2' Practices of a meditator
3' Actualizing practices
a" Practicing cause and effect and emptiness as inseparable
b" Practicing skillful means and wisdom as inseparable
c" Practicing appearance and emptiness as inseparable
b' Practice by meditation
1' Conduct [§166]
2' Actual practice
a" Meditative stabilization [§167–70]
1" Your own mind established as free from extremes
2" Appearances spontaneously established
3" Established without attachment or aversion
4" Established in sameness

5" Established indivisibly
b" Sustaining the meaning of that [§171–72]
1" Sustaining awareness in unclarity
2" Sustaining taking on concepts as allies
3" Sustaining all appearances and concepts as traceless
4" Sustaining awareness as carefree
5" Sustaining not being separated from realization [§173]
3' Conclusion
a" Undegenerated skillful means [§174]
1" Features of post-meditative experience
2" Restraining the sense faculties
3" Reliquishing activities [§175]
4" Purification and accumulation of merit [§176]
5" Relying on continuous mindfulness [§177]
b" Unmistaken signs of progress [§178]
3) Reversal of tendencies [§179]
4) Results [§180]
III. The thoroughly completed conclusion [§181]

Structural Analysis of Stages of the Path to Awakening is concluded.

3. General Meaning of the Stages of the Path

THIS CHAPTER comprise a general meaning (*spyi don; samudāyārthaḥ*) commentary on *Stages*. In Indian and Tibetan Buddhist exegesis, a general meaning commentary provides an overview of the subject matter. In addition to focusing on the general meaning, the colophon states that the commentary explains "the difficult points of the stages of the path to awakening" (*byang chub lam gyi rim pa'i dka' ba'i gnas*). The difficult points are actually explained in the later portion of the commentary (see below). The commentary cites a number of sūtras and tantras as proof to validate statements found in *Stages*. This work is by a Tibetan author and is the latest of the commentaries in the *Stages* manuscript. The author provides a lineage list (see introduction on page 27 above) that ends in the early to mid-thirteenth century.

Before the commentary proper, the *Stages* manuscript provides a brief description of its contents, which I have included in the translation. The commentary consists of three strands of exegesis that the author has woven together. The first part of the work focuses on how to study the holy Dharma (*dam pa'i chos; saddharma*). This consists of three main points: (1) a general presentation of the holy Dharma, (2) identifying the holy Dharma in its particularities, and (3) the manner in which to study and explain the holy Dharma.

In the latter section of the third part, the author suddenly shifts to an alternate style of commenting on *Stages* and outlines three different points of exegesis: (1) proclaiming the greatness of the work's author and (2) the greatness of the Dharma to be taught, and (3) indicating the meaning of the Dharma, which is endowed with greatness.

The first section provides an early biography of Atiśa and an early account of the lineage of teachings that he upheld. The second section discusses the magnitude of the holy Dharma, succinctly enumerating its distinct qualities. This section also mentions aspects of Buddhist lore untraceable in history and culture, such as how Buddhists in their use of writing are likened to the farmer's son named Lotus Crown. The third section, on indicating the meaning of the Dharma, provides further exegesis comprised of three main parts:

a preliminary introduction (*sngon du 'gro ba klad kyi don*), followed by "that which is wished for," the main body of the text (*mngon par 'dod pa gzhung gi don*; *abhiprārthayamāna*), and then the thoroughly completed conclusion (*yongs su rdzogs pa mjug gi don*). At the beginning of the third section of the commentary, the author discusses the Sanskrit title, the method and meaning of prostration, followed by the oath of composition. The commentary then very quickly lists a well-known hermeneutical framework comprised of four points (i.e., *anubandhacatuṣṭaya*). The author lists and describes *Stages'* (1) subject matter (*brjod bya*; *abhidheya*), (2) purpose (*dgos pa*; *prayojana*), (3) purpose of the purpose (*dgos pa'i dgos pa*; *prayojanaprayojana*), and (4) connection (*'brel ba*; *sambandha*).[174]

The author then quickly moves on to describing the main body of *Stages*. Here, the commentary cites sections of *Stages* containing points that are difficult to understand. The author comments on each of these sections with either a Buddhist framing story or a direct citation from scripture. The citations suggest the author's historical circumstances and lineage of study. The author cites the *Quintessential Instructions on All Dharma Practices Tantra* (*Sarvadharmacaryopadeśatantra*), a controversial work among post-twelfth-century Tibetan scholars that was known to have been popular at Vikramaśīla Monastery (Wangchuk 2016). The citation of this work implies that the author was a Kadam master in the lineage of Atiśa's scholasticism brought from Vikramaśīla, the famous monastic university in India where Atiśa resided and taught before coming to Tibet. The author also cites the *Guhyagarbhatantra* six times, a controversial tantra of the Mahāyoga class affiliated with the *Māyājālatantra* corpus.[175] The author's commentarial use of the tantra implies that he understood this work as an authentic and important scriptural source to validate teachings found in Atiśa's *Stages*. Even in the late eleventh century, this recognition of the *Guhyagarbhatantra* would have been controversial, due to its content and affliation with translations from the early dissemination period (*bstan pa snga dar*). The author's multiple citations of the *Guhyagarbhatantra*, without any polemical comments, may indicate that he composed the commentary before the tantra became more widely controversial in Tibet. Finally, the author cites, without attribution, a scriptural extract of the *Suvarṇaprabhāsasūtra* drawn from a ninth-century Tibetan commentary by the renowned translator Yeshé Dé. The citation in Yeshé Dé's commentary differs from the version of the *Suvarṇaprabhāsasūtra* in the Kangyur. In this manner, the author of *General Meaning of the Stages of the Path* used traditional Tibetan scholarship descended from the imperial period for his exegesis on Atiśa's *Stages*.

General Meaning of the Stages of the Path

The treatise has the following topical outline and various texts: four texts of special instructions; secret instructions; pointing-out instructions; hindrance elimination; rituals; and various texts.

Homage to the spiritual teacher!

This stages of the path to awakening has three main points:

I. A general presentation of the holy Dharma
II. Identifying the holy Dharma in its particularities
III. The way of explaining and listening to the holy Dharma

I. A general presentation of the holy Dharma

The first has two [topics]:

A. The Dharma of the subject matter
B. The Dharma of words, the means of expression

Moreover, the *Benefits of Reciting the Names* [*of Mañjuśrī*] says, "One will understand all the technical digests by way of meaning and letters."[176]

A. The Dharma of the subject matter

Among these, first: all objects of knowledge are objects within the two realities. The *Meeting of Father and Son* states, "All knowable things [**25b**] are included in the conventional and ultimate."[177]

B. The Dharma of words, the means of expression

The words that indicate or express this very meaning are the scriptures and treatises. In this regard, the *Question of the Devaputra Sūtra* states, "Dharmas are grouped within two categories: scriptures and treatises. These refer to what is well spoken along with the commentaries clarifying their intention."[178]

1. Scriptures

Scriptures have two topics:
a. The nature of scripture
b. Its divisions

a. The nature of scripture

First, whichever Dharma is produced by the empowering condition of the Buddha appears as the essence of the three collections and is virtuous in the beginning, middle, and end.

b. Its divisions

This has four topics:
1) The divisions of the dominant condition
2) The subject matter
3) The antidote for the disciple
4) The way of expression

1) The divisions of dominant condition

The first has three topics:
a) Scriptures that are actually taught orally
b) Scripture that is by the power of blessing
c) Scripture that is requested through permission

a) Scriptures that are actually taught orally

The first are disseminated orally, enunciated through white teeth.

b) Scripture that is by the power of blessing

The power of blessing is twofold: that not connected to the mental continuum and that connected to the mental continuum. The first is the preaching of Dharma that arises from space, mountains, rocks, or the sound of drums, as in the *Golden Light Sūtra*. Blessings that are connected have three types: blessing of the body, blessing of speech, and blessing of the awakened mind. The first is like explaining the *Ten Levels Sūtra* by placing the hand on the top of the head of Vajragarbha, or like emitting light rays upon Akṣayamati in the

Akṣayamatisūtra. The blessing through speech is, for instance, when Subhūti is told to speak with eloquence when commencing the perfection of wisdom in the chapter of Subhūti.[179] The blessing of the awakened mind is like in the *Heart of Wisdom Sūtra*, when the Blessed One fully enters the meditative concentration on the enumeration of dharmas called "illumination of the profound," and Śāriputra becomes empowered to request and Avalokiteśvara becomes empowered to explain.[180]

c) Scripture that is requested through permission

The scripture requested through permission blessing (*rjes su gnang ba'i bka'*) is, for instance, the request of Ānanda at the time of the Buddha's body attaining nirvāṇa. How is the scripture comprised? In six ways, according to whomever is to be disciplined. (1) First, by relying on the request of someone, an introduction (*nidāna*; *gleng gzhi*), which states "Thus have I heard at one time"; (2) next is the bestowal by word, (3) a connection with explanation, then at the end, (4) a teaching by the Bhagavan and a (5) praise (*abhyananda*; *mngon par stod*), followed by a (6) concluding imperative that comes of its own accord, such as, "You [**26a**] should rely on the elder Kāśyapa."

2) The subject matter

When classifying according to the subject matter, there are three successive Dharma wheels. The first body of scripture is principally taught for the training in superior morality and is called the "Dharma wheel on the four truths [of the noble ones]." The second one is principally taught for the training in superior meditative stabilization and is called the "Dharma wheel on the absence of characteristics." The final one is principally taught for the training in superior insight and is called "ascertaining the meaning."

3) The antidote for the disciple

When classified according to the antidote for the disciple, there are three precious scriptural collections as antidotes to the three poisonous afflictions. The main antidote for desire is the scriptural collection of the Vinaya. The main antidote for hatred is the scriptural collection of Sūtra. The main antidote for delusion is the scriptural collection of Abhidharma.

4) The way of expression

When classified according to the way of expression, there are twelve sets of discourses.[181] In all cases they are indicated as possessing four seals: all conditioned things are impermanent; all contaminated things are suffering; all things lack essence; all nirvāṇas are peaceful.[182]

2. Treatises

Treatises have four topics:
  a. The nature of treatises
  b. Etymology
  c. Divisions
  d. Purpose

a. The nature of treatises

First, the phenomena that are produced by dominant conditions for an individual below the tenth level appear as the nature of the three kinds of collections.

b. Etymology

The etymology is from the *Commentary on the Middle Beyond Extremes*: "It subdues all the enemy afflictions without exception and protects from existence in lower realms of rebirth. Because of the qualities of subduing and protecting, it is a *treatise* (*śāstra*). These two do not exist in other systems."[183]

c. Divisions

The divisions are three:
  1) A division empowered by the subject of the speech to be explained
  2) A division empowered by the actions to be performed
  3) A division according to its own content

1) A division empowered by the subject of the speech to be explained

This has both common and distinctive explanations. The common are treatises on grammar such as *vyākaraṇa*; four classes and so forth; the Seven Treatises on Valid Cognition and other works on reasoning; texts encompassing the main body of meaning of the excellent speech of the Buddha.

Explanations of distinct categories of speech are three: comments on the essential meaning of the Buddha's first teachings, second teachings, and final teachings. Among these, the first principally teaches the view of the ultimate according to the treasury of explanations of the Vaibhāṣikas and principally teaches the stages of conventional deeds, as in the Vinaya [collection], Sūtra [collection], and so forth. The primary teaching of the view of the ultimate of the second category is the six collections of [**26b**] Madhyamaka reasoning[184] and so forth; the principally indicated practices are those in *Ornament for Clear Realization* (*Abhisamayālaṃkāra*) and so forth. The comments on the essential meaning of the final teachings are principally the view of the ultimate as found in the upper Abhidharma and so forth; the principal practices to perform are found in *Bodhisattva Levels* (*Bodhisattvabhūmi*) and the works concerned with conduct (*spyod phyogs*).[185]

2) A division empowered by the actions to be performed

This division is threefold: treatises that delineate profound speech; treatises that compile the extensive; and treatises that organize the confused order of the text.

3) A division according to its own content

Regarding this division, it is said:

> Treatises may (1) be meaningless, (2) have backward meaning, or (3) be meaningful. Some treatises (4) are deceitful, some (5) lack compassion, and others (6) eliminate suffering. Some treatises are (7) devoted to worldly learning, some are (8) devoted to polemics, and others are (9) devoted to accomplishment. Among these treatises, we reject six and adhere to three.[186]

d. Purpose

Regarding the purpose: commentaries make comprehensible the meaning of scripture that is not understood and resolve doubts by unraveling the concealed intention and so forth of interpretable meaning (*neyārtha*) and definitive meaning (*nītārtha*); by putting the meaning into practice, an individual's mind is beautified with happiness.

II. Identifying the holy Dharma in its particularities

Identifying the particularities does not apply to scripture but does apply to treatises. Although there are many treatises, this [*Stages of the Path to Awakening*] is a treatise that is the essential endpoint of scripture. Furthermore, in teaching the stages of the path of the three types of individuals—that is, the small, middling, and supreme—when indicating bodhisattva activity, it is identified as concerned with conduct (*spyod phyogs*).

III. The way of explaining and listening to the holy Dharma

The way of explaining and listening has four topics:

A. An individual who is the basis of the practice
B. The actual way of explaining and listening
C. The result of explaining and listening
D. Indicating its purpose

A. An individual who is the basis of the practice

Individuals are two:

1. The accomplished master
2. The disciple

1. The accomplished master

First, Maitreya states, "Attend upon a spiritual friend who is tamed, peaceful, tranquil, greater in qualities, persevering, rich with transmission, skilled in speech through understanding reality, compassionate of nature, and has abandoned weariness."[187]

2. The disciple

Regarding the disciple, the *Quintessential Instructions on All Dharma Practices Tantra* (*Sarvadharmacaryopadeśatantra*)[188] states,

> Dedicated to the spiritual teacher, willing to part with what is to be let go, abandoning pride, faithful, [with] an unsatisfied mind, striving with purpose, and undergoing many hardships and suffering; an individual endowed with these seven qualities, I explain as one who is skillful in learning.

B. The actual way of explaining and listening

The way of explaining is by a teacher who eliminates incorrect exposition and correctly explains via the three doors of body, speech, and mind. A person with physical impurity is someone who has a sickness, such as leprosy and so forth, or even who has no sickness but incorrectly practices the path. A person with impure speech does not [27a] understand the meaning but teaches others nonetheless and so forth. *Differentiating the Sūtras* (*Mdo rab tu rnam 'byed*)[189] states,

> Śāriputra, as many sentient beings as there are in the three-thousandfold universe, some who have died, who have viewed the Dharma master as impure, when this view toward the master is demonstrated, this will produce a great amount of nonvirtue.
>
> Śāriputra, one with such a view of the person will have a great amount of downfalls. They will quickly understand all things with a nihilistic view. Those with impure thoughts, motivated by the three poisonous afflictions, for the sake of achieving their own purpose in this life of riches, honor, and fame abandon the Dharma teacher, while the Dharma teaching should be explained with correct body, speech, and mind, having turned away from previous faults with love, compassion, and the awakening mind for others.

The way a disciple properly listens is they abandon the three defects of a vessel and respectfully listen with three virtuous thoughts. The three defects to be abandoned are that like an upturned vessel, when your mind is not engaged with the Dharma; that like a vessel with a hole in it, when you are engaged but you do not seek the meaning; and that like a vessel with poison in it, when you seek the meaning but it is polluted by mental afflictions. The three virtuous thoughts are listening while thinking that you are sick, while thinking that the Dharma is like medicine, and while thinking that the teacher is like a doctor.

C. The result of explaining and listening

The result of explaining and listening, as stated in the *Bodhisattvapratimokṣa*: "Śāriputra, a renunciate bodhisattva, when teaching a four-lined verse, would generate greater merit than a householder bodhisattva who fills as many buddhafields as the sands of the Ganges River with the seven precious royal treasures."[190] The *Birth Stories of the Buddha* (*Jātaka*) state:

> Learning is the lamp that dispels the darkness of delusion, the supreme treasure that thieves or others cannot carry away, the weapon that conquers the enemy of all-obscuring ignorance, the supreme of friends who instructs with skillfulness and special instructions, a devoted spouse who will not leave if you are destitute. It is a mighty power that conquers the forces of evil. [**27b**] It is the supreme treasury of fame and glory; the perfect gift when one meets noble persons. It pleases the learned when among an assembly; it sweeps away the contempt and arrogance of rivals.[191]

Further, the *Inquiry of Nārāyaṇa* states,

> Son of good family, if you have learning, insight will occur. If you have insight, your mental afflictions will be pacified. If you have no mental afflictions, Māra will find no opportunity.
>
> If you have learning, realization will occur. If you have realization, you will have proper investigation. When you endeavor in investigation, Māra will find no opportunity.
>
> If you have learning, you will become free from wrong view. Correct view will arise, and when you engage it correctly, Māra will find no opportunity.[192]

The *Samādhi That Gathers All Merit Sūtra* also states,

> One cannot measure the amount of merit from giving, morality, and learning. One may be able to count each drop of water in a great ocean, yet the three merits of a bodhisattva cannot be enumerated. If asked what is the principal virtue among the three, that which is especially exalted as supreme is only learning. The measure of Mount Meru and of mustard seeds are made known by learning. An act of generosity that fills a three-thousandfold world system with gold does not compare to the benefit of reciting a single four-lined verse.[193]

The *Bodhisattva's Scriptural Collection* also states, "Learning increases with the desire to learn. Learning increases insight. Insight engages with the purpose. Once attaining purpose, they attain happiness. This attained purpose sharpens the mind. In this life, you reach nirvāṇa."[194] The *Collection of Purposeful Sayings* (*Udānavarga*) states,

Even if someone has intelligence,
if they do not hear the Dharma of vice and of virtue,
they cannot have wisdom.
Just as someone who has eyes,
if they bear also a lamp, can see all objects,
those who hear the Dharma of vice and of virtue
can become perfectly wise.

Those who listen understand the Dharma;
those who listen turn away from sin;
those who listen give up all harm;
those who listen attain nirvāṇa.[195]

D. Indicating its purpose

In this regard, indicating its purpose has three topics: a preliminary introduction (*sngon du 'gro ba klad kyi don*); that which is wished for, the main body of the text (*mngon par 'dod pa gzhung gi don*); and the thoroughly completed conclusion (*yongs su rdzogs pa mjug gi don*). [**28a**]

Alternately, this text may be understood through three points:

1. Proclaiming the greatness of the teacher, the author
2. Proclaiming the greatness of the Dharma to be taught
3. Presenting the meaning of the Dharma that is endowed with greatness

Furthermore, the ācārya Asaṅga has stated, "The purpose should be understood by commentators proclaiming the greatness of the teacher and the Dharma."

1. Proclaiming the greatness of the teacher, the author

In this regard, the author of this text is the venerable Lord [Atiśa]. His greatness has two topics:

a. The greatness of his lineage
b. The greatness of his good qualities

a. The greatness of his lineage

First, in Bengal in eastern India, in a city called Sahor Golden Banner, a king called Kalyanaśrī, the chief of 2,700,000 and a master of Secret Mantra Great Vehicle teachings, had three sons with the mother Śrīprabhā. The first was

Padmagarbha, the second was Candragarbha, and the youngest was Śrīgarbha. The Lord [Atiśa] was the middle one, Candragarbha.

b. The greatness of his good qualities

The greatness of his good qualities has five topics:

1) Mastery of the five fields of knowledge
2) A direct vision of his personal deity
3) Possession of supersensory knowledge
4) Possession of the special instructions of the lineages
5) Mastery of love, compassion, and the awakening mind

1) Mastery of the five fields of knowledge

First, he had knowledge of all eighteen types of crafts—weaving, painting, and other arts. He mastered the science of medicine, including healing elephants, all types of cloven-hoofed animals, and all single-hoofed animals, such as horses. With regard to human medicine, he had mastered the eight branches of medical treatment, which were translated into Tibetan. He also mastered the science of grammar, including many treatises of grammar—the *Indravyākaraṇa*, *Pāṇinivyākaraṇa*, *Ra tsa vyākaraṇa*, *Candravyākaraṇa* and so forth. He mastered many works of logic and epistemology, such as the *Pramāṇasamuccaya* of Dignāga and Dharmakīrti's Seven Treatises on Valid Cognition. With regard to inner science, he mastered the treasury of explanations of the Vaibhāṣika and so forth; the many collections of the Vinaya; the system of Śāntipa, which elucidated the Perfection of Wisdom as Mind Only (Cittamātra); and the system of Haribhadra, which elucidated the Perfection of Wisdom as Madhyamaka. He mastered many collections of the sūtras, the six collections of Madhyamaka reasoning, and the treatises of expansive deeds, such as the five divisions of the *Yogācārabhūmi*. He mastered many collections of the Abhidharma, such as the two compendium treatises [**28b**] and so forth.

Having mastered innumerable collections of tantras of secret mantra, the thought occurred to him, "I am the master of secret mantra in Jambudvīpa." Then, in a dream, when he was puffed up with pride with volumes in a temple, a goddess asked him, "Do you know the words in this tantra?" Then the thought occurred to him that a great number of secret mantra works are in the hands of ḍākiṇīs, and his pride was broken.[196]

2) A direct vision of his personal deity

He had a direct vision of his chosen deities. Early on, he saw Trisamayavyūharāja, then Venerable Tārā, Mañjuśrī, Maitreya, and so forth. He attained a complete blessing from Venerable Tārā, and she prophesized that "After this life, you will be reborn as the divine youth Stainless Space (Vimalākaśa) in Tuṣita heaven."[197]

3) Possession of supersensory knowledge

He was endowed with supersensory knowledge. In western India, Ḍombhipa requested Dharma from a certain paṇḍita. The paṇḍita said, "We have no connection. In eastern India there is one named Dipaṃkaraśrījñāna, and you should request Dharma from him." He went to see him in the east, and when he supplicated Lord [Atiśa], the Lord, due to his exalted knowledge, blessed Ḍombhipa with words.

4) Possession of the special instructions of the lineages

He was endowed with the special instructions of lineages: the lineage of view, including Nāgārjuna, Candrakīrti, Vidyākokila, Kusulu the elder, Kusulu the younger, and the Lord [Atiśa]. The lineage of extensive deeds from Maitreya: Asaṅga, Vasubandhu, Vimukisena, Bhadanta Vimuktisena, Paramasena, Viniyatasena, Vairocanabhadra, Haribhadra, Ratnabhadra, Ratnasena, Guṇamitra, Dharmakīrtiśrī, and the Lord [Atiśa]. The lineage of blessings from Tilopa: Nāropa, a yogin of the lowest caste, then Lord [Atiśa].

5) Mastery of love, compassion, and the awakening mind

He also trained in love and compassion. When a female dog was struck by others, Lord [Atiśa]'s eyes swelled with tears on witnessing the event. Atiśa was proclaimed the crown jewel of five hundred paṇḍitas of Vikramaśīla monastic university.[198]

From Atiśa, the teachings went to Gönpawa (1016–82), Gya Chakriwa (eleventh century), Dakpo Lhajé (Gampopa, 1079–1153), and then Phakmodrupa (1110–70). From him, the teachings went to both the Drigung and Taklung branches of the Kagyü and then to the Khamkom, the Khön, and myself.

2. Proclaiming the greatness of the Dharma to be taught

This has two topics:

a. The greatness of the holy Dharma in general
b. The greatness of this very Dharma in particular

a. The greatness of the holy Dharma in general

[29a] First, as the holy Dharma is endowed with the four seals[199] of the Buddha's teachings, it is distinct from the doctrines of non-Buddhists, and by indicating the threefold training[200] to be discussed, it serves as an antidote to the mental afflictions.

Since the holy Dharma is virtuous in the beginning, middle, and end, it gives rise to both temporary happiness and ultimate happiness. Furthermore, through writing, Buddhists are like the farmer's son Lotus Crown; through reciting, Buddhists are like the layperson Salu Sprout; through upholding, Buddhists are like the princess Utpala Ornament; through listening, Buddhists are like the son of the brahman Supreme Splendor; through explanation, Buddhists are like the monk Radiant Light; through meditation, Buddhists are like the sage King Beauty of Awareness; through worship, the Buddhists are like the monk Akṣobhya.

Moreover, when five hundred children who heard the Dharma once died with faith in the Buddha, they were reborn due to that in the Heaven of the Thirty-Three Gods. When a certain elephant that had heard the Dharma one time from the tathāgata Paramapuruṣa died, it was [also] reborn in the Heaven of the Thirty-Three Gods; as this shows, each time that you respect the Dharma, an auspicious result occurs.

b. The greatness of this very Dharma in particular

By indicating unmistakenly and purely the paths of the three types of individual—small, middling, and supreme—and each type of Dharma to be achieved, starting with taking refuge and guarding each and every shared vow, this teaching is complete in itself. As this Dharma also indicates all the meditation objects for each of the lesser and greater individuals, it is complete in itself. Finally, as all temporary and ultimate results, all happiness and well-being, arise from this Dharma, it is unmistaken and complete in itself.

3. Presenting the meaning of the Dharma that is endowed with greatness

This Dharma endowed with greatness is presented under three main headings:

a. A preliminary introduction, that which is wished for
b. The main body of the text
c. The thoroughly completed conclusion

a. A preliminary introduction, that which is wished for

Among them, the first has three topics:

1) Showing the title (*mtshan bstan pa*)
2) The prostration
3) The oath of composition (*bshad par dam bca' ba*)

1) Showing the title

First, *bodhi* means awakening, *patha* means path, and *krama* means stages.

The purpose [of the Sanskrit title] has four topics: indicating a pure source, establishing predispositions for the Sanskrit language, remembering the kindness of the translators, and promoting ease of understanding.[201]

The explanation [of the title]: *awakening*, in general, is of three types: the awakening of (1) śrāvakas and (2) pratyekabuddhas, who overcome the obscurations of mental afflictions. [**29b**] They attain the result of arhatship and the spiritual level of supreme wish-fulfilling happiness. (3) *Unsurpassed awakening* (*bla med kyi byang ba*) means complete purity (*byang ba*) from the obscurations, and *perfected* (*chub pa*) means accomplishing the salvation of others through expansive total pristine awareness. The *path* is the means by which you traverse or attain these results. *Stages* is like a stairway, from common refuge up to the level of a buddha.[202]

2) The prostration

Prostration has three topics:

a) The method of prostration
b) The purpose
c) The meaning of the words

a) The method of prostration

The first has two topics: prostration that seeks to receive realization and prostration that pays respect with the three doors.

i) Prostration that seeks to receive realization

First is the very realization of your own mind as free from extremes. The *Five Stages* states,

> Like putting water into water
> or like putting butter into butter,
> your own timeless awareness by yourself
> seen well by yourself—that is the homage here.[203]

ii) Prostration that pays respect with the three doors

Prostration that pays respect with the three doors [of body, speech, and mind] includes placing the five extremities of the body on the ground, the speech proclaiming words of praise, and the mind having devotion and humility with joy.

b) The purpose

The purpose [of prostration] has three points: to show faith in another by understanding the teacher as noble;[204] to complete the composition of a book through pacifying obstacles; and to complete the accumulations for the purpose of attaining buddhahood.

c) The meaning of the words

The meaning of the words (*tshig gi don*; *padārtha*) ["I pay homage to the supreme refuge, the spiritual master, and the Three Jewels"]: *Refuge* means protection from the suffering of saṃsāra and the Hīnayāna. *Supreme* is the spiritual master (*bla ma*). The *Piled Up Stūpas Tantra* states, "A body that comprises all the buddhas, the very nature of Vajradhara, the root of the Three Precious Jewels: I take refuge in the spiritual master."[205] The *Saṃvarārṇavatantra* states, "The spiritual teacher is the Buddha, the spiritual teacher is the Dharma, and the spiritual teacher is also the Saṅgha. The spiritual teacher is glorious Vajradhara."[206] The [*Sūtra*] *that Unifies the Intentions* [*of the Buddha*] states, "Understand that listening to the spiritual master is equal to the buddhahood of one hundred thousand eons. Why? The buddhas of an eon occur in reliance upon the spiritual master."[207] Thus the spiritual teacher (*guru*) constitutes the supreme refuge.

["Three Jewels" means] supreme rarity, [consisting of] the Buddha, Dharma, and Saṅgha. A buddha (*sangs rgyas*) has expanded (*rgyas pa*) pristine wisdom through purifying (*sangs*) all obstructions. In all of the worlds, even those of the gods, a buddha is as rare as an *udumbara* flower; a buddha is "supreme" since he is the supreme among humans. A buddha has three classifications: the Dharma body that is free from elaborations; [30a] the enjoyment body, as buddhas of the five families; and an emanation body—one supreme and one created through conscious rebirth.

The Dharma is unblemished, and it is that which protects from the sufferings of saṃsāra. It is as rare in all of the worlds, including those of the gods, as a flash of lightning. It is called "the supreme rare Dharma" since it is the supreme of that which is free from desire. The Dharma has three classifications: the ultimate Dharma free from elaborations; the Dharma of practice, the eightfold path of noble beings; and the Dharma that is the teachings, the twelve branches of excellent speech.

The Saṅgha leads others by liberating them through yearning for the unblemished Dharma. It is as rare in all of the worlds, including that of the gods, as a wish-fulfilling jewel, and it is the supreme among many collections. The Saṅgha has three classes: the Saṅgha of śrāvakas—the four pairs of persons, the eight kinds of superior beings; the Saṅgha of pratyekabuddhas, who are like a rhinoceros or a parrot; and the Saṅgha of bodhisattvas, from those of devoted conduct (*adhimukticaryā*) on the path of preparation up to those of pure motivation on the path of vision.

3) The oath of composition

The oath of composition has three topics:

a) Indicating the fourfold connected purpose
b) The necessity of teaching
c) Its application to the text

a) Indicating the fourfold connected purpose

The first has four topics:

i) The subject matter (*brjod bya*)
ii) The purpose (*dgos pa*)
iii) The purpose of the purpose (*dgos pa'i dgos pa*)
iv) The connection (*'brel ba*)

i) The subject matter

The subject matter is the complete, unmistaken paths for the three types of individuals.

ii) The purpose

The purpose is to practice, through understanding and realization, the paths of the three types of individuals.

iii) The purpose of the purpose

The final goal is to attain temporary and ultimate results through practice having understood [the paths].

iv) The connection

The connection is connecting one to another, by depending upon and through the text about these [paths].

b) The necessity of teaching

The necessity of teaching these four is so that individuals endowed with conceptual and analytical abilities will engage with this Dharma.

c) Its application to the text

The application to the text: the subject matter is called "stages of the path." The purpose is "for the sake of realization." The final goal is "awakening." The connection is "that to be explained" and depends on apprehending these.

b. The main body of the text

Now comes the sections presentating the text as a whole. The text states, "You should understand each of the three individuals to possess. . ." [in §3]. This means that the three complete paths have four qualities [**30b**] for each of the three types of individuals.

The text [in §8] states, "Do not relinquish refuge, even for the sake of life and reward." This is like the story of the Druna (*bru na*) king and the Kashmiri king. First, the Kashmiri king did not relinquish, he did not abandon going for refuge, when a haughty non-Buddhist said to him, "Kill!" Even when the non-Buddhist arrived at the king's eye, and having cut the skin from the crown of his head, he did not abandon going for refuge. Even when his body was scattered into five heaps, he dwelled like Vajrasattva in the east.[208] The king said, "May there be happiness," even with his slaughtered [body parts] all around [him]. The Kashmiri king did not reliquish, even when a non-Buddhist magical emanation gave him a hundred *srang* of gold to do so, saying, "You cannot bribe me to abandon going for refuge."

The "female servant of Śrāvastī" [in §9] refers to when an impoverished old servant-woman was requested by Ārya Katyāyana to make an offering. The impoverished old servant woman asked what she should offer, and he taught her that she should offer a bowl full of water to the Three Jewels, keeping the Buddha in mind and going for refuge. By doing so, she exhausted her evil karma and was reborn the same evening among the gods in heaven. Later, when that goddess along with a great retinue came to make offerings at the corpse of the old servant woman, people heard the sound of a symphony.

As to "like finding a treasure" [in §9]: The Bhagavan Hālāhala[lokeśvara] taught and then departed, showing how to escape. A certain man was to be punished by a king, but through taking up a treasure by remembering the previous teaching of Hālāhala[lokeśvara], he found refuge and was liberated from annihilation.

The text [in §9] states "joy": A certain laywoman was healing a man who had been tied to a tree trunk as punishment by a king. The king had forgotten [about the man], and the laywoman brought food to the man one evening, whereupon the king remembered his promise of a royal reward to whomever delivered the food. [The laywoman named] Joy arrived, after which the demonesses Alam, Lampa, and Blazing arrived, ready to feast, but instead they took refuge and went away without eating the man. A reward was bestowed [to Joy] by the king, who disbursed three pots of gold.[209]

The text [in §9] says, "eliminate bad conditions": The portents of death arose for the divine prince Stainless Jewel (Vimalamaṇiprabha), and he was to be reborn as a pig seven days after his passing. Recognizing that he would be reborn in the hells before continuing on for seven lifetimes as an animal, he sought refuge in Indra; then, by always seeking refuge **[31a]** in the Buddha, he was liberated from the lower realms of rebirth and reborn in a higher deity realm.[210]

The text [in §11] declares, "A few. . .": The *Moon Lamp Sūtra* (*Candrapradīpasūtra*)[211] states,

> If, for millions of eons as numerous as the sands of the Ganges River, one were to mentally offer parasols, seats, garlands of light, food, and drink, or if one were to pursue one training for one night at the time of destruction of this holy Dharma when the Tathāgata's teaching is ceasing, the merit of the latter would be more extraordinary.

The text [in §12] says, "as many imagined world systems as there are particles of dust" and so forth: The *Kindling the Power of Faith*[212] states,

> If one were to give as many hundred-flavor divine foods as there are grains of sand in the Ganges River to as many beings as there are atoms in all world realms, or if a layperson were for one night to give teachings to one who is not zealous in practice (*mi bsten pa*; *asevin*), the merit of the latter would be much greater.

Likewise, it is explained that the offering of a basic lamp by a layperson (*upāsaka*) exceeds the merit of offering lamps as large as Mount Meru [by one who is not zealous in practice]. Mentioning "abodes of bad rebirth" and so forth [in §13]: The *Flower Array Sūtra* (*Gaṇḍhavyūhasūtra*) states, "It is difficult to avoid the eight unfavorable conditions (*mi khom pa brgyad*). The complete freedoms are also difficult to meet. The arising of a buddha is rare as well."

The text [in §17] says "difficulty": The *Nanda's Ordination Sūtra* (*Nandaparivrajyāsūtra*)[213] states, "Say this great world were one large ocean, and upon that ocean a yoke with a single opening were driven by winds in various directions, and then say a blind, aged tortoise were to surface every one hundred years; it would be difficult for the outstretched neck of that turtle to enter the hole of that yoke, but harder still is finding a free, well-favored human birth."

The text [in §33] says, "For this reason . . . revealing the fundamental nature." The *Questions of Upāli Sūtra* (*Upālipariprcchāsūtra*) states, "What is the teaching of the Buddha? What is the holy Dharma? What is the Vinaya?" The Buddha said, "Upāli, when I give something that is a cause of higher rebirth and liberation, either directly or indirectly, to someone who is suitable or not suitable, that is the Buddha's teaching, that is the holy Dharma, that is the Vinaya. When I give something that is a cause for saṃsāra or lower realms of rebirth **[31b]** to someone who is suitable or unsuitable, that is not the Buddha's teaching, that is not the holy Dharma, this is not the Vinaya. Upāli, you should apprehend accordingly."

The text [in §77] says, "the creation of all good qualities." The *Teaching of the Great Magical Display*[214] states, "All sentient beings in the three thousand world systems should become renunciates for the sake of awakening.

For a complete eon with a mind undiscouraged, having given away spouses and sons, generate the resolution for awakening and train in following the Tathāgata; even a single step with a mind of renunciation is distinctively meritorious." Further, the sūtra states,

> Renunciation has been lauded, praised, and esteemed by all the tathāgatas; whosoever desires to worship all the buddhas should understand renunciation in the teaching of the Victorious One. Were you to give to the buddhas as many houses ornamented with precious jewels as there are grains of sand in the Ganges River or if you were to be a renunciate for one day with thoughts of impermanence, suffering, and selflessness, you would, as a bodhisattva who is a conscientious renunciate close to awakening, destroy the sphere of Māra and increase, not decrease, your virtuous qualities. A renunciate is praised by noble individuals for eliminating bad paths and conforming to the path. Indeed, he does not exhaust virtue, and he relinquishes grasping onto things. By being liberated from the household, his afflictions do not increase; liberated from the afflictions, he is no longer bound by Māra. A liberated mind happily engages in the practice of awakening. Engaging in the practices, awakening is not difficult to gain.

The *Mass of Jewels Sūtra*[215] states,

> If [on one hand] all the sentient beings in the world systems of three-thousand great thousand worlds were established in the Great Vehicle, and if all of them were endowed with the sovereignty of a universal monarch, and if then each universal monarch, one by one, were to set up lamp basins as vast as the great ocean, light wicks the size of Mount Meru, and offer the lamps at the shrine of the Tathāgata; or if, on the other hand, a bodhisattva who has renounced the household life were to make a lamp wick, place it in oil, light it, and offer the lamp at a [32a] shrine of the Tathāgata, the merit from the former lamp offering would not equal a hundredth part of putting that wick in a little bit of oil; it does not bear any comparison at all.
>
> Again, those universal monarchs might respectfully offer to the order of monks headed by the Buddha whatever is needed for their physical well-being; but if a bodhisattva who has renounced the household life makes his almsround and, thereafter, partakes of the

> almsfood after having offered others their share, [the merit of the latter action] would be far greater and more precious than that of the former.

The text [in §78] says, "Without discipline, you cannot eliminate evil states." The *Moon Lamp Sūtra* (*Candrapradīpasūtra*)[216] states,

> There have been no buddhas in the past, nor will there be any in the future or now in the present, who attain the highest, most supreme enlightenment while living inside their homes. Those who are addicted to their desires, who crave for children and wives, who are addicted to their revolting homes, will not attain unsurpassable, highest enlightenment.

Therefore a householder calls [a monk] "an arhat" and so forth. The *Prophecy of Mount Gośṛṅga* states, "Apart from those who have renounced the world, I do not hear, I do not see anyone who wears layman's clothes who attains the state of arhat or unsurpassable awakening."[217] The *Teaching of the Great Magical Display* also states, "The buddhas that have occurred in the past, those who now reside, and those who will occur in the future have not attained peaceful, unsurpassed awakening without abandoning the household with its many faults."[218]

The text [in §79] states, "grasp onto the Lower Vehicle discipline of a monk." The *Ordination Rite* (*lam karma sha taṃ*) says, "Even the king of the Śākyas, the lion of the Śākyas, that chief, went forth as a lord of renunciation."[219]

The *Lion's Roar of Queen Śrīmālā Sūtra* (*Śrīmālādevīsiṃhanādasūtra*) states,

> The two Dharmas called Pratimokṣa and Vinaya differ as words but have the same meaning. What is called Vinaya is a training for persons in the Great Vehicle. Why is that? Blessed One, it is because it is for the sake of tathāgatahood and for going forth to the religious life and monastic ordination. Blessed One, **[32b]** in this way, the terms called Vinaya, "the going forth to the religious life, and monk ordination" stand for the sum of the ethical moral rules of the Great Vehicle.[220]

The text [in §79] says, "Monastic moral disciple on the path of all vehicles." Those known as the "pratimoksa," the "shared vows," are common or general vows for all insider Buddhists (*nang pa sangs rgyas pa*) and are common together like water. Without dispute, they exist among śrāvakas, and they also exist among bodhisattvas. The *Medicine God Sūtra* states, "Those among bodhisattvas who have renounced the household life are called the supreme."[221] The *Abhidharma* states, "What is the moral discipline of the bodhisattva vows? It is condensed into the seven types of pratimokṣa."[222] The *Lion's Roar of Queen Śrīmālā Sūtra* states, "What is called Vinaya is a training for persons in the Great Vehicle."[223] It is also thus for the way of mantra. The *Vajra Pinnacle Tantra* (*Vajraśekharatantra*) states,

> Having faith in the Three Precious Jewels and not devoted to other gods, while inclined in this way, abandon killing, stealing, sexual relations, lying, and alcohol. From abiding in the household in this manner, a king following the way of mantra achieves. If you are a renunciate, you should reside in the three vows—that is, the vows of the pratimokṣa, the vows of bodhisattvas, and the vows of inner knowledge-holders (*vidyādhāra*).[224]

The *Complete Enlightenment of Vairocana Tantra* (*Vairocanābhisaṃbodhitantra*) states,

> Lord of Secrets, from that, a bodhisattva should turn away from killing living beings, taking what is not given, and sexual misconduct. He should turn away from lying, harsh speech, divisive speech, and frivolous talk. He should turn away from covetousness, harmfulness, and falsehood. These are called the trainings of a bodhisattva.

The *Vajraḍāka* also states, "Wise practitioners, for the sake of benefiting sentient beings, do not kill living beings. They do not take what is not given, they refrain from desire, and they do not tell lies. Alcohol, as it is the source of harm, is forsworn."[225] [33a] The *Hevajratantra* states, "First there should be public confession, then you should train in the ten points of conduct."[226]

As it is called *pratimokṣa* ("individual liberation") since it eliminates all sin and nonvirtue, all vehicles must eliminate such sin and nonvirtue. If you abandon the pratimokṣa, that will become a root downfall of the bodhisattva according to the *Ākāśagarbhasūtra*. In this way, as explained by all sūtras and tantras, you should have conviction in the speech of the Buddha and eliminate sin. The *Extensive Commentary on the Root Downfalls* (*Mūlāpattiṭīkā*) also states, "Abide with full engagement in the great yoga of the three vows. Householders and so forth should also abide in their own concordant vows."

The text [in §79] says "attaining the higher realms, liberation, and omniscience." The *Moon Lamp Sūtra* states,

> Supreme awakening will not be difficult to attain for those who shun desire as as they would a pit of fire, for those who abandon craving for children and wives and, frightened and terrified, leave their homes behind. Casting away a kingdom like a lump of phlegm, longing for solitude and living in the forests, eliminating the afflictions and defeating the *māras*, they will realize stainless, unconditioned awakening.[227]

The *Prophecy of Mount Gośṛṅga* also states, "Even all the past buddhas as numerous as the sands of the Ganges River abandoned the household life. Having gone forth, by this very path of practice, they found great awakening. I, as well, with this very path of practice, have gained the perfectly complete spiritual level, buddhahood."[228]

The text [in §107] states "merchants on an island of demonesses."[229] Five hundred merchants, having been shipwrecked, arrived on an island of demonesses. Not knowing they were demonesses, the merchants remained, married them, and had children with them. Avalokiteśvara taught the merchants in a dream,

> Since these women are demonesses, do not rely on them! Tomorrow morning, Balāhakāśvarājā ["the king of horses who has the power of the clouds"], having rolled about in the grains of golden sand [so as to integrate the earth element into his cloud-like nature], will come here and then go to Jambudvīpa. You should escape without looking back by holding onto his hair and be liberated!

Then the merchants said, "To escape, we must pass beyond without being attached to our sons." For those who did not look back, salvation was at hand; [**33b**] those who did not look were liberated.

[The text in §107 states], "sons of the sorceresses."[230] The men told their sons they were borne of flesh-eating cowherd demonesses. When they heard, "Your mother is a demoness," the sons lost faith in their mothers and disappeared. Then many flesh-eating demonesses gathered and cast away their jewelry in turn one by one. The cowherd demonesses revolted and descended on their sons. Some of [the demonesses] said, "That is not beneficial," but others whispered, "May they [the sons] be killed by this bull." Upon arising the next day, [one son] shot an arrow, struck the forehead of that bull, and the bull was felled. That night, removing the dead bull and bandaging the forehead of his mother, the son grew disgusted with his mother. Likewise having grown disgusted with saṃsāra, do not entrust your mind to it.

[When the text in §108 states], "reach the state of a stream enterer through the state of arhat," this refers to temporary and ultimate results. A stream enterer suppresses the mental afflictions and gives rise to his own path of vision (*darśanamārga*). The fruition [of this state] not only eliminates defilements, it also generates virtuous qualities. A once-returner hits the mental afflictions on the head [that is, he suppresses them] and enhances both previous realizations [of a stream enterer] and reaches the path of meditation (*bhāvanāmārga*). The fruition is the virtuous qualties of this state. A nonreturner, having enhanced both of the preceding realizations, suppresses the mental afflictions. The fruition is the virtuous qualities of this state. An arhat, having enhanced the previous realizations, eliminates the mental afflictions from the root. The result of that is mental concentration (*samādhi*), pristine awareness (*jñāna*), magical emanation, supersensory powers (*abhijñā*), and guiding disciples.

[The text in §109 states], "Above the paths of the small and middling individuals are the practices of the supreme individual, who practices the aspiring and engaging mind of awakening." The *Ten Wheels of Kṣitigarbha Sūtra*[231] states, "If sentient beings are not diligent in the qualities of both vehicles when they are instructed in the Great Vehicle, both [vehicles] will degenerate." Therefore you should build up from a foundation in the qualities of both the small- and middling-capacity individuals.

In this regard, since generating the mind of supreme awakening is what qualifies you to be in the Great Vehicle, it is classified in three ways: (1) classification according to boundary, (2) classification according to examples, and (3) classification according to the commitment procedure.

(1) *Ornament of the Mahāyāna Sūtras* states, "The generation of the altruistic thought is aspiration, pure higher resolve for the spiritual levels, and the desire to mature others. In this way, it eliminates obstructions."[232]

(2) The classification according to examples is from the *Ornament for Clear Realization*: "It is of twenty-two types: like earth, gold, moon, fire, treasure, jewel mine, sea, vajra, mountain, medicine, [34a] virtuous friend, wish-granting gem, sun, song, monarch, storehouse, highway, vehicle, a spring, love talk, river, and cloud."[233]

(3) The classification according to the commitment procedure is conventional or ultimate. The conventional [generation of the awakening mind] has two varieties: aspirational and engaging. In this regard, *Introduction to*

the Practice of Awakening states, "This awakening mind, in brief, is understood as twofold: the mind that aspires to awakening and the mind that proceeds toward awakening."[234] Furthermore, the aspiration is the commitment to attain the result of buddhahood and the desire to attain it for the sake of others. The engagement is the commitment, until buddhahood is attained, to creating its causes through any virtuous deeds whatsoever, such as the six perfections, for the sake of liberating sentient beings.

As for the ultimate [awakening mind], the *Hevajratantra* states, "The awakening mind is generated in both its ultimate and its conventional forms."[235] Not only this, [the text continues,] "As conventional, white as white jasmine; the ultimate in the form of bliss."[236] The ultimate in the very form of bliss is emptiness. The very same text states, "Bliss is in the form of selflessness, and that bliss is the great seal."[237] Furthermore, [the text states]: "The awakening mind is nirvāṇa in both conventional and ultimate forms."[238] Furthermore, [the text states]: "The nature of the realm of reality should be investigated with this very wisdom. That itself is the form of coemergence, the *yoginī* of auspicious great bliss."[239] You should commit to practicing emptiness.

[The text in §122 states], "the seven types of pratimokṣa vows," which are the basis of the bodhisattva vows. In investigating this, some say that "the desire to attain emptiness" and "one's own and others' welfare" are contradictory with the [pratimokṣa] vows. [Answer:] There is no contradiction; in benefiting others one must turn away from having a basis of harming others.

Some say, "There is no relation [between the two sets of vows]." [Answer:] There is a relation, for as the *Bodhisattva Levels* states, "What is the discipline of bodhisattva vows? It is comprised of the seven types of pratimokṣa vows."[240] Some say, "The [pratimokṣa] vows are necessary as a basis for generating [bodhisattva vows]. The [pratimokṣa] vows are not necessary as a basis of abiding." [Answer:] The [pratimokṣa] vows are not counted for a transformed state, yet their nature is necessary. Some say, "The [pratimokṣa] vows and bodhisattva vows are mutually inclusive, and there is a different cause [**34b**] of attaining emptiness." [Answer:] They are together.

The *Treasury of Abhidharma* states, "The vows of the pratimokṣa are lost through giving back the training, through death, by cutting off the roots of virtue, through the arrival of the end of the night, and by having become a hermaphrodite." [241] The Vinaya states, "When one confesses three times a day and three times a night, root downfalls that occur are declared void while those of bodhisattvas will not be void." Here it is accepted that the transformed nature of the vows has a basis of upwardly progressing good qualities (*yon tan yar ldan*).[242]

The root downfalls of the pratimokṣa do not void the bodhisattva vows, and if there is expiation, one will be free of faults; if one does not atone, there will be serious downfalls. This is known from the [story of the] bodhisattva ship captain (*sārthavāra, ded spon*) and the son of the brahman named Jyotis (*bram ze'i khye'u skar ma*) in the *Skillful Means of the Great Secret Sūtra*.[243]

[The text in §124 states], "The discipline of vows, the discipline of gathering virtuous qualities," indicates four points: (1) specification in number, (2) fixed sequence, (3) nature, and (4) characteristic.

(1) The fundamental vows eliminate what is to be eliminated and produce virtuous qualities through the practice of Dharma, and for this reason they benefit others.

(2) The sequence is that the initial vows, through eliminating what is to be eliminated, produce virtuous qualities; you then complete the causal factors of buddhahood in your own mental continuum, and then you benefit others.

(3) As for the nature, the initial intention to eliminate is enhanced by eleven virtues along with their seeds. The eleven virtues are faith, shame, embarrassment, nonattachment, nonhatred, nondelusion, effort, pliancy, conscientiousness, equanimity, and nonviolence. The nature of virtue creation (*dge ba chos sdud*) is the mind of application of virtuous qualities, along with their seeds, enhanced by the six perfections. The nature of acting to benefit sentient beings is the mind of application of virtuous qualities, along with their seeds, enhanced by the four immeasurables.

(4) The characteristic of the discipline of vows: in reliance upon correctly taking the vows, one who is characterized by eliminating transgressions is enhanced by types of karmic action that are compatible or incompatible [with the vows]. The characteristic of virtue creation: in reliance upon correctly taking the vows, all virtue of body, speech, and mind is performed nonconceptually within the three spheres [of agent, action, and object] and is embraced with an altruistic mind of emptiness and compassion. The characteristic of acting to benefit sentient beings [35a] is the happiness and benefit to yourself and others that was previously achieved in reliance upon having correctly taken the vows.

[The text in §124 states, "The vows are] promised through the ritual, and you should guard them, keeping them uncorrupted." You perform from the beginning a seven-limbed prayer according to the system of Nāgārjuna. Both the salutation and offerings are according to Asaṅga. You gather whatever you can afford according to Lord [Atiśa]. The procedure is similar to other [such rituals].

The ritual explained in the *Bodhisattvapratimokṣa* is either received from an ācārya or taken independently. First, those who have received precepts, holds the vows, and are assiduously devoted to meditation qualified by the bodhisattva trainings abide in having the vows. These are the general qualities of those who hold the vows: they recognize their transgressions of the training, they fear doubting the spiritual teacher's training instructions, and they are effortlessly respectful and happy.

As for taking [the vows] independently: aspiring to whichever training is suitable among the trainings from the very same [text of the *Bodhisattvapratimokṣa*], when there is no spiritual friend (*kalyaṇamitra*) present, visualize all the buddhas and bodhisattvas of the ten directions directly in front of you and declare, "I will uphold all the relevant vows."

Protecting uncorrupted [vows and pledges] has three topics: (1) what are protected, (2) the means of keeping them uncorrupted, and (3) repairing them again when corrupted.

(1) The first has two topics: (a) the system of Nāgārjuna and (b) the system of Asaṅga. The system of Nāgārjuna asserts three types: (i) defeating offenses (*pham pa*), (ii) serious violations (*sbom po*), and (iii) minor infractions (*nyes byas*).

(i) The first four [defeating offenses] explained below appear in the *Vairocanābhisaṃbodhitantra*; the remainder, the eighteen root downfalls, appear in the *Ākāśagarbhasūtra* and, lastly, the *Skillful Means of the Great Secret Sūtra* (*Sarvabuddhamahārahasyopāyakauśalya*). (ii) Serious violations means that the complementary branches are not all present. (iii) The minor infractions are forty-six. Asaṅga accepts four minor infractions that are like the defeating offenses, minor infractions that are related to other downfalls, and independent minor infractions.

(2) The means of keeping these uncorrupted are mindfulness, attentiveness, and conscientiousness. In this regard, *mindfulness* is not forgetting a familiar object[244] and all root downfalls and minor infractions, including all rules, codes, and conventions, are kept clearly in mind. With regard to *attentiveness*, the *Moon Lamp Sūtra* (*Candrapradīpasūtra*) states, "You make effort to counteract addictions, which lead to poverty, and to fears, which lead to being scorned. It is like [**35b**] how an aide endures hardship to please a wrathful king by taking time with a vessel filled with medical ointment while going across a slippery platform."[245] Regarding *conscientiousness*, the *Secret Tathāgata Sūtra* (*Tathāgataguhyasūtra*) states, "Who is conscientious? One who guards the sense faculties (*dbang po sdom pa*; *indriyasaṃvara*). One who does not grasp onto features when seeing forms with the eyes, who does not grasp on to secondary features with the mind."[246]

(3) To repair them again once corrupted, the *Ten Wheels of Kṣitigarbha Sūtra* states,

> There are two who do not degenerate in my teaching. One who is pure by nature and does not commit transgressions from the beginning, and one who commits transgressions but confesses each one with embarrassment and shame.[247] These two holy individuals have a very pure aspiration for my Dharma.[248]

The *Teaching on the Four Qualities Sūtra* states, "Maitreya, if a bodhisattva mahāsattva possesses four qualities, all evils that have been committed and accumulated will be overcome. What are the four? They are (1) the power of support, (2) the power of total remorse, (3) the power of renouncing transgressions, and (4) the power of thoroughly applying the remedy."[249]

Enumerating the root downfalls that are engaged in has two topics: refuting other mistaken systems and establishing our own unmistaken system. First, [other mistaken systems] assert twelve major transgressions and four transgressions that are like major transgressions. Among these, first, there are the four core pratimokṣa vows, and the first four are divided into eight.

To refute this: the four core vows of the pratimokṣa are not bodhisattva vows. If you are in accord with elimination [of the downfalls], the vows will become faultless. If you are not in accord with elimination, your vows will become faults. The *Skillful Means of the Great Secret Sūtra* states, "Even if a monastic bodhisattva destroys all four core vows, if he pays attention to counteracting this with skillful means, the bodhisattva is said not to have a downfall."[250] Also from the same text, "The son of the brahman named Jyotis, who maintained celibate conduct for forty-two thousand years, curtailed rebirth in saṃsāra for ten thousand eons by letting go of the celibate conduct for the sake of others."[251] Likewise, in the story of the bodhisattva ship captain given above, you would be woefully mistaken if you understood that he completed the accumulations of sixty eons by not killing.[252] [36a]

Also, it is mistaken to have the first among the four divided into eight. *Twenty Verses on the Bodhisattva Vow* (*Bodhisattvasaṃvaraviṃśaka*) states, "The faults of these are four." Also, Śāntarakṣita states, "There are four dharmas that function like sites of defeat,"[253] and so it is harmful to ask, "Are there really just four?" Even a little equivocation about these as four causes harm according to scripture.

[Opponent: Yes, but] the *Ākāśagarbhasūtra* states,

> Son of good family, a king has five fundamental downfalls of a crown-anointed royal lineage of consecration by which a crown-anointed royal king totally destroys all his previously planted roots of virtue; he is defeated, and having fallen from all happy abodes

> of gods and men, he will then transmigrate to lower realms of rebirth.[254]

Thus, because [this sūtra] teaches [five downfalls] for rulers and so forth, it is harmful [to assert only four vows].

[Answer:] Well, then, what about in this instance? Naktso inquired, "How many constitute the essence of the vows?" To this, [Atiśa] clearly explained: The basis of *Vairocanābhisaṃbodhitantra* and fourteen [vows] are taken from the *Ākāśagarbhasūtra*; the fifth one of the latter [i.e., *Ākāśagarbhasūtra*] is synonymous with the first [vow] of the *Vairocanābhisaṃbodhitantra*; not including the fifth [vow in the *Ākāśagarbhasūtra*] makes thirteen [vows]. You add [to that] the foresaking of the awakening mind, the first of the three from the *Skillful Means of the Great Secret Sūtra*, to make fourteen [vows]. [The fourteen are added to the four found in Asaṅga's *Bodhisattva Levels.*] With those vows, there are definitely eighteen.

Asaṅga and Candragomin accept [the core vows] as four. Infractions should be understood as threefold: afflicted, unafflicted, and changeable due to elimination. The others are easy to understand.

[The text in §128 states], "With a desire to produce the ultimate mind of supreme awakening"; this is explained in both sūtras and tantras. The *Seal for Ridding and Restoring* states,

> Not grasping aggregates, elements, and sense spheres, relinquish grasped objects and the grasping subject. In the equal essencelessness of all things, unproduced from the very beginning, generate the awakening mind as the nature of emptiness, saying, "I, who am named ___________, from now until I reach the essence of awakening, will generate the aspiration for awakening."[255]

The *Completely Pure Discipline Sūtra* states, "You should understand that all things are unproduced and unceasing."[256] Accordingly, this is also indicated for generating the awakening mind and so forth.

[The ultimate mind for supreme awakening] is also taught in tantras. The *Hevajratantra* states, "You generate the awakening mind in both its ultimate and its conventional forms."[257] **[36b]** Moreover, the *Guhyasamājatantra* states, "Due to the sameness of the essencelessness of things, your own mind—free of all entities, without aggregates, elements, sense spheres, and subject and object—[is] unproduced from the beginning, the very nature of emptiness."[258] The *Guhyagarbha*[*tantra*] also states, "This generation of the primordially awakened mind as gnosis is taught,"[259] and, "The ultimate and conventional mind is generated as gnosis."[260]

[The text in §158 states,] "There is nothing at all that is not indivisible from your own mind." The *Essence of the Perfection of Wisdom* (the *Heart Sūtra*) states, "Form is empty. Emptiness is form. Emptiness is not other than form. Form is not other than emptiness."[261] This is extensively explained in the completely pure Mother [Perfection of Wisdom scriptures] and so forth. The sacred *Golden Light Sūtra* (*Suvarṇaprabhāsasūtra*) also states, "It is not conceptual. It is not nonconceptual. That is the middle way." The *Verses That Summarize the Perfection of Wisdom* state, "This existence and nonexistence is a nondual Dharma"[262] *Teaching on the Inconceivable Properties of the Buddhas*[263] states, "A practitioner of yoga who seeks out an emptiness that is distinct from desire, hatred, and delusion is not a practitioner of yoga. Why is that? Because emptiness is not to be found divorced from desire, hatred, and delusion, as desire, hatred, and delusion are in fact emptiness."

Well then, what is [emptiness] connected with? It is separate from [desire, hatred, and delusion]; it is not both [desire and the emptiness of desire together]. The Mother [Perfection of Wisdom] states, "It is not endowed with desire; it is also not separate [from desire]."

[The text in §180 states, "buddhahood] endowed with the three bodies and five wisdoms." The *Guhyagarbha[tantra]* states, "The Dharma body is immeasurable, inexpressible. The enjoyment body is an inexhaustible precious treasure. The emanation body is inconceivable, tens of millions [of emanations]." As *Reciting the Names of Mañjuśrī* states, "A buddha in his nature of five bodies, an overlord by his nature of five types of wisdom."[264] A buddha has five bodies: the Dharma body, enjoyment body, vajra body, truly awakened body (*abhisaṃbodhikāya*), and emanation body.[265] The five types of wisdom [**37a**] are mirror-like wisdom, realm-of-reality wisdom, wisdom of sameness, conventional wisdom,[266] and accomplishing wisdom.

[The text in §180 states], "with various awakening activities." The *Guhyagarbha[tantra]* states,[267] "To discipline all migrators without exception, a variety of bodies appear in accord with their needs." Furthermore,

> Entirely endowed with inconceivable bodies, entirely endowed with inconceivable minds, entirely endowed with inconceivable speech, countless inconceivable forms are manifested in the ten directions.
>
> All [these emanations] act in the following manner: they edify by the power of their instruction in the vehicle of gods and humans,

> in the vehicle of śrāvakas, in the vehicle of pratyekabuddhas, and in the vehicle of bodhisattvas, the unsurpassed vehicle. They have taught, are teaching, and will teach the eighty-four thousand doctrines as antidotes for the eighty-four thousand afflictions, which are conceptual thoughts comprised of ignorance.
>
> Also, all these [vehicles] address, respectively, the dichotomy of subject and object, the inner dependent arising, the productive nature of karma and its results, and the conclusion revealing that which is uncovered, will not be covered, and cannot be covered by deeds or the results of deeds.
>
> The supreme great seal (*phyag rgya che mchog*) of the buddha body, without straying from the real expanse (*de bzhin dbyings*), emerges as the buddha body of form, which confers genuine liberation; and in order to train living beings without exception, it reveals as appropriate the diverse buddha bodies. [12]
>
> This teacher is a magical display or optical illusion, a modality that essentially does not stray from the expanse. But when multiplied without straying, he manifests in dissimilar, diverse [buddha bodies], corresponding to the different [needs of diverse beings]. Although he is uncontrived by the real, he appears distinctly through the residue of deeds, as, for example, [images in] a mirror or the moon [reflected] in water. [13]
>
> At this moment, he is appearing to all six classes of living beings in forms that inspire them to renounce negativity: to the pious attendants in the form of an arhat, [15] and to solitary victorious ones in the solitary way of a rhinoceros. [16] Moreover, this is according to the sequence of the supreme vehicle.[268]

Furthermore, "Buddhas do not pass into final nirvāṇa; their doctrine also does not decline. In order to instruct the ignorant through acts that mature them, [buddhas] emerge and then demonstrate the passing into nirvāṇa."[269] Futhermore, "The sages demonstrate birth, renunciation, austerity, buddhahood, the subjugation of Māra, the turning of the wheel of Dharma, **[37b]** the demonstration of great miracles, the passing into nirvāṇa, and so forth."[270] The *Inconceivable Secrets Sūtra*[271] states,

> Then the fabricated body, fabricated speech, and fabricated mind do not appear, and they accomplish all the deeds of a buddha. Furthermore, [a buddha] acts effortlessly and without obstacles, without volitional impulses. Why is that? Oh, Śāntamati, complete

> buddhahood is the clear realization of all dharmas as the natural feature of emanation through a tathāgata. After complete, perfect buddhahood is clearly realized, [a buddha] also teaches out of his compassion for all sentient beings. Oh Śāntamati, this is true for the hidden mind of a tathāgata. He is inconceivable, because without leaving his abode of meditative stabilization, he leads all sentient beings to knowledge (*rnam par rig pa*).

The *Limitless Doorways Sūtra*[272] states, "A tathāgata does not have nonknowledge or even slight nonvision, as a tathāgata abides in the limitless vision of self-arisen gnosis (*svayaṃbhūjñāna*; *rang 'byung gi ye shes*); since he is free from any darkness of errors, he is without obscurations."

Are a buddha's three bodies permanent or impermanent? The *Descent into Laṅkā Sūtra* states,

> A tathāgata is neither permanent nor impermanent. If he is permanent, he will be connected with a creator. Mahāmati, a creator, for non-Buddhist thinkers, is uncreated and permanent, and thus something uncreated is permanent, but the tathāgata is not permanent. If he is impermanent, he will be connected with created, impermanent things. As long as there is conceptualization via words (*tshig gi rnam par rtog pa; vāgvikalpa*), there will be the faults of permanency and impermanency. Destruction of the conceptualizing mind overturns the view of things as permanent or impermanent.[273]

The *Golden Light Sūtra* also states,

> Son of good family, since the three bodies have the aspect of permanency, they are called "permanent." As they have the aspect of impermanency, they are also called "impermanent." The emanation body is permanent because he continuously turns the wheel of Dharma, understood precisely in all abodes, with skillful means. **[38a]** As the excellent great deeds do not manifest where there is no basis, he is called "impermanent."
>
> The enjoyment body is uninterrupted because he has the [eighteen] excellent qualities of all buddhas, and since sentient beings are inexhaustible, his deeds are inexhaustible. In this way he is permanent. As the excellent great deeds do not manifest where there is no basis, he is called "impermanent."

The Dharma body is not a conditioned thing and is free of diverse phenomenal marks; since that is its basis and foundation, it is permanent.

Son of good family, there is no gnosis of an ārya apart from non-conceptual gnosis. Therefore, since the Dharma body has pure wisdom and a pure sphere of activity, it is called excellence in purity. The state of great concentration (*mahāsamādhi*) and even total great gnosis will directly appear based on the Dharma body. In this way, the two bodies, based on concentration and wisdom, will directly appear.

Since he relies on the state of great concentration, he is called "blissful." Since he relies on great gnosis, he is called "completely purified." Therefore the Tathāgata dwells permanently, has self-control, enjoys happiness and contentment, and is completely purified.

Furthermore, "Endowed with concentration and wisdom, the Dharma body like this transcends all phenomenal marks, is not attached to phenomenal marks, is nonconceptual, and is neither permanent nor impermanent; that is the middle way."[274] The *Ornament of Mahāyāna Sūtras* states, "The Dharma body is permanent by nature since it does not change. The enjoyment body is undegenerated permanency since the great enjoyment of Dharma is uninterrupted. The enjoyment body is a permanence of continuity since it appears again and again."[275]

Some sūtras state that you should have faith in the explanation of the Dharma body as permanent, some in the explanation as impermanent, some in the explanation as existent, some in the explanation as nonexistent, and some in the explanation as neither [existent nor nonexistent]. Not relying on merely the words, you should realize the practical purpose (*dgos pa'i don*) and apprehend [these teachings] accordingly. The *Sūtra Illuminating Appearance of All Things Distinctly without Their Departing from Their Essential Nature, Emptiness,* states,

Through the blessings of [the Blessed One's previous] aspirations and compassion, audiences perceive hearing teachings perfectly suited to their individual thoughts and inclinations. [**38b**] They think, "The Blessed One is teaching the Dharma to me and not to others."

Furthermore, among the multitude in the surrounding audience, some think the Dharma taught indicates that all things exist

> just as they appear, and they imagine and grasp with respect to that.
>
> Some think the Dharma taught indicates that all things do not exist except as mind only, and they imagine and grasp with respect to that.
>
> Some think the Dharma taught indicates that even the mind itself is unproduced, and they imagine and grasp with respect to that.
>
> Some think the Dharma taught indicates that all things are established like an illusion, and they imagine and grasp with respect to that.
>
> Some think the Dharma taught indicates that all things are naturally unproduced, intrinsically unabiding, free from all extremes of karmic activities, transcending conceptual thought and the domain of conceptual thought, completely pure of elaborations from beginningless time, and they imagine and grasp with respect to that.[276]

These are inconceivable teachings. In this way, since his body, speech, and mind are inconceivable, the Buddha's performance of deeds that fulfill the immeasurable aims of migrating beings leads to an excellent result.

This explanation of just a few of all the difficult points of the stages of the path to awakening is now complete.

Supplementary Material: Two Sūtra Citations

The *Sāgaramatisūtra* states,

> There are four actions close to the heinous actions entailing immediate retribution: with a nonvirtuous mind, killing a pratyekabuddha; engaging in impure conduct with an arhat nun; stealing donations of precious things previously offered; and causing discord with bad views.[277]

The *Inquiry of Pūrṇa* states,

> Pūrṇa, the Tathāgata is without interruption since he is always endowed with the power of miraculous emanation like this. The śrāvakas see the explanation of the Dharma as residing with only this Tathāgata. In reality, I teach the Dharma in all worldly realms of the ten directions and perform buddha deeds without interruption

in as many world realms in the ten directions as there are sands of the Ganges River.[278]

[39a] This [teaching] is the practice domain of the Kadam textual tradition.[279] The conventional is the essence that appears. Achievement is the essence of practice. Practice is the essence of training. Application is the essence of the vows. This set of four essences is the essence of the Three Baskets. It is the practice domain when establishing the Abhidharma and expanding upon it with the *Introduction to the Practice of Awakening* (*Bodhicaryāvatāra*). Having established engaging in practice based on the *Introduction to the Practice of Awakening*, when one expands upon the Abhidharma, it is the essential cycle (*snying po bskor*).

4. Instructions for Select Disciples

IN TEACHING and transmitting the stages of the path system, the Kadampas made a distinction between public discourses (*tshogs chos*) regarding the path and personal instructions on meditation given from spiritual master to disciple (*lkog chos*). The following work, attributed to oral teachings given by Atiśa himself, is a teaching directly articulating meditations and practices of the three types of individuals in the stages of the path system. The colophon gives an alternative title to the work as *Practical Guidance on the Special Instructions of the Stages of the Path to Awakening* (*Byang chub lam gyi rim pa'i gdams ngag dmar khrid*). The term I have translated as "practical guidance" is literally in Tibetan a "red instruction" (*dmar khrid*). The Tibetan name for this type of teaching is a metaphor for how the spiritual teacher guides a disciple through a teaching as a physician might excise a cadaver and directly point out various internal organs. In other words, the teacher directly instructs by laying bare the essential reality of the subject matter. The colophon also states, "This is the special instruction of the practice domain of the Kadam textual tradition" (*bka' gdams pa'i gzhung pa'i spyod phyogs kyi gdams ngag*). This statement might provide insight into the antiquity of the work in that "the entrusted holders of the lineage" (*bka' babs kyi brgyud 'dzin*) of Kadam teachings are considered by tradition to be the "three Kadam brothers"—Potowa Rinchen Sal, Chengawa Tsultrim Bar, and Phuchungwa Shönu Gyaltsen (Jinpa 2008, 8), all eleventh-century disciples of Dromtönpa. Potowa was considered the entrusted holder of the textual tradition (*gzhung*).

Instructions for Select Disciples contains internal evidence for Atiśa's authorship of the teaching. Atiśa resided and taught in both India and Tibet, and the treatise mentions cultural examples comparing India and Tibet in two different sections of the work. Early in the commentary's discussion of death, the author mentions burial grounds in India and the lack of burial grounds in Tibet. In a later section on meditating on appearances as illusion, the author describes how illusions are a suitable example for meditation, since illusions exist in India while dreams serve as a better example in Tibet. These examples illustrate the author thinking about both Indian and Tibetan culture in his teaching. Along these lines, the commentary mentions the superhuman figure Nārāyaṇa, regarded as the creative energy of the Hindu deity Viṣṇu, as an example of a powerful being who is unable to turn back death. The use of this example would more than likely come from an Indian author. The instructions also advocate using the hundred-syllable mantra of Vajrasattva for purification (folio 47a), a practice found in the *Sarvatathāgatatattvasaṃgraha* (Chandra 1981) and *Kriyāsaṃgraha* (Skorupski 2002, 142). Atiśa composed a text on the hundred-syllable mantra of Vajrasattva, as found in his collected works.[280]

Instructions for Select Disciples supplements Atiśa's *Stages* with points of guidance related to the meditations and realizations of the three types of individual—those of small, middling, and supreme capacities—found in the stages of the path system. The documented oral teaching outlines four qualities for each of the three types of individuals, comprising their specific practices (*lag len*), meditation objects (*bsgom rgyu*), reversals of tendencies (*blo ldog*), and results (*'bras bu*).

Instructions for Select Disciples discusses pointing-out instructions (*ngo sprod*) in its latter sections for the individual of supreme capacity. As a type of advanced meditation guidance, "pointing-out instruction" generally signifies an introduction to the nature of mind by a spiritual teacher to a qualified disciple (see chapter 5). In its layered overview of the *Stages*, the *Structural Analysis* summary in chapter 2 indicates where pointing-out instructions may be found in Atiśa's *Stages* and how these sections correspond with the pointing-out instructions in *Instructions for Select Disciples*. In correlation with teachings found in *Stages*, *Instructions for Select Disciples* furnishes pointing-out instructions for the actual practice of serenity, pointing out the mind (*sems ngo sprad pa*) in the practice of insight, and pointing out the cultivation of union (*zung 'jug bsgom pa*). As indicated in its outline structure, *Instructions for Select Disciples* contains pointing-out instructions for each of these types of advanced practices.

In Atiśa's stages of the path system, serenity is characterized by nonconceptuality, clarity, and blissful experience. As with later pointing-out instructions of mahāmudrā found in the works of scholars such as Gampopa, *bliss* (*bde*) does not connote a tantric meaning but is the blissful experience that flows from the practice of serenity (Sherpa 2004, 175; Brunnhölzl 2014, 193). *Instructions for Select Disciples* illustrates Atiśa's teachings to his advanced students on serenity and insight with a focus on pointing out the nature of one's own mind, a nature equivalent to the realm of reality (*dharmadhātu*). These instructions significantly differ from the analytical insight using reasoning found in *Lamp for the Path to Awakening*. As Roger Jackson (2019, 71) notes when citing corresponding passages from *Stages*, "although the term *mahā-*

mudrā is not specifically applied to this practice, it is very much in line with earlier Indian . . . contexts in which the term is used." Along these lines, Mathes (2006, 23–24) has discussed how pointing-out instructions for insight in not-specifically-tantric meditation manuals among Kagyüpa scholars differ from practices of insight advocated in traditional works of meditation in Indian Madhyamaka. Traditional works, as described by Mathes, "require an analytical or intellectual assessment of emptiness . . . mainly based on Madhyamaka reasonings," while insight in mahāmudrā pointing-out instruction is "an investigation performed by the inward-looking mental consciousness on the basis of direct cognition." Atiśa's *Instructions for Select Disciples* instructs the practitioner to "look directly" (*cer lta*) to gain an experiential vision of emptiness in line with an approach through direct cognition by an inward-looking mental awareness.

Instructions for Select Disciples provides an extended discussion in its corresponding instructions for directly pointing out union (*yuganaddha*). The text presents instructions for union in terms of the union of the ground, union of the path, and union of the result. The triadic division of the tantric way into ground (*gzhi*), path (*lam*), and result (*'bras bu*) is considered by Tibetan traditions to derive from the *Guhyasamājatantra* (Broido 1984, 5, and Broido 1985) and is often used in advanced exegesis of Mahāyāna and Vajrayāna works. According to Atiśa, based on these passages, the union of the *ground* is the ever-present nonconceptual nature of emptiness, equated with the unobstructed radiance of one's own awareness. The union of the *path* is embodied by the emptiness that pervades all, like sesame oil pervades a sesame seed. The union of the result is the pure realm of reality, which is ever-present from the very beginning, like a cloudless sky with a luminous essence.

A fourth component, the yoga of signlessness, is only discussed in *Pointing-Out Instructions* (chapter 5) and briefly mentioned in Atiśa's *Stages*. Rather than focusing on signlessness, *Instructions for Select Disciples* has an extended discussion of the practice of union in terms of the indivisibility of causality and emptiness (*rgyu 'bras dang stong pa dbyer med*), the indivisibility of skillful means and wisdom (*thabs dang shes rab dbyer med*), and the indivisibility of appearances and emptiness (*snang ba dang stong pa dbyer med*). According to the content structure in the *Structural Analysis* (in chapter 2), these topics correlate to *Stages* in sections §162–63 on causality and emptiness, section §164 on skillful means and wisdom, and §165 on appearances and emptiness.

In addition to pointing-out meditation instructions, *Instructions for Select Disciples* contains many meditation instructions found in later Kagyü manuals, such as *sustaining* (*bskyang ba*) the meaning of the instruction and *eliminating pitfalls* (*gol sgrib*) to various stages of the practices. The text also uses many analogies and metaphors found in the later Kagyü tradition, such as the analogy of water and waves[281] and the analogy of the brahman's thread.[282] *Instructions for Select Disciples* also contains novel features not found in other Indo-Tibetan meditation manuals. The first is the analogy of the skillful cowherd (*mkhas pa ba glang skyong ba*) in using mindfulness to maintain insight. *Ba glang skyong ba* (*gopālaka*; Skorupski 1996, 222; Shukla 2008, 400) is a term referring to a low Indian caste that tends cattle. I have only located this analogy in *Stages of the Path, Instructions for Select Disciples*, and *Pointing-Out Instructions*, all works attributed to Atiśa. *Stages* [§170] instructs the reader to sustain one's mind "free from elaborations," to "hold with mindfulness, like a skillful cowherd, be free by resting naturally without projecting, without concentrating."[283] Finally, *Pointing-Out Instructions* instructs the practitioner to have a bodily posture for meditation that is described in terms of the "five-point posture of Amitābha" (*snang mtha' yi chos lnga ldan*) rather than the more common "seven points of Vairocana" (*rnam snang chos bdun*) (Callahan 2019, 180–82).

In sum, *Instructions for Select Disciples* significantly contributes to understanding the advanced forms of meditation taught in Atiśa's stages of the path system. The work also provides insight into the historical development and practices of Indo-Tibetan Buddhist forms of meditation related to mahāmudrā.

Supplementary Material: Citations of Sūtras

In the *Stages* manuscript, *Instructions for Select Disciples* is followed by two citations from the *Upālipariprcchāsūtra*, a listing of the seven jewels of a cakravartin king, and a citation from the *Sāgaramatisūtra*. The citations from the *Upālipariprcchāsūtra* consist of verses requested by Upāli, traditionally listed as one of the top ten disciples of Śākyamuni and the upholder of the monastic code. The first citation of verses establishes the Buddha's teaching on nonconceptuality. The second citation is a brief statement to recognize the Buddha's teaching.

Instructions for Select Disciples

[Atiśa]

[39a2] Here are *Instructions for Select Disciples* (*Lkog chos*).

Homage to the holy spiritual teachers!

These special instructions on the stages of the path to awakening should be understood to have three general topics, which consist of the sets of teachings on:

I. The small-capacity individual
II. The teachings on the middling individual
III. The teachings on the supreme individual

I. The small-capacity individual

In this regard, first, the so-called small individual is one who is inclined to not have interest in this life and who is interested in future lifetimes. There are four qualities with respect to this individual:

A. Practices
B. Meditation objects
C. A reversal of tendencies
D. Results

A. Practices

The first has three topics:

1. General taking of refuge
2. Temporary vows (*bsnyen gnas, upavāsa*)
3. The vows up to and including pure, chaste conduct

Once suitable vows have been taken, they should be uncorruptedly protected.

B. Meditation objects

Meditation objects has three topics:

1. Freedoms and favorable conditions
2. Impermanence
3. Karma and its results

1. Freedoms and favorable conditions

Among these, the first has two topics:

a. Contemplating the difficulty of finding freedoms and favorable conditions

b. Contemplating not wasting what has been gained

a. Contemplating the difficulty of finding freedoms and favorable conditions

First, the difficulty of finding the opposite from the eight unfavorable conditions[284] and being endowed with the ten freedoms has four topics:

1) Difficulties by means of number

2) Difficulty by means of cause

3) Difficulty by means of example

4) Difficulty according to scripture

1) Difficulties by means of number

Among these, first, there are an inconceivable number of sentient beings among the six lines of transmigration. Among animals alone, for instance, there are said to be 36 billion different species. When we contemplate these [numbers, we see that freedoms and favorable conditions are] rarely met.

2) Difficulty by means of cause

The difficulty by means of cause is that among these numbers of sentient beings, a few virtuous wholesome actions have a rare result.

3) Difficulty by means of example

This is explaining the difficulty through a meditative illustration. The *Nanda's Ordination Sūtra* (*Nandaparivrajyāsūtra*) says,

> If this great world were one large ocean, and upon that ocean there was a yoke possessing a single opening and driven in various directions by winds, and a blind, old tortoise [**39b**] were to surface every one hundred years, it would be difficult for the outstretched neck of that tortoise to enter the hole of that yoke; but greater than that is the difficulty of finding a free, well-favored human birth.[285]

4) Difficulty according to scripture

The explanation from scripture is stated in the *Flower Array Sūtra* (*Gaṇḍhavyūhasūtra*): "It is difficult to meet with reversal from the eight unfavorable conditions (*mi khom pa brgyad*). The complete freedoms are also difficult to meet with. The occurrence of a buddha is difficult to meet with," and so forth. This is mentioned many times. *Introduction to the Practice of Awakening* (*Bodhicaryāvatāra*) states, "This well-favored freedom and wealth is extremely difficult to find."[286]

b. Contemplating not wasting what has been gained

Not wasting the opportunity: this rarely gained opportunity is like a precious jewel, since it is the foundation of achievement when achieving happiness, liberation, and omniscience; it is devasting to waste such an opportunity. Moreover, it is like a ship for crossing over. *Introduction to the Practice of Awakening* says,

> Relying upon the boat of human rebirth,
> cross over the great river of suffering.
> As this boat is difficult to find later,
> O fool, there is no time for sleep.[287]

Thus this precious, free, and well-favored human birth should not be wasted, since within the span of one's life, when friends, wealth, and the eight worldly concerns distract one's body and mind, many activities become mixed with evil deeds; when one dies, the opportunity is wasted. Therefore, since there is nothing other than great foolishness or misfortune [when wasting this opportunity], when one contemplates this well-favored opportunity, one contemplates making effort in meaningful, virtuous actions and strives as much as possible for virtuous action. As much as one can, one eliminates evil deeds, karma, and mental afflictions.

2. Impermanence

The meditation on impermanence has two topics:

a. External impermanence
b. Internal impermanence

a. External impermanence

External [impermanence] is the impermanence of the creation and destruction of the worldly environment (*bhājanaloka*) and so forth, the changing of the four times,[288] the blossoming and dying of grass, trees, leaves, and so forth.

b. Internal impermanence

Internal impermanence is the impermanence of the sentient inhabitants [of the world]. In this regard, there are three reasons:

1) The definiteness of death
2) Death strikes without warning.
3) Death is not averted in any case.

1) The definiteness of death

First, there is no one who does not die; death is definite. Further, there are three reasons for the inexhorability of death:

a) Due to birth as a sentient being
b) Due to being conditioned
c) Since life draws to an end

a) Due to birth as a sentient being

First, one neither hears about nor encounters someone who says, "This person did not die." All people die. [40a] Furthermore, in India, when one goes to burial grounds, one first sees some who have died who are like oneself; now in this manner there are dead people. One meditatively cultivates the thought, "I am no different from the deceased." In Tibet, although there are no burial grounds, one can see and hear about those who are old, young, or close to one's own age who have died, and upon reflection, [one may] meditatively cultivate the thought, "I am like this as well."

b) Due to being conditioned

Since [the body] is conditioned, death is definite. One meditatively cultivates [the thought] that this body of temporary causes and conditions is like an illusory, unreal conventionality that definitely dies. Since life draws to its end, there is death and there is no extension or way of cheating. The days, months, and years are illustrated by the example of white and black mice in Tsaphung;

since time does not sit still as life draws to its end, one meditatively cultivates the thought that death is definite.

c) Since life draws to an end

Death is definite. In the earlier part of life, one conqueres enemies, protects friends, and accumulates wealth; later one wonders what Dharma to practice. In this way, the activities to be done at the time of death become immeasurable. Furthermore, there are three reasons:

i) There are many opposing conditions.
ii) Lifespan is uncertain.
iii) Since the body is without essence, death strikes without warning.

i) There are many opposing conditions.

Among these, first, external opposing conditions such as enemies, demons, fire, water, poison, pitfalls, and even not meeting with food are causal conditions of death. As for internal opposing conditions, this body dies through the causal conditions of the 404 sicknesses of wind, bile, phlegm, and so forth.

ii) Lifespan is uncertain.

Since the span of life is uncertain, death strikes without warning. Although it is certain in the three continents [other than our own], it is uncertain here at this place. From a lifespan of immeasurable years until a lifespan of ten years, there is increase and diminishment. Nowadays, one is worn out at sixty years of age, and it is not even certain that one can reach that [age]. Some die of old age, some die in their youth. Since death is in one's destiny, it is unnecessary to use scripture and reasoning for this; it is clear when it is directly perceived. It is not known when death will come—from a certain year, a certain month, or a certain day.

iii) Since the body is without essence, death strikes without warning.

The body has no essence, like a plantain tree. There is no essence at all of a solid, hard tree. It is like a water bubble, which is unable to endure even the slightest [contact]. [40b] Since death occurs without effort, even under the slightest of conditions, think that the time of death is unpredictable, relinquish this life, and strive for the sake of the future.

3) Death is not averted in any case.

Contemplating that one is unable to avert death in any case has three topics:

a) You are unable to avert death.
b) Protector deities and so forth are unable to avert death.
c) Other influential beings are not able to avert death.

a) You are unable to avert death.

In this regard, it is like the evening shadows or like a butter lamp exhausting its oil at the inevitable time of death. Therefore, [even if] you are courageous and powerful like Nārāyaṇa, a powerful athlete, a tiger, a lion, and so forth, you cannot avert death. The poisonous tongue of the learned, who are fearful, do not have a place of refuge [from death]. You cannot turn back [death] with power; the clever are unable to hide from death; the wealthy cannot avoid [death] with their wealth. Therefore you should contemplate that even you are unable to avert death.

b) Protector deities and so forth are unable to avert death.

Protector deities and so forth are unable to avert death. Even relying on virile tutelary deities, war gods, violent demons (*yakṣa*), and so forth, you cannot avert death. Whatever special mantras [you recite], of Amitāyus and so forth, and whatever special substances [you use], such as the precious wish-fulfilling jewel or the six precious substances, these are unable to avert death.

c) Other influential beings are not able to avert death.

Other influential beings—even political leaders, who have many friends and attendants or who lead an army—are unable to turn back death. No one is able to turn back death. Being surrounded by dear and near relatives does not help to avert death. Rulers of the land cannot subdue [death]. Therefore, since you are unable to turn back death, you should contemplate relinquishing achievement in this life and relinquish apprehending things as permanent; you should achieve your future aim.

Although you achieve comfort and happiness in this life, you must cast those aside; such pursuits are like renovating in order to revive something that is no longer there. Even the suffering of this lifetime does not subsist for a long time. Therefore cast aside both happiness and misery, which are joined with virtuous and negative actions; discard the notions of this life, and continually meditate until the signs of progress on the path arrive. Merely uttering the words is like explaining something for an aunt's amusement; the meaning does not penetrate the mental continuum. Therefore know that all happiness and misery arise through conditions, and meditate on impermanence.

If you possess signs of progress on the path in your mental continuum, it is not necessary to meditate. [**41a**] If you do not possess signs of progress, since great pride is not beneficial, you should contemplate impermanence.

3. Karma and its results

Contemplating the causes and consequences of karmic actions is as follows: due to impermanence there is death; accordingly, when you contemplate that all will die, in addition to death not being beneficial, there is also rebirth. When you are reborn in a lower realm of rebirth, there is no method to endure suffering. Thus you should eliminate nonvirtue, the cause of rebirth there, and engage in virtue, the cause of rebirth in higher realms. You should contemplate karma and its effects.

Even though you may think karma and its effects are not at all real, karma and its effects are nondeceptive as mere conventionalities. The *Close Placements of Mindfulness Sūtra* (*Smṛtyupasthānasūtra*) states,

> Actions never disappear,
> even after hundreds of millions of eons.
> Having reached completeness [of the right conditions] and the
>   [right] time,
> [they] certainly yield fruit for embodied beings.[289]

The *Sūtra on the Householder Śrīgupta* also says,

> Previously performed virtue and nonvirtue can never be lost. Relying on the wise can never be lost. The elegant teachings of the assembly of the venerable can never be lost. Repaying kind actions can never be lost. [Those which are] well done are virtuous actions. Acting badly is nonvirtue. Furthermore, they mature into a result. Without any doubt, results come to fruition.[290]

Actions that one has done do not perish; one does not experience a karmic result of an action one has not done; actions done by oneself ripen upon oneself. One should contemplate karma and its results. Karma and its results has two topics:

a. The causes and effects of evil deeds
b. The causes and effects of wholesome deeds

a. The causes and effects of evil deeds

The first has two topics:
1) Causes
2) Effects

1) Causes

The causes are all sinful actions one has committed, such as the ten nonvirtuous actions and so forth, which are motivated by the mental afflictions and by those [factors] contradictory with vows that prompt the misdeeds of broken vows.

2) Effects

The effects of these are the dominant results that are causally concordant with their maturation. The maturation effects of those are the three lower realms of rebirth. Various results occur, as there are greater or lesser natures of sinful actions depending on their motivations, [their] objects being wholesome or unwholesome and so forth.

In this way, hell is experienced due to excessive sinful deeds. In general, there are eighteen hell realms.[291] To indicate a few of them here, there are hot hells and cold hells. The hot hells have a ground of burning iron below, nets of blazing iron above, and four gates; they are surrounded by mountains of burning iron. [**41b**] All eight hot hells have these features.

Among these, first, there is the suffering of Reviving Hell: the guardians of that hell do not actually exist, but due to the agitation of one's own mind, a killer nearby [appears to] kill one there; when a cool wind arises from space, one is reanimated; [a voice] says, "May one be revived," and by doing as before, suffering occurs [again]. As there are guardians in the Black Line Hell below that, one has a black threaded line drawn on one's body and then is smashed into pieces. In the Hell of Crushing Pain, one is crushed by mountains, struck with hammers, trampled by elephants, and so forth. In the small Wailing Hell, one is scorched in a blazing place and burned in an iron building without doors. In the Great Wailing Hell, one is burned in two iron buildings. In the Hot Hell, after being burned in a pit of blazing fire, one is pulled out, beaten, pierced with tridents, and boiled in an iron kettle. In the Exceedingly Hot Hell, after being burned in a pit, one is pulled out, beaten, fried on an iron pan after being cut into small pieces, hoisted upon pointed stakes, and boiled in a five-hundred-yojana iron kettle. In the Relentless Agony Hell, one is pinned down with five stakes on the blazing ground and struck with stakes from one hundred tongues; one's skin is taken off, and one is run over by chariots, scooped out with a winnowing vessel, placed upon a mountain of blazing fire, and the trembling retinue is eaten by many birds and so forth.

There are eight cold hells that have suffering concordant with their name: the Arbuda hell ("the hell of chilblains"), the Nirarbuda hell ("the hell of enlarged chilblains"), the Atata hell, the Hahava hell, the Huhuva hell, the Utpala hell ("the hell of the blue lotus"), the Padma hell ("the hell of the crimson lotus"), and the Mahāpadma hell ("the hell of the great crimson lotus"). As the neighboring hells and occasional hells are clearly explained in texts, only a little will be indicated here.

There is no means for withstanding the suffering when one is reborn in these hells. Nowadays, one suffers even due to a tiny spark or the prick of a needle. Therefore one should now keep in mind not to commit sinful actions. A Dharma practitioner who is at all cavalier about committing sinful action is at fault for not being conscientious. To be conscientious, one should take care to avoid even small misdeeds. Therefore contemplate again and again, since this contemplation is vital.

When committing a moderate amount of nonvirtuous evil deeds, [**42a**] one is born as a hungry ghost. Those [hungry ghosts] whose obstruction is external do not find any food or drink whatsoever. Even if they do find [food and drink], they are powerless to protect themselves against individuals brandishing cudgels. Some do not appear to those who view them. Some, who see [food as] pus and blood, do not desire to eat. Those [hungry ghosts] whose obstruction is internal have hunger and thirst due to having a great appetite and small necks; while they eat and drink with parched throats, the hunger and thirst cause their bodies to burst apart. As the intrinsic essence of food is an obstruction [for them], all food and drink becomes blazing fire. They suffer from eating their own flesh as they are pained by hunger and having only snot and mucus [to eat].

When committing a small amount of evil deeds, one is born as an animal. Those who live in the ocean [suffer as follows]: when in the ocean, crocodiles of the continent, large fish, and so forth eat the sentient beings, the small living beings who have poured into the water. When the small ones eat the scales on the large ones, the pain is overwhelming, and they cry and shake, experiencing the suffering of swimming in bloody ocean water.

Moreover, animals that live among humans, such as deer and so forth, suffer from fear and panic. Fish and so forth die due to drought, bugs and ants are eaten by flocks of birds, and so forth. Some suffer due to the immeasurable sufferings of being subjugated and bound into servitude. Due to meditating on the sufferings of the three lower realms of rebirth, one should have a sense of revulsion and refrain from evil deeds.

At present, even the slightest pain, a little harm from another, cold, hunger, and so forth are unbearable, to say nothing of the sufferings of the lower realms of rebirth. Therefore contemplate these sufferings of the lower realms of rebirth; contemplate again and again to refrain from committing evil deeds.

As the concordant and dominant causes for liberation from the lower realms of rebirth are clear in the authoritative scriptures, one should don the armor that intends to eliminate the subtle evil deeds that are the causes of these, and one should eliminate them.

b. The causes and effects of wholesome deeds

The cause and effect of wholesome deeds are such that as you protect the ten naturally virtuous actions and the pure vows that you have taken, you will attain the supreme body of a human or god. The ultimate goal is that by attaining liberation and omniscience, you will set out to benefit others. Therefore, [**42b**] with the desire to achieve happiness, you should make effort in virtuous actions. With a desire to abandon suffering, you should eliminate nonvirtuous actions and mental afflictions. As this is attested in authoritative scriptures, you should strive with energetic diligence to achieve virtuous deeds and eliminate evil deeds. Those who pridefully brag that they make no effort to achieve virtuous deeds and eliminate evil deeds deviate from the path. In this way, you should make effort to achieve [virtue] and eliminate [misdeeds].

C. Reversal of tendencies

In this way, give rise to the three aspects of the reversal of tendencies, signs produced in the mental continuum through meditation: (1) abandoning the eight worldly perceptions of this life, (2) abandoning laziness and future plans, and (3) abandoning subtle evil deeds and becoming enthusiastic for virtue.

D. Results

Accordingly, meditation gives rise to three results: the result of *separation*, which eliminates rebirth in the three lower realms; the result of *maturation*, which brings the leisure and fortune of higher rebirth as a king among gods and humans and so forth; and the *causally concordant* result, in which one eliminates nonvirtue and makes effort in virtue due to conviction in the law of karmic cause and effect.

II. Middling individual

The middling person is one who is not inclined to seek the welfare of cyclic existence and who searches instead for the welfare of liberation. There are four qualities with respect to this individual:

A. Practices
B. Meditation objects
C. Reversal of tendencies
D. Results

A. Practices

There are three practices:

1. The complete lay practitioner's vows (*upāsaka*)
2. The marks of a novice monastic (*śrāmaṇera*)
3. The vows of a monk (*bhikṣu*)

These are to be protected by upholding as many vows as one can.

B. Meditation objects

There are three meditation objects:

1. The faults of cyclic existence
2. The causes of these cyclic existences
3. The path that liberates from cyclic existence

1. The faults of cyclic existence

Among these, the first has two topics:

a. General faults
b. Specific faults

a. General faults

General faults are three:

1) Suffering due to total delusion
2) Unpredictable suffering
3) Suffering due to being unsatisfied

1) Suffering due to total delusion

Among these, first, generally all sentient beings of the six realms of transmigration—due to not knowing the object, the two realities; due to not knowing objects of knowledge; and due to apprehending entities as real and permanent—perform various nonvirtuous actions of the three doors [of body, speech, and mind] in order to fulfill their own desires. Although they desire happiness, they are bewildered by the persistence of suffering.

Specifically, various kinds of animals scattered about have the misfortune of being food for other animals. Humans, due to various nonvirtuous actions performed under the sway of mental afflictions for the sake of fulfillment in this life, [**43a**] having amassed a great maturation of sinful deeds, are deluded with the death of individual selfhood, and great suffering ensues.

2) Unpredictable suffering

As for unpredictable suffering, one experiences various pains and pleasures among the six realms of rebirth. Even experiencing the happinesss of a king among gods and humans and so forth is impermanent, and one falls into the three lower realms of rebirth. The opposite also occurs, and [lower-realm beings] fall into the higher realms. For humans as well, based on the smallest conditions, an enemy becomes a friend or a friend becomes an enemy. The powerful and wealthy become poor and the opposite of that: the poor become wealthy. In brief, you should keep in mind that since all happiness is impermanent, it should be renounced as nothing other than suffering.

3) Suffering due to being unsatisfied

As for suffering due to being unsatisfied: habitual attachment to the five sense desires is as dissatisfactory as salt water. Due to that, you perform a great amount of sinful karmic deeds for the sake of achieving the objects of the five senses, bringing the result of great suffering; Therefore desire should be eliminated. If it is not eliminated, you will later be disturbed by attachment to a single form, like a deer disturbed by sound, a honeybee disturbed by scent, or an elephant disturbed by touch.

As humans enjoy all five senses together, [the five sense desires] are dissatisfactory. As one may transmigrate to lower realms of rebirth [in the next lifetime] due to enjoying sense desires in this lifetime, [the enjoyment of sense desires] is a fault of cyclic existence. You should be totally endowed with the good conduct of a monastic person who has eliminated desire, like an arhat.

Although you feel pleasure from the great pride of understanding much Dharma and practicing Dharma, being attached to your spouse, children, and wealth will lead to many sinful deeds. Even if you create virtuous qualities, you will still generally migrate to the lower realms of rebirth without leisure.

b. Specific faults

The specific faults are the direct experiences of suffering of the six realms of rebirth. You should again contemplate the teachings in the section on the small-capacity individual regarding the sufferings of the lower realms of rebirth. From the perspective of the higher realms of rebirth, there are even many sufferings when you are born as a human.

When condensed, there are eight [types of suffering]. The first of these is the suffering of birth: there is physical craving from the time that one has not yet found a body. Once a body is found, your mother's womb is black darkness, you are heated like a cooked husk, and so forth. When newborn, you are pulled out as if by a wooden nose-string and drawn out by the head with closed eyes; being placed on a seat is like being put down on a bed of thorns; [**43b**] the suffering of birth is fierce. After this, even masters who are paṇḍitas and so forth have to train in learning the alphabet; this too is a fault of cyclic existence.

The sufferings of aging are immeasurable: your skin tone degenerates, your body's physical strength is lost, all shape and color of the body changes, merit is depleted, your accumulated wealth is useless, the sense faculties degenerate, others are disgusted when they see you, even your son and grandson are ashamed before others, no one listens to your words, your past deeds are remembered; since others show disrespect, you feel aversion when thinking about yourself. As you are powerless, you remain silent from despair; this again is a fault of cyclic existence.

The suffering of sickness is as follows. As your body is pervaded with intense sharp pains, your mind is oppressed by great suffering. As your mind does not engage with any objects, the sense faculties are withdrawn. The daytime is not completed, nor is the nighttime completed. You are not happy with even a nicely made bed; even food that is well prepared and offered stinks. Smoothly spoken speech is unpleasant. The body's appearance changes. Food and wealth become actual demons. You lift your darkened hands to the doctor to indicate the suffering of the fears of death; this again is a fault of cyclic existence.

The sufferings of death are as follows: at the end, laid low by serious illness, you are surrounded by relatives. The doctor, medicine, and food are cast aside. Some say at this time they have done nothing wrong and conceal their wealth.

Some speak as if nothing has changed and persist in their desires. Some cling to their own wealth. Some cannot bear to be seperated from husband, wives, relatives, and so forth. Some continually stare down death [with their eyes open]. Activities of enjoyment and so forth do not satisfy. Your body is discarded. You ruminate on and are frightened by what is on the other side [of death]. Your speech degenerates and your body smells. The appearance of this life ceases. The Lord of Death takes hold [of you]. The Lord of the Dead manifests before you. You have no place where you can escape. You exclaim, "Oh, friend!" and your breath is cut off. What shall become of a body like this? This again is a fault of cyclic existence.

When you seek for what you lack, [44a] you do not find it. A person from the southern region gives to one of Jang Tsakha a whip for an actual horse.[292] A servant, with the blood and marrow of their hands, even exhausting the flesh of their body, prepares food and clothes while wearing worn-out tattered clothing, and boasts [that their appearance] is pleasing to living beings.

With the suffering of maintaining what one has, [whatever one may possess is] carried away by friends, robbed by others, cultivated for the sake of enemies, thieves, and so forth. Whether taken by a corrupt or a clean hand, since [whatever one may possess] does not endure, it is suffering.

When encountering hostile enemies, one experiences fear. Much killing can take place over something of little value. The violence of theft and so forth is suffering. When you are separated from friends and loved ones, you forget their faults; by remembering their virtuous qualities, attachment arises. Being distressed through one's own neediness, sorrow, lamentation (*śokaparideva*), and so forth is suffering. Even gods and demigods, who transmigrate, have moral failings, quarrel, reconcile, and so forth and thus have suffering. One should understand all these as faults of cyclic existence, contemplate repeatedly, and become digusted (*yid 'byung bar bya*).

2. The causes of these cyclic existences

The cause of birth in cyclic existence is, first, not cognizing that one's own mind is separated from the extremes; this is called "ignorance that is deluded with regard to suchness." Then, through "ignorance of the imaginary" (*kun tu brtag pa'i ma rig pa*), grasping at a self is produced. Through "arising," improper mental activity (*tshul bzhin ma yin pa'i yid la byed pa*; *ayoniśomanaskāraḥ*) occurs, from which ensues inclinations toward desire. Because of this, hatred arises. In this way, the three poisonous mental afflictions cause the ten nonvirtuous karmic actions to be enacted everywhere, producing all the sufferings of cyclic existence.

Therefore, since the root cause of cyclic existence is ignorance, it should be eliminated with the three wisdoms of learning, reflection, and meditation. As learning eliminates coarse ignorance, reflection eliminates moderate ignorance, and meditation eliminates subtle aspects of ignorance, one should train in learning, reflection, and meditation in the presence of a learned preceptor.

3. The path that liberates from cyclic existence

Cultivating the path that liberates from cyclic existence is as follows. Generally, the three wisdoms of learning, reflection, and meditation that eliminate ignorance, the cause of birth in cyclic existence, are the path. All the virtuous actions [**44b**] performed that eliminate evil deeds and mental afflictions are the path. Specifically, cultivating the four applications of mindfulness is the path. With respect to this, there are the mindful establishments of body, mind, sensations, and phenomena.

First, since the body is unpleasant, attachment to it should be overcome by meditating that it is an impure thing, full of filth, and a skeleton, which is impermanent. One should meditate that the external body will become a decomposed corpse in the cremation grounds. By meditating that the nature of the internal body as well "does not pass beyond the nature like this," that it is unclean, impermanent, and so forth, one will overcome attachment to the outer and inner body. As for the application of mindfulness to the mind (*cittasmṛtyupasthānam*), the mind is impermanent like autumn clouds, momentary, and readily changing. Sensations likewise should be understood as suffering. Since the sensation of happiness changes, it is suffering. Phenomena should be meditated on as lacking a self, and belonging to a self (*bdag dang bdag gi med pa*; *ātmātmīyarahita*) as emptiness. In this way, by meditating on ceasing the cause of suffering, from ceasing ignorance up through ceasing aging and death, the result is the truth of cessation.

C. Reversal of tendencies

Accordingly, meditating gives rise to three marks: the mind turns away from the entirety of cyclic existence, eliminates attachment to the five sense desires, and turns away from clinging to a self.

D. Results

The result is separation from all the sufferings of the three realms; the fruition is attaining nirvāṇa, the resultant arhatship; and the causal outpouring is emanations, supersensory perceptions, and doing as much as possible for the benefit of others.

III. Supreme individual

[The supreme individual has:][293]

[A. Practices]
B. Meditation objects
C. A reversal of tendencies
D. Results

A. Practices

First, train well in the precepts, having taken the vows of the aspirational awakening mind, the vows of the engaged awakening mind, and the vows of the ultimate awakening mind.

B. Meditation objects

The meditational objects are:

1. Meditating on skillful means
2. Meditating on wisdom
3. Meditating on union

1. Meditating on skillful means

Meditation on skillful means has two parts:

a. Meditating on love, compassion, and the awakening mind
b. Meditating on all appearances as illusion

a. Meditating on love, compassion, and the awakening mind

Among these, the first is the meditation on love. Attaining one's own liberation is not sufficient; one must attain the welfare of all mother sentient beings. If one does not attain that aim, there is no person more miserable than that, [**45a**] the durability is not briefer than that, the time period is not smaller than that; therefore love must be cultivated. Furthermore, all sentient beings have been one's parents. Although the exact number of each of these mother beings is not known, it is said many times, "There is not enough soil in the world to make a tiny pellet the size of a mere juniper berry for each of your past mothers."[294] One should establish kindness wishing to protect their life and protect them with a loving mind. Give food and clothing. One should gather whatever wealth is needed, avoiding bad deeds and sufferings. Whatever happiness is experienced by the son is due to their kindness.

With respect to that, since it is necessary to administer help in order to repay kindness, it is not sufficient to repay it with food and clothing; one must have great love. Furthermore, by [first] cultivating [love with respect to] one's present mother, the previous meditation is easy to produce. Therefore gradually cultivate [love] for your parents, children, and so forth and then for all sentient beings. Then, meditatively cultivate [it for all of them] simultaneously. At intervals, cultivate it toward objects who are dear. In this manner, remind yourself to be endowed with happiness. Being endowed with happiness, you should happily empathize with others and have compassion for those sentient beings who are endowed with suffering. [Sentient beings who are] endowed with the cause of suffering are unskillful in allowing the cause to emerge. Remind yourself that these beings who lack the favorable circumstance of being accepted by a spiritual friend should be freed from suffering. Happily empathize with the beings in freeing them from suffering.

With regard to the awakening mind: think that all sentient beings should attain buddhahood; that is, [generate] the aspiring awakening mind. The endeavor in physical, verbal, or mental virtue for that purpose is the engaging awakening mind; to the extent that it is maintained, it is a cause of buddhahood. Moreover, however much one endeavors to one's ability in the six perfections—up to and including even the most subtle giving; effort in any virtuous actions; eliminating evil deeds and moral downfalls; physically, verbally, and mentally benefitting others—production of the awakening mind, achievement of virtue, and elimination of evil deeds by others should be celebrated with happiness.

b. Meditating on all appearances as illusion

Meditating on all appearances as illusion eliminates suffering by ceasing apprehension of the reality of entities. In this regard, since illusions exist, meditation is indicated by that example in India. In Tibet, although there are illusions, [**45b**] meditation is indicated by the examples of dreams, reflections, and so forth. In this regard, during a dream, although something exists as a mere delusive appearance, there is no real entity whatsoever. Nothing other than a mere object is remembered upon waking. Likewise, there is no real entity whatsoever with respect to a reflection appearing in a mirror or the way that a reflection of the moon in water, a mirage, and so forth appears. Likewise, since an appearance in accord with these examples does not exist as a real entity but is merely a deceptive, impermanent, unreliable, transient conjunction of causes, circumstances, and connections, one should cognize [these appearances], definitely keep in mind [their nature], and refrain from relying on attachment, hatred, and suffering for any entity.

2. Meditating on wisdom

The cultivation of wisdom has two topics:
- a. Preliminary practices
- b. Actual practices

a. Preliminary practices

The first, preliminary practices, has two topics:
- 1) Relying on the spiritual teacher
- 2) Practicing in solitude

1) Relying on the spiritual teacher

First, relying on the spiritual teacher, has three topics:
- a) Eliminating all displeasing activities
- b) Practicing pleasing activities
- c) Having genuine devotion and requesting special instructions.

2) Practicing in solitude

Practicing in solitude has three topics:
- a) Bodily isolation (*kāyavyapakarṣa*)
- b) Mental isolation (*cittavyapakarṣa*)
- c) Avoiding harm

a) Bodily isolation

First, bodily isolation consists in abandoning activities, distractions, and cities and being in a hermitage without noisy people during the day and without noisy sounds during the night.

b) Mental isolation

Mental isolation means being without mental afflictions and discursive thoughts. In this regard, one should also have pure moral conduct, have a mind without regrets, and eliminate the eight worldly concerns, concerns with food and clothing, perceptions concerned with this life, and so forth.

c) Avoiding harm

Avoiding harm is to reside in a place without savages, carnivorous animals, demonic spirits, terrestrial antagonists (*sa dgra*),[295] and so forth.

b. Actual practices

The actual practice of meditation has two topics:
1) The cultivation of meditative serenity
2) The cultivation of insight

1) The cultivation of meditative serenity

The first has two topics:
a) The method of cultivation
b) Dispelling hindrances to cultivation

a) The method of cultivation

The first has three topics:
i) Preliminaries
ii) Actual practice
iii) Practices subsequent to meditation

i) Preliminaries

The first has two topics:
a' Relying on conducive conditions
b' Meditative equipoise

a' Relying on conducive conditions

The first has three topics:

1' Sever external ties of attachment
2' Gather internal necessities
3' Restrain the sense faculties

1' Sever external ties of attachment

First, eliminate ties with debt, arenas of discourse, [worldly] activities, and so forth. [46a]

2' Gather internal necessities

The internal necessities to be gathered are food, drink, firewood, medicine for recuperation, and so forth.

3' Restrain the sense faculties

Restraining the sense faculties, including the eye and so forth, is not engaging in distraction with sense objects and posting a guard against perceiving things incorrectly.

b' Meditative equipoise

Meditative equipoise has three topics:
1' Bodily meditative equipoise
2' Giving rise to the awakening mind
3' Meditating that the spiritual teacher is above one's head

1' Bodily meditative equipoise

From these, you should first have the five aspects of the posture of Amitābha: legs in a cross-legged sitting posture, hands in meditation gesture, spine straight, eyes directed toward the nose, and chin tucked slightly toward throat.[296]

2' Giving rise to the awakening mind

Giving rise to the awakening mind, think, "I will attain buddhahood for the sake of all sentient beings, and for that purpose I will strive in virtuous actions of body, speech, and mind."

3' Meditating that the spiritual teacher is above one's head

Meditating on the spiritual teacher is to show devotion and respect by thinking that the spiritual teacher is sitting on sun and moon disks atop a lotus above your head and seeing him as a buddha.

ii) Actual practice

The actual practice has two topics:
a' Meditative equipoise
b' Directly pointing out serenity

a' Meditative equipoise

The first has three topics:
1' Relax the body and mind
2' Settle in an unaffected manner
3' Remain in nonconceptuality

1' Relax the body and mind

First, remain tranquil, without tightening the body and mind like the twisting of a brahman's thread.

2' Settle in a unaffected manner

Settle in a manner free of artifice, like the limpidity of calm water, to naturally establish the mind without the contrivance of various ideas about tenets and the like.

3' Remain in nonconceptuality

Nonconceptual means that one does not evaluate traces of the past, anticipate the future, or grasp the surface of present awareness. Settle free from conceptual thought without cultivating, without thinking anything at all.[297]

b' Directly pointing out serenity

Directly pointing out has three topics:
1' Nonconceptuality

2' Clear awareness
3' Blissful experience

1' Nonconceptuality

First, regarding nonconceptuality, one resides with one-pointedness of mind (*cittaikagratā*), nonconceptually, by ceasing all subtle and gross discursive thoughts based on external objects and all subtle and gross conceptualization based on the mind within.

2' Clear awareness

Regarding clear awareness: one resides with one-pointedness of mind in non-grasping, self-luminous awareness, which at first does not engage with conceptually grasping onto vivid sense objects and later is freed from identifying with the luminous nature of the lucidity of one's own mind.

3' Blissful experience

[**46b**] The experience of emptiness and lucidity, which is free from all the torments of afflictions and conceptuality in previous experience, resides, due to halting even slight feelings of suffering, with one-pointedness of mind in naturally occuring unconditioned bliss.

iii) Practices subsequent to meditation

Practices subsequent to meditation has two topics:
a' Undegenerated practice
b' Unmistaken signs of progress on the path

a' Undegenerated practice

The first, undegenerated practice, has three topics:
1' Eliminate afflicted conceptual thoughts
2' Remain in solitude and forgo activities
3' Practice without distraction through mindfulness

1' Eliminate afflicted conceptual thoughts

First, do not give rise to conceptual thoughts of desire, hatred, or delusion. If they arise, eliminate them with an antidote.

2' Remain in solitude and forgo activities

Next, discard activities of body, speech, and mind associated with farming, commerce, and so forth and remain in a solitary place, such as a hermitage and so forth.

3' Practice without distraction through mindfulness

Always, in every situation, establish the mind upheld throughout with mindfulness inseparable with previous meditative experience. When meditative stabilization gradually degenerates due to forgetfulness, practice undistracted mindfulness.

b' Unmistaken signs of progress on the path

Unmistaken signs of progress on the path has three topics:

1' Not engaging the mind with sensory objects
2' Developing equanimity toward the eight worldly concerns
3' Refraining from the causes and consequences of karmic actions, and taking joy in solitude

1' Not engaging the mind with sensory objects

First, the mind remains unattached to any sensory object, and clinging and attraction do not arise. If they arise, they are eliminated.

2' Developing equanimity toward the eight worldly concerns

Next, one is without joy, attachment, and clinging to gain, fame, praise, and happiness, and one is without displeasure, hatred, and so forth to loss, disgrace, slander, and suffering.

3' Refraining from the causes and consequences of karmic actions, and taking joy in solitude

Refraining from the causes and consequences of karmic actions, and taking joy in solitude, results in the elimination of subtle evil deeds by understanding the results of virtuous and nonvirtuous actions, practicing even subtle virtues, and residing in isolation while eliminating being distracted by crowds and so forth.

b) Dispelling hindrances to cultivation

Dispelling hindrances has three topics:
i) The hindrances of moral downfalls
ii) The hindrances of obstructions
iii) The hindrances of distractions

i) The hindrances of moral downfalls

First, with regard to the hindrances of moral downfalls, if any of the vows that one has taken are damaged by root downfalls and there is degeneration, whether or not meditative stabilization has arisen, one should confess, restrain, and so forth. [47a]

ii) The hindrances of obstructions

The obstructions are desire and aspiration, harmfulness, agitated excitement, sloth and torpor, and doubt.

iii) The hindrances of distractions

Distractions are the multitude of outer and inner activities that affect the purity of body and mind. Distractions should be eliminated.

2) The cultivation of insight

Insight has two topics:
a) The method of meditation
b) Eliminating hindrances

a) The method of meditation

The first has three topics:
i) Preliminaries
ii) Actual practice
iii) Practices subsequent to meditation

i) Preliminaries

Preliminaries has two topics:

a' Specific preliminaries
b' General preliminaries

a' Specific preliminaries

The first, specific preliminaries, has three topics:
1' Uninterrupted, intense desire to produce insight
2' Activities, such as reciting the hundred syllables, to create merit and purify obscurations
3' Earnestly supplicating a qualified spiritual teacher with correct, authentic devotion

b' General preliminaries

General preliminaries has three topics:
1' Keeping the body and mind in seclusion
2' Generating the mind set on supreme awakening
3' Establishing the body and mind in the meditative equipoise of serenity

ii) Actual practice

The actual practice has two topics:
a' Pointing out the nature of the mind
b' Sustaining the meaning of that

a' Pointing out the nature of the mind

Pointing out has three topics:
1' Pointing out the mind as empty
2' Pointing out conceptual thought as empty
3' Pointing out whatever appears as empty

1' Pointing out the mind as empty

First, one's own mind is emptiness. Since the mind is not at all established as having shape, color, and so forth, remaining in emptiness from the very beginning, emptiness is not undermined by reasoning, destroyed by antidotes, purified by mantras, or cultivated by meditative stabilization. It is not mind-made emptiness. It is empty by nature, inherently empty. Since establishment as a mind of male, female, neuter, high realms, or lower realms does not exist even in the slightest, it is not seen, has not been seen, nor will be seen by the buddhas of the three times.

Accordingly, the mind that is empty is pure since it is not polluted or subject to any noxious influence of birth, death, pleasure, pain, and so forth. It is spontaneously present since the beginning as it is not established through effort and striving. The emptiness of one's own mind such as this is called "unproduced," "the realm of reality," and "ultimate reality." It abides from the very beginning [**47b**] as the emptiness of inherent existence.

As to the method to realize the meaning of that: by looking directly into your own mind during nonconceptual meditative stabilization in serenity, practice not meditating on anything at all while dwelling in lucidity as empty. Again, practice looking directly. With effort, realize that there is emptiness.

By producing strong effort with respect to that, a meditative stabilization mixed with feeling and conceptual thought arises, pure like space. Become firmly established in the certainty of that [state].

2' Pointing out conceptual thought as empty

Accordingly, even if you realize your own mind as emptiness, if you think while sitting that the subtle and coarse conceptual thoughts that arise from conditions are the unhindered, fleeting movement of thoughts, point out that the fleeting movement of thoughts itself is empty. By looking directly into the manner of fleeting movement, the haziness disappears without a trace, just as a self-arisen cloudy sky vanishes of its own accord.

Just as waves and foam on an ocean are without differentiation from the water, since conceptual thoughts themselves are empty, conceptual thoughts do not need to be negated. Like snow falling into water, the ally [of awareness] that is empty is simultaneously empty fleeting movement. Since awareness [and its movement are] simultaneously empty, it is sufficient to look directly into all conceptual thoughts.

3' Pointing out whatever appears as empty

Then all cultivation, body, and appearances should be understood as emptiness. For example, just as the appearance of the moon in water is without an inherent nature, the body is understood as lacking an intrinsic body nature, all appearances are cognized as without intrinsic appearance, and entities are not apprehended as real. Attachment and aversion do not accumulate in relation to sense objects. All things are contemplated as dreams and illusions.

b' Sustaining the meaning of that

Sustaining the meaning of these [points] has three topics:

1' Sustaining undistracted mindfulness
2' Sustaining the identification of the fleeting movement [of thoughts]
3' Sustaining appearances as naturally free

1' Sustaining undistracted mindfulness

Among these, first, one should do whatever is suitable during the four daily activities.[298] The experience of the realization of emptiness that takes place is to be held contiuously with mindfulness. For example, like a mother who is inseparable from a dying, cherished son, realization should be sustained. Otherwise, later it is sufficient to meditate at times of leisure and solitude, when free of sickness and without mental afflictions and other suffering. Now, if one thinks that meditation will not suffice, that is a sign **[48a]** that one has not realized emptiness and is, moreover, without special instruction. Perhaps, since [thinking that meditation will not suffice] is a blessing by a demon, one should refrain accordingly [from that blessing]. If nonconceptual thought is present but one is endowed with special instructions and demonic forces are not present, one will not be harmed by any conditions. All conditions of suffering and happiness are sufficient to be recollected as empty. Since any efforts at physical postures and particular focal objects and so forth are unnecessary, as it is sufficient to hold with mindfulness all daily activities as abiding from the beginning as empty, one should sustain and uphold with undistracted, correct mindfulness.

2' Sustaining the identification of the fleeting movement [of thoughts]

By directly looking into elaborated, unsupressed, fleeting movements of subtle and coarse conceptual thoughts regarding external and internal things, and by understanding that none whatsoever are established by nature, since [at that time] there is no greater fault than the desire to stop fleeting movements, one does not refute them; the fleeting movements are themselves the luminous clarity of one's own mind.

If one desires to repudiate [conceptuality], that signifies a lack of understanding. The absorption of cessation[299] is that desire. Therefore, since conceptuality is meditation, do not view conceptual thought as a fault. For example, like a thief of an empty house, it is unnecessary to counter something that naturally dissipates. It is sufficient by sustaining through union with the fourth time.[300] In this regard, the time of fleeting movement, the time of viewing with mindfulness, the time of emptiness, the time of being free, and the fourth time are sustained at the same time.

3' Sustaining appearances as naturally free

When sustaining appearances as naturally free, everything whatsoever that is perceived is apprehended with mindfulness as lacking inherent existence. For example, like consecrating a mantra on poison, [when one applies emptiness to appearances and] one understands appearances as empty, then holding things as real, attachment, and hatred are brought to cessation, and one recognizes appearances as powerless.

One should sustain the understanding of intrinsic emptiness as naturally evanescent, like throwing a stick into water without creating any ripples or like clouds disappearing in the sky. Furthermore, the *Teaching of the Armor Array* states, "Do not see the empty in emptiness; do not see emptiness other than emptiness; just this, which is called 'seeing emptiness,' is what is seen."[301]

iii) Practices subsequent to meditation

Practices subsequent to meditation has two topics:

a' Developing whichever conceptual thoughts occur
b' Signs of progress on the path

a' Developing whichever conceptual thoughts occur

The first has three topics:

1' Tempering metal for the sake of realizing emptiness
2' Testing on the basis of conditions
3' Eliminating discordant [**48b**] conditions

1' Tempering metal for the sake of realizing emptiness

First, don the armor that intends to strive for the prerequisites of realization, renounce the world, strive for solitary meditation, sustain with mindfulness all appearances as dreams and illusions, and eliminate all discordant conditions.

2' Testing on the basis of conditions

Try a test: meditate upon, reflect upon, and view the eight worldly concerns in terms of your own mind: Do you cut off or [merely] watch the conceptual thoughts of attachment and hatred toward the experiences of joy and sorrow? Do you view with an agitated or unagitated mind contempt toward others, insults, and minor injuries? Check and see, and then practice, [whether] your own mind has attachment or nonattachment for praise, honor, and gain.

3' Eliminating discordant conditions

Sustain by eliminating discordant conditions accordingly: when sitting uninterruptedly after examining the above, meditate in solitude and strive in the actual practice. When interrupted, first, continue through [the actual practice] as a powerful god and demon, forsaking self-grasping, and abide in emptiness. Then, continue through the ground of producing attachment for friends and hate for enemies and so forth and, apprehending with mindfulness while thinking everything is emptiness, disperse appearances. You should practice at times being interrupted, at other times uninterruptedly, at times remaining in meditative equipoise, at times sustaining.

b' Signs of progress on the path

Signs of progress on the path are threefold: (1) The suppression of mental afflictions diminishes. (2) Attachment to entities diminishes, and one becomes liberated from grasping at them as solid. (3) Whatever joys, sorrows, and so forth appear, any grasping at the attachment and aversion, happiness and suffering, that occurs is undermined.

3. Meditating on union

The meditation of union (*zung 'jug*; *yuganaddha*) has two topics:

a. Directly pointing out union
b. Practicing its meaning

a. Directly pointing out union

Directly pointing out has three topics:

1) The union of the ground that is the basis
2) The union of the path that is indicated
3) The union of the result that is achieved

1) The union of the ground that is the basis

First is the union of the ground that is the basis. Its three characteristics are that there is no buddha that is made manifest through realization; there is no mistaken sentient being through nonrealization; and remaining spontaneously perfected from the very beginning, the natural condition is in itself the general ground of all of cyclic existence and nirvāṇa. Its own nature dwells in emptiness. The hindrances to be dispelled are three: despising the body of the spiritual teacher, abandoning the holy Dharma, and committing a heinous evil deed. These three should be eliminated: those uncreated should not be created, and what has been created should decline.

The nature abides lucidly; the characteristic abides indivisibly. Among these, first, its *own nature* (*rang bzhin*) dwells in emptiness; there is no emptiness that is destroyed, [49a] entrusted, or purified. It abides as emptiness of inherent nature from the very beginning, free from all phenomenal marks, such as shape and color. There is no realization that apprehends a nonexistence within. Unobstructedly be aware of the radiance of your own awareness. Abide like the sun rising in pure space or the wind of pure space. The *characteristic* (*mtshan nyid*): the indivisibility of lucidity and emptiness, inseparable like a conch shell and its whiteness, abides primordially free from conceptuality.

2) The union of the path that is indicated

The union of the path that is indicated has three topics:

a) The inherent nature, emptiness
b) The essence, clarity
c) The characteristic, indivisibility

a) The inherent nature, emptiness

First, one's own mind, primordially pure, resides in the realm of reality, all-pervading just as it appears. Although emptiness is not lucid when it appears while ignorance presides, emptiness timelessly abides, pervading all that appears, like [sesame oil] pervades a sesame seed.

b) The essence, clarity

The luminous essence is clear in three appearances:

i) Karmic appearance
ii) Delusive appearance
iii) Meditative appearance

i) Karmic appearance

First, [karmic appearances] are all the appearances of happiness and suffering of the six realms of rebirth. These are not appearances that are established as external objects. Since one's own karmic action is a conjunction of circumstances and connections of virtue and evil deeds, like an illusion and so forth, it is like a reflection.

ii) Delusive appearance

Delusive appearance is grasping at an external object that is not understood as one's own perception; it is like seeing a rope as a snake.

iii) Meditative appearance

Meditative appearance is the appearance of one's own mind at the time of abiding in nonconceptual meditative stabilization. Though an appearing external object ceases, the factor of clarity does not cease the appearance of the mind within. Like a mirage, smoke, a star, drops of light, and so forth, subtle and coarse colors and shapes mostly appear but are utterly empty, like a cloudless sky.

In brief, all karmic appearances, delusive appearances, and meditative appearances are the luminous essence of one's own mind.

c) The characteristic, indivisibility

The indivisibility characteristic: since all karmic appearances and so forth, all appearances seen as subject and object, are pervaded by the emptiness of inherent nature, and since the appearance itself is empty and emptiness is appearance, [**49b**] they are without any differentiation, like water and waves.

3) The union of the result that is achieved

The union of the result that is achieved has three topics:

a) The inherent nature, emptiness
b) The essence, clarity
c) The characteristic, indivisibility

a) The inherent nature, emptiness

Among them, first, [as to the inherent nature, emptiness,] since it abides as inseparable from the condition of twofold purity—actualizing the meaning of being free from the momentary defilements and being the realm of reality that is pure from the very beginning—it is like a cloudless sky.

b) The essence, clarity

The luminous essence (*ngo bo gsal ba*) is all the appearances of the body, wisdom, pure realms, celestial palaces, and so forth just as they appear; they are not established from without. The very embodiment of the awakening mind, one's own mind, is the luminous essence of pristine wisdom, the wisdom that appears like the moon reflected in water and like a rainbow in the sky.

c) The characteristic, indivisibility

The indivisibility characteristic: all the bodies, pure realms, celestial mansions, and so forth; the appearances of true pristine wisdom, which are like an illusion; and the actualized realm of reality just as it is are inseparably merged. It is like the inseparability of the sky and a rainbow. The good qualities and activities that manifest from that inseparability mature and liberate those to be trained.

b. Practicing its meaning

The practice of union has two topics:
1) The practice of vision
2) The practice of meditation

1) The practice of vision

First, the practice of vision has three topics:
a) Accepting appearances and emptiness as inseparable
b) Accepting causality and emptiness as inseparable
c) Accepting skillful means and wisdom as inseparable

a) Accepting appearances and emptiness as inseparable

This practice requires an elevated realization of emptiness, so one obtains firm control in the meditative cultivation of wisdom so that union will happen without effort. First, the realization of emptiness becomes firmly established, and then one integrates skillful means and wisdom. Union happens when skillful means and wisdom are integrated.

Furthermore, the seal of emptiness is placed upon whatever is perceived. One places the seal of appearance on emptiness. From that, since appearance and emptiness are inseparably mixed, with multiplicity as a single taste, there occurs the realization of nothing whatsoever other than the nature of one's own mind, free from extremes. It is said that during all one's daily activities, one should not stray into intellectualizing that which is not separable. It must be possible to hold [this vision] with mindfulness. Since it is possible not to be necessary [to hold this vision with mindfulness], [50a] practice without separating from that vision. As one apprehends whatever appearance that arises—attachment, hatred, and so forth—as empty of inherent nature, one will not fall under the sway of the mental afflictions. One should practice by recognizing all appearances in this way. Similarly, for the time of practice, as one's own mind is free from extremes, one resides as if there is nothing whatsoever among all things established as an external object. Then one risks chasing after the ordinary by thinking that it is not necessary to make any effort to meditate and so forth. Therefore one should not separate from meditation.

Sometimes [one may think], there does not exist a cause to abandon saṃsāra. A buddha does not exist to be achieved. Since the spiritual teacher is oneself, there does not exist an object of respect and devotion. Since there do not even exist causes and consequences of karmic actions, it is unnecessary to eliminate and achieve. Since there is no duality of the reason for meditation and one who meditates, one will come to think that meditation is not necessary. At that time, demons may descend and pointless chatter will flow. Even if one cannot respect and have devotion toward an [actual] spiritual teacher, one should generate respect and devotion in a similar way to being in a dream or an illusion and one should display effort in spiritual practice, striving in meditation practice, [understanding of] cause and effect, and so forth.

b) Accepting causality and emptiness as inseparable

In this practice, as there is stability in the realization of emptiness, one does as much as one can to achieve virtuous karmic deeds and eliminate evil karmic deeds. One should eliminate even the subtlest evil deed and achieve the subtlest virtue. Only suchness is emptiness. Only emptiness is cause and effect. If one says that emptiness contradicts cause and effect, and that cause and effect contradicts emptiness, it is improper, as one will not realize union. Therefore emptiness manifests as cause and effect. Since cause and effect itself engages as emptiness, causality and emptiness are not distinct; they are not differentiated and are inseparable.

In this way, when there is an elevated realization, an illusion-like result will occur. Furthermore, when the realization is elevated, space-like cause and effect will occur. Due to this, since cause and effect is nondeceptive even at the level of a buddha, as there exists an elevated realization of union, one should make effort to eliminate [evil deeds] and achieve [virtue] regarding the causes and consequences of karmic actions.

c) Accepting skillful means and wisdom as inseparable

To practice the inseparability of skillful means and wisdom is to purify love, compassion, and the awakening mind. Without that, the Great Vehicle is not practiced. Even unsurpassed [**50b**] awakening will not be attained. Emptiness is a meditation for śrāvakas. Since mere illusory appearances are meditated upon by ordinary individuals, this union [of skillful means and wisdom] is a practice of ārya beings. Therefore one should purify love, compassion, and the awakening mind while observing sentient beings and phenomena, and without observing a basis. At all times, purify any disturbances with emptiness. Both [sentient beings and phenomena] are emptiness.

Since love, compassion, and the awakening mind are only emptiness, one should practice skillful means and wisdom as inseparable. If skillful means and wisdom are contradictory, it is a cause of going astray on the path, and even buddhahood will not be attained. One must complete both skillful means and wisdom to attain buddhahood. For example, like the two wings of a bird in flight or two legs traversing a path, one must complete both skillful means and wisdom. Therefore one should make effort to purify the conventional awakening mind, eliminate evil deeds, and achieve virtue, and one must by all means respect and venerate the spiritual teacher.

Since any one of those [practices] is marked with the seal of emptiness, as skillful means and wisdom become inseparable, one should accordingly recognize and practice [that everything is marked with the seal of emptiness]. Furthermore, the various virtuous methods are not sealed [with emptiness only] after they have been enacted. Such action is a practice of ordinary individuals and a pitfall of yogis. Here, skillful means is sealed with wisdom; wisdom is sealed with skillful means. The meaning is that skillful means and wisdom are integrated simultaneously. Therefore skillful means and wisdom are not distinct; they are undifferentiated and inseparable.

2) The practice of meditation

Practicing meditation has two topics:

a) The means of meditation
b) Clearing away hindrances

a) The means of meditation

The first, the means of meditation, has three topics:

i) Preliminaries
ii) Actual practice
iii) Practices subsequent to meditation

i) Preliminaries

The first, preliminaries, has two topics:

a' Prerequisites
b' Meditative equipoise

a' Prerequisites

The first, prerequisites, has three topics:

1' Meditating on emptiness
2' Developing aspiration
3' Accumulation and purification

1' Meditating on emptiness

One should sustain emptiness according to the explanation in the section on insight.[302]

2' Developing aspiration

Aspiration is the fervent wish to generate union.

3' Accumulation and purification

As the supreme form of accumulation and purification is devotion [**51a**] to the spiritual teacher, earnestly request [instruction] from the spiritual teacher and be devoted by perceiving him as a buddha.

b' Meditative equipoise

Meditative equipoise has three topics:
1' Body
2' Mind
3' Guru yoga

1' Body

As mentioned previously, the body should have the five qualities of Amitābha.

2' Mind

The mind should eliminate afflictions and conceptual thought through being established in serenity.

3' Guru yoga

Guru yoga is to meditate [that the spiritual teacher is sitting on a lotus with sun and moon disks] above one's head.

ii) Actual practice

The actual practice has two topics:
a' Meditative equipoise
b' Sustaining that state

a' Meditative equipoise

The first, meditative equipoise, has three topics:
1' Establishing as inseparably established
2' Establishing as free from extremes
3' Establishing without adopting and rejecting

1' Establishing as inseparably established

The first, inseparably established, is to establish conceptual thought, non-conceptual thought, appearance, emptiness, rejection, acceptance, hope, fear, the object of meditation, meditation, and so forth as being one taste, in equal nature, without distinction.

2' Establishing as free from extremes

[Establishing as] free from extremes is to not fall to the extremes of permanence and annihilation while establishing the nature of one's own mind as free from extremes by not meditating on objects of observation or phenomenal marks at all.

3' Establishing without adopting and rejecting

For this, one does not avoid the afflictions, conceptual thoughts, suffering, and so forth of cyclic existence. They are one's own mind. Achieving nirvāṇa and desiring happiness is also one's own mind. No matter what, one's own mind abides primordially in union, established without adopting and rejecting.

b' Sustaining that state

Sustaining that state has three topics:

1' Sustaining appearances as unceasing
2' Sustaining by bringing appearances and conceptual thoughts along as allies
3' Sustaining union as inseparable

1' Sustaining appearances as unceasing

First, whatever appearances and conceptual thoughts arise are all sealed with emptiness as unceasing. Awareness is freshly established, without projecting, without concentrating, without tightly holding, like a skillful cowherd (*mkhas pa ba glang skyong ba*). As appearance and emptiness are inseparable, one sustains by recognizing the multiplicity [of things] as having the single taste [of emptiness].

2' Sustaining by bringing appearances and conceptual thoughts along as allies

As everything that appears is covered with emptiness, all appearances and conceptual thoughts are like a stick stirring water in which the ripples vanish without a trace. The flourishing amity of the wisdom of all that appears is a friendship that increases realization of the ephemeral as like snow falling into water or [the path of] a bird flying through the sky.

3' Sustaining union as inseparable

One makes sure to attain this with mindfulness, holding with continual mindfulness, like the mother of a dying son, by freely establishing awareness as naturally dissipating, like a bird flying up from a boat or a thief leaving an empty house. Any fixing of the mind and so forth, any particular posture and so forth, is not necessary. Any walking, moving around, lying down, and sitting [**51b**] in any situation is suitable to uphold with mindfulness.

iii) Practices subsequent to meditation

Practices subsequent to meditation has two topics:
a' Uncorrupted method
b' Unmistaken signs [of successful practice]

a' Uncorrupted method

The first, uncorrupted method, has three topics:
1' Renouncing activities
2' Accumulation and purification
3' Protecting with mindfulness

1' Renouncing activities

Renouncing activities is to practice in solitude while abandoning all activities and actions of body, speech, and mind. When one is distracted with activities, realization degenerates.

2' Accumulation and purification

Although virtue and nonvirtue do not exist in the nature of realizing one's own mind, one should make effort to achieve even the subtlest virtue and eliminate the subtlest nonvirtue.

3' Protecting with mindfulness

All appearances and conceptual thought are made into knowledge of the path, the path is made into union, and one does not distractedly engage with any external or internal things. Getting lost in conceptual thought when distracted is delusion; because of that, attachment, hatred, and so forth are produced; then realization degenerates, negative actions and downfalls increase, and one falls into lower realms of rebirth. Therefore one should continuously rely on mindfulness to eliminate mental distraction.

b' Unmistaken signs [of successful practice]

Signs of progress on the path has three points:

1' Confidence in positive and negative karma
2' Understanding appearances as unreal
3' Generating compassion for those of no understanding

1' Confidence in positive and negative karma

Confidence in positive and negative karma is refraining from the subtlest non-virtuous evil deeds and striving with energetic diligence in virtuous actions of body, speech, and mind.

2' Understanding apperances as unreal

One does not generate attachment to even the most excellent desirable conditions that may occur. If they do arise, one eliminates [attachment]. One does not generate hatred for undesirable conditions that may occur. If they arise, one eliminates [hatred]. For any appearances such as these, one understands them as mere illusions and dream appearances, without clinging to them as real.

3' Generating compassion for those of no understanding

One naturally produces compassion for those who do not understand.

In this way, these [three points] are unmistaken signs of progress on the path. Accordingly, when signs contradictory to progress on the path occur, since these are strayings from the path that are fueled by demons, one should request special instructions in front of the spiritual teacher.

b) Clearing away hindrances

The hindrances to be cleared away are threefold:

i) Not placing trust in virtuous and evil deeds
ii) Apprehending appearances and emptiness as distinct
iii) Not enjoying meditation

i) Not placing trust in virtuous and evil deeds

First, if you think that there is no reason to abandon nonvirtue and achieve virtue because virtuous or nonvirtuous karma only exist in one's own mind, you engage in a great evil deed, and whatever virtue is not performed gets lost in pointless chatter. [**52a**]

ii) Apprehending appearances and emptiness as distinct

By thinking that all things are empty, you apprehend cause and effect of karmic actions as nothingness for all appearances; alternately, you see real entities through apprehending the cause and effect of karmic actions as real.

iii) Not enjoying meditation

Not enjoying meditation is a great hindrance and is a sign of being overpowered by demons. If that should occur, generate enthusiasm for meditation by making effort in the special instructions of taming demons through various methods.

Generally, all these special instructions eradicate [hindrances]; by making effort to listen to a great amount of Dharma while sitting in the presence of a spiritual teacher, creating [merit], purifying [obscurations], and being devoted to a spiritual teacher, [hindrances] will be eradicated.

C. Reversal of tendencies

In this way, through relying on the practices of the path of the supreme individual, three reversals of tendencies occur. In this regard, (1) one reverses the tendency for mental afflictions and all motivations for one's own welfare, while motivations for others' welfare emerge; (2) through reversing the tendency to always apprehend all external and internal entities as real, one realizes that whatever appears is like a dream or an illusion; and (3) through reversing the tendency to always apprehend extremes like permanency, nihilism, and so forth, one gains a firm realization, free from effort, without accepting or rejecting views, free from extremes.

D. Results

Results has three topics:

1. The separation effect (*visaṃyogaphala*) is that one is free from all obscurations of karma, afflictions, and obstacles to knowledge.
2. The maturation effect (*vipākaphala*) is being endowed with the major and minor marks of a [buddha's] body, being endowed with the sixty aspects of speech,[303] and being endowed with the five wisdoms of a [buddha's] mind.
3. The correlative effect (*niṣyandaphala*) is that one guides all beings to be trained by way of five aspects of enlightened activity.

The practical guidance on the special instructions of the stages of the path to awakening has been set forth. The teaching from the mouth of the Paṇḍita Dīpaṃkaraśrījñāna is thus completed. These are the special instructions of the practice domain of the Kadam textual tradition.

Supplementary Material

Verses requested by Upāli to establish nonconceptuality and recognize the Buddha's teaching

The *Questions of Upāli Sūtra* (*Upāliparipṛcchāsūtra*) states,

> Forever happy in this world are these men who know the inconceivable Dharma.
> There is no distinction between thing (*dharma*) and nonthing (*adharma*): all [things] are free from differentiation by thought. (50)
>
> If we eliminate the knowledge of existence and nonexistence,
> everything turns out to be inconceivable; everything turns out to be unreal.
> But those who are enslaved to the power of thought, the childish, [**52b**]
> ah! they are unhappy for hundreds of countless lives. (51)
>
> Monks who would not worship the Buddha
> as inconceivable and nonexistent, their thought would be incorrect.
> The Buddha is a product of the imagination,
> but this imagination itself is unreal. (52)
>
> Even one who thinks that things are empty
> would also be a simple one who went wrong.

With words, we proclaim that things are empty;
with words also, we say that something is unspeakable. (53)

If we think that things are appeased, completely appeased,
this very thought never existed.
Any differentiation is only a conjecture of thought;
this is why we consider that things are inconceivable. (54)

All these things are outside thought and its efficiency (*niścetanā*);
to the extent that they are unthinkable; they are empty.[304] (55ab)

The *Questions of Upāli Sūtra* also states,

> What is the teaching of the Buddha? What is the holy Dharma? What is the Vinaya? The Buddha said, "Upāli, when I give something that is a cause of higher rebirth and liberation, either directly or indirectly, to someone who is suitable or not suitable, that is the Buddha's teaching; that is the holy Dharma; that is the Vinaya. When I give something that is a cause for saṃsāra or lower realms of rebirth to someone who is suitable or unsuitable, that is not the Buddha's teaching; that is not the holy Dharma; this is not the Vinaya. Upāli, you should accordingly apprehend."

Wheel, elephant, horse, queen, jewel, steward, and minister. The *Sāgaramati-sūtra* states, "Think to apply to the afflicted what is associated with the roots of virtue. Engage with the three realms for the sake of fully ripening sentient beings."

5. Pointing-Out Instructions in Sets of Five

THE ADVANCED INSTRUCTIONS on meditation known as *Pointing-Out Instructions in Sets of Five* (hereafter, *Pointing-Out Instructions*) are based upon Atiśa's *Stages of the Path* and are historically attested to have circulated independently of the *Stages* manuscript (see below). The work represents an initially oral tradition of pointing-out instructions transmitted by early Kadampa communities. It may well be that Atiśa himself bestowed it to his early followers.

In Indian and Tibetan forms of Buddhism, "pointing-out instructions" (*ngo sprod*) generally signifies an introduction to the nature of mind by a spiritual teacher to a qualified disciple. Previous scholarship has noted that the verb *ngo sprod* means "to indicate, indentify, point out, introduce, or recognize" (Jackson 2019, 91n297), as well as "confront" (Achard 1999, 58) or "encounter" (Guenther 1993). As Kapstein (2000a, 180) summarizes, "introduction (*ngo sprod/sprad*) . . . in its technical sense, refers to instruction that, if skillfully delivered to an appropriately receptive disciple by an appropriately qualified master, catalyzes an immediate intuitive grasp of the instruction's content." The impact of this type of instruction by the teacher is thought to "bring about direct insight into the ultimate nature of mind . . . without the disciple's having first traversed the entire sequence of tantric initiation and yogic practice" (Kapstein 2000, 77).

As these citations suggest, pointing-out instructions are primarily associated with tantric Buddhist lineages of meditation and yogic practice. The practice of bestowing such instruction has a long, yet uncharted, history in tantric forms of Indian Buddhism and may have its beginnings in the *siddha* culture during the Pāla dynasties (760–1142) in northeastern India. The currently known evidence for pointing-out instructions among *siddhas*, such as Saraha, Tilopa, and Maitrīpa, suggests concise, unsystematic, and perhaps spontaneous, direct verbal and/or nonverbal acts of revealing realization to disciples (Sherpa 2004, 175; Brunnhölzl 2014, 193). Female and male yogic masters used this technique for directly introducing the nature of the mind (Shaw 1994, 98–99), and the technique was closely associated with the practice and realization of mahāmudrā. In Tibetan forms of Buddhism, pointing-out instructions have been primarily affiliated with the Nyingma and Kagyü lineages. In Nyingma lineages pointing-out instructions are connected to varied Great Perfection (*rdzogs chen*) traditions, where one confronts the natural state (*gnas lugs ngo sprod*).[305] Kagyü and other Tibetan traditions of the new sects (*gsar ma*) associate pointing-out instructions with the practice of mahāmudrā.

Among prominent figures within Kagyü lineages, Gampopa Sönam Rinchen (1079–1153) moved mahāmudrā "to the heart of Kagyü tradition and to a place of great prominence in philosophical and meditative discourse in Tibet" (R. Jackson 2019, 92). The influence of Gampopa's mahāmudrā teachings in Tibet was such that, as Roger Jackson suggests, "all Kagyü reflection on mahāmudrā is really but a series of footnotes to Gampopa" (2019, 88). In his teachings of mahāmudrā, Gampopa was most renowned for what Mathes has termed a "not-specifically-tantric mahāmudrā practice" (2006, 201), whereby "a disciple need not receive tantric empowerment in order to attain awakening; hearing the guru's experiential introduction to the nature of mind through a 'pointing-out instruction' (*ngo sprod*) will suffice" (R. Jackson 2019, 91). This style of teaching mahāmudrā was called "introduction to the [nature of] mind" (*sems kyi ngo sprod*), and the important role of "pointing-out" in Gampopa's system was characterized by other twelfth-century Tibetan figures such as Lama Shang (Zhang g.yu brag pa Brtson 'grus grags pa, 1123–93) as "pointing-out *mahāmudrā* in the Tradition of Dagpopa" (*dags po ba'i lugs kyi phyag rgya chen po ngo sprod*; D. Jackson 1994, 2, 13). The chapter that follows demonstrates that pointing-out instructions for "not-specifically-tantric mahāmudrā practice" did not originate with Gampopa. Structured pointing-out instructions are also neither derived from, nor influenced by, other Buddhist traditions such as Chan. Rather, systematized and structured "not-specifically-tantric" pointing-out instructions are intimately related to Atiśa's *Stages of the Path* (chapter 1), *Instructions for Select Disciples* (chapter 4), and the teachings found in *Pointing-Out Instructions in Sets of Five*.

Pointing-Out Instructions comprises approximately thirteen folios, which are copied out in the same scribal hand as the rest of the *Stages of the Path* manuscript. The colophon also provides an alternative title: *The Great Pointing-Out Instructions in Sets of Five that Eliminate the Extremes of One's Own Mind* (*Rang sems mtha' gcod kyi ngo sprod lnga tshoms chen mo*). The colophon additionally states, "These are special instructions of the Kadam textual lineage or practice lineage" (*bka' gdams gzhung pa'am / spyod phyogs kyi gdams ngag*). This indicates that this work circulated among early Kadampa communities. On the other hand, contextual evidence as well as a brief historical note suggest that *Pointing-Out Instructions* circulated independently, as oral teachings of Atiśa. An episode in the biography of Mokchok Rinchen Tsöndrü (1110–70), a disciple of Khyungpo Naljor (Mei 2009), recounts how he went to request teachings on mahāmudrā from the Kadampa Geshé Gar (ca. twelfth century), who held lineage teachings from both Atiśa and Milarepa. The biography states,

> He fully received the [teachings of the] lineage from Lord [Atiśa] and those of Milarepa. Those teachings he requested from Geshé Gar. Then he offered Geshé Gar some silk cloth. He requested all the teachings on mahāmudrā without exception. [Geshé Gar] said, "Since you are in harmony with the Dharma of Lord [Atiśa], I will give teachings to you" . . . Moreover, he requested many pointing-out instructions . . . He was granted without exception instructions on mahāmudrā used by the spiritual teacher himself, including the *Twofold Armor*, the *Fivefold Pointing-Out Instructions*, the *Eight Lines of Verse*, *Taking the Three Bodies as the Path*, and so forth.[306]

The *Twofold Armor* (*Go cha rnam gnyis*) is a nonextant text attributed to Atiśa in later historical works (Apple 2017, 23–24), and the mention in this episode of the *Fivefold Pointing-Out Instructions* may be a reference to the very *Pointing-Out Instructions* included in this chapter. Whether *Pointing-Out Instructions* was given by Atiśa in its current form or organized by his early Kadampa followers and circulated independently, these instructions are based on Atiśa's *Stages of the Path* and its related commentarial literature.

Pointing-Out Instructions within Atiśa's Stages of the Path System

Pointing-Out Instructions, in terms of its subject matter, presents instructions in sets of five, as reflected in the title of the work. This indicates that *Pointing-Out Instructions* was initially a teaching disseminated orally, as sets of fivefold categories serve as a mnemonic technique in oral recitation. The larger structure of the work within which these sets of five appear is arranged in three general points and four actual practices. The three general points consist of (1) general preliminaries, (2) the actual practices, and (3) the distinctive features of the actual practices. The four actual practices consist of the yogas of (1) serenity, (2) insight, (3) union, and (4) signlessness. These four yogas differ from the four yogas found in Atiśa's mahāmudrā instructions to his disciple Gönpawa (Apple 2017), as well as from other well-known sets of four yogas or meditations (Bentor 2002; Katsura 2018).

The four yogas discussed in *Pointing-Out Instructions* have a discernable relation to the content of Atiśa's *Stages.* In its layered overview of *Stages*, the *Structural Analysis* summary (in chapter 2) indicates sections in *Stages* where pointing-out instructions may be found. In my translation of *Stages,* I have correlated these with section numbers. These indicate which portions of *Stages* were considered pointing-out instructions for Atiśa and his early Kadampa followers. Namely, the *Structural Analysis* indicates pointing-out instructions in the contexts of the actual practice of serenity, the practice of insight, and the cultivation of union. The fourth yoga of signlessness discussed in *Pointing-Out Instructions* is only briefly mentioned in *Stages.*

The pointing-out instructions for the actual practice of serenity are found in *Stages* §142–44. These sections of *Stages* are elucidated in *Pointing-Out Instructions* in section II, Actual Practices, under heading A, Serenity. Instructions for the next yoga, pointing out the mind in the practice of insight, are located in *Stages*, §145–47, and *Pointing-Out Instructions* outlines guidance on insight in section II under heading B, Insight. The pointing-out instructions for union in *Stages* are in §158–59. These sections in Atiśa's *Stages* and *Instructions for Select Disciples* (chapter 4) are elucidated in *Pointing-Out Instructions* under heading C, Union. As mentioned, the fourth yoga of signlessness, though briefly mentioned in *Stages*, is only discussed in *Pointing-Out Instructions.* The differences in exegesis between *Instructions for Select Disciples* and *Pointing-Out Instructions* indicate alternative ways of understanding *Stages* and different points of emphasis in meditation practice.

The yoga of signlessness is alluded to in *Stages* §167, which states, "One's own mind free from extremes, the Great Middle Way, free from conceptuality with signs and without signs." The initial passage of this citation evokes a phrase from the alternate title of *Pointing-Out Instructions*: "eliminate the extremes of one's own mind" (*rang sems mtha' gcod*). Atiśa also refers to this state as the "Great Middle Way" (*dbu ma chen po*), a term he uses throughout his works on Madhyamaka and the path (Apple 2018, 50–52, 58–60). It is tempting to compare this fourth yoga of signlessness with other systems, such as the fourth stage in Ratnākaraśānti's *Prajñāpāramitopadeśa*, which is described as "signless emptiness" (*nirnimittā śūnyatā*) (Katsura 2018). However, as mentioned, Atiśa's system of four yogas in *Pointing-Out Instructions* is different from all currently known types of fourfold meditations as studied in Bentor (2002). The discussion of signlessness in *Pointing-Out Instructions* is also found in section II, under heading D, Signlessness.

Pointing-Out Instructions is a key document for illustrating the nature of Kadam pointing-out instructions. It contains a number of features that indicate a tantric orientation, archetypal features that influence later Kagyü meditation manuals, and anomalies that illustrate unique teachings not found in other Indo-Tibetan meditation traditions. The tantric orientation of *Pointing-Out Instructions* is indicated through mention of practices that are explicitly found in Buddhist tantras. For example, *Pointing-Out Instructions* advocates use of the hundred-syllable mantra of Vajrasattva for purification (fol. 53a), a practice found in the *Sarvatathāgatatattvasaṃgraha* (Chandra 1981) and *Kriyāsaṃgraha* (Skorupski 2002, 142). *Pointing-Out Instructions* also instructs the practitioner in multiple sections to meditate on the spiritual teacher as a buddha (56b) and to attain union in order to gain a vision of one's deity (63b). In the final section of the work, attainment of the great clear light (*'od gsal chen po*; 64a and 65a) is discussed as the result of attaining a great level in signlessness meditation. Clear light (*prabhāsvara*) is discussed in Atiśa's other works in relation to the *Cakrasaṃvaratantra* and mahāmudrā teachings (Apple 2017). Although *Pointing-Out Instructions* contains elements demonstrating a tantric orientation, however, it does not directly cite any Buddhist tantra or specify instructions for receiving consecration or empowerment.

The teachings of *Pointing-Out Instructions* serve as a prototype for later Kagyü meditation manuals on mahāmudrā. Like those manuals, *Pointing-Out Instructions* presents the subject matter in terms of preliminaries (*sngon 'gro*), actual practices (*dngos gzhi*), and subsequent practices (*rjes*) (Callahan 2019). In addition to pointing-out instructions, the text contains other techniques that are found in subsequent Kagyü manuals, such as sustaining (*bskyang ba*) the meaning of the instruction, enhancement (*bogs 'don pa*) of the practice, and eliminating pitfalls (*gol sgrib*) to various stages among the practices. It also uses analogies and metaphors frequently mentioned in Kagyü manuals, such as water and waves, sugar and its taste, water and ice, a statue made of gold, and a brahman's thread.[307] As mentioned above, Atiśa's *Instructions for Select Disciples* also contains novel features not found in other Indo-Tibetan meditation manuals. *Pointing-Out Instructions* also outlines stages of meditative experience in terms of the gradual approach (*rim gyis pa*), crossing over (*thod rgal ba*), and the simultaneous approach (*cig car ba*), a typology found in Kagyü traditions of mahāmudrā instruction (Broido 1984, 11; Callahan 2019, 175–77).

Pointing-Out Instructions also has several novel features that I have not so far found in other Indo-Tibetan meditation manuals, including the analogy of the skillful cowherd in using mindfulness to maintain insight (57b; II.B.2.d.1). *Instructions for Select Disciples* (see chapter 4) has a similar description. Finally, as discussed in chapter 4, *Pointing-Out Instructions* instructs the practitioner to adopt a bodily posture for meditation that is described in terms of the "five-point posture of Amitābha" rather than the more frequent "seven-point posture of Vairocana." In sum, *Pointing-Out Instructions* significantly contributes to our understanding of the advanced forms of meditation taught in Atiśa's stages of the path system and provides insight into the development and practices of mahāmudrā-related forms of meditation in Indo-Tibetan Buddhist history.

Pointing-Out Instructions in Sets of Five

[Attributed to Atiśa]

I pay homage to the holy spiritual teachers!

The great pointing-out instructions that eliminate the extremes of one's own mind in sets of five has three general points: (I) general preliminaries, (II) actual practices, and (III) their distinctive features.

I. General preliminaries

This has five topics: (A) following a spiritual teacher, (B) guarding moral conduct, (C) accumulation and purification, (D) having contentment [with few desires], and (E) knowing how to ration food.

A. Following a spiritual teacher

In dependence upon a spiritual teacher with all the virtuous qualities, with a wish to give rise to special realization, request special instructions as much as you can with veneration and devotion to a spiritual teacher who is endowed with four characteristics. [**53a**] Namely, [a spiritual teacher is] one who understands the nature of things, does not cling to selfish vested interests, bears the burdens of others' welfare, and subdues the mind with blessings.

First, one who understands the nature of things understands the general and specific characters of things and realizes the meaning of suchness.

One who cuts off clinging to selfish, vested interests does not strive for wealth, food, servants, the eight worldly concerns, and so forth in this life.

One who bears the burdens of others' welfare by means of great compassion pursues others' welfare by enduring the ingratitude of audiences while not being attached to his own happiness.

One who subudes the mind with blessings is able to produce virtuous qualities in the minds of others who have admiration and respect.

Through being supreme in possessing these four characteristics, they attain the title of *precious one* (*rin po che*). They are able to accomplish others' welfare in great measure. Even if they do not possess all these characteristics, if they have realization, they can inspire others to practice meditation.

Those who have authentic veneration and devotion to the spiritual teacher see him as a buddha and listen closely to whatever is taught with confidence.

As the spiritual teacher is the root of all qualities or the principle of prerequisites for producing virtuous qualities, one should make effort in this regard. If one does not have respect and devotion, even though one may have spiritual instructions and blessings, virtuous qualities will not be produced. Although one may have respect and devotion, since virtuous qualities will not be produced without blessings, one must be endowed with respect and devotion as well as blessings.

One will not understand the practices, dispel hindrances, or gain improvement if the special instructions are not complete; one should therefore request complete special instructions.

B. Guarding moral conduct

One must have moral virtue that blocks afflictions and nonvirtuous karma. Without that, one does not give rise to meditation because one is polluted with faults and downfalls; therefore one should not be polluted by faults and downfalls. The *Moon Lamp Sūtra* (*Candrapradīpasūtra*) states, "Quickly attaining the comprehension of awareness when free of mental afflictions: this is the benefit of pure moral conduct."

C. Accumulation and purification

Since the path is not produced in the mental continuum when one has karma, mental afflictions, and knowledge obstructions from beginningless lifetimes, one should recite the hundred-syllable mantra and so forth. If one does not accumulate merit, the path will not arise.

As the *Verses That Summarize the Perfection of Wisdom* state, "As long as one does not complete the roots of virtue, [**53b**] this most excellent emptiness will not be attained."[308] One should therefore accumulate whatever collections can be gathered, offer offerings and so forth, offer maṇḍalas, recite the hundred syllables, and so forth.

D. Having contentment with few desires

When one is not content, one does not give rise to meditation, as the mind is distracted by desires for food, wealth, and so forth. Thus one should meditate on being content with simple food and clothing while reversing the tendency toward desire.

E. Knowing how to ration food

One should rely on agreeable food and eliminate harm in sickness due to food that is connected with sickness in wind-bile and so forth.

II. Actual practices

There are four topics with regard to the actual practices: these are the yogas of (A) serenity, (B) insight, (C) union, and (D) signlessness.

A. Serenity

This first [yoga] has three topics: (1) preliminaries, (2) actual practice, and (3) subsequent practice.

1. Preliminaries

Among them, the first has five subtopics: (a) residing in solitude, (b) restraining the sense faculties, (c) cultivating the awakening mind, (d) meditating on the spiritual teacher, and (e) developing aspiration.

a. Residing in solitude

If one does not relinquish whichever subtle or coarse causal conditions that distract the body, speech, and mind, meditation will not be cultivated. One should demonstrate activities that cause production of those conditions to weaken.

Since it is not beneficial for one not to reside in solitude, then even if one relinquishes activities, one must also reside in solitude. Furthermore, [one should reside in] a place that is without human noise during the day, without the sounds of chatter during the night, not overrun by poisonous nonhumans, and not on a busy road. The place to reside should have previous spiritual attainments, be endowed with a plaintain tree, be free of harm by savages and carnivores, and give rise to joyful experience.

Moreover, since bodily solitude is not beneficial if one is distracted mental afflictions, one should eliminate all subtle and coarse mental afflictions and conceptual thoughts.

b. Restraining the sense faculties

Impediments to meditation are created due to the arising of hatred and attachment from all sorts of conceptual thoughts when objects appear to the eye sense faculties and so forth. Therefore one should make sure to attain conscientious mindfulness that guards the sense doors, not engaging the sense faculties with regard to appearances of the six sense objects.

c. Cultivating the awakening mind

The oaths of the aspiring and engaging [awakening mind] are gathered together, and they cause one's path to transform into the path of the Great Vehicle while not falling into the Lower Vehicle. One should give rise to the supreme awakening mind; it thus becomes a means for attaining [**54a**] buddhahood and achieving extensive benefit for others.

d. Meditating on the spiritual teacher

One shows devotion and respect by meditating on the spiritual teacher as sitting above one's head and giving rise to the perception of him as a buddha. Perception of him as a buddha completes an immense accumulation of merit, gives rise to meditation, and generates respect and veneration toward oneself as a student.

By giving rise to meditation through completing an immense accumulation of merit and earning respect and veneration for oneself as a student, the welfare of others will be achieved and buddhahood will be attained.

e. Developing aspiration

In general, the desire for Dharma is aspiration. Since it is a principal cause, here the fierce aspiration desiring to give rise to meditation is the developing aspiration. Without that, although one may have other prerequisites, meditation will not be developed. Therefore aspiration should be continuously attended to.

2. Actual practice

This has five topics: (a) meditative equipoise, (b) the stages of arising in the mental continuum, (c) pointing out, (d) sustaining the meaning that has been pointed out, and (e) enhancement.

a. Meditative equipoise

First, have a bodily posture with the five qualities of Amitābha—that is, with the legs in a cross-legged sitting posture, hands in meditation gesture, spine straight, eyes directed toward the nose, and chin tucked slightly toward throat. Five methods of settling the mind should be established: (1) deeply relaxed, (2) nonartificial, (3) nonconceptual, (4) discarding conceptual thought, and (5) without effort.

(1) Deeply relaxed: awareness should be left in its own place, the body and mind remaining tranquil, like spinning a brahman's thread without holding it tightly.

(2) Nonartificial: fresh awareness left naturally as it is is like the transparency of calm water, unspoiled by various conceptual thoughts and so forth in meditation.

(3) Nonconceptual: do not evaluate traces of the past, do not welcome the future, and do not grasp the surface of the present awareness in eliminating all subtle and coarse internal and external conceptual thoughts. A stupid person establishes this as being unconscious for whatever [meditative] basis, and the meaning gets lost.

(4) Discarding conceptual thought: when subtle, internal fleeting movements, the robbers that are conceptual thought, arise without conditions, identify and discard them like crumbs of food and establish nonconceptuality.

(5) Effortlessness: establish your own mind at ease, like a person who has completed a deed without expending any effort to accomplish it.

In brief, establish into your own undestanding the five meditation methods as one group.

Then, with regard to the object of observation of mind, do not disrupt the taking of food in the body for the mind. In between, while [**54b**] not engaging with other conceptual thoughts, each time make a dedication for unsurpassable awakening.

[b. The stages of arising in the mental continuum]

Accordingly, the stages of experience arising by meditative equipoise are five: (1) lesser experience, (2) middling, (3) very best, (4) crossing over, and (5) simultaneous.

(1) As to the first among these, by stopping conceptual thought that arises from external objects at the time of meditative equipoise, internal, mental, conceptual thought is recognized, and awareness moves fleetingly, without abiding, like water flowing downhill. Then, having pacified conceptual

thought, the mind remains in nonconceptuality, like a stream of water reaching a pool. Then, sometimes one abides, and sometimes one does not abide.

(2) Regarding middling experience: one produces virtuous qualities, like a reflection in sparkling water. One is unharmed by subtle distractions while in a cognizant, yet nonconceptual, continuous meditative experience.

(3) As to the very best meditative experience: due to uniting luminosity and emptiness (*gsal stong*), the experience continuously occurs by way of mental pliancy and the cognition of the lack of inherent existence in that very luminous experience itself.

(4) As to crossing over: while giving rise to higher and lower meditative experience, at times one does not think "I am meditating" and comes to be free from engaging in cognition. At times, one thinks there can be nothing that exceeds this meditation.

(5) Regarding the simultaneous: there occurs a continuous, undiminishing, produced-from-the-very-beginning experience of the inseparability of luminosity and emptiness, although there exists a little bit of conceptual thought.

[c. Serenity pointing-out instructions]

Directly pointing out has five topics: (1) nonconceptuality, (2) luminous awareness, (3) blissful experience, (4) single-pointed nature, (5) and steadfast recognition.

(1) *Nonconceptuality*: Having ceased the subtle and coarse conceptual thoughts relying on external objects and the subtle and coarse conceptuality arising from the mind within, there is nonconceptuality, like a statue.

(2) *Luminous awareness*: First, one engages with apprehending inner conceptual thought for the luminosity of various and distinct objects. Later on, the self-luminous, objectless, transparent awareness of one's own mind does not grasp self-luminous awareness, which is free from any identification like a reflection in a mirror.

(3) *Blissful experience*: When one is free from all mental afflictions and conceptual thought while having the previous meditative experience, one becomes endowed with the meditative experience of emptiness and luminosity, free from all discomforts of conceptual thought and so forth. This ceases **[55a]** the sensation of indifference to suffering and has self-arisen unconditioned bliss, like a monk generating the meditative absorption of the first concentration (*prathamadhyāna*).

(4) *Single-pointedness* is the nature of meditative stabilization. That, having ceased subtle and coarse external and internal conceptual thought, is mental

stability, undistracted from the state of bliss, clarity, and nonthought, while a person distracted by many indeterminate things is like a parrot.

(5) *Steadfast recognition*: With a peaceful and tamed mind, freed from doubt by having the nature of the previous meditative experiences, one has mastery in concentration, like the power mastered by a king.

d. Sustaining the meaning that has been pointed out

This has five topics: (1) eliminating hindrances, (2) renouncing activities, (3) residing in solitude, (4) engendering energetic diligence, (5) continuous nondistractedness.

(1) First, the hindrances are five: desire and aspiration, harmfulness, excitement and remorse, sleep and torpor, and doubt.

First, *desire and aspiration* are mental distractions through the desire for food, wealth, fame, and so forth for this life.

Harmfulness is the intention to harm through malice and regarding [someone] as an enemy, in nine or ten stages of a hostile attitude (*kun nas mnar sems pa*).

Excitement and remorse is the body, speech, and mind being excited with distraction and being unhappy due to recalling one's previous evil deeds, downfalls, and so forth.

Sleep and torpor is the nature of laziness and delusion, which occurs from not overtly increasing thoughts of virtue.

Doubt is one's attention becoming split due to forgetting the quintessential teaching and so forth and forgetting to maintain the elimination of these five hindrances.

(2) As to renouncing activities: one should eliminate any subtle and coarse bodily, vocal, and mental activities whatsoever that are distracting.

(3) Regarding residing in solitude: one should eliminate floating to objects with one's sense faculties amid large crowds and so forth; eliminate the body being distracted with many activities; eliminate from the mind the multiplicity of conceptual thoughts, such as the afflictions and so forth; and meditate while residing in solitude in a hermitage and so forth.

(4) Energetic diligence is to have mental enthusiasm for meditation and to abide in methods of settling the mind, inseparable from the maintenance of the body.

(5) Continuous nondistractedness is to have a nondistracted mind [**55b**] even during times of nonmeditation and to sustain concentration without forgetting, like the mother of a dying son.

[e. Enhancement of serenity]

Enhancement (*bogs 'don pa*) has five topics: (1) clearing away the defects of saṃsāra, (2) renouncing the world, (3) confessing faults and downfalls, (4) accumulating merit, and (5) remaining in solitude while giving up activities.

(1) *Clearing away the the defects of saṃsāra*: Since rebirth in whichever of the six realms of rebirth is without bliss and happiness, one should have revulsion to saṃsāra, like seeing vomited food.

(2) *Renouncing the world*: When one thinks about food, clothing, talk, and so forth—the eight worldly concerns and so forth, the conceptualization of this life—since one will commit evil deeds as mental afflictions proliferate, one should eliminate any conceptualization for this life that arises.

(3) *Confessing faults and downfalls*: One should confess through means of purification and maturation, because there are many obscurations and evil deeds from beginningless lifetimes.

(4) *Accumulating merit*: One offers whatever one has to the spiritual teacher—precious treasures. One should make effort with one's own body in activities for the spiritual teacher. One should gather whatever suitable accumulations, such as [the offering of] maṇḍalas and so forth, like the water and manure of a farmer.

(5) *Renouncing activities*: One should meditate while remaining idle, like a wild animal; eliminate distracting conditions of body, speech, and mind; and restrain the sense faculties. These [practices] will bring progress.

[3. Subsequent practices of serenity]

Subsequent practices has five topics: (a) eliminating pitfalls, (b) eliminating mental afflictions, (c) stopping sensory enjoyments, (d) leveling out the eight worldly concerns, and (e) making the body and mind serviceable.

[a. Eliminating pitfalls to serenity]

The first, pitfalls, has five topics. Since one may (1) fall into the formless realm when attached to nonconceptuality, (2) fall into the form realm when attached to clarity, (3) fall into the desire realm when attached to bliss, (4) fall into cessation when attached to one-pointedness, or (5) fall into cyclic existence when attached to an ascertaining consciousness, one should not become attached to the taste of concentration.

[b. Eliminating mental afflictions in serenity]

Eliminating mental afflictions has five topics: (1) attachment, (2) aversion, (3) delusion, (4) pride, and (5) jealousy.

(1) One should eliminate *attachment* to the mind within and external wealth.

(2) *Aversion* is a malicious attitude that regards others as enemies through nine stages of vindictiveness (*mnar sems*).

(3) *Delusion* is behavior that becomes a contradictory condition for concentration, since one does not understand what to do and what not to do.

(4) *Pride* is an inflated attitude that is not respectful toward others, [**56a**] that scorns others, and so forth.

(5) *Jealousy* is to become tattered and have overtly unhappy thoughts regarding the gain and so forth of another.

Accordingly, since pitfalls and afflictions obscure concentration, these should be identified and eliminated.

[c. Stopping sensory enjoyments]

Stopping sensory enjoyments has five topics: (1) leaving the eye as it is in having neither attachment nor aversion for forms. (2) Likewise, neither attachment nor aversion should occur for the ears in regard to sound, (3) the nose in regard to smell, (4) the tongue in regard to taste, and (5) the body in regard to touch.

[d. Leveling out the eight worldly concerns]

Leveling out the eight worldly concerns has five topics: (1) being unattached to the four desirables, (2) not being hostile to the four undesirables, (3) equalizing these factors, (4) the reason for leveling out these factors, and (5) the benefits of equanimity.

(1) With regard to the first, the desirables—gain, fame, praise, and pleasure in this life—one should not be attached to these four when they occur.

(2) The undesirables are loss, disgrace, slander, and suffering in this life.

(3) As to equalizing these factors: if the four desirables should arise of their own accord without one trying to achieve them, one should be without attachment and clinging; if the four undesirables should arise, one should not become cowardly, hateful, or have an unpleasant mind [toward them].

(4) What is the reason for leveling out these factors? They should be understood as not truly existing.

(5) What are the benefits of equanimity? One will achieve virtue by being disinterested in these for this life, through not giving rise to attachment and hatred and suppressing other mental afflictions.

[e. Making the body and mind serviceable]

Making the body and mind serviceable has five topics: (1) striving for virtue, (2) gaining mastery, (3) becoming steadfast, (4) generating happiness, and (5) producing virtuous qualities.

(1) *Striving* is overtly exerting the mind in concentration and meditating without abandoning meditative stabilization.

(2) *Mastery* is steadily abiding in concentration, [both] with a focal object and without a focal object.

(3) *Steadfastness* is remaining in steadfast concentration through circumstances, subtle distractions, and subtle errors and obscurations.

(4) *Happiness* comes from harnessing the mind and body and having clarity of understanding in the mind, being competent with pleasurable sense-objects without the discomforts of mental afflictions and discursivity.

(5) *Producing virtuous qualities* provides a basis for giving rise to supersensory knowledge, miraculous emanations, and the realization of the true nature of reality.

B. Insight

This has three topics: (1) preliminaries, [**56b**] (2) actual practice, and (3) subsequent practice.

[1. Preliminaries for insight]

The first, preliminaries, has five topics: (a) renouncing a worldly mind, (b) residing in solitude, (c) engendering aspiration, [(d) generating the awakening mind,][309] and (e) meditation on the spiritual teacher.

[a. Renouncing a worldly mind]

Renouncing a worldly mind consists of the cultivation and avoidance of the eight worldly concerns and eliminating the motivation to accomplish desires and aspirations for food, clothing, and so forth.

[b. Residing in solitude]

Residing in solitude is remaining isolated in a hermitage and so forth while eliminating periods of abiding with bodily and mental distraction, eliminating busyness with many activities, and eliminating many afflictions and fabricated discursive thought.

c. Engendering aspiration

Engendering aspiration is to single-pointedly, sincerely aspire for realization to emerge.

[d. Giving rise to the awakening mind]

Giving rise to the awakening mind is condensed as the promise of aspiration and application.

[e. Meditation on the spiritual teacher]

Meditation on the spiritual teacher is to meditate on the spiritual teacher as sitting at the crown of one's head and, with devotion and veneration, see him as a buddha.

[2. Actual practice of insight]

The actual practice has five topics: (a) the method of stabilization, (b) stages of producing [insight] in the mental continuum, (c) directly pointing out, (d) sustaining the meaning of that, and (e) enhancement.

[a. The method of stabilizing insight]

The method of stabilization has five topics: (1) remaining in a state of natural freshness, (2) remaining without reference points, (3) remaining as empty, (4) remaining without any support, and (5) remaining traceless.

(1) Remaining in a state of natural freshness is to remain in bodily serenity while having the mind relaxed in an undistorted, unartificial way without being subject to the noxious influences of reference points and views.

(2) Remaining without reference points is to refrain from focusing whatsoever on tenets of views, meditation, and so forth, or on mental observations of the mind, while abiding without a fixed object.

(3) Remaining in emptiness, as discussed above, is since nothing whatsoever is established, one should remain like empty space, in a pure clarity in not meditating on anything during this state.

(4) Remaining without any support is to clearly remain, without any support whatsoever, as a source of awareness, like a bird flying unsupported in the sky.

(5) Remaining traceless, at the time of remaining posited above, is to remain in luminosity and emptiness with unobstructed awareness and without ephemeral fleeting movements, like soothing coolness.

In brief, the five methods of stabilization are to be brought together as one. One should have one's own mind settle in limpid clarity, free from elaborations.

[b. Stages of producing insight in the mental continuum]

The awareness that arises has five topics: (1) ordinary, (2) middling, (3) superior, [57a] (4) crossing over, and (5) simultaneous.

(1) In *ordinary* [awareness], although there is the mere realization of one's own mind as emptiness at the time of giving rise to ordinary special insight, the awareness of conceptuality and experience is not realized as empty. Emptiness, furthermore, is at times clear and at other times not clear. Although the profound and extensive Dharma is seen, it is not understood. At that time, one should be inseparable from the spiritual teacher. Through nourishing this [awareness], realization will become middling.

(2) When a *middling* realization arises, all mind and conceptual thought is realized as emptiness. The thought of accepting and rejecting cyclic existence and nirvāṇa does not exist. Meditation becomes elevated or base; sometimes one doubts even the special instructions and the spiritual teacher. At times, having realized emptiness, one resides in that state. Through nourishment, that [awareness] will become superior.

(3) When *superior* [awareness] arises, by realizing all mind, conceptual thought, and experiential awareness as empty, causes for transmigration into the hell realms become nonexistent. Even the cause for attaining buddhahood does not exist. This action of a buddha's Dharma body (*sangs rgyas chos sku*) is the source (*kha*). Even having the actual spiritual instructions and meaning of the Dharma, one thinks "this meditation of mine has not been reached."

Thinking that devotion to the spiritual teacher alone is sufficient, with little attachment to one's own meditation and special instruction, all previous Dharma trainings become an outer husk of chaff. Even when asleep, one is not separated from realization.

(4) When *crossing over*, meditation does not become elevated or base. Since uncertainty arises, realization is unstable.

(5) Having produced the ultimate, supreme meditation from the very outset, by abiding continuously and steadily, one sustains *simultaneous* [awareness] indefinitely.

[c. Directly pointing out the instructions for insight]

Directly pointing out has five topics: (1) the mind itself is directly pointed out as empty, (2) conceptual thought is directly pointed out as empty, (3) experiential awareness is directly pointed out as empty, (4) appearing objects are directly pointed out as empty, and (5) everything is directly pointed out as free from elaborations.

(1) First, [the mind itself is directly pointed out as empty]: No nature of the mind whatsoever is established. Even the buddhas of the three times [of past, present, and future] have not seen, do not see, and will not see [the mind], because the mind does not exist. This emptiness, moreover, is not an emptiness that is nihilistic, destructive, purified in meditation, and so forth. It resides as empty by way of its own nature, and in this regard, since any phenomenal marks of color, shape, and so forth are not established, it is like the sky free from clouds.

(2) Conceptual thought is [directly pointed out as] empty: Although the mind itself accordingly abides as empty, if one thinks that conceptual thought does not cease, [**57b**] one should see whether there is any nature to any given fleeting movement of conceptual thought. In so doing, that very fleeting movement is recognized as empty, so it is not necessary to cease conceptual thought. As one uproots the fundamental basis of the mind, the haziness disappears without a trace. Since the self-arisen nature subsides of its own accord, like clouds in the sky, the [mind's] fleeting movements are not great faults, and by understanding the emptiness of fleeting movements at all times, one remains in self-cognizant wakefulness (*ye shes rang gsal*).

(3) Experiential awareness is [directly pointed out as] empty: By looking directly into the awareness that is the experiencer of the previous realization, as nothing is identified with respect to that since the experience is empty, the inseparability of awareness and emptiness is realized.

(4) The emptiness of apparent objects [is directly pointed out]: All appearances of external objects of the six sense faculties lack inherent existence. To illustrate, it is like the happiness and suffering that appear in a dream and so forth: they appear unhindered; they lack inherent existence. One should understand all apparent objects as like an illusion.

(5) [Directly pointing out that everything is] free from elaborations: Accordingly, one realizes everything as emptiness, and the lucidity of awareness and appearance is unhindered. Since the lucidity also does not have a nature, it is free from all elaborations of extremes such as permanence, nihilism, and so forth.

In this way, one should directly point out in stages.

[d. Sustaining the meaning that has been pointed out]

Sustaining the meaning that has been pointed out has five topics: (1) sustaining unwavering mindfulness, (2) sustaining against oppressive conditions by antidotes, (3) sustaining change without leaving a trace, (4) sustaining a serene awareness, and (5) sustaining appearances as one's allies.

(1) First, *sustaining unwavering mindfulness*: While being inseparable from the experience of serenity and the manner of preparing the body during disturbed meditation, one should have mentally relaxed awareness, like a skillful cowherd; one should maintain correct mindfulness and sustain without distraction at all times.

(2) *Sustaining against oppressive conditions by antidotes*: When conditions such as mental afflictions, conceptual thought, or suffering and so forth occur during disturbed meditation, one should clear them away, contemplating with the mind that all that occurs lacks inherent existence. Or, in another way, by directly looking into whichever conditions occur, like discovering a thief, they naturally dissipate and will be realized as emptiness. In another way, one should eliminate with individual antidotes through individually discriminating wisdom.

(3) *Sustaining change without leaving a trace*: With middling realization, one should understand all conceptual thought that arises as leaving no trace—like a stick stirring water or a bird flying through the sky. Like an unafflicted friend of wisdom, after the [**58a**] conceptual thought is discarded, they naturally vanish just as they arise.

(4) *Sustaining a serene awareness*: Relax the body and mind, and do not grasp the mind through elevated realization. By remaining in the state of conceptualizing while alternating between dwelling, the path of activity, and focal points, [concepts] will naturally dissipate, like a bird flying up from a boat, and will be unnecessary to apprehend with mindfulness. In general, although unncecessary, by giving rise to virtuous qualities when apprehending, one apprehends [concepts] with mindfulness.

(5) *Sustaining appearances as one's allies*: Since all conceptuality that appears through discursive thought is understood as unhindered emptiness and established as naturally free, like a mantra consecrating poison [as medi-

cine] or snow falling on a hot spring, all conceptualized appearances should be understood as allies of wisdom, and the realization [should be] increasingly sustained.

[e. Enhancement of insight]

Enhancement has five topics: (1) accumulating and purifying, (2) eliminating clinging, (3) renouncing a worldly mind, (4) eliminating clinging to a self, (5) having devotion and veneration toward a spiritual teacher.

(1) *Accumulating and purifying*: Although one has amassed evil deeds and downfalls across innumerable lifetimes, one should confess them by means of the four opponent powers, like clearing obstacles from a farmer's irrigation ditch. Having given away as charity one's material wealth and so forth, one should make effort until achieving the meditation of concentration, like the water and manure of a farmer.

(2) *Eliminating clinging*: One should eliminate everything that gives rise to attachment and hatred through clinging—such as friends, enemies, and physical resources that are apprehended as "I" and "mine"—as well as appearances of happiness, suffering, and so forth that are apprehended as real.

(3) *Renouncing a worldly mind*: One should abandon rejection and achievement related to the eight worldly concerns; desires and aspirations for food, clothing, and pleasant conversation; and all concepts of achievement for this life, and one should pursue the happiness of the future.

(4) *Eliminating clinging to a self*: Since all the suffering of cyclic existence arises when there is clinging to a self in the continuum of the five aggregates, one should relinquish clinging to the pride of a self and offer one's body to demons, forcefully eliminating self-cherishing, while offering service to the spiritual teacher.

(5) *Having devotion and veneration toward a spiritual teacher*: In relation to the enhancement, as before, firmly make requests and offer material resources, directly seeing [the spiritual teacher] as the Dharma body. [**58b**] Those requests and offerings should be gradually fulfilled and perfected; by meditating as before, it will bring progress.

[3. Subsequent practice]

Subsequent practices after insight meditation has five topics: (a) the means of preventing degenerated actual practice, (b) special instructions on protecting with mindfulness, (c) eliminating pitfalls, (d) sustaining appearances as unreal, and (e) unerring signs of progress on the path.

[a. The means of preventing degenerated actual practice of insight]

Among these, first, the means of preventing degenerated actual practice has five topics: (1) eliminating adverse circumstances, (2) studying the holy Dharma, (3) accumulating and purifying, (4) eliminating evil deeds and downfalls, and (5) remaining in solitude.

(1) *Eliminating adverse circumstances*: One should avoid places and situations that give rise to afflictions—cities, villages, and so forth; meetings with friends that fuel one's afflictions; quarreling and fighting; places where many noisy people are gathered; the good realms of beings who are not relatives; and so forth.

(2) *Studying the holy Dharma*: One should listen to the profound and extensive special instructions; investigate and consider various sūtras, tantras, treatises, and pith instructions; and discuss the vast and extensive Dharma and reflect upon its meaning.

(3) Accumulating and purifying: One should make efforts in virtuous actions of body, speech, and mind by reciting the hundred syllables, offering maṇḍalas, practicing the perfections of giving and so forth, and listening to Dharma teachings.

(4) *Eliminating evil deeds and downfalls*: One should purely protect vows that have been taken, eliminate all subtle and coarse natural nonvirtues, and refrain from evil deeds and mental afflictions.

(5) *Remaining in solitude*: One should eliminate physical activity in cities, the countryside, and so forth. One should remain in a hermitage and so forth, which averts many afflictive thoughts and so forth.

[b. Special instructions on protecting insight with mindfulness]

Protecting with mindfulness has five topics: (1) essential points concerning physical posture, (2) restraining the faculties, (3) nourishing serenity, (4) protecting realization with mindfulness, and (5) engendering energetic diligence.

(1) *Essential points concerning physical posture*: By remaining in a physical [meditation] posture even when residing while not meditating, one produces virtuous qualities of meditative stabilization and so forth.

(2) *Restraining the faculties*: At all times, by not pursuing objects while not engaging objects that appear to the eye and so forth, one does not register identifying qualities.

(3) *Nourishing serenity*: One establishes the mind in the nonconceptual state during the time of serenity.

(4) *Protecting realization with mindfulness*: The realization of emptiness in all behaviors in the activities of walking around, traveling, lying down, sitting, and so forth [**59a**] one protects with mindfulness.

(5) *Engendering energetic diligence*: One arouses enthusiasm for meditation, bringing about physical and mental effort and striving in the antidotes to the laziness of lacking enthusiasm for meditation.

[c. Eliminating pitfalls during susequent practice after insight]

Eliminating pitfalls and obstructions has[310] five topics: (1) getting distracted in mere darkness, (2) deviating from the fundamental nature, (3) getting distracted through sealing things and experiences, (4) getting distracted in antidotes, (5) getting distracted along the path.

(1) *Getting distracted in mere darkness*: Through realizing both virtue and evil deeds as empty, up to and including middling realization, you get carried away in nihilistic views in which elimination and achievement are not accomplished.

(2) *Deviating from the fundamental nature*: You think it is not necessary to cultivate emptiness, since all things are emptiness, and you think it is not necessary to make use of antidotes, since virtue and evil deeds are also empty.

(3) *Getting distracted through sealing things and experiences*: You cultivate a mind-made emptiness and do not observe afterward the practice of virtue.

(4) *Getting distracted in antidotes*: By cultivating a mind-made emptiness that annihilates and purifies, you cultivate the thought that the object to be abandoned is emptiness.

(5) *Getting distracted along the path*: By means of cultivating meditation on nonarising, clear light, the Dharma body, nonobservation, the Great Middle Way, and so forth, *mind-made* cultivation quickly attains buddhahood.

[d. Sustaining appearances as unreal]

Sustaining appearances as unreal has five topics: (1) sustaining conceptual thought as unreal, (2) sustaining mental afflictions as unreal, (3) sustaining pleasure and suffering as unreal, (4) sustaining whatever appears as unreal, and (5) sustaining experience and realization as unreal.

(1) *Sustaining conceptual thought as unreal*: All desire, attachment, and so forth that may arise—whatever arises—is not let go in itself.[311*] One should refrain from reanimating previous attachment to happiness and suffering for any entity that arises by recognizing conceptual thoughts as unreal fleeting movements of the mind.

(2) *Sustaining mental afflictions as unreal:** By seeing [unreal fleeting movements of the mind] itself, one should cognize [afflictions] as rootless or otherwise skillfully dissolve them with antidotes.

(3) *Sustaining pleasure and suffering as unreal*: One should not give rise to attachment or aversion and so forth for any pleasurable conditions—such as the riches and honor of food, wealth, and so forth, power, health, and so forth—or for any unpleasurable conditions that are the opposite of those, as one should consider that happiness and suffering are to be understood as unreal.

(4) *Sustaining whatever appears as unreal*: All conditions of pleasure and suffering that appear through the six objects of the eye and so forth should be understood as unreal appearances, like an illusory dream, and one should not be ensnared by afflictions and so forth.

(5) *Sustaining experience and realization as unreal*: One should not be attached to [**59b**] the taste of concentration, the experiences of bliss, clarity, nonconceptuality, and so forth, and one should eliminate attachment (*mngon par zhen pa*; *abhiniveśa*) to the realization of emptiness.

[e. Unerring signs of progress on the path]

Signs of progress on the path has five topics: (1) suppressing the mental afflictions, (2) not attaching to sense pleasures, (3) leveling out the eight worldly concerns, (4) having conviction in cause and effect, (5) generating compassion for sentient beings.

(1) *Suppressing the mental afflictions*: As one understands all things as unreal, all conventional elaborations are seen as the chaff of an outer husk, and the mental afflictions become few.

(2) *Not attaching to sense pleasures*: One is unattached and without fixation by the five sense faculties, the eye and so forth, on the five sense objects, form and so forth.

(3) *Leveling out the eight wordly concerns*: Free of attachment, one does not fixate on accomplishing the four harmonious factors (gain, fame, praise, and pleasure of this life). Free of discouragement, one does not focus on discarding the four nonharmonious factors (loss, disgrace, slander, and suffering of this life).

(4) *Having conviction in cause and effect*: Through understanding that virtuous and nonvirtuous actions arise as pleasurable and painful effects, one eliminates and achieves by not discounting (*khyad du mi gsod pa*; *aparibhavanatā*) the subtlest causes and effects.

(5) *Generating compassion for sentient beings*: Accordingly, by extension, one generates compassion for sentient beings who lack realization, and one engages with effort to secure the welfare of others.

[C. Union]

The development of union has three topics: (1) preliminaries, (2) actual practice, and (3) subsequent practices.

[1. Preliminary practices for union]

There are five topics with regard to the preliminaries: (a) generating the mind for supreme awakening, (b) accumulating and purifying, (c) nurturing insight, (d) generating aspiration that desires unity, and (e) practicing devotion and veneration for the spiritual teacher. These are similar to the previous [preliminaries].

[2. The actual practice of union]

The actual practice has five topics: (a) the method of stabilization, (b) the stages of arising, (c) directly pointing out, (d) sustaining the meaning, and (e) enhancement.

[a. The method of stabilizing union]

First, there are five topics with regard to methods of stabilization: (1) leave it as it naturally is, (2) remain in the free relaxation of the six aggregates (*tshogs drug*) of consciousness, (3) remain indivisibly, (4) remain without attachment or aversion, and (5) remain free from extremes.

(1) *Leave it as it naturally is*: One remains free from suppressing or straining, like the activity of a small child who is free from any noxious influences of views, meditation, or benchmarks.

(2) *Remain in free relaxation of the six aggregates*: One does not bind the six sense faculties. Like the sun free from clouds, one leaves whatever objects are perceived as they are and does not keep apprehending phenomenal marks in objects.

(3) [60a] *Remain indivisibly*: Whatever appears remains as the indivisibility of appearance and emptiness, like water and waves, having a single taste with emptiness.

(4) *Remain without attachment or aversion*: Appearances are unhindered and emptiness is unestablished. As appearances and emptiness are undifferentiated, like sugar and its taste, one remains without accepting and rejecting.

(5) *Remain free from extremes*: One does not abide in any extremes of appearances, emptiness, and so forth, remaining like a skillful listener.

In brief, the five methods of stabilization should be construed as one group, the multiplicity remaining as one taste.

[b. The stages of generating union]

The stages of generating has five topics: (1) lesser, (2) middling, (3) superior, (4) crossing over, and (5) simultaneous.

(1) *Lesser* union: Having realized one's own body, mind, and appearances as indivisible, although one enters into meditation, sometimes [union] is not clear. Sometimes one has ascertainment; sometimes appearances are real or solid. One does not refrain from karma and its effects. One does not forsake envy. Sometimes one thinks, "This is the ultimate." Sometimes unwholesome behaviors cannot be hidden. Sometimes meditation happens to reside in union.

(2) *Middling*: Having integrated body, mind, and appearances into one, the thought occurs that there is nothing other than this meditation, where one has dissolved into the state in which whatever appears is the mind. Whether or not sentient beings and one's own spiritual teacher are suitable, one thinks there is no need for compassion, devotion, or veneration. Having thoughts that karmic cause and effect, and even the causes of abandonment and achievement, do not exist—these are strayings on the path that are hard to avoid. Sometimes, however, one understands and does not go astray on the path.

(3) *Superior*: When this [stage] arises, appearances, mind, and ultimate reality are realized as one, as one has cognized the equality of saṃsāra and nirvāṇa. One pacifies based on superior roots of virtue, and one's experience and realization can no longer diminish.

(4) *Crossing over*: One has high or low experiences, up to and including middling [realization], that are not reliable.

(5) *Simultaneous*: One never separates from generating the superior realization from the very beginning.

[c. Directly pointing out the instructions for union]

Directly pointing out has five topics: (i) the basis, the union of the ground; (ii) appearances, the union of the path; (iii) achievement, together with the result; (iv) realization, along with experience; and (v) demonstrating the condensed meaning.

[i. The basis, the union of the ground]

The actual basis has five topics: (1) the inherent nature that is emptiness, (2) the essential nature that is clarity, (3) the characteristic [60b] that is indivisibility, (4) the unchanging quality, and (5) the unobstructed activity.

(1) *The inherent nature*: It primordially abides as emptiness and abiding as emptiness from the beginning. It is not destroyed, suppressed, purified, or developed, and so forth, like the purity of space.

(2) *The essential nature lucidly remains*: It is the unobstructed, natural radiance of emptiness, which is not an object of the sensory faculties, like the sun appearing in the sky.

(3) *The characteristic of the mind remains as indivisible*: Since clarity is the essential nature of emptiness and emptiness is the inherent nature of clarity, remain in indivisible clarity and emptiness like the moon reflected in water.

(4) *The unchanging quality*: Since saṃsāra and nirvāṇa do not go beyond indivisibility, to whatever extent saṃsāra and nirvāṇa unchangingly remain with the mind, they are included together with the characteristic.

(5) *The unobstructed awakened activity*: The essential nature of that indivisibility remains the nonattached, unobstructed, soothing coolness of self-arising awareness. It is nonconceptual, objectless, and together with the luminous essential nature.

[ii. Appearances, the union of the path]

There are five topics with regard to union of the path: (1) inherent nature, (2) essential nature, (3) characteristic, (4) quality, and (5) activity.

(1) The *inherent nature*: Ever-present emptiness, everything in the way that it appears, is a spontaneous manifestation. In this way, like sesame oil in sesame seeds, all that appears, even ignorance, is pervaded by emptiness.

(2) There are four topics with regard to the luminous *essential nature*: karmic appearance, delusive appearance, meditative appearance, and personal experience. The first, *karmic appearance*, is all appearances of happiness and suffering among the six realms of rebirth. Moreover, [the appearances] are not established as external objects; like the appearances in a dream, the results of each individual virtuous and nonvirtuous action merely appear, like illusions. *Delusive appearance* is the arisal of attachment and hatred due to grasping at an external object through not understanding one's own perception as empty, like seeing a rope as a snake. *Meditative experience* is like smoke, a mirage, fireflies, drops of various colors, and pure space.[312] In *personal experience*, accordingly,

all appearances are the appearances of one's own mind, like the example of a reflection.

(3) The *characteristic*, indivisibility: One should understand that all appearances of karmic appearances and so forth are integrated with emptiness, like water and ice.

(4) The *quality*, unchangibility: Just what appears is unchangeably indivisible from one's own mind, like a statue made of gold. [**61a**]

(5) The *activity* is unobstructed: The manifestation of a virtuous or nonvirtuous mind arises as happy and painful results, like a reflection in a mirror or an echo.

[iii. Achievement, together with the result]

There are five topics regarding the result: (1) inherent nature, (2) essential nature, (3) characteristic, (4) quality, and (5) activity.

(1) *Inherent nature*: Since the realm of reality is primordially pure and free from all subtle and coarse adventitious stains, actualized emptiness is like space free from clouds.

(2) *Essential nature*: The very embodiment of the awakening mind, the appearances of merit and wisdom, appearances of the body, wisdom, celestial mansions, and so forth, and the appearances of correct exalted wisdom are like the moon reflected in water.

(3) The *characteristic*: The wisdom of knowing things as they are and the knowledge that perceives all possibly existing things are indivisibly mixed with emptiness, like a rainbow.

(4) The *quality*: The powers, fearlessnesses, minor and major marks, and other qualities are indivisible from emptiness.

(5) The *activity*: Pacifying, increasing, magnetizing, subjugating, and so forth produce[313] benefit that tames beings according to their needs.

[iv. Realization, along with experience]

Realization has five topics: (1) indivisible from experience, (2) indivisible from realization, (3) indivisible from appearance, (4) indivisible from cause and effect, and (5) realization indivisible from skillful means and wisdom.

(1) [*Indivisible from*] *experience*: Through realizing bliss, clarity, nonconceptual experience, and all appearances of elevated or base experience as mixed with emptiness, there is the unity of experience and realization.

(2) *Indivisible from realization*: By realizing all subtle and coarse conceptual thoughts of attachment and aversion, which apprehend the dualism of

outer object and inner subject as empty, there will be unity of emptiness and realization.

(3) *Indivisible from appearance*: Through realizing whatever is experienced of the unceasing appearances of objects and mind as emptiness, there is unity of appearance and emptiness.

(4) *Indivisible from cause and effect*: Even while realizing all things as emptiness, one abandons evil deeds and accomplishes virtue through the inevitable relation between karma and its results as merely conventional. This is realizing their indivisibility from emptiness.

(5) *Realization indivisible from skillful means and wisdom*: Although any perceiver and object, any outer and inner things, are not established, one does not abandon the means—great compassion—and the awakening mind. That is the indivisible unity of means and wisdom.

[v. Demonstrating the condensed meaning]

Demonstrating the condensed meaning has five topics: (1) spontaneously present, (2) unconditioned, (3) free from elaborations, [**61b**] (4) neither arising nor ceasing, and (5) free from thoughts and words.

(1) *Spontaneously present*: It is unnecessary to practice any effort or exertion, as it is primordially established as wisdom.

(2) *Unconditioned*: All causes, conditions, and so forth from one's own mind are established from the very beginning as unproduced.

(3) *Free from elaborations*: The abode that is one's own mind is free from all extremes of permanency, annihilation, and so forth.

(4) *Neither arising nor ceasing*: All phenomenal marks of shape, color, concepts, and so forth are unarisen, and all of those are unceasing.

(5) *Free from thoughts and words*: One's own mind, accordingly—the actuality of thinking with the mind of existence and nonexistence, eternalism and nihilism, and so forth—does not exist. Also none of these exist as expressed.

[d. Sustaining the meaning]

Sustaining the meaning of these has five topics: (1) sustaining whatever appears as empty, (2) sustaining whatever appears as unreal, (3) understanding whatever appears as one's own mind, (4) taking appearances and concepts as allies, and (5) sustaining undistracted mindfulness.

(1) The first, [*sustaining whatever appears as empty*]: One arrives naturally at unity by primarily meditating on emptiness while recalling the conceptual idea of insight, like the additional effect conveyed by boasting.

(2) [*Sustaining whatever appears as*] *unreal*: Since any real entity of mental and physical appearances does not exist, any conditions of attachment, aversion, and so forth that arise are also unreal. Recognizing them as being like an illusion should be sustained.

(3) *Understanding whatever appears as one's own mind*: All entities of appearing objects and so forth are not external objects but are objects of one's own mind. For example, since they are like a reflection, appearances and mind (*snang sems*) are mixed with the conceptuality of attachment, aversion, and so forth. They should be sustained in the condition of nonduality.

(4) *Taking appearances and concepts as allies*: All appearances and concepts of happiness, pain, and so forth are recognized as false appearances. Recognizing them as allies of emptiness, the concepts of attachment and aversion should be recognized as naturally evanescent and unproduced, and understood like [snow] falling into a hot spring.

(5) [*Sustaining*] *undistracted mindfulness*: All previous experience and realization should be held and sustained with mindfulness. Integrate the practice in the morning and evening. Integrating in the daytime, integrating at night, one upholds it even when that is unnecessary, without distraction, like carrying a bowl of oil on a slippery platform.

[e. Enhancement of union]

[**62a**] Enhancement has five topics: (1) relinquishing attachment to one's body and wealth, (2) relinquishing self-grasping, (3) cutting the ropes of pride, (4) alternating residing in a friendly place, and (5) giving rise to devotion and veneration to the spiritual teacher.

(1) *Relinquishing one's body and wealth*: Offer whatever you can of the body and wealth to the spiritual teacher. Make offerings to the Three Jewels. If one has wealth, property, and offerings, one should become destitute. One should eliminate attachment.

(2) *Relinquishing self-grasping*: One should sacrifice one's body to others in the presence of *yakṣas* and relinquish grasping one's five aggregates as a self. What is the use of anything unless all subtle and coarse conceptual thought is undistracted from the state of selflessness, motivated by the awakening mind?

(3) *Cutting the ropes of pride*: One should cut the ropes of pride with regard to all coarse conceptual thoughts of attachment, aversion, and so on; the abandonment and development of happiness or suffering; attachment to the eight worldly concerns; grasping at experience and realization; and all subtle and coarse conceptual thoughts that surface on the path to immortality.

(4) *Alternation of residence*: At times, meditate amid a gathering of peo-

ple. At times, sit on the ground with unharmonious circumstances and cut off mental afflictions that arise from that. At times, sit on the ground and cut off afflictions of fierce gods and demons. At times, reside in solitude in a hermitage and so forth. At times, remain in a fixed posture. At times meditate while walking about, or lying down. Reside in [a variety of] places like this while abiding on the path of conduct. At times, see the increase of experience and realization through engagement, and [at other times] meditate to increase [experience and realization].

(5) *Giving rise to devotion and veneration to the spiritual teacher*: View the spiritual teacher as the embodiment of the three bodies of a buddha and offer whatever wealth and resources that you are able. Energetically offer maṇḍalas.

[3. Subsequent practices of union]

Subsequent practice has five topics: (a) the methods keeping the actual practice undiminished, (b) eliminating fundamental pitfalls and obstacles, (c) continually sustaining, (d) signs of progress on the path, and (e) beneficial qualities.

[a. The methods keeping the actual practice of union undiminished]

The first has five topics: (1) eliminating major transgressions and downfalls, (2) gathering the accumulations, (3) meditating on everything as unreal, (4) taking objects and circumstances as allies, (5) unceasing devotion and veneration for the spiritual teacher.

(1) *Eliminating major transgressions and downfalls*: All the basest downfalls, such as having contempt for the embodiment of the spiritual teacher and so forth; the greatest transgressions, such as the heinous acts entailing [**62b**] immediate retribution; and the acts of abandoning the holy Dharma and so forth should be eliminated.

(2) *Gathering the accumulations*: One offers whatever wealth one can afford to the spiritual teacher, offers maṇḍalas, shares all wholesome roots of virtue and wealth with sentient beings, and dedicated this all to unsurpassed awakening.

(3) *Meditating on everything as unreal*: One recognizes all that appears as unreal, like an illusion, and eliminates attachment and aversion.

(4) *Taking objects and circumstances as allies*: Through practicing in reliance upon the six objects of the sense faculties and in reliance upon all conceptual thoughts of joy and sorrow, goodness and badness, one takes [objects and circumstances] as allies of meditation.

(5) *Unceasing devotion and veneration for the spiritual teacher*: One establishes continuous devotion and veneration [to the spiritual teacher] at all times.

[b. Eliminating fundamental pitfalls and obstacles of union]

[Eliminating] fundamental pitfalls and obstacles has five topics: (1) not having compassion, (2) not having devotion and veneration, (3) not eliminating evil deeds, (4) not performing virtuous deeds, and (5) deviating in term of the fundamental nature.

(1) *Not having compassion*: One thinks that since external sentient beings are not established and there is only one's own mind when appearances and mind become a unity, there is no external object of compassion, and one becomes compassionless.

(2) *Not having devotion and veneration*: One comes to have no devotion or veneration by thinking that an external object of devotion and veneration is not established since, although there [seems to be] a spiritual teacher, there is [actually] only oneself.

(3) *Not eliminating evil deeds*: One thinks that since the cause to eliminate does not exist since evil deeds are not externally established and only one's own mind exists, evil deeds are not to be eliminated.

(4) *Not performing virtuous deeds*: One thinks that since the cause to be achieved does not exist due to virtue remaining as one's own mind, virtuous deeds are not to be performed.

(5) *Deviating in terms of the fundamental nature*: Having relied on the fundamental nature as one understands it, without the special oral instructions, with mere equanimity that is not embraced by insight and means, one deviates into the ordinary and does not perform virtuous actions such as explaining, listening, and so forth. These are demonic forces.

These [demonic forces] are also possible for both the individuals of lesser and middling capacity. These do not occur for those who heard previous teachings and have the special instructions. One should eliminate [these demonic forces] with effort, since the iron hook of Māra will occur if one has not heard previous teachings and special instructions.

[c. Continually sustaining union]

Continually sustaining has five topics: (1) apprehending with correct mindfulness, (2) [**63a**] remaining in solitude, (3) meditative stabilization, (4) integrating mind and appearances, and (5) sustaining things as unreal.

(1) First, even if apprehension with mindfulness is not necessary, one should *apprehend with correct mindfulness.*

(2) *Remaining in solitude*: Even if having no distraction at all, one should reside in solitude.

(3) *Meditative stabilization*: One should practice meditative stabilization even if meditation and subsequent meditation do not exist for one as separate.

(4) *Integrating mind and appearances*: While alternating abodes, allies, paths of activity, focal objects, and so forth, since all mental afflictions and conceptuality are the emptiness of one's own mind, then attachment, aversion, and apparent objects should not be apprehended independently; the multiplicity should instead be understood as one taste.

(5) *Sustaining things as unreal*: All manifestations that appear everywhere should be sustained as unreal, like an illusory dream, and mental afflictions and their latent tendencies should be subdued and made powerless.

[d. Signs of progress on the path of union]

Signs of progress on the path has five topics: (1) pacifying jealousy, (2) leveling out the eight worldly concerns, (3) understanding things as unreal, (4) hitting the mental afflictions on the head, and (5) gaining conviction in virtuous and evil deeds.

(1) First, [*pacifying jealousy*]: By realizing the [true] nature as indivisible when giving rise to great unification, when one has pacified all dualistic appearance, jealousy disappears and all other afflictions are overpowered.

(2) *Leveling out the eight worldly concerns*: Attachment to the four desirable qualities does not exist, since all things are realized as nondual. One cognizes the four undesirable qualities with steadfast[314] and courageous equanimity.

(3) *Understanding things as unreal*: By understanding all forms and sounds as like an illusion, nothing whatsoever is apprehended as real, and one is unfettered by any entity.

(4) [*Hitting the mental afflictions on the head*:] All coarse afflictions, such as attachment, aversion, and so forth, that are due to previous conceptual thoughts overwhelmed by mental afflictions are subdued and unable to arise. Even if they arise, they are quickly pacified.

(5) *Gaining conviction in virtuous and evil deeds*: Since all things are understood to be indivisible, by integrating virtue and evil deeds with emptiness, one strives to eliminate evil deeds and achieve virtue.

[e. Beneficial qualities of union]

Beneficial qualities has five topics: (1) supersensory powers appear, (2) vision of one's sacred deity appears, (3) love and compassion for sentient beings arise, (4) outer and inner dependent arising appears, and (5) one greatly benefits others.

(1) *Supersensory powers appear* with the realization of union. [**63b**] After a long time, the six uncontaminated supersensory powers will manifest.

(2) *Vision of one's sacred deity* appears through direct seeing or in a dream.

(3) *Love and compassion [for sentient beings]* instinctively arise without meditation.

(4) *Dependent arising*: Many inner and outer causes and effects will manifest without training.

(5) *One greatly benefits others*: Many transmigrating beings will receive extensive benefits from one, and all one's activities will be able to produce realization for others by their generating faith and apprehending what one utters as true.

[D. Signlessness yoga]

Signlessness meditation has three topics: (1) preliminaries, (2) actual practice, and (3) signs of achievement.

[1. Preliminaries for signlessness meditation]

The first, preliminaries, has five topics: (a) eliminating intense grasping, (b) renouncing the body and so forth, (c) giving rise to aspiration, (d) devotion and veneration toward the spiritual teacher, (e) generating distinctive skillful means.

a. Eliminating intense grasping

One should relinquish all grasping at views of union without any attachment.

b. Renouncing the body and so forth

One should offer all bodies and material possessions to the spiritual teacher. One should offer gifts and offerings to the Three Jewels.

c. Giving rise to aspiration

One should assiduously give rise to aspiration that desires for signlessness to manifest.

d. Devotion and veneration toward the spiritual teacher

One should thoroughly supplicate to directly see the spiritual teacher as the Dharma body.

e. Generating distinctive skillful means

One should relinquish subtle aspects of self-grasping in the presence of fierce gods and demons. One should imagine giving away all bodily flesh and blood, and be without fear and self-grasping.

[2. Actual practice of signlessness meditation]

The actual practice has three topics: (a) lesser, (b) middling, and (c) great signlessness.

a. Lesser signlessness meditation

Through only meditative equipoise on signlessness in reliance upon preliminary practices, one is unchanged from the state that is devoid of meditation and post-meditation, having spontaneously realized signlessness without need of meditation.

b. Middling signlessness meditation

Without meditation and post-meditation phases, the condition of awareness due to meditative equipoise, which cuts off disputation entirely, immerses one in signlessness. Free from the duality of meditation and meditator, without activities and the potential for action, one mentally resides in the nature of emptiness.

c. Great signlessness meditation

One is devoid of all grasping at signlessness, from fine subtle aspects of [**64a**] grasping at unity and nonmeditation, the realization of signlessness, and the great clear light. Like the sky free from clouds, or like snow melting in water, neither that which is to be eliminated nor the antidotes exist. Having become completely immersed in the Dharma body and free from all exertion of activities, one actualizes the path of real exalted wisdom, released from extremes to be eliminated, having realized suchness. Outwardly one is called "Buddha."

[3. Signs of achievement in signlessness meditation]

Signs of achievement has two topics: (a) internal signs and (b) external signs.

a. Internal signs

(1) The lack of apprehended and apprehender appears, (2) extensive all-knowing wisdom—through spontaneous realization that is unchanged from correct exalted wisdom, the Dharma body—manifests, (3) the dependent arising of karmic cause and effect is directly realized, (4) one generates great compassion for sentient beings, and (5) one emerges unmoved from the realm of reality (*dharmadhātu*).

b. External signs

(1) Others see one as having many bodies, one is seen surrounded by *ḍaka*s and *ḍākiṇī*s, and one will be seen as a buddha by pure disciples. (2) Sometimes [one is] seen by others as performing childish deeds. (3) The impure see [the aim of] one's life as having been achieved. (4) Some see one as an emanation (*sprul ba*) [or "magical display"]. (5) Some see one as devoid of physical and mental activities.

That period is the phase of performing the welfare of sentient beings. Some say that the benefit of the teachings is for one's own disciples while physical activities are to benefit others. The blessings arise for those with devotion and veneration, wherever they may reside. At that time, since one is a Buddhist, one will accomplish extensive benefit for transmigrating beings.

[III. Distinctive features of the four yogas]

The distinctive features of these four yogas has three topics: (A) the distinctive features of serenity and insight, (B) the distinctive features of insight and union, and (C) the distinctive features of signlessness and union.

[A. The distinctive features of serenity and insight]

Among these, the first, has three topics: (1) the distinctive features of what is eliminated, (2) of realization, and (3) of virtuous qualities.

1. The distinctive features of what is eliminated

One eliminates all attachment to desirable qualities of serenity, the eight worldly concerns, and the perceptions of this life, and one suppresses the mental afflictions. Insight eliminates the five fears—the fear of death and so forth—and one is free from grasping to tenets, and the mental afflictions are subdued.

2. The distinctive features of of realization

[64b] *Śamatha* abiding in the uppermost serenity pacifies the subtle and coarse external and internal conceptualizations. These experiences are understood to be like an illusion. They are supremely realized by an aspect of the mind. The least insight realizes the mind itself. Middling [insight] also realizes conceptual thought as empty. The best [insight] realizes body, appearances, and aspects as empty. In brief, the meaning of emptiness is either realized or not realized in an excellent manner.

3. The distinctive features of virtuous qualities

With serenity the body is light, the mind is blissful and happy, pliable in action, and the five supersensory knowledges manifest. With insight, appearances are realized as empty and understood as unreal; suffering ceases; and with the slightest manifestation of internal dependent arising, one gains conviction in cause and effect and instinctively generates compassion for sentient beings.

[B. The distinctive features of insight and union]

The distinctive features of insight and union has three topics: the distinctive features of (1) what is eliminated, (2) realization, and (3) virtuous qualities.

1. The distinctive features of what is eliminated

The first are similar to those of insight, which was discussed above. Objects eliminated in union are apprehension of separateness between saṃsāra and nirvāṇa, things abandoned and their antidotes, acceptance and rejection, emptiness and appearance, and so forth; jealousy is eliminated and other manifest afflictions are subdued.

2. The distinctive features of realization

The distinctive features of realization for insight are as stated above. By realizing union, all happiness, suffering, abandonment, acceptance, emptiness, appearance, and so forth are realized as illusory personal experiences (*rang snang*) through the single taste of the undifferentiatedness of one's own mind. In brief, the apprehension of dualistic appearance does not exist. The distinctive features of virtuous qualities are like the previous [virtuous qualities] for insight.

3. The distinctive features of virtuous qualities

The virtuous qualities of unity: by realizing external dependent arising, one becomes beneficial for disciples, the six supersensory knowledges are suitable to arise, love and compassion arise instinctively, and all appearances are understood as unreal.

[C. The distinctive features of union and signlessness]

The distinctive features of union and signlessness are three: (1) objects to be abandoned, (2) realization, and (3) virtuous qualities.

[1. Objects to be abandoned]

First, [what is eliminated by union] are as stated above. Signlessness eliminates the subtle factors of apprehending deceitful appearances and so forth, does not differentiate between meditation and post-meditation, and eliminates all mental afflictions from the root.

[2. Realization]

For union, [the distinctive features of] realization are like what was stated above. Realizing signlessness is like purifying the sky of clouds or like melting snow in water. One realizes the Dharma body as one consummate whole, distinguishing neither things to abandon nor their remedies within the state of the great clear light. [**65a**] In brief, there is no grasping to appearances as illusory.

[3. Virtuous qualities]

For union, the virtuous qualities are like what was stated above. In signlessness, supreme all-knowing wisdom appears along with the actual state of knowables. Internal and external dependent arising are realized; pure disciples see one as a buddha; one's body is seen as many; one has the capacity do things for others through whichever actions of body, speech, and mind; and the effects of previous altruism ripens. At that time, one has the capacity to greatly benefit others due to having attained the result.

[Conclusion]

The *Great Pointing-Out Instructions in Sets of Five that Eliminate the Extremes of One's Own Mind* is concluded. These are special instructions of the Kadam textual lineage or practice lineage.

Supplementary Material

Instructions for lesser, middling, and superior meditators

The low-level meditator must eliminate mental afflictions and misdeeds. The middling meditator must eliminate grasping at "I" and "mine." The great meditator must eliminate dualistic grasping and self-centeredness.

Even if one does not possess these while practicing meditation, [one should avoid the following] errors in meditation: being tenser than a trapped animal, having less endurance than a child, having pride greater than a mountain, having disdain greater than a king, and being unconscious like an imbecile.

Like this, one should observe whether one's mental continuum possesses signs of progress on the path.

Mantra for overcoming bad dreams

Nama sarva buddha / sama prati hara shasana / tadyatha / kha kha khāhi khāhi / hūṃ hūṃ / jvala jvala / tiṣṭha tiṣṭha phaṭ svāhā.

Mantra for overcoming bad omens

Sod ku ru nan / ti ni pra ma shi / zhi zhi ru ru khu ru nan.

Mantra for guarding against infectious disease

Oṃ shig tri shig tri hūṃ phaṭ / oṃ hūṃ phyi mar shig shig / gnod pa'i 'dre dum bur bya ba / oṃ lis khri li mi ha la sa sang sang / che ge la rakṣa rakṣa svā hā / oṃ lis khri li mi li ha la svāhā / oṃ sarva byid svāhā / oṃ āḥ hūṃ.

Write out the essence of the causation mantra above. Consecrate it and keep it on the body.

Citation from the Ratnakūṭa collection and the *Compendium of the Teachings Sūtra*

From the Ratnakūṭa: "Kāśyapa, it is preferable [for someone] to have a view of the person (*pudgaladṛṣṭi*) that is as massive as Mount Meru rather than for a person who is inflated with pride to have a view of emptiness (*śūnyatādṛṣṭi*). [**65b**] Why is that? Kāśyapa, when it is an emptiness that emerges like that, Kāśyapa, I explain that view of emptiness alone as incurable."[315]

The *Compendium of the Teachings Sūtra* states, "A buddha collects the cause, a buddha arises from ripening, a buddha arises from meditative stabilization, a buddha arises from aspiration, a buddha arises from thought, a buddha arises from intrinsic nature, a buddha completes an enjoyment body, a buddha completes an emanation body, a buddha is established in one's presence."[316]

Part 3
Performance and Ritual Texts

6. Enhancing Practice and Removing Obstacles on the Path

Atiśa's avid followers of his *Stages* system were acutely aware of the obstacles that can arise when practicing the path to awakening. The following work, composed by an anonymous Kadam master, focuses on removing obstacles and enhancing practice while engaged in the stages of the path system of meditations. Tibetan editors of the manuscript have applied the title *General Meaning of the Special Instructions on the Stages of the Path to Awakening* (*Byang chub lam gyi rim pa'i man ngag gi spyi don*) based on the first sentence in the text. However, the title in the colophon, from which this chapter's title is derived, is *Cycle of Enhancing Practice and Removing Obstacles in the Circumstances for Meditating on the Stages of the Path to Awakening* (*Byang chub lam rim sgom pa'i cha rkyen gegs sel bogs 'don kyi bskor*; hereafter, *Enhancing Practice and Removing Obstacles on the Path*). The colophon also mentions that the text consists of special instructions of the Kadam textual tradition of practice (*spyod phyogs*), indicating how Kadam lineage holders classified these teachings, as noted in the chapters above.

Enhancing Practice and Removing Obstacles on the Path is comprised of three main divisions: (I) clearing away obstructive situations, (II) praying for the enhancement of experience and realization, and (III) incidentals that occur. Each section offers practices and prescriptions for removing a variety of potential obstacles and offers techniques for improving practice on the path. The first division focuses on removing (A) external obstacles and (B) internal obstacles. The commentary classifies external obstacles as (1) human-made obstacles, (2) obstacles to favorable conditions, (3) obstacles due to distraction, and (4) obstacles due to harmful spirits. Internal obstacles are comprised of (1) obstacles due to mental afflictions, (2) obstacles due to sickness, (3) obstacles to meditative stabilization, and (4) obstacles due to virtuous qualities.

A long section of *Enhancing Practice and Removing Obstacles on the Path* focuses on obstacles of sickness. The text elaborates on this topic in terms of (a) protecting against sickness, (b) pacifying sickness, and (c) integrating sickness into the path. Protecting against sickness includes (1) protecting against sickness with medicine, (2) protecting against sickness with mantras, and (3) protecting against sickness with common medicinal mantras. Protecting against sickness with medicine includes two types of medicine: (a) that which is applied to the body and (b) medicine that is taken within. Medicine applied to the body includes a reference to Ācārya Chakdum (A tsa ra Phyag rdum), an important figure in the history of Tibetan medicine. Ācārya Chakdum, also known as Kyebu Melha (Skyes bu me lha), is a doctor "who is said to have come from a country to the west of Tibet and who was active in Tibetan regions during the eleventh century."[317] This section also includes a reference to the *Nine-Ingredient Black Pill* (*ril bu dgu nag*) attributed to a formulation made by Nāgārjuna. The discussion on consumed medicine outlines formulations of seven-ingredient and four-ingredient medications for treating infectious disease.

The section on protecting against sickness with mantras includes (a) using mantras applied to the body for protection and (b) consuming the mantra by drinking blessed water. The use of mantras applied to the body offers (i) protection from spirit-related diseases (*gnyan nad*) and (ii) protection from diseases related to poison (*dug nad*). The protection from spirit-related diseases uses a circle of protection (*srung gi 'khor lo*), one of the most important protective devices in Tibetan Buddhist culture.[318] The circle of protection in this manucript consists of a pattern drawn on paper with the symbolic emblem of a pig (see the figure below). This is then hung on the body to ward off spirit-related diseases. Protection by mantras through consumption of blessed water also includes use of a circle of protection, also depicted in the figure below, while visualizing oneself as the bodhisattva of wisdom, Mañjuśrī.

The section on pacifying sickness offers three techniques for subduing sickness: (1) pacifying with mantras, (2) pacifying the body through exercises and stretches, and (3) pacifying through meditation. The text briefly discusses a variety of illnesses, including hot diseases, colds, nose germs, and dental parasites. Bodily exercises and stretches are recommended for nervous disorders and disturbances due to heat. Pacifying through meditation involves various meditation techniques to pacify and clear away illnesses. The section on integrating sickness into the path consists of contemplations that seek to transform illness by assimilating it into one's spiritual development.

The section on obstacles to meditative stabilization discusses removing hindrances that occur in meditation, such as (a) the hindrances of laxity and agitation due to deliberate effort, imbalance in bodily elements, or harmful spirits. Another obstacle the commentary focuses upon at great length is that of (b) drowsiness. The commentary discusses the causes and conditions for drowsiness as well as the signs that drowsiness may occur, such as the imbalance of bodily elements in correlation with various types of dreams. Various lines of treatment (3) are prescribed against drowsiness and sickness. The section on drowsiness discusses (i) techniques for clearing away bodily sickness, which comprise (a) physical exercise, (b) practicing channel (*nāḍī*) and vital wind (*prāṇa*) meditation, and (c) "empty hole" meditation; and (ii) clearing away faults of the mind through (a) modifying the object of observation of meditative stabilization, (b) requesting blessings for the profound Dharma, and (c) relying on various types of focal objects. The last part of this section provides a brief overview of (iii) treatments for common physical and mental faults.

The final topic in the first division of the commentary focuses on the (4) obstacles due to virtuous qualities. This section discusses how different types of virtuous qualities may become a distraction on the path rather than serving as antidotes against mental afflictions. The topics covered include how (a) virtuous qualities of conventional words, (b) the energy and power of blessings, or (c) experiences, realizations, and signs of accomplishment may become impediments on the path.

The second main division, (II) praying for the enhancement of experience and realization, discusses five topics with brief guidance on their practice. The five topics are: (A) accumulating [merit] and purifying [misdeeds], (B) rigorously meditating, (C) eliminating self-grasping, (D) integrating negative conditions as allies, and (E) directly subjugating unfavorable conditions.

The final division in the commentary (III) briefly outlines prescriptions for incidentals that may occur on the path. The concise discussion includes a brief ritual for protection against enemies and a technique for binding wild people, concluding with brief rituals to cultivate wisdom and bring about a sharp intellect. The commentary ends with poetic stanzas concerning the nature of obstacles, explaining that only students endowed with faith should be given the instructions.

Supplementary Material: A Refutation of Those Who Say There Is No Explanation for Generating the Ultimate Awakening Mind

After *Enhancing Practice and Removing Obstacles on the Path*, the manuscript contains a short discussion regarding textual sources for generating the ultimate awakening mind. This topic will be important in the chapter that follows, *A Ritual for Generating the Awakening Mind*. The concise text cites the *Hevajratantra*, *Guhyagarbhatantra*, the *Sūtra on the Fully Pure Monastic Code*, and the *Hundred Salutations Repairing Breaches* as proof that the ultimate awakening mind is explained in both sūtras and tantras. Asaṅga's *Compendium of Higher Knowledge* (*Abhidharmasamuccaya*), is also quoted, focusing on vows. Several of the citations on the ultimate awakening mind are also quoted in *General Meaning of the Stages of the Path to Awakening* (chapter 3). As will be discussed in chapter 7, the ritual for generating the ultimate awakening mind was controversial in Tibet in the thirteenth century. The Kadam lineage holders of the stages of the path teachings may have included these brief notes to recollect the primary authentic sources that substantiated their tradition's claims regarding the ultimate awakening mind. These notes may have had a pedagogical function to prepare the Kadampa audience for the ritual procedures outlined in chapter 7.

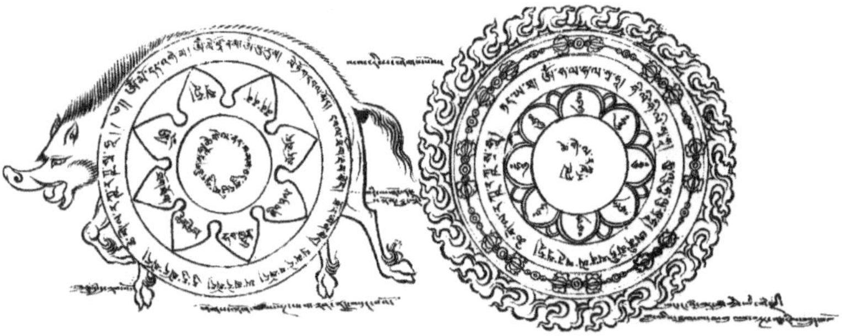

Two circles of protection for clearing away obstacles on the stages of the path (reproduced from *Byang chub lam gyi rim pa*, folio 65b).

Enhancing Practice and Removing Obstacles on the Path

[66a] Homage to the holy spiritual teachers!

This special instruction on the stages of the path to awakening has three general points:

I. Clearing away obstructive situations
II. Praying for the enhancement of experience and realization
III. Incidentals that occur

I. Clearing away obstructive situations

The first has two topics:

A. External obstacles
B. Internal obstacles

A. External obstacles

External obstacles has four topics:

1. Human-made obstacles
2. Obstacles to favorable conditions
3. Obstacles due to distraction
4. Obstacles due to harmful spirits

1. Human-made obstacles

Among them, first, there are two topics regarding human-made obstacles: (a) those that arise gently and (b) those that arise forcefully.

a. Those that arise gently

Obstacles that arise gently include turning away from the Dharma due to meeting with friends and so forth; undertaking worldly affairs; seeking out messengers, nurses, and so forth while protecting a place of rest in recuperation from sickness; and obstacles that hinder access to Dharma, such as having involuntarily been entrusted to perform village rituals and so forth. These should be abandoned through recognizing them as obstacles.

b. Those that arise forcefully

Obstacles that arise forcefully include harm and so forth that occurs through conditions arising between oneself and one's peers. When hatred, quarrels, heated conversations, and so forth arise as obstacles, one should reflect as follows. In response to myself and my friends and so forth having been harmed, this is due to the ripening of the karma of previous lifetimes, and it is the nature of sentient beings. Reflect, as well, that the results of hatred are frightening and do not accumulate misdeeds, which are worthless with regard to this life. Contemplate cultivating love and compassion for enemies.

2. Obstacles to favorable conditions

The obstacles to favorable conditions occur when one has not acquired [resources] for a long time, having engaged in Dharma but being destitute of food, clothing, and so forth. The spiritual teacher and fellow practitioners become of little importance, and one may resort to deprecating them and so forth. But gossip is hateful, leaving one with no helpers at all.

Because conditions of suffering arise from sickness and so forth, one's mind seeks to satisfy the desires for food and clothing. Obstacles can arise when hiring a servant that one desires, distracting one from the Dharma, thus in securing food and clothing, even if one thinks of practicing Dharma, it is not possible for Dharma to occur. [The servant] will become an obstacle, since [the servant] becomes a dependently arisen mishap.

To eliminate these obstacles, [recognize that] because all these sufferings are one's own previous negative karma, [**66b**] the mere ripening of experiences by manifesting the stains of negative karma related to practicing Dharma, this is only cleared through the confession of misdeeds. Since this obstacle to favorable conditions is created through negative karma, meditate on that with joy, and from the start give rise to forbearance with regard to suffering. When making effort in spiritual practice, and respecting one's need to be fed and clothed, it is said that one will be free from these hindrances in one year.

Where there are virtuous qualities, any obstacles to favorable conditions are pacified. For this reason, when there are obstacles, there is a lack of virtuous qualities. With respect to this, when one persists, virtuous qualities arise. Furthermore, even the very first Buddha himself underwent hardships in his quest for awakening.

Since the superior *siddhas* attained achievement by undergoing hardships, and since you have achieved stable happiness at this time of attaining a well-favored human rebirth, you should achieve awakening while enduring hardships. Prior experiences of immeasurable, pointless sufferings in the lower realms of saṃsāra have been of no benefit to you. But now, since great meaning can be achieved by enduring even slight hardships, one should make effort in spiritual practice. For all the unharmonious conditions and so forth that arise along the path, spiritual practice is how one produces the virtuous qualities that liberate from such hindrances.

3. Obstacles due to distraction

With regard to obstacles due to distraction, some Dharma practitioners with little faith and so forth seek to satisfy the aims of this life, and awareness slips away. Even though one must gather conducive conditions, one should understand nonessential farming, commerce, stone masonry, hermitage maintenance, the superficial activities of laypeople, the distractions of love for friends and hate for enemies, and the many other insignificant, meaningless activities that hinder virtue as obstacles and eliminate them. One should reflect and contemplate a great deal on the common path and establish achievement in this life, all while avoiding the karma of increasing misdeeds. From the *Extensive Play Sūtra* (*Lalitavistarasūtra*):

> Through viewing worldly deeds, one see all activities as pointless,
> a cause of suffering.
> Not seeing the benefit, one asks "Why?" One should become
> accustomed to examining one's own mind [in this manner].[319]

Recognizing that one has been distracted toward this life and so forth, toward things that will disperse just like a gathering, all subtle and coarse activities should be relinquished, and Dharma should be achieved.

4. Obstacles due to harmful spirits

The obstacles related to external harmful spirits [**67a**] has two topics: (a) those that arise gently and (b) those that arise forcefully.

a. Those that arise gently

The first has two topics: (1) identifying the obstacle and (2) clearing away the obstacle.

1) Identifying the obstacle

In the case of obstacles that arise gently, the quality that arises at first is elation. Having experienced supersensory knowledge or dream omens, or having seen the face of one's chosen deity, pride and conceit arise. Externally, many people who have aroused faith may support one with offerings, causing one's fortune to swell and distracting one's body and mind in sensory enjoyments. Since they thereby greatly increase one's mental afflictions, misdeeds, and downfalls, they become an obstacle to spiritual practice.

2) Clearing away the obstacle

To eliminate this, how does one identify the signs of harmful spirits and qualities? When a virtuous quality arises, spiritual practice increases without conceited and pride. Mental afflictions are not produced; renunciation arises; the world is relinquished. There is little attachment to sensory enjoyments. Love, compassion, experience, and realization all increase. But when a harmful spirit is at work, it turns back these former qualities, becoming an obstacle to virtue. These [obstacles] should be recognized and eliminated.

b. Those that arise forcefully

Obstacles that arise forcefully has two topics: (1) identifying the obstacles and (2) transforming these obstacles into achievements.

1) Identifying the obstacles

With regard to the first, [the forceful obstacles are] fear arising in the yogin's mind, having fear and despair, having hair stand on end, becoming disheartened, experiencing madness, having indications of bad dreams and so forth, not desiring the essential part of spiritual practice and so forth, being overwhelmed by the darkness of delusion, being rutted with lust, burning with generalized hatred, and practicing nonvirtuous actions to achieve [aims] in this life while avoiding spiritual practice.

Obstacles due to harmful spirits are those that arise out of the blue, such as at the beginning of a practice session in the evening at the first [watch of the] night, or when one is healthy. Those that arise due to conditions, such as when starting a practice session at the time of bad elements in the morning, are not due to harmful spirits, so the conditions and so forth should just be cleared away and discarded.

2) Transforming these obstacles into achievements

Transformation of great obstacles into achievements has three topics: (a) cultivating spiritual practice as a friend, (b) transforming the aggregates into a food offering, and (c) bringing to mind experience and realization.

a) Cultivating spiritual practice as a friend

As for the first, one should take joy in not abandoning any signs of obstacles that occur and understand them as beneficial, since they are like a spiritual friend in that they [**67b**] encourage spiritual practice; then one should engage in spiritual practice. Furthermore, some abandon the generation stage of the deity and abandon the wrathful approach.[320] Some, while engaging in the spiritual practice of purifying their own mind, have the excellent previous practice of loving kindness toward a harmful spirit.

Again, one should let [obstacles] come. It is beneficial for oneself; like a chosen deity, this harmful spirit assists in exhorting virtue. Again, whichever omen of a harmful spirit occurs, resolve that just this is for spiritual practice. Later, when the omen of a harmful spirit occurs, engage in spiritual practice while not diminishing the previous resolve. Accordingly, when you have progressed in the practice of reflecting upon the obstacle as advantageous, afterward, since the harmful spirit will not come, the obstacle will have been transformed into an achievement.

b) Transforming the aggregates into a food offering

Become joyful when a sign of a harmful spirit occurs, and cultivate love and compassion for all sentient beings, who are thus taken as most dear thanks to that harmful spirit. Contemplate being severed from your physical body and being generous to the harmful spirit; as your contemplation increases, [contemplate] offering your body out of doors. Then place yourself on the ground. Then go to a haunted place and offer [food] to high-ranking demons. Afterward, make a dedication for great awakening.

Due to this practice, negative conditions become allies; since negative omens are included as enriching obstacles, they are transformed into achievements; since faults become virtuous qualities, the hindrances of harmful spirits are dispelled.

c) Bringing to mind experience and realization

When thoughts of harmful spirits occur, [reflect that] since the harmful spirit does not actually exist externally as a real object and does not have concrete existence within itself, then the conceptuality of apprehending it as a harmful spirit also has no concrete existence. Reflect as follows: since all conceptions of the harmer, oneself, and the subject and object are unproduced, since they are empty, and since emptiness is unable to harm emptiness, due to the condition of clearing away conceptuality, one's mind is freed from elaborations, obstacles are transformed into achievement, and negative conditions become friends.

B. Internal obstacles

There are four topics with regard to internal obstacles:

1. Obstacles due to the mental afflictions
2. Obstacles due to sickness
3. Obstacles to meditative stabilization
4. Obstacles to virtuous qualities

1. Obstacles due to the mental afflictions

Among the first, obstacles due to mental afflictions, there are three topics:

a. The faults and defects of the mental afflictions
b. The benefits [**68a**] of subduing the mental afflictions
c. Methods for taming the mental afflictions

a. The faults and defects of the mental afflictions

There are five poisons of the mental afflictions, due to which all failings and defects arise. All external obstacles, distractions both human and nonhuman, and all internal obstacles, distractions both mental and physical, are caused by mental afflictions. All sickness and sufferings, nonvirtuous misdeeds, and downfalls arise due to mental afflictions.

All obstacles to virtue are also caused by mental afflictions, obstacles to both liberation and omniscience. They produce all the sufferings of saṃsāra and the lower realms of rebirth. Since every fault of this life and beyond is caused by mental afflictions, they are the root of all faults, defects, and obstacles.

b. The benefits of subduing the mental afflictions

If mental afflictions did not exist, all the previous faults and defects would not occur. It is like when a fire is completely extinguished, the smoke is cut off. The ripening of karma is not induced. Moreover, humans and nonhumans will have faith, and there will be physical and mental happiness, an increase in virtue, the arising of excellent experience and realization, the abandoning of lower realms of rebirth, and the attainment of awakening.

c. Methods for taming the mental afflictions

The methods for taming the mental afflictions has three topics: (1) relying upon antidotes, (2) using the path, and (3) understanding them to be unproduced.

1) Relying upon antidotes

When the afflictions arise gradually, in a gentle manner, separate from them with small potency. When the afflictions arise suddenly, in a forceful manner, quickly separate [from them] with fierce potency. These will no longer become obstacles. In this regard, for mental afflictions that gradually arise, an inferior intellect needs to rely on an antidote. There are (a) general antidotes and (b) specific antidotes.

a) General antidotes

As to the first, [general antidotes]: contemplation of death and impermanence, of karmic cause and effect, and of the faults of saṃsāra eliminates whichever afflictions arise.

b) Specific antidotes

Specific antidotes are the meditation on separating from repulsiveness when lustful desire arises; the meditation on love and patience when hatred arises; and the meditation on karmic cause and effect, dependent arising, and emptiness for delusion. For pride, one cultivates humility and strives to remain humble, and to counter jealousy and so forth, one generates an altruistic mind. One should definitely eliminate [afflictions] for one's awareness.

2) Using the path

When an individual with middling faculties has mental afflictions arise suddenly, like the son of a merchant following after a friend,[321] accordingly the mental afflictions that have arisen for that individual are neither eliminated nor do they fade away. One must fiercely aspire, without distraction [**68b**], as follows: "Through my mental afflictions, may all the obscurations of mental afflictions and karma of all sentient beings become purified." Then the mental afflictions will be pacified and will become suitable to dedicate for supreme awakening. Moreover, when one does likewise for all internal discordant factors and so forth, all faults will become virtuous qualities and will be transformed into the attainment of awakening.

3) Understanding them to be unproduced

An individual with superior faculties, by understanding that whatever mental afflictions and discordant conditions occur are unproduced and baseless, simultaneously becomes liberated upon their occurrence. Since they arrive as a reminder of suchness, he does not see mental afflictions as a fault.

All mental afflictions, suffering, and so forth that arise are discarded as naturally evanescent and are practiced as self-cognizant wakefulness.

2. Obstacles due to sickness

Clearing away the obstacles due to sickness has three topics:

a. Protecting against sickness
b. Pacifying sickness
c. Integrating sickness into the path

a. Protecting against sickness

Among these, the first has three topics:

1) Protecting against sickness with medicine
2) Protecting against sickness with mantras
3) Protecting against sickness with common medicinal mantras

1) Protecting against sickness with medicine

Among these, the first, protecting against sickness with medicine, has two topics:

a) Medicine applied to the body
b) Medicine taken internally

a) Medicine applied to the body

First, the key instructions of Ācārya Chakdum (a.k.a. Kyebu Melha): nutmeg (*dza ti*), musk (*gla rtsi*), sweet flag (*shu dag*), mineral drug (*shu zur*), sulfur (*mu zi*), white garlic (*sgog skya*), wild aconite (*bong nga*), *yu nga*, myrobalan (*a ru ra*), *juta*, sandalwood (*tsan da*), garlic extract (*shing kun*), and black frankincense (*gu gul nag po*). After these [ingredients] have been wrapped with cotton, when [the ingredients wrapped in cotton] are applied to the body, any infectious diseases will certainly be subdued.

Further, even better than this is as follows. Medicinal bezoar (*'gi waṃ*) is the salve of the nine-ingredient black pill of Ācārya Nāgārjuna: myobalan, *tsenduk* (*tsan dug*), sweet flag, musk, *ruta* (*ma nu ru rta*), *zer*, sulfur, garlic extract, and frankincense (*gu gul*) based on Chinese ink. When these are applied and smeared, since even a little lump suffices, all sicknesses from nāgas, earth spirits (*sa bdag*), tree spirits, white and black anthrax (*lhopa dkar nag*), black pox, *gyuser* (*rgyu gzer*), running horse bile (*mkhris pa rta rgyug*), and infectious disease will be subdued, and the eighteen great evil spirits who afflict children will be repelled.

b) Medicine taken internally

Now, as to [medicine for] ingesting, there are two:
i) Seven-ingredient [medicine]
ii) Four-ingredient [medicine]

i) Seven-ingredient [medicine]

First, myrobalan, medicinal bezoar, dark frankincense, sweet flag, musk, white garlic, and garlic extract are thoroughly ground and made into pills (*ril bu*). Consuming just enough to take the place of a meal on an empty stomach subdues infectious disease.

ii) Four-ingredient [medicine]

The fourth application [**69a**] has the ingredients of one part goat poison,[322] five parts wallich spurge,[323] yellow myrobalan, and molasses. Taking about half each morning internally definitely subdues all infectious disease.

These earlier [ingredients] subdue whatever [sickness] is in turn suitable.

2) Protecting against sickness with mantras

Protection by mantras includes:
a) Applied to the body
b) Taken internally

a) Applied to the body

The first has two topics:
i) Protection from spirit-related diseases (*gnyan nad*)
ii) Protection from diseases related to poison (*dug nad*)

i) Protection from spirit-related diseases

First, on the circumference of a wheel drawn on top of a [drawing of a] pig, write: *oṃ mo dang gho ma / oṃ mo dznyā na ma / oṃ mes su ru ma / me tog dbal sod / dbal thog rngam sod / tho ra me na sod / sra ma de ba sod / a ma de sod / du du sod sod sva hā*. On the eight spokes of the wheel, write: *oṃ thog thog / chem chem / hab khyur / zhib nyal / sod sod / nan nan / svāhā*. In the center of the wheel, write: "May so-and-so be protected from all diseases, fever, inflammation, and dysentery, *svāhā*!" Hang the drawing on the body. This will subdue only diseases that are spirit-related.

ii) Protection from diseases related to poison

For protection from a poisoned state, write this in single lines of golden letters on dark blue paper: *oṃ ka li ku ku ri haṃ 'u / bhu dza bhi te se / ban dha bhis / bha gang 'ung / a na bhis / rdes ka 'ung / bhis pa ri ka 'ung / bhis gang he bhis / ha ra ha ra ri ma 'ung / kṣa sa dha srab 'ba ra bhis / la hi ra ki / a gri ta ka ri / sa ri na ho / ma ha dhe ho / ni lan kan ta / do hor ha re bhis / dan dhi bhis*. Through applying that to the body, thirty-two thousand different types of poisons will be subdued. By reciting the mantra twenty times before a meal, all diseases from poison will be averted.

b) Taken internally

Taking internally is done through blessing water. For that, first recite over some water: *tadyatha / oṃ hala hala svāhā / hili hili svāhā / hulu hulu svāhā / animo tipana ye phaṭ*.

Write [this mantra] on a wheel drawing, place that on the tongue, and visualize oneself as Mañjuśrī. Think of all diseases as food, then drink and urinate while convalescing.

When protecting another person, [they should also] drink and urinate while convalescing. That will subdue all diseases, including infectious disease and so forth.

Furthermore, stating *oṃ nye snya sad / nye puruṣa sad / nye la sad / oṃ nye oṃ dzwa shi lo nyi lo du sad* before a meal, drink urine and spit it out on the ground. That will subdue all hot infectious diseases.

Further, state *oṃ khri yag sha huṃ* while placing drops of urine on the forehead and drink [blessed water] on an [**69b**] empty stomach. That will subdue all plagues.

3) Protecting against sickness with common medicinal mantras

Regarding protection with a common medicinal mantra, one should protect with the three—*yu du sad*, sweet flag, and black aconite—while reciting this mantra a hundred times: *oṃ bi tsa ra tsa ye svā hā*. Ideally, one recites it five hundred times and applies [an inscription of] it to the body. That will subdue all infectious disease.

For protecting children from infectious disease, recite *oṃ kun dhe la kun baṃ laṃ brum shal shal svā hā*. Write out this mantra with vermillion and maroon dye and red dye from a vine, cover it with red pieces of cotton, weave it into a red rope, and adorn the body with it. This is called "wrapped up with five reds." It will subdue infectious disease.

To protect someone from spirit-related diseases, thoroughly grind equal parts of garlic extract, musk, and sulfur and preserve some for a day in two pints (*bre*) of beer. Then, one should meditate as being like a white mouse in a pile of yak hair[324] and recite [the following] one hundred times into the beer: *oṃ pa ku tse cig tuṃ svā hā*. Then one should drink it. Then, near a swamp, expel impure air and shake the body and pass a little gas.

Dissolve the medicine [added to the beer] and eat food; that will subdue a one-year plague.

Moreover, having recited this mantra for great medicine a mere hundred times, eat just enough food in the morning and then recite: *oṃ sad / chu sad / dur dha sad / snying mgo chod / kha la tsa shag tra rbad*. When the medicine is too potent, then treat the sickness with eightfold myrobalan. Drink a great amount of cold water. That will subdue a plague.

For protection from poison made of mixed substances, recite *oṃ trig le trig le huṃ* five times onto the fingers of the right hand. Four times over, recite seven times each for the two words [of *trig le trig le*] on the ring finger. That will subdue all types of poison.

For protection to subdue sickness from ingesting poisoned meat, recite *oṃ ha sing ha sa / ka ling / ka ma ra / tsi svā hā* a hundred times.

For protection against nervous disorders, recite *oṃ tram pa ra na hūṃ hūṃ svāhā* on oil and apply it to the body; this will be beneficial.

b. Pacifying sickness

Pacifying sickness has three topics:

1) Pacifying with mantras and so forth
2) Pacifying through training the body
3) Pacifying through meditation

1) Pacifying with mantras and so forth

As to the first, heat, bile, phlegm, tumors, indigestion, colic, upper blockage, loss of appetite, urinary retention, and constipation are measured based on the intake of food [70a]; arrange four *dré* (*bre*) of rice on top of a clean woolen cloth and so forth. On that cloth, write *oṃ āḥ hūṃ*. On top of that, pour four *dré* of water. Then place fragrant smelling salts on it. Recite the following mantra over that a thousand times: *oṃ bha ra hi / khag kra bha ra hi / tsa mu kri bha ra hi*. Recite it a hundred more times, and place the rice in the water. Accordingly, recite the mantra a thousand more times upon the water and drink the water. Then if, at the time of digesting the water, there is some upper respiratory viral infection, one will vomit. If there is some lower disease, it will be purged [through excretion or urine]. If the disease has been purified, one's urine will be clear yellow.

If the disease is not purified, ingest more water. If the disease is purified, stop drinking water. One will be agreeable with others after purging. This method will pacify [the disease].

To pacify the plague called "unsuitable" (*mi rung ba*), take musk or black frankincense orally. Moreover, treat the plague with the mantra for great medicine [explained above]. That should be beneficial. Furthermore, recite *oṃ ke na lo 'di ma ha man dra ma ha man dra / kṣi pa kṣi pa ro ma ya hụm phaṭ*, casting it upon the water. Then place the water on the swelling and so forth. That will pacify [the disease].

When there is a fever, recite *ba la si si ha ra baṃ svā hā* onto tree leaves; when placing them on the chest, [the disease] will be pacified.

For cold disease, recite *a su na re ṣi pa ra li yar tsa byi raṃ khyed mi raṃ svāhā*. When reciting, contemplate the ground burning with fire; this will be beneficial.

For mental disease, recite *oṃ hūṃ ra nan pa ra ni nan svāhā*. After reciting this many times onto water, drinking it will pacify hot mental sickness.

For nose germs, recite *oṃ bal tri bal tri sad / srin pa ta svāhā*. When giving [the mantra with the breath] blown onto salt water, the disease will be pacified.

For cataracts, recite *oṃ theb lo / neb lo / sa di lo nyal nyil bur bur snying la rbad*. Recite it twenty times for the interior of each eye; when this is performed for three mornings, [the eyes] will become fresh.

For dental parasites, recite *oṃ tsa li mi li sod / cib cib sod / ya ma na ba sod / so'i srin bu sod*. By giving frankincense for demons and molasses or fat for nāgas, while checking the pulse like a watchman, the disease will be pacified.

For colds, recite *oṃ kha ra kha ra / ha sa ha sa raṃ svā hā*. Apply that before meals from the right nostril on down, [and the cold] will become healed.

For toothaches, recite *oṃ a ta ra nan / a ma du khye nan* [70**b**] *shan te u tan nan / rtag svā hā*. Applying ground salt will also be beneficial.

2) Pacifying through training the body

First, abandon the activities of body, speech, and mind and massage (*sku mnye*) the body. Then, sitting in a cross-legged position, generate the supreme awakening mind. Make your hands into fists, and place them on top of the knees. Release the breath three times, then hold the breath within three times.

Then, for a nervous disorder, first, massage the arms and shoulders three times as if washing them.

Second, twist and turn so as to massage the chest and back with both hands.

Third, place one hand on top of the thigh, and with the other hand hold the first hand at the wrist, and then shake the torso.

Fourth, cross the arms, cover the shoulders [with the hands], and twist the torso right and left.

Fifth, position your arms as if drawing an arrow in a bow.

Sixth, clenching both hands into fists, fiercely stretch them out and draw them in.

Seventh, gather both arms in and strike blows [into the air] with the right and left [fists].

Eighth, bend the arms back onto the chest.

Ninth, while sitting in vajra posture, hold the big toes of both legs and flutter them.

Tenth, sitting cross-legged with hands on the kneecaps, rotate the belly left and right.

Eleventh, stretch out both hands and bend the body.

Twelfth, gently shake the torso.

Thirteenth, rotate the head and neck.

Fourteenth, move all four [limbs], the arms and legs, to and fro without engaging your voice.

Perform each one of these in three sets of three.

Moreover, when one investigates this with reasoning one will discern it to be efficacious.

[Perform these exercises] in this way, every day for a half month, with the intention of purifying the body.

If the body becomes hardened due to the conditions of purification, pacify the body by washing many times gently on the ground. Later, purify occasionally. Sentient beings who are disturbed by heat and so forth are not suitable to be purified, and [attempting to use this method on them] may cause harm.

The basis of any sickness, such as that due to rigid meditation, irregular breathing, and so forth, can be purified by meditating on suchness. Hereafter, [**71a**] I will not explain this, but one should purify in accord with the above whichever of the sicknesses [one has] and investigate the result with reasoning.

3) Pacifying through meditation

Pacifying through meditation has two topics:

a) Meditating with general antidotes to sickness

b) Meditating with specific antidotes to sickness

a) Meditating with general antidotes to sickness

As to the first, arrange a physical contemplation place, and in the field of meditation meditate on the spiritual teacher himself as the Medicine Buddha or, alternatively, meditate on the Medicine Buddha himself. Then, with the intention desiring to pacify sickness arisen from contemplation, offer a maṇḍala of actual medicine and strongly supplicate for the pacification of sickness. Then, establish your awareness in nonconceptuality. Moreover, meditate on an area that is empty or that has many holes wherever the sickness is. Alternatively, the sickness can be pacified by drinking a great amount of one's own urine together with meditating on one's breath.

Generally, all sickness is the mind, and the mind is not real. "Unreal" means that the sickness is not established. Think that since the self of a sick person is not established, it is empty. And if the sickness is particularly intense and acute, one should meditate on this from the bottom of one's heart.

As indistinctly contemplating without engagement for a mere bit of time is not suitable, one should contemplate for a long time and strongly think that it would better to die happily while meditating one-pointedly on suchness. When generating certainty in one's being, one may lie down with [meditation] remaining to be done. To meditate more and more clearly is also permissible.

b) Meditating with specific antidotes to sickness

As to the specific antidotes, when there is the contamination of filth, recite: *oṃ i ho shuddhe shuddhe / vi shuddhe shuddhe / ram ho shuddhe shuddhe / ho ram vi shuddhe shuddhe / a a a svā hā.* Having recited the mantra 108 times into water, when cleansing with it, all filth and contamination will be washed away.

When the contamination is great or is not purified when one recites, they will be washed away by reciting many times and dedicating the recitations for others. This is a vital point, if [the contaminations] are very numerous and in quick succession. For heat, blood, and bile disease, meditate while counting up to one thousand mantras. Contemplate a very cool river of nectar arising from the letter *aḥ* upon a moon at the heart and spreading throughout the entire body.

With the breath, let out a whistling sound. Furthermore, if the body becomes numb and until mucus begins running down, eat cool food. Abandon rigorous physical activity and sleeping [**71b**] during the day. Accordingly, no matter how many days the sickness has been going on, [the sickness] will be pacified.

Place the body in an upright, straight sitting posture and contemplate the entire lower body blazing with fire; see it as pervaded by fire below the navel. Firmly contemplate the engulfed body uniting with the breath. Eat nourishing food and wear warm clothing. In physical activity, merely break a sweat. This will pacify [the sickness].

If you are flatulent, eat nutritious food. Integrate relaxation into one's practice. Let the consciousness relax, remaining in a nonconceptual state. Then, do not become distracted, knowing that within a mere third of an armspan, there is a yellow pit below one's self.[325] Wear warm clothing. Keep control over one's constitution. This will pacifiy [the sickness].

For diseases of phlegm, edema (*rmu chu*), tumors, indigestion, and so forth, manipulate and massage the belly, avoid walking with a full belly for a long time in the woods, and so forth.

Consider placing the chin on the breastbone. Let the focal points of the body energetically circulate. Abandon eating food; that will cure [the disease].

For sicknesses such as distention of the stomach due to obstructed flatulence (*pho ba sbos pa*), sickness in the nose, or sickness with shooting pains (*glang 'thab*), warm [the affected area] with fire from shards of pottery and burn incense on the finger.

Take fire as one's focal object to press down the breath. Drink thin soup made from salty water. Exercise while seated on the ground. This will pacifiy [the sickness].

For a headache, use a lower object of meditation. Contemplate the head suddenly being on the ground. Generate and release air energy.

Avoid taking delight with the head and hand.

Meditate on the blocked passageways or internal wounds as empty, generate a small image of the spiritual teacher within them, and contemplate scorching the disease with blazing fire. Contemplate that they are filled up and that nectar arises within the emptiness of the wound. That will clear away [the illness].

c. Integrating sickness into the path

When one relies on sickness to consider something harmful as a friend, transform faults into virtuous qualities, and transform obstacles into achievement, it becomes the cause to attain buddhahood. With regard to this, there are five topics:

1) Extinguishing evil deeds
2) Developing renunciation
3) Relinquishing along the path
4) Reminding oneself of realization
5) Attaining buddhahood

1) Extinguishing evil deeds

As to the first among these, contemplate as follows when the suffering of illness occurs. Since this suffering of illness is the manifestation of the stains of previous karma, [**72a**] [illness] is a sign that the stains are being cleansed. By exhausting the maturation of this certain experience, later happiness will occur. Therefore one should happily meditate on the suffering and sickness. The *Bodhicaryāvatāra* states, "Is it not well for one who experiences a little bit of human suffering to escape hell?"[326] Thus, since [illness] is the cleansing of misdeeds, even when confessing misdeeds, one should happily meditate to extinguish misdeeds.

2) Developing renunciation

In dependence on this sickness and suffering, one should develop disenchantment for saṃsāra. Furthermore, review the topics of karmic cause and effect, impermanence, and the faults of saṃsāra, and develop the holy Dharma in one's continuum by happily meditating on all sickness and suffering, viewing them as a spiritual friend.

3) Relinquishing along the path

While meditating on love and compassion for all sentient beings, one should think that "All the sickness and suffering of sentient beings will be pacified through this sickness and suffering of mine." Then, each time one does this, one should dedicate for great awakening. However, one's previous sickness and suffering will not be pacified.

4) Reminding oneself of realization

Through analyzing the nature of sickness, understand that sickness lacks intrinsic nature. Through analysis of the self of the sick person, understand that the self is not established. By understanding that a self and what pertains to a self are not established, relinquish the mind of self-grasping and establish awareness in the emptiness of the selfless state.

When understanding in this way, one is reminded of the unproduced, emptiness; the forceful purification of pristine wisdom occurs. By understanding that achievement is acquired by way of obstacles, by transforming faults into virtuous qualities, and through bad conditions becoming part of the path, one is liberated from bondage, and the hindrances of evil spirits are cleared away.

5) Attaining buddhahood

The result is the attainment of buddhahood. By relying on sickness and suffering, one purifies misdeeds, enters the path of the Great Vehicle by developing the path of renunciation in the continuum, liberates the mind from bondage, and attains the result of perfectly complete buddhahood.

Therefore, since one clears away the obstacle of sickness by happily engaging with sickness, one should understand that sickness is a spiritual friend and should not engage with suffering unhappily.

3. Obstacles to meditative stabilization

The obstacles to meditative stabilization has three topics:
a. The hindrances of laxity and agitation
b. The obstacle of drowsiness [**72b**]
c. Eliminating clinging to things

a. The hindrances of laxity and agitation

The first has three topics:
1) Deliberately contrived laxity and agitation
2) Laxity and agitation that upset the elements
3) Laxity and agitation caused by harmful spirits

1) Deliberately contrived laxity and agitation

When one is drowsy due to the conditions of wearing warm clothing while in inferior sleeping quarters blackened in darkness; overeating; experiencing physical exhaustion; feeling lethargic for a long time; having a flawed focal object; or a meditating too intensively, these conditions should be cleared away by eliminating them.

As for deliberately contrived agitation, when one is agitated due to many discussions of gossip, is committed to the eight worldly concerns, has many conceptual thoughts of desire and delusion regarding this life, or is mentally distracted by many deeds and activities, one should clear away and eliminate anything that causes mental scattering.

2) Laxity and agitation that upset the elements

As to being drowsy due to upsetting the elements, when there is overwhelming heaviness of body, lethargy, and sleep, sit in a high place wearing light clothes and with an expansive, clear view. Dispel the sleepy body, eat cool food, focus the object of observation, stimulate the mind, and clear away [laxity] by meditating on the creation stage and the dependent arising of cause and effect.

If agitated due to upsetting the elements—say one is scattered, with much conceptual thought; does not desire mental stillness; is agitated, drunk, or with buzzing ears; or is scattered, with many conceptual thoughts that desire not to remain in mental stillness—then, in a low place, rely on warm clothing, darkness, and nourishing food. Drink the minimum at the right time, and do not let the body break into a sweat. Then, relax the cognition, discard conceptual thought, and remain in a state of ease. Clear away [agitation] by relaxing in spiritual practice and living in solitude.

3) Laxity and agitation caused by harmful spirits

On drowsiness caused by harmful spirits, should there occur sleepiness, physical or mental heaviness and fogginess, non-enactment of any virtue, laziness, procrastination, despair, thinking it would be better to die, or irritation, then clear those [conditions] away with a spiritual practice of determined awareness that naturally clears these away, such as the wrathful essence, giving the body to demons, bringing harmful spirits into the path, and so forth.

As for agitation caused by harmful spirits, if there arises much scattering of conceptual thought due to attachment, aversion, and mental afflictions; the elements feeling irritated and restless; the lack of desire for essential spiritual practice [**73a**]; an unhappy mind desiring to go [somewhere]; or struggles, then clear away harmful spirits with respect to this.

b. The obstacle of drowsiness

The obstacle of drowsiness has three topics:

1) The assembled causes and conditions
2) The assembled signs
3) Lines of treatment

1) The assembled causes and conditions

The assembled causes [of drowsiness] are previous nonvirtuous karma, such as corrupted vows. As to the conditions: due to the occurrence of fierce suffering and due to the arising of fierce desire, [the vows] are not established. Moreover, the life-sustaining energy becomes paralyzed with fright owing to various suitable secondary conditions.

2) The assembled signs

Various signs of drowsiness occur when the winds of the collected five elements that reside in the life channel of the heart center become paralyzed.

Among these [signs], when the vital wind of *earth* is paralyzed, sleep and rest cannot renew the strength of the body, the body is heavy and foggy, and sleepiness also occurs. Pacifying the unhappy mind clears away that awareness. In a dream, one goes to a high plain, dreams that the body is possessed with a great burden, and becomes weary and disheartened.

When the vital wind of *water* becomes paralyzed, the thin, limpid, cold body is like giving water to parched land; the state of the body is such that flashes and pox disease will occur; mere mental distress causes unhappiness; and an empty, cold heart arises. In a dream, one crosses a lake, river, or mountain; one builds a boat or a bridge; water disappears or is carried away; and so forth.

When the vital wind of *fire* is paralyzed, there is heat in the upper part of the body, and pain and sickness flare up. The mind becomes unhappy and irritatable. Quarrels ensue, with a restless and short-tempered mind. In a dream, a building or orchard catches fire, the fire is extinguished, and so forth.

When the vital wind of *wind* is paralyzed, [one experiences] headaches, agitation, congestion in the upper part of the body, and a burning sensation; one cannot be firmly established on the ground for long and ardently wishes to go; one's heart throbs, one scratches oneself, experiences pain in the front and back, and one's seventh vertebra emerges.[327] The mind becomes unhappy, lacking a cleansing flow, the heart loses heat, the mind is stupefied, there is a great amount of scattered conceptual thought, much talk emerges from the mouth, [**73b**] one sees cyclones in dreams, and so forth.

When the vital wind of *space* is paralyzed, one is diaphanous and empty, one does not engage in any activities, one's mind swims about, one always has shallow aspiration, and one's body is light and slouched. Even dreams occur as empty, and earthen pots and so forth appear in the sky.

When all these elements are paralyzed, all these signs occur. Understand the various relationships among these symptoms and the frequency and intensity of their occurrence. Regarding all of these, some are due to previous karma, some are from upsetting the elements, some from harmful spirits, and some completely arise at the same time. They should be understood and cleared away. When you engage in spiritual practice at dawn or at dusk and an unhappy mind occurs, it is a harmful spirit.

In the event that [drowsiness occurs] due to faulty meditation, when the meditation is faulty due to being tired and exhausted, you should relax the practice and abandon nourishing food. Since when this occurs, it is the elemental forces that agitate the body, there is always a line of treatment for that. In this manner, when [nourishing food] is not beneficial, you should bring this [practice abandoning nourishing food] into the path, since there is no other definite way to experience [benefit].

3) Lines of treatment

The lines of treatment has three topics:

A) Preparation
B) Actual practice
C) Subsequent practices

A) Preparation

As to the first: gently stretch your body and mind and sit on a low seat, accumulate whatever merit you can manage, offer feast gatherings and tormas, generate the mind of supreme awakening, settle the body in the posture, and expel the stale air.

B) Actual practice

The actual practice has three topics:

i) Clearing away bodily sickness
ii) Clearing away faults of the mind
iii) Treatment for common physical and mental faults

i) Clearing away bodily sickness

Among these, the first has three topics:

a' Physical exercise
b' Practicing channel (*nāḍī*) and vital wind (*prāṇa*) meditation
c' "Empty hole" meditation

a' Physical exercise

These [three topics] can be combined into one practice. First, when the body is without sickness, physically exercise. Through meditating on emptiness and the vital winds, sickness will not occur.

b' Practicing channel and vital wind meditation

If it is the entire upper part of the body that is struck when sickness occurs, ingest cinnamon and firmly practice letting out the vital wind through physically training the upper part of the body. Meditate on the upper part of the body as hollow.

c' "Empty hole" meditation

Meditate on many holes in the upper part of the body. When penetrating [through meditating] into the flesh of the body and boring into the front and back, physically exercise while lying on the ground. Practice letting out [breath] when it is difficult to breathe. When the [vital wind] is not unified within, suppress the vital wind. [74a] This will clear away the majority of upper-body sicknesses. When there is sickness of the lower body and so forth, while physically exercising on the ground, expel the vital wind from the holes as explained above.

ii) Clearing away faults of the mind

Rectifying the mind has three topics:

a' The focal object of meditative stabilization
b' Requesting blessings for the profound Dharma
c' Relying on various objects

a' The focal object of meditative stabilization

Regarding the first, when the vital winds of earth and water are fiercely paralyzed, meditate on being a skeleton from above the teeth. Contemplate the interior [of the body] and the head as empty cavities. Contemplate earth and water vaporizing from the heart center, exiting from the head like incense smoke, and rising into the sky. When both fire and wind are paralyzed, meditate on the arising of a small image of one's spiritual teacher and chosen deity at the heart. Then, contemplate that you cause the warmth of the vital wind of fire to arise, which then descends into the lower part of the body, and then continues descending a fathom below the ground. Most of the fierce faults of the mind will be cleared away by this practice.

b' Requesting blessings for the profound Dharma

One should study the Dharma that is both vast and profound, give discourses on the Dharma that is both vast and profound, and investigate the sūtras, tantras, and so forth.

c' Relying on various objects

Observing crowds of people gathered together, observing musicians, participating in whatever amusements there may be, and wandering directionless through the country will purify [the faults of the mind].

iii) Treatment for common physical and mental faults

The treatment for common physical and mental faults has three topics:

a' Purifying harmful spirits and obstructions
b' Secret practices of body and speech
c' Spontaneous practice

a' Purifying harmful spirits and obstructions

Among these, regarding the first, since there are harmful spirits causing faults everywhere, they should be cleared away. Then, since there are evil deeds and obstructions of negative karma, you should confess them in order to purify their maturation.

b' Secret practices of body and speech

These secret practices [include] dwelling at night in the rugged country having gone into solitude, relinquishing self-grasping, acting fearlessly, and physically leaping, jumping, and running around, and so forth. Verbally proclaim intensely Ha!, Hūṃ!, and Phaṭ!

When tired and fatigued, sit cross-legged and establish the mind in nonconceptuality. The body is relinquished by offering it to demons. You should practice this as mentioned above.

c' Spontaneous practice

As to spontaneously practicing, [you should state out loud,] "What use are desires?" Cry out, be exuberant, [**74b**] sing and dance, spark your awareness, jump around, chant loudly, and so forth, and sharpen your attention in not suppressing any recollection.

When you become tired, and your energy has scattered, freely sit down and expel the stale breath. Rely on nourishing food. Massage the body. It is cleared away with the count of several days.

C) Subsequent practices

As for subsequent practices, command your entire awareness to be established in nonconceptual awareness. Then dedicate this toward supreme awakening.

c. Eliminating clinging to things

To eliminate clinging to things, eliminate grasping a self and what pertains to a self, establish the awareness in emptiness, and since all sufferings of saṃsāra arise from clinging to things, understand all things as not truly existent. Whatever happiness and suffering appears, understand it to be illusory like a dream. Furthermore, by understanding that things lack intrinsic existence, clinging ceases.

When there is a great deal of clinging, since that involves a high amount of conceptuality, and since the remains [of conceptuality] are the intellectual understanding of words, understand [concepts] as selfless and empty, be free from suppressing or cultivating anything, and do not be fettered by any conceptuality of happiness and suffering.

4. Obstacles to virtuous qualities

The obstacles to virtuous qualities has three topics:

a. The virtuous qualities of conventional words
b. The energy and power of blessings
c. Experience, realization, and signs of accomplishment

a. The virtuous qualities of conventional words[328]

Among these, the first is as follows. Certain great meditators, who have been distracted by the study of many scriptures due to clinging to conventional words; who are not inspired through studying the meaning of tantras; who are not enthusiastic to meditate on the meaning; who in their arrogance do not seek special instructions; who generate pride and conceit regarding words and deprecate others, such as siblings, fellow practitioners, and so forth; who think they are more knowledgeable than the accomplished master: for them, doctrinal knowledge does not become an antidote for the mental afflictions, and falling into the perceptions of this life—the eight worldly concerns—becomes a hindrance to great meditation. You should eliminate these [faults], and you should settle the meaning with the right amount of study and reflection. Seek out the special instructions on meditative stabilization to eliminate pride, and make vigorous effort in meditation.

b. The energy and power of blessings

The energy and power of blessings can become a hindrance for some great meditators [75a] for whom a little energy and power of blessings occur due to spiritual practice. These qualities of the energy and power of blessings do not become antidotes to the mental afflictions. [Such energy and power leads to] generating desire for food and resources. [One engages in activities like] going to town, protecting against hailstones, rearing a demon child, subduing evil spirits of sickness, protecting against the faults of beer, engaging in the rites of reversing circumstances, reciting texts for money, [forecasting] omens in dreams, clairvoyance, divination, divining auspicious circumstances, and so forth. [With] the mind having fallen into desire, one speaks to flatter others, one violates [one's practice] with biased eyes for the sake of the food and wealth of dying people and benefactors.

Since this attachment and clinging to desire, in wandering through towns to offer [trade in commerce such as] weights and measures, is an obstacle for a great meditator, these should be cleared away, and one should relinquish the mind aiming for this life. One should contemplate the difficulty of finding leisure and fortune, death and impermanence, karmic cause and effect, the faults of saṃsāra, and so forth and reverse the tendency toward desire.

These topics—leisure and fortune and so forth—are the path; these topics strike the iron of the path. They also remove obstacles. Since they are practices that enhance, one should contemplate them. Having seen the faults of desire, spiritually practice in solitude.

c. Experience, realization, and signs of accomplishment

As to experience, realization, and signs of accomplishment, for some great meditators, when good experience and realization occur due to an increase of spiritual practice; when the energy and power of blessings occur; when they see the face of their chosen deity; when many signs of achievement, such as clairvoyance, magical powers, and so forth occur, for them exultation, pride, and conceit arise, and wherever they look, there is excessive attention to oneself.

First one hears; then, in the middle, one contemplates the object of meditation; and finally, one meditates, departing from signs of achievement and so forth, passing beyond others. When there occurs the thought that the spiritual forefathers are too difficult to understand [and should be discarded], it is an obstacle of Māra. That should be cleared away, and since all virtuous qualities are due to the kindness of the spiritual teacher, one should again generate devotion and respect.

Generate for others love, compassion, and the altruistic mind. Since the slightest good qualities occur from the kindness of the spiritual teacher and from oneself meditating for just a while, [**75b**] do not have pride, conceit, and exultation but rather generate devotion and respect for the spiritual teacher and make effort in spiritual practice.

The meaning of the mind itself being free from elaboration is that the "I" and "self" do not exist. The exultation, "I am the greatest and the most powerful" and so forth is grasping at a self and what pertains to a self, and when there is grasping to a self and to that which pertains to a self, it is the root of suffering. When there is attachment to signs of achievement and so forth, it is Māra. Therefore eliminate grasping to a self and what pertains to a self, pride, and conceit, and again make effort in spiritual practice.

II. Praying for the enhancement of experience and realization

Enhancement has five topics:

A. Accumulating [merit] and purifying [misdeeds]
B. Rigorously meditating
C. Eliminating self-grasping
D. Integrating negative conditions as allies
E. Directly subjugating unfavorable conditions

A. Accumulating [merit] and purifying [misdeeds]

As to the first, when there are misdeeds and downfalls, hindrances, and missed gains, since it is very important to confess faults and downfalls, make an effort to confess using whichever methods are suitable, such as the special instructions of the four opponent powers.

Since not gathering the accumulation of merit is like having a field without water and manure, and there are missed gains, accumulate the appropriate stores of merit and offer body and wealth to the spiritual teacher. Worship the Three Precious Jewels. Accrue accumulations that are suitable, such as the offering of maṇḍalas and so forth.

B. Rigorously meditating

Due to spiritually practicing in a location in which powerful gods and demons reside, thoughts of anxiety and despair may occur. Therefore meditate with disciplined awareness to bring progress.

C. Eliminating self-grasping

Relinquish self-grasping and offer up the body to demons. When conceptual thoughts of fear and so forth occur, if one directly subjugates them by residing in a terrifying place, they will completely vanish.

As to eliminating self-grasping, since the root of all the sufferings of saṃsāra and lower realms of rebirth is grasping at a self and what pertains to a self, relinquish grasping to a self and what pertains to a self, and give up the body, as if it were a corpse. Establish the mind as empty, like space. Eliminate all conceptual thoughts of being unable to bear separation from comfort and unable to experience attractive things. Equalizing joy and sorrow [**76a**] will bring progress.

D. Integrating negative conditions as allies

Conditions that cannot be stopped by blocking them and any unfortunate circumstances that arise should be integrated as allies on the path in not eliminating them; this includes anything that is the experience of enemies, demons, joys, and sorrows.

Since these are the appearance of one's own mind and are not externally established, and since the mind is empty, all negative conditions are also empty. Through recalling the instructions on emptiness, any appearances whatsoever become allies on the path. Moreover, by relying on whichever conditioned appearances and meditating on whichever Dharma tradition is suitable, the integration of all negative conditions as allies on the path will bring progress.

E. Directly subjugating unfavorable conditions

To directly subjugate unfavorable conditions, one should entirely cast out, with absolute determination, forceful clinging and desirous craving for food, clothing, residence, and so forth as well as the self-cherishing that grasps I and mine. All cold, hunger, fear, anxiety, despair, attachment, and aversion to a self and what pertains to a self should be cast out entirely. Refrain from any affirmations and negations and hopes or fears.

If one does not understand all negative and unfavorable conditions as allies on the path, this [lack of understanding] is the residue of great pride and intellectual understanding. Like the water of a mirage, or like a deep ravine in a dream that completely vanishes when jumped over, directly subjugating negative and unfavorable conditions will liberate one from being bound, and experience and realization will progress.

III. Incidentals that occur

Next, to protect the path from incidentals that may occur, [recite the mantra] *oṃ aḥ ti pa ti gung pa ti sarva tri ti i ti i si svā hā.* [Then,] draw on the ground in front of you a bow and arrow shooting twenty-one notched arrowheads arrayed across the ground in the direction of beings; enemies will not come.

For binding wild people, state: *hri ti mi tra ti ta ban dha ha sa ha tas ka ma ra sa la tha.* Cast [the mantra] twenty-one times with the right hand and robbers will not occur. Subdue other occurences with the thumb. By doing this, the beings will be confounded.

To cause great wisdom to come about, recite: *tadya tha ka pa tsa ka na la la ye svā hā.* After casting [the mantra] seven times into water, drink it, and [**76b**] all individuals will become happy and have great wisdom.

To cause sharp intellect to come about, state: *na mo si sha prad nye svā hā.* When drinking after casting [the mantra] into the water of a precious vessel during a lunar eclipse, a sharp intellect will develop.

The cycle of enhancing practice and removing obstacles in the circumstances for meditating on the stages of the path to awakening is completed.

> This special instruction of clearing away obstacles,
> the inner and outer obstacles that may occur
> while achieving unsurpassable awakening,
> when directly apprehended from the heart,
> accomplishes in the interval of not showing signs [of progress].
> Experienced by oneself,
> do not teach it to others
> except students endowed with faith.

These are the special instructions of the Kadam textual domain of practice.

Supplementary Material

A refutation of those who say that there is no explanation for generating the ultimate awakening mind

If someone says, "There is no [scriptural] explanation for generating the ultimate awakening mind," the fourth chapter of the *Hevajratantra* states, "One generates the awakening mind in both its ultimate and its conventional forms."[329] That is not all; the same text continues, "As conventional white as white jasmine, ultimate in the form of bliss."[330] Thus, if someone asks, "Is the bliss of the essential drop designated as the ultimate?" [the answer is that] the ultimate in the very form of bliss is emptiness.

The very same text states, "Bliss is in the form of selflessness, and that bliss is the great seal."[331] Furthermore, [the text states,] "The awakening mind is nirvāṇa in both conventional and ultimate form."[332] [The text also states,] "The nature of the realm of reality should be investigated with this very wisdom. That itself is the form of coemergence, the yoginī of auspicious great bliss."[333] The second chapter of the *Guhyagarbha*[*tantra*] also says, "This generation of the primordially awakened mind as gnosis is taught,"[334] and, "The ultimate and conventional mind is generated as gnosis."[335]

Moreover, this is also explained from sūtras. The *Sūtra on the Fully Pure Monastic Code* states, "When someone generates the thought saying, 'I understand all things as unproduced and unceasing' while in the meantime not falling into instances of views, this is the fourth action entailing immediate results."[336] The *One Hundred Salutations Repairing Breaches* also states,

> Upholding from this time, I take refuge [77a] in the Three Jewels until the fundamental state of awakening. Offering my own body, may those endowed with great compassion always partake. I offer to all the buddhas and bodhisattvas of the [three] times. I relinquish the grasped object and grasping subject while not embracing aggregates, elements, and sensory spheres. The primordially unproduced is equal with the essencelessness of things and the selflessness of persons. Generating the awakening mind as the nature of emptiness, I, having the name of so-and-so, from this time until the fundamental state of awakening, will generate the awakening mind. May I never forsake the supreme awakening mind and never be separated from the holy spiritual friend.[337]

The *Compendium of Higher Knowledge* (*Abhidharmasamuccaya*) says,

> The vows according to the code of discipline (*pratimokṣasaṃvara*), the vows of absorption (*dhyānasaṃvara*), and uncontaminated vows (*anāsravasaṃvara*). Regarding that, the code of discipline has eight types: [1] vows of the monks (*bhikṣusaṃvara*), [2] vows of the nuns (*bhikṣuṇīsaṃvara*), [3] vows of those who are in training (*śikṣamāṇasaṃvara*), [4] vows of male novices (*śramaṇerasaṃvara*), [5] vows of female novices (*śramaṇerīsaṃvara*), [6] vows of male lay disciples (*upāsakasaṃvara*), [7] vows of female lay disciples (*upāsikāsaṃvara*), and [8] vows through fasting (*upavāsasaṃvara*).[338] The vows of absorption are abstention in a person free from desire of the desire realm at the time of weakening the mental afflictions. It is abstention in a person free from desire of the fourth absorption.[339] Uncontaminated vows are the uncontaminated abstention that sees reality.[340]

7. A Ritual for Generating the Awakening Mind

Atiśa is renowned as the illuminator of the awakening mind. He taught numerous audiences in India and Tibet on this topic and composed many works elucidating the cultivation of this gateway to the Mahāyāna path. *Open Basket of Jewels*, an earlier commentary he composed in India, provides one of the most thorough overviews on the awakening mind in Indian Buddhist literature. Atiśa's *Lamp* and its autocommentary discuss the awakening mind in some detail as well.[341] As illustrated in chapter 1, Atiśa's *Stages* discusses the awakening mind in many sections.[342] The following chapter is comprised of a ritual procedure for generating the awakening mind based on the system of *Stages*. The anonymous Kadam ritual manual states in its colophon that it was composed according to the system of Lord Atiśa, and that it is a practice manual belonging to the Kadam textual domain of practice.

Atiśa composed a similar ritual procedure on the awakening mind while residing at Tholing, in the western Tibetan region of Ngari. The work was entitled *A Ritual for Generating the Awakening Mind and for the Bodhisattva Vow*.[343] This ritual complements the conservative Mahāyāna path overview outlined in *Lamp* and its autocommentary, in which Atiśa briefly outlines a ritual for the awakening mind but specifies that one should consult manuals of Indian Buddhist scholars for details.[344] *A Ritual for Generating the Awakening Mind and for the Bodhisattva Vow* is a formal Mahāyāna manual that outlines a procedure for intermediate-level monks and laypeople. The ritual references a short Mahāyāna sūtra, the *Inquiry of Avalokiteśvara on the Seven Qualities*, a discourse that provides instruction on practices to be cultivated after generating the awakening mind and that specifically advocates celibacy.[345]

On the other hand, the awakening-mind ritual procedure translated in the present chapter complements the advanced meditation teachings found in *Stages*. The ritual manual also cites numerous sūtras and tantras in its prescriptive method for manifesting the awakening mind. In this regard, the differences between the ritual procedure for the awakening mind explained in *Stages* and in the text composed in western Tibet illustrate the previously discussed Kadampa dichotomy between public teachings (*tshogs chos*) and advanced teachings for select disciples (*lkog chos*). That is, the western Tibet ritual procedure is imperially commissioned, is translated by court-appointed monks like Ma Gewai Lodrö, and is an officially registered canonical work. *A Ritual for Generating the Awakening Mind and for the Bodhisattva Vow* and *Lamp* are public teachings. On the other hand, the *Stages* manuscript ritual procedure is not officially translated, is only attributed to Atiśa, and is not an official canonical work found in the Tibetan Tengyur. Like *Stages*, *Ritual for Generating the Awakening Mind* circulated among select Kadam followers.

The content of the *Stages* manuscript ritual for generating the awakening mind begins with recollection of the mental trainings of the small- and middling-capacity individuals on the stages of the path. These meditations include recollecting the difficulty of achieving the precious human rebirth and recalling the impermanence of conditioned existence and the reality of death. One then contemplates that the source of happiness for oneself and others is attaining buddhahood and that the cause of buddhahood is the awakening mind.

Based on these preliminary meditations, the ritual text then outlines the ritual procedures and contemplations for generating the mind for supreme awakening (*byang chub kyi mchog tu sems bskyed pa*). The use of extensive citations of sūtras and tantras within its ritual prescriptive instructions and contemplations may indicate or aid the pedagogical aim of the manual for the teacher to instruct disciples as the ritual is being conducted. The text is comprised of numerous divisions and subdivisions within the ritual procedure. Sections of the work often consist of three sections outlining preliminaries (*sbyor ba*), actual practice (*dngos gzhi*), and subsequent practices (*rjes*) for each stage of the ritual.

The main body of the ritual manual outlines generation of the supreme awakening mind. This is covered in two divisions: (I) generating the conventional awakening mind (*kun rdzob byang chub kyi sems*) and (II) generating the ultimate awakening mind (*don dam byang chub kyi sems*).

The section on generating the conventional awakening mind is divided into two categories, which are commonly found in Mahāyāna technical digests: (A) generation of the aspiring mind (*smon pa sems*; *praṇidhicitta*) and (B) generation of the engaging mind (*'jug pa sems*; *prasthānacitta*). The generation of the aspiring mind is outlined with the three steps of (1) preliminaries, (2) actual practice, and (3) subsequent practices.

The preliminaries for generating the aspiring mind consist of two areas of focus, (a) the cause of generating the aspect and (b) the cause of generating the intention. Generating the aspect is comprised of four components: (1) accumulating merit, (2) extraordinary going for refuge, (3) cultivating the four immeasurables, and (4) offering one's body to the spiritual teacher. The cause of generating the intention has four topics: (1) contemplating the virtuous qualities of the Buddha, (2) contemplating the beneficial qualities of the awakening mind, (3) supplication, and (4) making an inquiry to determine potential impediments to generating the awakening mind.

The actual practice of the generation of the aspiring awakening mind consists of a contemplation on dependent arising. Contemplating dependent arising familiarizes one with the notion that the awakening mind arises from an accumulation of causes and conditions.

The subsequent practices contain a ritual recitation repeated three times, which commits the reciter to generating the awakening mind. The teacher then utters words of confirmation, and the disciple responds, "It is wonderful."

The next procedure in the ritual manual initially begins with the generation of the engaging mind, having two topics: (1) praising the glory of the awakening mind and (2) describing its training. The text lists five topics of training but only briefly discusses the first: (a) training the mind to not abandon sentient beings.[346] The manual then suddenly shifts to outlining the generation of the engaging mind within the three steps of (1) preliminaries, (2) actual practice, and (3) engagement, similar to the previous sections of the manual.

The section on the preliminaries has four subtopics: (a) supplication for accruing the accumulations of merit, (b) expressing the great extensive basis of training, (c) conducting an inquiry to determine potential impediments for a suitable vessel, and (d) offering exhortation to the teacher to correctly bestow vows of bodhisattva morality. The manual instructs on the actual practice of the engaging mind by contemplating the virtuous qualities of the Buddha and the beneficial qualities of the awakening mind. The student is then instructed to hold a flower while repeating after the teacher the wish to fully receive the vows of bodhisattva morality. The last section of this part of the ritual manual outlines the engagement to proclaim at the end of the ritual. The engagement addresses four areas: (a) requesting that notice be taken that disciples have been empowered with vows, (b) engaging with vision and pristine cognition, (c) not proclaiming precipitously the vows that have been taken, and (d) summarizing the interior of training and understanding it. The latter section summarizes the three topics related to the bodhisattva vows: observing moral discipline, collecting virtuous qualities, and acting on behalf of sentient beings

The second major division of the ritual manual focuses on generating the ultimate awakening mind. This begins with recollecting the importance of the practitioner being endowed with means and wisdom. The section on generating the ultimate awakening mind likewise consists of three sections on

(A) the preliminaries, (B) the actual practice, and (C) subsequent practices. The preliminaries center on taking supreme refuge as embodied in the spiritual teacher. The ritual manual cites three different tantras on this point and instructs one to contemplate the spiritual teacher as the Dharma body of the Buddha. One then recites a confirmation statement of this type of refuge three times. The actual practice of the ultimate awakening mind is based on a stanza from the *Guhyasamājatantra*. The practice entails a meditation and recitation pointing out that one's mind is in reality the same as the unconditioned, changeless, spontaneously present essencelessness of things and persons. The ultimate reality that is pointed out is one's own awakening mind. This portion of the ritual succinctly enacts the advanced pointing-out instructions found in chapters 4 and 5. The subsequent practices consist of requesting the teacher for consideration, followed by several Kadam-based contemplations. These include meditating that all sentient beings are also one's mother, followed by one's chosen deity appearing suddenly, and then recollecting the spiritual teacher as abiding above one's head. The practitioner then meditates that the mind is emptiness. A statement is then recited that resembles the practical advice given in *Stages* concerning the cultivation of virtue even while realizing emptiness or nonduality. Following these contemplations and statements, the teachings are entrusted, and offerings of thanksgiving are presented. The ritual procedure concludes with the teacher proclaiming, "Train well in the precepts," and the disciple responding, "Thank you for your kindness." Afterward, all roots of virtue are dedicated to supreme awakening.

From the perspective of Tibetan Buddhist history, the most controversial—and perhaps most intriguing—section of the ritual manual is its prescriptions on and discussion of the ultimate awakening mind. Sakya Paṇḍita brought to the forefront issues that he considered problematic in the Tibetan practice of ritually generating the awakening mind. Among these was the question of whether the ultimate awakening mind could be ritually produced. Sakya Paṇḍita rejected this as an impossibility in both his *Clear Differentiation of the Three Codes* and *Clarifiying the Sage's Intent*.[347] The ritual translated in this chapter demonstrates the type of Kadam-based ritual generation of the awakening mind that Sakya Paṇḍita so vehemently rejected. Sakya Paṇḍita also differentiated between a Madhyamaka system (*dbu ma'i lugs*) and Cittamātra system (*sems tsam pa'i lugs*) in the ritual procedure for the awakening mind.[348] The earlier Kadampa master Sharawa has a long discussion in his *Stages of the Path* arguing against the claims of some Tibetans that Nāgārjuna and Asaṅga had different systems of generating the awakening mind.[349] Sharawa's discussion demonstrates that some twelfth-century Tibetans scholars differentiated systems of the ritual procedure for the awakening mind before the time of Sakya Paṇḍita. However, the following Kadam ritual does not make any distinctions in terms of Madhyamaka or Yogācāra. Rather, it claims to follow the syncretic system of Atiśa, which combines sūtra and tantra and ritually induces the conventional and ultimate awakening mind.

Supplementary Material: Ancillaries to the Awakening Mind Ritual

The Kadam manuscript includes several short ancillary texts that follow the awakening mind ritual. These include concise notes on the special components related to the aspirational and engaging awakening mind practices. The first is a summary of the five fundamental downfalls that may occur in relation to the aspirational awakening mind. The second names six limbs in common with cultivating the aspirational and engaging awakening mind. These two summary lists appear to be pedagogical notations whose meaning is not fully elaborated.

The notations regarding the awakening mind are followed by a list of Sanskrit name equivalents to Atiśa and four early Kadam masters. An unknown commentator has marked the Tibetan name equivalents under the line of the text in the manuscript. I have placed the Tibetan name equivalents in brackets next to each Sanskrit name. The Tibetans mentioned in the list are Dromtön Gyalwai Jungné, Potawa Rinchen Sal, Chengawa Tsultrim Bar, and Gönpawa Wanghuck Gyaltsen. Notable in this list is the archaic spelling of Potawa's name as "Putopa" and the listing of his Dharma name (*chos ming*) as *rin chen dga' pa* ("joyful treasure") rather than *rin chen gsal* ("radiant treasure"). The Sanskritization of these Tibetan names, as well as the listing of Atiśa's name Dīpaṃkaraśrījñāna, may represent an early stages of the path name-mantra (*mtshan sngags*) lineage list. In Indo-Tibetan Buddhist traditions, a name mantra is thought to embody specific buddhas and spiritual teachers; these mantras are likened to physical relics (Bentor 2003). The name mantra is formed based on the Sanskrit equivalent of the spiritual teacher's Tibetan name and bestows blessings through its enunciation.

The list of Sanskrit names is followed by two verses from the *Higher Teaching* (*Uttaratantra*) and a list regarding four certainties. The citation of these verses and the list appear to be pedagogical notations for the Kadam lineage holder. After these pedagogical notations, the Kadam manuscript contains three short ritual texts: *A Common Ritual of Taking Refuge*, *A Ritual for the One-Day Precepts*, and *A Ritual for Establishing Someone as a Lay Disciple.* Atiśa discusses taking refuge in his *Autocommentary to the Lamp* (Sherburne 2000, 59–65) and has a separate explanation in his *Teaching on Taking the Refuges* (*Śaraṇagacchāminirdeśa*; Sherburne 2000, 430–37). In the latter work Atiśa states that one should request the specific ritual from a spiritual teacher. The next ritual concerns the vows of *upavāsa* discipline, or the one-day precepts, known also as the "fortnightly assembly with its eight constituents" (*aṣṭāṅgasamanvāgataṃ upavāsaṃ*; *yan lag brgyad pa'i gso sbyong*; Buswell and Lopez 2014, 73). As mentioned in the ritual text, on special days Buddhist laypeople would take precepts to nurture the spirit of renunciation embodied by fully ordained Buddhists. This discipline would involve the laity vowing to uphold eight prohibitions against (1) taking life, (2) stealing, (3) sexual activity, (4) lying, (5) consuming intoxicants, (6) resting on a high or luxurious bed, (7) enjoying dance, music, ointments, or jewelry, and (8) eating at improper times. In this ritual the lay practitioner upholds these prohibitions while pledging to follow after the example of noble arhats. Notable about this eleventh-to-twelfth-century Kadam ritual is that in the history of Tibetan Buddhism, the practice of *upavāsa* was eventually replaced by the "Mahāyāna fast" (*theg chen gso sbyong*) in Tibet (Cabezón and Dorjee 2019, 35). Finally, *A Ritual for Establishing Someone as a Lay Disciple* is a short ritual in which a layperson pledges to uphold five prohibitions, refraining from (1) killing, (2) stealing, (3) sexual misconduct, (4) lying, and (5) consuming intoxicants. These basic rituals in the *Stages* manuscript may have been enacted after Kadam masters performed the ritual of the awakening mind or after giving teachings on the stages of the path.

A Ritual for Generating the Awakening Mind

One who wishes to generate the mind for supreme awakening, having first trained the mind in the path of both the lesser and middling individuals, should meditate on the path of the supreme individual, including the four immeasureables and so forth, and reflect upon the benefits of the awakening mind and the virtuous qualities of the Buddha.

Generally, this precious human body endowed with leisure and freedoms is difficult to attain, and one should make effort in virtue and eliminate misdeeds, not wasting one's life, which easily disintegrates. Since, without the good fortune of Dharma practice, life does not have leisure and freedom, one should be endowed with the meaning of leisure and freedom. Furthermore, one should refrain from laziness and procastination. Since conditioned things are impermanent, the time of death is unpredictable. Now is the time of short lifespans, and there are many conditions for death. [**77b**] Therefore, since we won't stay long in this very lifetime, there is the danger of dying quickly. The *Secret Night Sūtra* states,

> Who can know that one won't die tomorrow?
> So from this very day, act as if this is so.
> You are certainly not an ally
> of the Lord of Death and his great army.[350]

Since one cannot know if death will occur tomorrow morning, life is impermanent. After dying, when one is reborn in this ocean of saṃsāra, since there does not at exist even a mere bit of happiness and comfort, the source of happiness for oneself and others is omniscient buddhahood. Moreover, since [buddhahood] does not occur without a cause, and the certain cause is generating the mind for supreme awakening, one should generate the awakening mind.

Generating the supreme awakening mind has two topics:

I. Generating the conventional awakening mind

II. Generating the ultimate awakening mind

Furthermore, the *Hevajratantra* states, "One generates the awakening mind in both its ultimate and conventional forms."[351]

I. Generating the conventional awakening mind

Generating the conventional awakening mind has two topics:
A. Generation of the aspiring mind
B. Generation of the engaging mind

A. Generation of the aspiring mind

The aspiring mind has three topics:
1. Preliminaries
2. Actual practice
3. Subsequent practices

1. Preliminaries

The first has two topics:
a. The cause of generating the aspect
b. The cause of generating the intention

a. The cause of generating the aspect

The first has four topics:
1) Accumulating merit
2) Extraordinary going for refuge
3) Cultivating the four immeasurables
4) Offering one's body to the spiritual teacher

1) Accumulating merit

First, [generation of the awakening mind] arises from accumulating merit. All the buddhas of the past accumulated the prerequisites and became awakened by generating the awakening mind. Furthermore, the *Fortunate Eon Sūtra* states,

> Tathāgata Yaśas, when he was a weaver, offered woven tassels and generated the awakening mind; Tathāgata Flaming One (*arciṣmant*; *'od 'phro can*), when he was a city beggar, offered grass torches and generated the awakening mind; Tathāgata Duṣpradharṣa, when he was a timber merchant, offered toothpicks and generated the awakening mind, and so forth. Maitreya has also paid repect to buddhas.

> He has sown the roots of virtue. The spiritual friend created protection. This is the vessel of a ferryman.[352]

Thus this is an indication of having previously [78a] accrued accumulations. Now, as well, accumulate whatever provisions are necessary to support the spiritual teacher and the Three Jewels. Then recite the seven-limbed prayer.[353] Furthermore, the *Śikṣāsamuccaya* states, "Carrying the burden of all suffering beings without exception, pay homage, make offerings, confess misdeeds, rejoice in merit, request the buddhas to teach, and dedicate for awakening."[354] Specifically in the context of offering, arrange material objects, do not take hold of ownership, worship with the meditative stabilization called "magical display of Samantabhdra" and offer in worship all your body and possessions.

2) Extraordinary going for refuge

Then take extraordinary refuge. Directly in the presence of the buddhas, contemplate taking the perilous journey of the victorious ones. Generate the mind of supreme awakening, being born into the lineage of the victorious ones. Think, "A beggar like me, born human, who has faith for the perilous journey known by the Buddha, for the awakening mind, is not yet in the lineage of the victorious ones, and so forth."

Having thought, "Well then, I have faith," take refuge and generate the awakening mind. Having risen up seven Palmyra trees[355] in height is explained as attaining the level of irreversibility. The *Jewel Torch Dhāraṇi* also states, "If you have faith in the Victorious One and the Victorious One's Dharma, faith in the Dharma of the Buddha's sons, and faith in supreme awakening, that is generating the mind of great beings."[356] Thus you should take extraordinary refuge. That has three topics:

A) Preliminaries
B) Actual practice
C) Subsequent practices

A) Preliminaries

First, clean your residence, make preparations for a religious service with physical symbols of the Three Jewels, pay homage, and offer worship.

B) Actual practice

In regard to the actual practice, state:

> Teacher, please take heed of me, I with the name so-and-so, from this time onward until attaining the essence of awakening, take refuge in the Bhagavan Buddhas, the supreme of all humans. I take refuge in the Dharma of nirvāṇa, the ultimate peace, [**78b**] supreme of things free from desire. I take refuge in the spiritual community of great beings, irreversible ārya bodhisattvas, supreme of assemblies.

Utter three times,

> I, with the name so-and-so, take refuge from this time onward until the essence of awakening. May the teacher please accept me as a layperson who has taken refuge.

The teacher says, "It is the method."
The disciple says, "So be it! Wonderful."

C) Subsequent practices

Subsequently, do not relinquish the Three Jewels for the sake of your life. Refrain from embracing duality. Whatever difficult activities occur, do not seek another means. Having taken refuge in the Buddha, do not seek to venerate other deities. Having taken refuge in the Dharma, eliminate harming sentient beings. Having taken refuge in the spiritual community, do not associate with non-Buddhists (*tīrthika*).[357]

3) Cultivating the four immeasurables

As to the four immeasurables, *love* is the roots of virtue of nonhatred and the wish for all sentient beings to be endowed with happiness. *Compassion* is the roots of virtue of nonharmfulness and the wish for all sentient beings to be free from suffering. *Sympathetic joy* is the roots of virtue of nonenvy and the wish [for beings] not to be separated from happiness at any time. *Equanimity* is the roots of virtue of being free from like and dislike and cultivating equally and impartially for all sentient beings. Further, the nature, aspect, meditation object, and merit are immeasurable. Love causes gods and humans to love; they even will protect oneself. [It] causes much pleasure and happiness, saves from harm by poison or weapons, causes you to achieve goals without effort, to be born in the Brahmā worlds, and finally to attain buddhahood.

4) Offering one's body to the spiritual teacher

It is of utmost importance to see the spiritual teacher as a buddha and to offer your body as a servant of the spiritual teacher. Furthermore, Lord [Atiśa] has taught that when you do not see the spiritual teacher as a buddha, vows do not arise, and there is doubt in the vision to attain the spiritual levels. Therefore you should see [the spiritual teacher] as a buddha and offer one's body. **[79a]** Moreover, the *Indestructible Tent Tantra* (*Vajrapañjaratantra*) states, "The one called Vajrasattva himself takes the form of the spiritual master and abides in an ordinary form while observing and benefitting sentient beings." The *Vajra Rosary* states, "The nature of the spiritual teacher is Vajradhara. Therefore correctly worship the spiritual teacher. The attainment of that state, moreover, should be understood from the mouth of the spiritual teacher."[358]

b. The cause of generating the intention

The cause of generating the intention has four topics:

1) Contemplating the virtuous qualities of the Buddha
2) Contemplating the beneficial qualities of the awakening mind
3) Supplication
4) Inquiring to determine potential impediments

1) Contemplating the virtuous qualities of the Buddha

As to the first, a buddha has inconceivable virtuous qualities; having reached the wisdom that exactly knows the manner of reality (*yathāvadbhāvika*) to its fullest possible extent (*yāvadbhāvikatā*), he leads all beings to be disciplined and, when they are endowed with happiness and free from suffering, to complete buddhahood.

2) Contemplating the beneficial qualities of the awakening mind

The beneficial qualities of the awakening mind are stated from the *Marvelous Array Sūtra* (*Gaṇḍavyūhasūtra*):

> Son of good family, the awakening mind is like the seed of all buddha qualities. It is like a field of increasing virtuous qualities for all beings. It is like a foundation that supports all worlds. It is like Vaiśravaṇa, who purifies all offerings. It is like a father who protects

> all bodhisattvas. It is like a wish-fulfilling jewel, since it achieves all aims.[359]

The *Introduction to the Practice of Awakening* also states,

> When the awakening mind has arisen in him, a wretch, captive in the prison of existence, he is straight away hailed as son of the sugatas, to be revered in the worlds of gods and men.
>
> Taking this base image, it transmutes it into the priceless image of the Buddha Jewel. Grasp tightly the quicksilver elixir known as the awakening mind, which must be thoroughly worked.[360]

Further,

> Like the plantain stem, all other good things assuredly shed their fruit and then wither, whereas the awakening mind is a tree that constantly bears fruit. It does not wither but continues to produce.[361]

The *Liberation of Maitreya* also states,

> Son of good family, it is as follows: for example, a precious vajra, even though broken, surpasses with its brilliance [**79b**] an exalted golden ornament; the title of precious vajra is not discarded, and all other offerings are turned away. Mañjuśrī, it is as follows: for example, a chick of an Indian cuckoo within its eggshell, although it has not broken out and is still within its eggshell, cries out with the voice of an Indian cuckoo. Mañjuśrī, likewise, a bodhisattva within the eggshell of ignorance, even though they have not broken out of the view of a self and emerged from the three realms, has the voice of a buddha and cries out with the sound of emptiness, signlessness, and wishlessness.

The *Samādhi of Heroic Progress* (*Śūraṅgamasamādhi*) also states,

> When [the Buddha was] moving and teaching the awakening mind as a cause of buddhahood, Māra said, "What is the use of mentioning the awakening mind and making various virtues?" In order to turn away the seven hundred daughters of the gods from generating the awakening mind and for the sake of causing a hindrance to the

> Buddha, [Māra] went near and appeared to be bound by five bonds. Māra requested to be liberated and was liberated having generated the supreme awakening mind. The Buddha made a prediction, and even though [Māra] was not endowed with the activity of an ordinary individual, he generated the awakening mind and gained the blessing for attaining buddhahood. Therefore one should generate the awakening mind.[362]

3) Supplication

Always request from the heart to generate the awakening mind at the assembly occuring in the autumn.

In this context, offering at this time, state, "Teacher please take heed of me."

Then state three times: "Just as previous tathāgatas, arhats, completely perfect buddhas, the bhagavans and great beings, the bodhisattvas who have throughly entered into the higher stages, developed the mind set on supreme awakening, likewise I request with the teacher to generate the mind of unsurpassable, completely perfect awakening."

4) Inquiring to determine potential impediments

Conduct an inquiry to determine potential impediments. In particular, inquire by stating, "Are there sentient beings who have not crossed over who wish to cross over? Are there beings who are not liberated who wish for liberation? Are there beings without comfort who wish for relief? Are there beings who have not [80a] thoroughly passed beyond sorrow who wish to thoroughly pass beyond sorrow? Are there beings who wish to not interrupt the lineage of the Buddha?" Well then, specifically, you should firmly establish the awakening mind and [your] chosen deity.

2. Actual practice

As for actual practice, accordingly, the generation of the awakening mind is due to an accumulation of causes and conditions. That is none other than dependent arising, the occurrence of results from the accumulation of causes and conditions. Moreover, the Ācarya Nāgārjuna states, "[By] imputing any sort of annihilation in anything, however subtle, such an unwise individual does not see the meaning of arising from conditions."[363]

Thus this momentary, conceptual consciousness is the root or cause of all happiness and suffering within saṃsāra and nirvāṇa. All saṃsāra and nirvāṇa is the manifest material form of that. It is called "the causes and consequences of karmic actions." The *Vinaya* states, "Since all things arise from causes"; [conceptual consciousness] is the spontaneous manifestation of the results of virtuous or harmful deeds—there is nothing outside of that. Furthermore, the *Introduction to the Practice of Awakening* states,

> Who fashioned the pavement of scalding iron? And who sired those sirens? Every single thing arises from the evil mind, sang the Sage.[364]

Thus all the happiness and suffering of saṃsāra and nirvāṇa is not established externally. It is the manifesting result of the virtues and misdeeds made by one's own mind. Therefore the cause of happiness is the virtuous mind. May all sentient beings be endowed with happinesss.

Since the buddha who is free from suffering also, by instantly arising the mind for supreme awakening, manifested a great result from a small cause, and since one makes a realization in the mental continuum like that, generating the awakening mind also arises from previous causes. As buddhahood arises from the awakening mind, since it is an actual cause, you should generate the awakening mind. Furthermore, you should repeat without distraction, repeating three times:

> May all the buddhas and bodhisattvas residing in the ten directions please consider me. May the spiritual master please consider me. I, having the name so-and-so, from beginningless time up until the present moment, may the roots of virtue [**80b**] having the essence of giving, the essence of morality, and the essence of meditation, those that have been performed, are being performed, and will be performed, be rejoiced in. Just as previous tathāgatas, arhats, completely perfect buddhas, the bhagavans and great beings, the bodhisattvas who have thoroughly entered into the higher stages, developed the mind set on supreme awakening, likewise, may I with name so-and-so, from this time up until the essence of awakening, generate the great unsurpassable perfectly complete awakening mind. May those beings who have not crossed over cross over. May beings who are not liberated become liberated. May beings without comfort have relief. May beings who have not thoroughly passed beyond sorrow thoroughly pass beyond sorrow.

The teacher says, "It is the method."
The disciple says, "So be it! Wonderful."

B. Generation of the engaging mind

The engaging mind has two topics:
1. Praising the glory of the mind
2. Describing its training

1. Praising the glory of the mind

First, [the *Introduction to the Practice of Awakening* states,]

> Today, my birth is fruitful;
> my human life is justified.
> Today I am born into the family of the Buddha;
> now I am the Buddha's son.[365]

Thus, strive to enact the meaning. The *Heap of Jewels* (*Ratnakūṭa*) states,

> For example, Kāśyapa, as soon as the chief queen consort of a universal monarch has given birth to a son [endowed with the marks of a cakravartin], everybody will do obeisance to him—guild leaders, citizens, people from the provinces, and vassal princes. Similarly Kāśyapa, no sooner has a hero intent on awakening started aspiring after [supreme awakening] than the world, including its celestials, does obeisance to him.[366]

2. Describing its training

Training has five topics:
a. Training the mind to not abandon sentient beings
b. Abandoning the four negative qualities and training in the wholesome qualities
c. Training in the beneficial qualities of the awakening mind
d. Training in purifying the awakening mind
e. Earnestly training in the effort to accrue the two accumulations

a. Training the mind to not abandon sentient beings

Even though one possesses the vows of aspiration, since merit from that does not arise continuously, one must [81a] engage [the awakening mind]. Moreover, the *Introduction to the Practice of Awakening* states,

> Even in cyclic existence, great fruit comes from the mind resolved on awakening. But it cannot compare to the uninterrupted merit that comes from that resolve when put into action.[367]

Thus, in order to increase and fully complete the aspiration, you must generate the engaging mind, which gives rise to immeasurable merit. The *Introduction to the Practice of Awakening* states,

> With a resolve that cannot be turned back, from that moment on, though he may doze off or be distracted many times, uninterrupted streams of merit like the endless sky continuously pour forth.[368]

If the previous vow is breached, this teaches that by taking a vow it comes again from the preceptor. Therefore the engaging awakening mind is vitally important.

[Training in the] engaging mind has three points:

1) Preliminaries
2) Actual practice
3) Engaging

1) Preliminaries

The first has four topics:

a) Supplication for accruing the accumulations
b) Expressing the great extensive basis of training
c) Conducting an inquiry to determine potential common and distinctive impediments for the sake of making a suitable vessel
d) Offering exhortation

a) Supplication for accruing the accumulations

As for the first, it is of great importance to accumulate merit. Amitābha offered many precious jewels in order to appear in Sukhāvatī. Śākyamuni, due to small offerings, appeared in this degenerate age. Since at present one generates the vow and later a good result occurs, you should accrue the accumulations. The *Twenty Verses on the Bodhisattva Vow* states, "Make prostration with reverence and offer what you can to the victors along with their sons, who abide in all space and time."[369] Therefore you should offer whatever donations you can afford; perform the seven-limbed prayer; offer with no concern for your wealth; worship with all offerings. Pay homage holding a flower, and request,

> Teacher, please consider me. Teacher, I ask you to correctly receive the vows of bodhisattva conduct. I ask you to have compassion for me in not doing any harm. It is suitable to seek and hear a little knowledge.

State this three times and throw the flower.

b) Expressing the great extensive basis of training

Expressing the great extensive basis of training has three topics:
i) Expressing the factors of activity
ii) The faults of corrupted vows [**81b**]
iii) The beneficial qualities of vows

i) Expressing the factors of activity

Among these, for the first, think as follows: For the number of sentient beings that can possibly be found, for that many beings I should carry out altruistic actions; since this is the activity of bodhisattvas, I am willing and able to make it so. For the number of buddhas that can be found, for that many I should serve and worship; since this is the activity of bodhisattvas, I am willing and able to make it so. For the number of objects of knowledge and fields of science that can be found, for that many I should study and train; since this is the activity of bodhisattvas, I promise and vow to make it so.

ii) The faults of corrupted vows

The faults of corrupted vows are explained from the *Sāgaramatisūtra*,[370]

> A bodhisattva saves sentient beings who are not saved, liberates beings who are not liberated, gives relief to beings without relief, and leads to nirvāṇa beings who have not attained nirvāṇa. All sentient beings are satisfied to learn much and to possess some virtues other than that, but when a bodhisattva does not make effort in the factors conducive to awakening and does not speak accordingly, that is deceptive to the world along with its gods. In this way, when the gods who saw previous buddhas see, they condemn one who deceives and deprecates. Therefore, since a bodhisattva will have the fault of deceiving the world along with its gods, demigods, and men, you should be frightened, even terrified, to have a fault like this.

iii) The beneficial qualities of vows

The beneficial qualities of vows are explained from the *Inquiry of Vīradatta* (*Vīradattaparipṛcchā*): "If the merit of the awakening mind possessed physical form, it would completely fill all of space, and exceed even that."[371] Thus, since [the awakening mind] has the merit of however many buddhas and sentient beings can be found, I must be willing and able to make it so.

c) Inquiring to determine potential impediments

As to inquiring to determine potential impediments, accordingly, do you wish to save sentient beings who desire to be saved? Do you wish to liberate beings who are not liberated? Do you wish to give relief to beings who do not have relief? [**82a**] Do you wish to lead to nirvāṇa beings who have not attained nirvāṇa? Do you wish not to cut off the lineage of the buddhas? You must wish it to be so.

Conduct a specific inquiry: Son of good family, are you able to hear the scriptural collection of the Abhidharma? Do you understand it? Do you have faith in it? Are you able to protect it? You must be willing and able. Son of good family, do you make the aspiration for awakening? Are you a bodhisattva? Make it so. Son of good family, do you have the basis of training of all bodhisattvas called "I am called a bodhisattva"? Do you wish to hear about the morality of bodhisattvas? You must request it.

d) Offering exhortation

To offer exhortation, hold a flower and say three times, "Teacher please quickly bestow the correctly taken vows of bodhisattva morality to me." State, "The teacher has made it just so." Think how wonderful it is to have generated the bodhisattva vows that are like a wish-fulfilling jewel, a great treasure of merit, in your mental continuum and sit freely as you like.

2) Actual practice

As to the actual practice: recollect the virtuous qualities of the Buddha and the beneficial qualities of the awakening mind, and generate the specific mental practice of the three equalizations, being free from the four certainties. The four certainties are the certainties of branches, object, time, and lifespan.[372] Then, holding a flower while sitting, pay homage and offer worship to the teacher and the Three Jewels. It is not necessary to repeat this if you are focused without distraction.

> Son of good family, you with the name so-and-so, you who have the bodhisattva name so-and-so, who have become the basis of training of all bodhisattvas of the past, you who have transformed morality, who will become a basis of training of bodhisattvas of the future, who will transform morality, you who become a basis of training of all bodhisattvas who presently dwell in the ten directions, [**82b**] who transform morality, who are the basis of training: among those who have morality, who transform the training of all past bodhisattvas, who transform the training of all future bodhisattvas, who transform the training of all bodhisattvas who presently reside in the ten directions, do you wish to receive the total basis of training of present-day disciples, all bodhisattva morality, the morality of vows, the morality that gathers virtuous qualities, and the morality that achieves the aims of sentient beings?

The teacher states this three times.
The student accepts, "I wish to receive."
The teacher says, "It is the method."
The disciple says, "So be it! Wonderful."

3) Engaging

There are four topics regarding the qualities to proclaim at the end:
a) Requesting that notice be taken
b) Engaging with vision and pristine cognition
c) Not proclaiming precipitously the vows that have been taken
d) Summarizing the body of the training and understanding it

a) Requesting that notice be taken

Among these, regarding the first, link hands with all teachers and think, "I and all sentient beings should emerge from the ocean of saṃsāra." Stand up all at once and, beginning from the eastern direction, prostrate three times in the ten directions, scatter flowers in each direction, and devotedly supplicate in each direction.

Then, all the teachers and disciples stand up, raise the palms together above their heads, and then sit down. The teacher looks in the eastern direction and says the following words three times:

> This bodhisattva named so-and-so and I, the bodhisattva called so-and-so, have correctly received up to three times the vows of bodhisattva morality. The bodhisattva so-and-so has correctly taken the vows of morality with the bodhisattva so-and-so, and in limitless pure world realms in the ten directions I have been empowered. May the hidden assembly of ārya beings please grant knowledge to the hearts of [**83a**] unobscured sentient beings everywhere.[373]

b) Engaging with vision and pristine cognition

Due to this, in the eastern direction and so forth, in buddhafields beyond inconceivable numbers of world realms, omens such as earthquakes, trembling seats, radiant light, scents of incense, rainfalls of flowers, assemblies of rainbows, thunder, and so forth occur. Then, from among these bodhisattvas, the chief student becomes empowered, asking the bhagavan [of that realm], "Why are there omens like this?" [The bhagavan replies,]

> From here, passing beyond immeasurable world realms in the western direction, there is a world realm called Endurance (*Sahā*). In that world realm resides the Bhagavan Śākyamuni. In a great monastery, there is a teacher having a small retinue named so-and-so and a disciple named so-and-so; they have received and are empowered with the bodhisattva vow.

Since that time, all the buddhas have considered these bodhisattvas as chief disciples, and the bodhisattvas are considered as brothers. Furthermore, *Twenty Verses on the Bodhisattva Vow* states, "At which time, because of the virtue in that, the victorious ones and their disciples with their virtuous minds always consider you their beloved son."[374] Thus all the virtuous qualities of this will increase and will not degenerate.

c) Not proclaiming precipitously the vows that have been taken

For the sake of practice and protection, all restoration [of vows] should be performed in secret. As a bodhisattva has merit equal to space, when accumulating misdeeds with respect to this, even a small misdeed [needs to be corrected].

Accordingly, if your teacher has not kept vows, to say nothing of yourself, you should be secretive for the sake of protecting others.

d) Summarizing the body of the training and understanding it

For proclaiming the body of the training, learn as much as possible about the three vows, being free from the four certainties, and make effort to be faultless. Further, the moral discipline of vows eliminates all misdeeds together with their natures, and the vows of individual liberation are grouped into seven types. [**83b**] Protect against the faults of the fundamental downfalls explained from among these seven types and make virtue with the eleven friends.[375]

Regarding collecting virtuous qualities: it is necessary, as much as possible, at whatever time, to create virtue; even a small amount of giving from this point forward can include the six perfections, ten virtues, and so forth within your own mental continuum. The *Kṣitigarbhasūtra* states,

> One becomes a buddha with these ten paths of virtuous actions, but as long as one lives, if even just one virtuous path is not practiced and one says, "I am a Mahāyāna practitioner and I seek unexcelled, true, and complete awakening," that individual is disgusting, a hypocrite, a speaker of great falsehoods, a nihilist who deceives the world in the presence of all the bhagavan buddhas. When dying with delusion, they will fall into the lower realms of rebirth.[376]

As to acting on behalf of sentient beings: all activities whatsoever of body, speech, and mind that are done for the sake of achieving buddhahood for the benefit of others should be accompanied by the four immeasurables and the four means of gathering disciples. Accordingly, one must train in the three sets of vows as much as possible. Such a person is without fault in the inability to achieve [buddhahood for the benefit of others]. Moreover, they are without fault in establishing limited equanimity for the purpose of accomplishing an important matter.

II. Generating the ultimate awakening mind

Accordingly, both the aspiring and engaging minds are conventional means; now, you should enact what is called ultimate wisdom. Accordingly, you must be endowed with means and wisdom. The *Saṃcaya*(*gāthā*) states, "In this way, one must be endowed with means and wisdom. Without skillful means, deficient in wisdom, one falls into śrāvakahood."[377] The *Gayāśīrṣa Hill Sūtra* also states, "Wisdom free from means is Māra. Means free from wisdom is Māra."[378] Thus you must be endowed with both means and wisdom. The *Dohā*[*koṣa*] also states, "One who enters emptiness free from compassion will not discover the supreme path. One who is capable of joining both [compassion and emptiness] will reside neither in saṃsāra nor in nirvāṇa."[379] Thus you should generate the ultimate awakening mind with means and wisdom unseparated, like the wings of a bird. This has [**84a**] three topics:

A. The preliminaries
B. The actual practice
C. Subsequent practices

A. The preliminaries

First, take supreme refuge. Moreover, the Three Jewels transform into the supreme spiritual teacher. In this regard, the *Piled Up Stūpas Tantra* states, "A body comprised of all the buddhas, the very nature of Vajradhara, the root of the Three Precious Jewels: I take refuge in the spiritual master." The *Saṃvarārṇavatantra* states, "The spiritual teacher is the Buddha, the spiritual teacher is the Dharma, and the spiritual teacher is also the Saṅgha. The spiritual teacher is glorious Vajradhara."[380] The [*Sūtra*] *that Unifies the Intentions* [*of the Buddha*] (*Dgongs 'dus*) also says, "The buddhas of a thousand eons should be understood as the exalted spiritual master. Why are there eons of buddhas? They arise due to having relied on spiritual masters."[381] Thus it is the spiritual teacher who constitutes the Three Jewels. Since he causes one to attain the supreme in this life, the spiritual teacher is the supreme refuge. Moreover, since it is said that the ultimate of renunciates is the object of realization of faith, viewing the spiritual teacher as the Dharma body of the Buddha is the offering of all offerings. Dīpaṃkara paid homage by prostrating his body on the ground. Offer whatever donations you have. Then, take supreme refuge:

> Teacher, please consider me. I, named so-and-so, from this time forward until the great ocean of saṃsāra becomes empty, take refuge in the holy body of the spiritual teacher, whose nature is the body of all buddhas of the three times. I take refuge in the speech of the holy spiritual teacher, whose nature is the speech of all the buddhas of the three times. I take refuge in the mind of the holy spiritual teacher, whose nature is the mind of all the buddhas of the three times.

Say this three times.

[The teacher says,] "It is the method."

[The disciple says,] "Wonderful."

Then, meditate on your own body and the entire world of all appearances and possibilities as suddenly appearing. At that time, the ordinary has not gone anywhere, and the deity has not come from anywhere. All is one's own mind.

B. The actual practice

As for the actual practice, the *Guhyasamāja*[*tantra*] states, "Due to the sameness of the essencelessness of things, one's own mind—free of all entities, without aggregates, elements, sense spheres, and subject and object—[is] unproduced from the beginning, [**84b**] the very nature of emptiness."[382] Thus the mind is generated as emptiness itself: the ultimate. Generate the perception of the spiritual teacher as the Buddha's Dharma body, and pay homage, worship, and repeatly recite as follows:

> Teacher, please consider me. Just as previous tathāgatas, arhats, and perfectly complete buddhas have developed the mind set on supreme awakening as the very nature of emptiness, unproduced from the very beginning, the nature of one's own mind, the sameness of the essencelessness of things free from all aggregates, elements, sense spheres, and subject and object, likewise, I named so-and-so generate the mind for supreme awakening.

Say this three times.

[The teacher says,] "It is the method."

[The disciple says,] "Wonderful."

In this manner, point out the mind for those of sharp faculties. For those of middling [faculties], generate intellectual understanding. For those of the lowest [faculties], understand nothing whatsoever and establish good fortune.

As for the actual practice, a brief elaboration of the meaning of this: one's own mind is pointed out. One's own mind—ultimate reality, the unconditioned, changeless, and spontaneous presence, the essencelessness of things and persons—is your own awakening mind. Since it is pristine wisdom that cognizes that mind, you should cultivate the perception of not seeking out another buddha. "The Buddha himself did not find a Dharma other than one's own mind."[383] The *Guhyagarbha*[*tantra*] [also] states, "The mind itself is complete buddhahood; do not seek another buddha. Even though a buddha will not be found anywhere within the worlds of the ten directions, since a buddha is the realization of one's own mind, do not seek a buddha anywhere other than that."[384] No matter what occurs among the four bodily activities, or happiness and sadness, since there is no other refuge except cultivating one's own mind, you should meditate on realizing the mind.

C. Subsequent practices

First, recite the following benediction three times,

> Teacher, please consider me. Every day, in all my lifetimes, may I not forsake the awakening mind; may I be inseparable from the spiritual friend who generates the awakening mind.

Then, set the body in meditative equipoise, and contemplate that abusive enemies, hindrances that cause harm, and all obstacles to liberation and omniscience [**85a**] are your mother. Contemplate that all sentient beings are also your mother. Contemplate that these mothers—principally all sentient beings, my mothers, whose number is unfathomable like the sky—have happiness, become free from suffering, and attain precious, unsurpassable, perfectly complete awakening. Then meditate that your chosen deity suddenly appears. Recollect the spiritual teacher above your head. Then, look directly at the fleeting movements of your own mind. Observe that everything without exception is not established. Further, [everything without exception] is unproduced from the very beginning, does not abide with any identity in the middle, and at the end is unhindered everywhere. It is not established as color or shape. Since your mind is emptiness, which the buddhas of the three times have not seen, do not see, and will not see, do not engage the mind in any conceptual thought within that emptiness. Then, make a dedication. Later, as well, you should meditate accordingly. In this way, recite one time,

> Even while meditating to realize all things as emptiness, one should eliminate misdeeds and attain virtue. Even while realizing self and others as equal, one should consider how to benefit others. Even while abiding in the condition of equanimity, one should remain isolated. Even while realizing the meaning of nonduality, one should not denigrate things. Even while not having hopes and fears regarding happiness and suffering, one should strive for virtuous actions. Even while attaining the result of the three bodies, one should be in conformity with other practices. Always, in every situation, one should eliminate wrong views.[385]

Then, offer tormas in the proper sequence, and request the Dharma protectors to protect. Entrust the teachings [to the faithful protectors]. Following this, peacefully present offerings of thanksgiving. Then, since the ultimate and conventional awakening mind is an attainment, understand the attainment as an attainment. [The teacher] proclaims, "Train well in the precepts." The student proclaims, "Thank you for your kindness." Following this, dedicate the roots of virtue that arise from these [practices] to supreme awakening.

A Ritual for Generating the Awakening Mind is concluded. It is the system of Lord [Atiśa]. This is a practice of the Kadam textual domain of practice.

Supplementary Material

[**85b**] The four special limbs for rectifying the five fundamental downfalls of aspiration are: (1) contemplation, (2) object, (3) actuality, and (4) the past without regret. These are clear in the texts. The four limbs of engagement are also clear in the texts. The six limbs shared by aspiration and engagement are: (1) naturally abiding in contemplation, (2) naturally abiding in training, (3) not being a beginner, (4) not being unable to bring about effects, (5) not having the circumstance of forsaking the small for the sake of achieving a great aim, and (6) surpassing whatever suitable body, speech, and mind have arisen from five inferior contemplations.

[*jo bo*] Dīpaṃkaraśrījñāna [*mar me mdzad ye shes*], [*'brom ston*] Jayākara [*rgyal ba'i 'byung gnas*], [*pu to pa*] Ratnamabhapa [*rin chen dga' pa*], [*spyan snga pa*] Śīlajvala [*tshul khrims 'bar*], [*dgon pa ba*] Shvararāja [*dbang phyug rgyal mtshan*].[386]

The *Higher Teaching* (*Uttaratantra*) states,

> One should know the potential as having two aspects,
> like a treasure and the tree grown from the fruit:
> that naturally present since beginningless time and that perfected
> through proper cultivation.
> This twofold lineage is the desire to attain the three bodies of a buddha:
> [from] the first one, the first body, and from the second, the latter two.[387]

The four certainties: some adapt the limbs, some do not adapt the limbs. Some consider to protect or not protect, here abiding on the object. The occasion is day and night, during the rainy season and winter. The timespan is until the attainment of buddhahood.

A Common Ritual of Taking Refuge

This common ritual for taking refuge has three sections:

I. Preliminaries
II. Actual practice
III. Subsequent practices

I. Preliminaries

Prepare physical supports [of enlightened body speech and mind] and offerings. The bathed student should pay homage and make offerings. The physical supports and teacher should remain in place while being venerated.

II. Actual practice

[The student says,]

> Venerable teacher, please consider me.
> I, named so-and-so, from this moment for as long as I live, take refuge in the Buddha, supreme among bipeds.
> I take refuge in the Dharma, supreme among things free from desire.
> I take refuge in the Saṅgha, the supreme of assemblies.
> I, named so-and-so, from this moment for as long as I live, may the venerable one accept me as a layperson who has taken refuge.

One says this three times to the teacher.
The teacher says, "It is the method."
The student says, "So be it! Wonderful."

III. Subsequent practices

The subsequent practice is to recite the precepts: Do not forsake the Three Jewels for the sake of life and rewards; do not embrace two; whatever difficult hardships occur, do not seek another way; having taken refuge in the Buddha, do not seek to venerate other gods; having taken refuge in the Dharma, abandon harm to sentient beings; having taken refuge in the Saṅgha, train in not associating with non-Buddhists. Furthermore, those who arrive at the time of the ritual should learn the precepts of recollecting the virtuous qualities of the Three Jewels while repeatedly going for refuge, offering the first portion of food and drink to the Three Jewels, offering extensive worship on auspicious days, and paying homage to the buddha of whichever direction you are going in.[388]

Thus there are the three common [to all the Three Jewels], three specific, and four other than that. One should always train in these ten points of training.

[The ritual is] concluded.

A Ritual for the One-Day Precepts

The one-day precepts has three topics:

I. Preliminaries
II. Actual practice
III. Subsequent practice

I. Preliminaries

First, set out physical supports for worship. If worship, veneration, and so forth have not been established, the bathed student should bow three times to the teacher, who remains seated.

II. Actual practice

The actual practice is as follows. Say three times to the teacher:

> Venerable teacher, please consider me.
> I, named so-and-so, from this moment until the end of my life, take refuge in the Buddha, supreme among bipeds.
> I take refuge in the Dharma, supreme among things free from desire.
> I take refuge in the Saṅgha, supreme among assemblies.
> May the one-day precepts upheld at the time of the arriving new and full moon and the eighth auspicious day of the month that I, named so-and-so, take from this moment and for as long as I live be accepted by the venerable one.

III. Subsequent practice

Afterward, state the training precepts:

> Teacher, please consider me. Just as noble arhats have abandoned taking life, have turned away from taking life [**86a**], likewise, I, named so-and-so, from this time and for long as I live, during the new and full moon and the eighth auspicious day of the month, (1) abandon taking life and will turn away from taking life. With this first constituent, I will follow in the training of noble arhats. I will follow their achievement. I will practice following them.
>
> Moreover, just as the noble arhats abandoned and turned back

from (2) taking what is not given, (3) leading an unchaste life, (4) speaking falsely, (5) becoming intoxicated from barley beer and cooked beer, which brings on all failings,[389] (6) enjoying dance and music, wearing garlands, ointments, or jewelry, (7) sitting on high seats or a luxurious bed, and (8) eating at improper times, I, named so-and-so, from this moment until the end of my life, during the new and full moon and the eighth auspicious day of the month, abandon and turn back from taking what is not given; from leading an unchaste life; from speaking falsely; from becoming intoxicated from barley beer and cooked beer, the cause of all failings; from enjoying dance and music, wearing garlands, ointments, or jewelry; from sitting on high seats or a luxurious bed; and from eating at improper times.

With these eight constituents, I will follow in the training of noble arhats. I will follow their achievement. I will practice following them.

[The teacher says,] "It is the method.
[The student says,] "So be it! Wonderful."

A Ritual for the One-Day Precepts is concluded.

A Ritual for Establishing Someone as a Lay Disciple

A ritual for establishing a lay disciple (*upāsaka*) has three parts:

I. Preliminaries
II. Actual practice
III. Subsequent practices

I. Preliminaries

First, prepare physical supports and offerings. The bathed student should pay homage, make offerings, and so forth, and then sit down.

II. Actual practice

As for the actual practice, say three times:

> Venerable teacher, please consider me.
> I, named so-and-so, from this moment until the end of my life, take refuge in the Buddha, supreme among bipeds. [**87a**]
> I take refuge in the Dharma, supreme among things free from desire.
> I take refuge in the Saṅgha, supreme of assemblies.
> May the complete lay disciple precepts that I, named so-and-so, take from this time and, for long as I live, be accepted by the venerable teacher.

III. Subsequent practices

Afterward, recite the precepts:

> Teacher, please consider me. Just as noble arhats, for long as they live, (1) abandon taking life and turn back from taking life, likewise, I, named so-and-so, from this moment until the end of my life, abandon taking life and turn back from taking life. This first constituent I will follow in the training of noble arhats. I will follow their achievement. I will practice following them.
>
> Moreover, just as noble arhats have turned away from (2) taking what is not given, (3) leading an unchaste life, (4) speaking falsely, and (5) becoming intoxicated from barley beer and cooked beer, which brings on all failings, likewise, I, named so-and-so, from this

moment until the end of my life, turn away from from taking what is not given, leading an unchaste life, speaking falsely, and becoming intoxicated from barely beer and cooked beer, which brings on all failings.

With these five constituents, I will follow in the training of noble arhats. I will follow their achievement. I will practice following them.

[The teacher says,] "It is the method."
[The student says,] "So be it! Wonderful."

[The ritual is] concluded.

8. Essence of the Bodhisattva Vows

Essence of the Bodhisattva Vows is an original composition by Atiśa outlining the fundamental principles of practicing bodhisattva ethical moral discipline. The work complements the *Stages* system of bodhisattva conduct. The beginning of the work mentions the Indian-language title as *Bodhisatvasaṃvarahṛdaya*,[390] followed by the title in Tibetan (*Byang chub sems pa'i sdom pa'i snying po*). In general, providing an Indian-language title at the beginning of a Buddhist composition is an imperially sanctioned Tibetan practice that authenticates a work as included among official translations of Buddhist works into Tibetan.[391] However, *Essence of the Bodhisattva Vows* was never included in any Tibetan Tengyur or any other official register of Tibetan Buddhist canonical texts.

The colophon specifies that the text was composed by Śrīdīpaṃkarajñāna, an old form of Atiśa's ordination name. It also states the title of the work as *Fifty Verses on Essence of the Bodhisattva Vows*. According to the *General Meaning of the Stages of the Path* commentary (chapter 3), the work was composed after Naktso Lotsāwa Tsultrim Gyalwa requested Atiśa to explain the bodhisattva vows. Among the fifty verses of the composition, verses 9–26 closely match sections 125–27 of *Stages*. The parallel wording between the two documents may indicate that Atiśa first composed *Essence of the Bodhisattva Vows* at the request of Naktso Lotsāwa and then later incorporated this material into *Stages*, which was written for Drömtonpa. These parallels may also indicate that Atiśa worked with Naktso Lotsāwa in the translation of these works.

The subject matter of *Essence of the Bodhisattva Vows* correlates with material found in the later sections of *Stages*. *Stages* culminates with the practice of bodhisattva conduct and meditation. As witnessed in earlier chapters, Atiśa outlines progress in the stages of practice and meditation in correlation with the maintenance of vows. Different types of vows are applicable to the three different capacities of individuals on the path. The supreme-capacity individual takes whichever are suitable among the seven types of pratimokṣa vows as a foundation for the bodhisattva vows. Atiśa specifies in section 124 of *Stages* that the three types of bodhisattva moral discipline are the moral discipline of vows, the discipline of gathering virtuous qualities, and the discipline of benefitting sentient beings. This threefold division of discipline is based on the *Chapter on Right Conduct* in Asaṅga's *Bodhisattva Levels* (*Bodhisattvabhūmi*).[392] Among his early major works, Atiśa briefly discusses the threefold division of discipline in his *Open Basket of Jewels* in the context of increasing the awakening mind. He also discusses it in his *Lamp* and in his *Commentary on the Difficult Points of the Lamp for the Path to Awakening*.[393] Discussion of the threefold division of bodhisattva discipline will encompass several sections of *Essence of the Bodhisattva Vows*.

Essence of the Bodhisattva Vows consists of fifty stanzas on bodhisattva ethical moral discipline. After a verse of homage to the bodhisattva of wisdom, Mañjuśrī, the second verse provides an overview of the three types of discipline and then specifies trainings for the aspirational, engaging, and ultimate awakening minds. Verses 3–8 describe the points of training for the aspirational awakening mind, followed by stanzas on training in the engaging awakening mind in stanzas 9–26. In the engaging awakening mind section, verses 9–13 enumerate the eighteen downfalls of a bodhisattva, while verses 14–26 list the forty-six faulty actions of a bodhisattva.

As mentioned above, *Stages* lists the eighteen root downfalls (§125) and forty-six faulty actions of bodhisattvas (§126) in relation to individuals of supreme capacity. Although both *Essence of the Bodhisattva Vows* and *Stages* enumerate these downfalls and faulty actions, they are not listed in *Lamp* and its commentary. Indian Buddhist authors had various intepretations of the precise number of bodhisattva root downfalls (Wangchuk 2007, 188–94), and the enumeration of the root downfalls and faulty actions was also not clear to Atiśa's early Kadam followers. The *General Meaning of the Stages of the Path* commentary clarifies Atiśa's manner of counting, and its textual sources, for the downfalls and faulty actions (see chapter 3).

Verses 27–28 of *Essence of the Bodhisattva Vows* summarize points of training for the ultimate awakening mind. The discipline of gathering virtuous qualities, second among the three disciplines, is covered in verses 29–46. In this section of the text, Atiśa describes practices that enhance the six perfections and explains the discordant factors that should be eliminated. Training in the third type of discipline, the discipline of benefitting sentient beings, is treated briefly in verses 47–49. *Essence of the Bodhisattva Vows* concludes in its fiftieth verse with a dedication for all beings to generate the awakening mind and quickly attain buddhahood, having become well practiced in the conduct of bodhisattvas.

Supplementary Material

Four minor works follow *Essence of the Bodhisattva Vows* in the manuscript. These include two citations from scripture and two summaries for practice. The first text, *A Citation from the* Sāgaramatisūtra *on the Benefits of the Upholder of Dharma*, succinctly outlines the beneficial qualities accrued by one who practices the Buddha's teachings. The scriptural citation presumes multi-life benefits, as the text mentions the qualities of a dutiful practitioner's rebirths. The *Summary of Essence of the Vows* that follows is a brief topical outline of *Essence of the Bodhisattva Vows*. The succinct text was probably used as a mnemonic device for the Kadam lineage holder to quickly recall the content of Atiśa's text on bodhisattva ethical conduct. *A Method for Countermeasures to Downfalls* is a brief text that provides a ritual procedure for confessing and remedying bodhisattva vows that have been transgressed. Finally, *Ceasing to Count Good or Bad for Dharma as Cited from the Sūtra Gathering All Fragments* describes the kind of faulty behavior that results in abandoning the Buddha's teaching as well as behavior that is faulty against the transmitter of the Buddha's teaching, the Dharma preacher.

The manuscript concludes with guidance for the practitioner to train in one of four types of indivisibility. Emphasizing the union of wisdom and conduct, the text advocates either training in the practice of the indivisibility of causality and emptiness, the indivisibility of means and wisdom, the indivisibility of conventional and ultimate reality, or the indivisibility of suchness and pristine wisdom. The training in causality and emptiness correlates to the types of indivisibility realized by individuals of small and middling capacity. The three other types of indivisibility are applicable to the trainings realized by individuals of supreme capacity.

Essence of the Bodhisattva Vows

[ATIŚA]

In the Indian language: *Bodhisatvasaṃvarahṛdaya*
In the Tibetan language: *Byang chub sems dpa'i sdom pa'i snying po*

I pay homage to the noble youthful Mañjuśrī!

[1.] Having paid homage to the omniscient protector Mañjuśrī, I will give a condensed explanation of the bodhisattva vows.

[2.] In this regard, there are three types of morality in training. One abandons the ten common nonvirtues, takes refuge [**87b**] along with the vows of individual liberation, and specifically trains in the aspiring, engaging, and ultimate [awakening mind].

[3.] [§1] At the beginning, the precepts of aspiration are briefly stated, and one vows to never abandon sentient beings. One praises and worships the spiritual teacher and so forth while refraining from deception.

[4.] Without regret or remorse, do not slander one who has an awakening mind. Eliminate deceptive behavior toward all sentient beings. Cultivate the loving mind as an antidote to these, and do not speak false words for the sake of body and life.

[5.] The awakening mind is established in virtue by the Great Vehicle transmigrator. Respect and declare the virtuous qualities for the awakening mind. Straightforwardly, without deceit, contemplate benefiting others.

[6.] Having contemplated the beneficial qualities of the awakening mind, enthusiastically train in purifying the awakening mind. Dedicate the awakening mind with the threefold purity [of not conceptualizing subject, object, and action].

[7.] [§2] If fundamental downfalls occur, restore them within a third of a day by applying regret and the antidote.

[8.] If passed beyond that, retake the vow. Confess misdeeds in the presence of the Three Jewels. If one confesses three times a night, three times a day, then [vows] will be uncorrupted. Uncorrupted vows with exhausted misdeeds have immeasurable merit. One attains a happy state, ending with buddhahood.

[9.] [§3] To briefly explain the points of training related to the engaging awakening mind: (1) [due to seeking] honor and gain, praising oneself and deprecating others; (2) causing suffering to the unprotected; not giving

Dharma and wealth; (3) not listening to apologies with anger; (4) giving up the Great Vehicle and appearing to teach the excellent Dharma;

[10.] (5) stealing the property of the Three Jewels; (6) completely abandoning the sacred Dharma; (7) causing harm to the life and so forth of a monk; (8) deliberately committing the five heinous acts;

[11.] (9) holding wrong views, being ignorant of cause and effect, and so forth; (10) destroying cities and kingdoms; (11) proclaiming emptiness while not training in the Great Vehicle;

[12.] (12) turning away from engaging in highest awakening; (13) abandoning the pratimokṣa vows while practicing the Great Vehicle; (14) engaging in desire and so forth and not eliminating them through training; (15) speaking falsely, saying "I know the profound";

[13.] (16) persecuting a monk while donating to the Three Jewels; (17) giving up serenity and appropriating wealth; and (18) forsaking the awakening mind; these are the root downfalls.

[14.] [§4] (1) Passing a day and night without offering to the Three Jewels; (2) following desires; (3) voluntarily accepting riches and honor;

[15.] (4) not having respect for elders, with conceit and so forth; (5) speaking joyfully while not offering a reply to questions; (6) not accepting an invitation for a feast and not accepting gold, wealth, and so forth; (7) not giving to those seeking the holy Dharma; (8) forsaking those with offensive qualities and so forth; (9) not training for the sake of producing faith; (10) not protecting the mind; (11) not obtaining wealth for the benefit of others;

[16.] [§5] (12) not committing a nonvirtuous action with compassion for others' welfare; (13) earning a living through wrong livelihood; (14) wasting time on frivolous actions and distracting others and so forth; (15) not having joy for liberation; (16) not being fearful of afflictions and so forth;

[17.] (17) not forsaking taints that are not well known; (18) not correcting a mind that is capable but endowed with afflictions; (19) replying to exposure of one's faults by striking with abuse; (20) neglecting those who are angry with you;

[18.] (21) refusing to accept the apologies of others; (22) keeping the arousal of anger in one's mental continuum; (23) gathering disciples out of desire for material gain and respect; (24) wasting time and not countering laziness;

[19.] (25) relying on frivolous talk; (26) not seeking mental concentration while having pride and so forth; (27) not abandoning obstacles such as desire, aspirations, and so forth; (28) viewing the enjoyment of concentration as a virtuous quality;

[20.] (29) abandoning the doctrines of the Śrāvaka Vehicle and being of the Great [Vehicle] while making effort in the Śrāvaka Vehicle; (30) making effort in outsider practices while not making effort in Buddhist practices and making effort in outsider practices for their own sake;

[21.] [§6] (31) abandoning the vast Great Vehicle; (32) praising oneself and belittling others with a turbulent mind; (33) not attending Dharma ceremonies or increasing the teachings; (34) disparaging a Dharma preacher and not relying on his words; (35) not assisting those who need help; (36) avoiding the duties of caring for the sick;

[22.] (37) not working to alleviate those who suffer; (38) not teaching to those who are careless; (39) not repaying the kindness of others; (40) not alleviating the distress of others;

[23.] [§7] (41) not giving to those who desire food and resources; (42) not caring for one's companions with Dharma and material resources; (43) not acting in accordance with others' wishes; (44) not praising those who have good qualities; (45) not preventing harmful acts permitted by circumstance;

[24.] (46) not wishing to act on others' behalf and so forth while having miraculous powers. These will become faulty actions of bodhisattvas. Continuously having fetters and having little shame and modesty while viewing [them] as joyful, pure, and good qualities.

[25.] Although admonishing, passing a day without overturning is a great downfall. Furthermore, accepting to aspire to the Three Jewels and so forth while turning away from admonishing incomplete fetters is an intermediate downfall.

[26.] Slight self-reverting and confessing one or three times is not an affliction other than worshiping forgetfulness. Afflictions such as attachment, hatred, and so forth should be confessed with the four opponent powers by one's own mind.

[27.] To briefly summarize the points of training in the ultimate awakening mind: you should achieve virtue, eliminate misdeeds, and realize emptiness; realize the equality of self and other and practice benevolence; abide in a state of integration and keep to secluded places.

[28.] Although you realize nonduality, you should abandon deprecating the Dharma. Although you are without hope and fear, eliminate misdeeds and achieve virtue. Although you attain the result—the three bodies—act in accordance with others. Eliminate wrong views at all times and in any situation.

[§8] Creating virtuous qualities, the six perfections:

[29.] Having an intention with unusually strong attachment to desire; being egotistical with little altruism; being entagled in miserliness without generosity. One should eliminate these unfavorable conditions for giving.

[30.] [§9] Having generated love, compassion, and the awakening mind, endowed with a pure field, thought, and objects, give the gift of Dharma without fear of any turbulence, dedicating to awakening with the threefold purity [of not conceptualizing subject, object, and action].

[31.] Give rise to happiness and benefit, and clear away suffering in oneself and others. [**89a**] With little miserliness, spread and give fortune, and be devoid of destitution. Perfect generosity while increasing virtue as well. Remember to increase and generate wisdom and to attain buddhahood.

[32.] The improper mode of mental activity is a close object. Fully developing mental afflictions, practicing impious actions, not knowing the precepts of training, and having careless disrespect are factors discordant with morality; they should be eliminated.

[33.] With mindfulness and conscientiousness, reverse from these, maintain the vows of individual liberation, eliminate the threat of mental afflictions, gather the two accumulations by unifying with uncontaminated concentration, and establish acts other than that to perform on behalf of sentient beings.

[34.] Quickly attain suitable meditative stabilizations from contemplation. Realize the meaning of selflessness, and be endowed with serenity and insight. Be endowed with the morality that eliminates nonfree states of rebirth and gains leisure and fortune. Finally, attain buddhahood that possesses the ten powers.

[35.] Strong adherence to self-grasping and self-cherishing, having hatred and resentment after arising anger, attachment to objects, not realizing the meaning of selflessness, and not understanding karmic causation—these are discordant factors to be eliminated.

[36.] Endure suffering for the sake of spiritual practice. Meditate on love for what causes harm; overturn vindictiveness. Refrain from enraged thoughts on karmic causality and the meaning of selflessness. Do not conceptualize the three spheres [of subject, object, and action], and make dedications to supreme awakening.

[37.] [§10] Being free from the pain of hatred or attraction to others brings in the future a pleasing face and form, lovely to look upon, and a good nature. Increasing the factors of virtue and eliminating mental afflictions and misdeeds leads finally to attaining buddhahood, endowed with the major and minor marks.

[38.] Discouragement, attachment to negative actions, lethargy, attachment to pleasure, disdain for oneself, not proliferating virtue, and increasing laziness—these factors discordant with diligence should be eliminated.

[39.] Contemplate the meaning of karmic causality; with enthusiasm for virtue, refrain from discarding the fourfold dress of great armor (*saṃnāha*). Make enthusiastic effort in total virtue and be insatiable with regard to virtue, as if drinking salt water.

[40.] [§11] With diligence, increase, and do not diminish, virtue. The assistance of total virtue increases other virtues. In the future, familiarizing with this leads to being endowed with diligence. Realize the meaning of the two realities [**89b**] to quickly attain buddhahood.

[41.] [§12] Desires and aspirations and so forth; obstructions to concentration, the five faults [to serenity], laziness, forgetfulness, and so forth; mental afflictions, distraction, and so forth—these factors discordant with concentration should be totally eliminated.

[42.] Eliminate discordant factors with conscientiousness, mindfulness, and nondistraction. Nonconceptuality, clarity, residing one-pointedly without grasping, pliable body and mind—these attain mastery in being without mental afflictions. Apply the continuity of nonconceptualizing the three spheres [of subject, object, and action], and dedicate to supreme awakening.

[43.] Overturn attachment to the eight worldly concerns and sensory enjoyments. Suppressing the mental afflictions, being untainted by misdeeds, further develop awareness, supersensory knowledge, and meditative stabilization. Generate special insight and gradually attain buddhahood.

[44.] Apprehending entities as real, not recognizing the meaning of reality, not understanding karmic causality, engaging in mistaken practice, not making effort in learning, reflection, and meditation, and overwhelming delusion—these discordant factors to insight are to be eliminated.

[45.] Enthusiastically make effort in learning, reflection, and meditation. Eliminate reification (*dngos 'dzin*; *bhāvagraha*) while realizing emptiness. Train in the specific meaning of whether causes and effects are virtuous or harmful. Understand the meaning of the indivisibility of causality and emptiness.

[46.] Generate the three types of wisdom in the mental continuum, and reach the perfected path of nondelusion with regard to all knowables. Quickly attain omniscient buddhahood. With objectless compassion, achieve the welfare of sentient beings.

Achieving the aim of sentient being while eliminating selfish aims,

[47.] Cultivating the four immeasurables is the cause for success in benefiting beings. An altruistic mind with the four means of gathering [disciples] is the condition for success in benefiting beings. With the awakening mind and the six perfections, directly or indirectly, do as much as possible to benefit beings.

[48.] [§13] Since empty earnest aspirations and so forth are not capable, what is the use of the altruistic mind generation to undergo others' welfare? [§14] As perfect, noble intentions are empty, enact others' welfare as much as possible and abandon self-interest.

[49.] [§15] Train in whichever vow [you have taken] on every occasion. Investigate the practice of the awakening mind with awareness. What is the use of spiritual practices and so forth? First, generate the awakening mind. **[90a]** In actual practice, practice the threefold purity [of not conceptualizing subject, object, and action]. Afterward, make dedications to highest awakening.

[50.] With all the merit I have accumulated in writing this, may all sentient beings, having generated the awakening mind, become well practiced in bodhisattva conduct and quickly attain omniscient buddhahood.

Fifty Verses on the Essence of the Bodhisattva Vows by Śrī Dīpaṃkarajñāna is concluded.

Supplementary Material

A Citation from the Sāgaramatisūtra *on the Benefits of the Upholder of Dharma*

Regarding the benefits for the upholder of Dharma, the *Sāgaramatisūtra*[394] states,

> One who upholds the holy Dharma of the Tathāgata has great extensive insight, is endowed with pervasive wisdom, and is skilled in eliminating the mental afflictions along with their latencies. The faults of Māra will not take hold of him. He will not have any fetters or even small obstructions. He is never born in empty [buddha]-fields, and in all births he sees a victorious one. Having seen [a victorious one], he attains complete faith. He recollects giving rise to the great magnimity of Dharma. Again and again, he becomes a monk. He performs the essential achievement of perfectly pure conduct. In learning morality, he has noble religious practice. Skillfully he quickly gains the five supersensory powers. With supreme concentration, he attains liberation. He masters realization of the profound Dharma. He cuts off the doubts of all living beings. With a happy and peaceful mind, he attains awakening.

Thus and so forth, it is explained.[395]

Summary of Essence of the Vows

This essence of vows has three general points:

I. Introduction
II. Body of the text
III. Conclusion

I. Introduction

The first has three topics:

A. Teaching the characteristics
B. Paying homage
C. Promise to explain

II. Body of the text

The body of the text has two topics:
A. Brief explanation of the body
B. Extensive explanation of the parts

A. Brief explanation of the body

The first has three topics:
1. The discipline of vows
2. The discipline of gathering virtuous qualities
3. The discipline of benefiting beings

1. The discipline of vows

The first has three topics:
a. Aspiration
b. Engagement
c. Ultimate

a. Aspiration

The first has three topics:
1) Root downfalls (*rtsa ltung*)
2) Infractions (*nyes byas*)
3) Countermeasures to impairments (*nyams na phyir bcos pa*)

1) Root downfalls

The first is twofold: the actual root downfalls and relying on their antidotes.

b. Engagement

Engagement has three topics: root downfalls, infractions, countermeasures to impairments.

2. The discipline of gathering virtuous qualities

"Gathering virtuous qualities" refers to the six perfections. The words "three times" should be applied to each one of these, for each discordant class, **[90b]** for each of the perfections, and for each of the benefits.

3. The discipline of benefiting beings

The discipline of benefiting beings has three topics:

a. Essence of causes and conditions
b. Training whichever being in whatever circumstance
c. The special instructions for all activities

b. Training whichever being in whatever circumstance

[Training whichever being in whatever] circumstance has three topics: training with earnest aspiration, training with pure motivation, and training in connection with the great and small purposes.

The *Summary of Essence of the Vows* is concluded.

A Method for Countermeasures to Downfalls

Unimpaired expulsory offenses are a great contamination. When this downfall occurs, retake the vow. Whether you are connected with a teacher or not, it is suitable to retake [the vow].

An impaired, fundamental downfall is a middling coarse contamination. An individual able to speak and understand the meaning confesses in the presence [of venerable ones] three times and states,

> Venerable ones, please consider me.
> I, named so-and-so, have committed an error of gross contravention transgressing the bodhisattva disciplinary code. (State the actual transgression.) I confess these to the venerable ones openly and without concealing.
> Confessing without concealing, I am at ease; not confessing or concealing, I would not be at ease.[396]

[The venerable ones state,] "That is the method. Thank you. Perceive the stained vow."

If a downfall of a small entanglement occurs, confess in front of a single individual, as follows:

> Venerable one, please consider me.
> I, named so-and-so, have committed a small infraction. (Then state the actual transgression.) These I openly confess, without concealing them, to the venerable one.

> Confessing without concealing, I am at ease; not confessing or concealing, I would not be at ease.

In regard to general confession without a person present for confessing downfalls and so forth, confess the actual transgression along with your name and lineage. Any degeneracy of aspiration, engagement, and so forth should be accordingly confessed.

A Method for Countermeasures to Downfalls is concluded.

Ceasing to Count Good or Bad for Dharma as Cited from the Sūtra Gathering All Fragments

The *Sūtra Gathering All Fragments* (*Sarvavaidalyasaṃgrahasūtra*) states,

> One abandons the holy Dharma when perceiving the Dharma taught by the Tathāgata as good or bad.
>
> Abandoning the holy Dharma deprecates the Tathāgata. [**91a**] It is abusive words to the Saṅgha.
>
> These foolish people express this about my Dharma to the śrāvakas.
>
> This is expressed to the pratyekabuddhas. This is the training of bodhisattvas.
>
> When one states, "This is not the training," the holy Dharma is abandoned.
>
> When saying, "This is not the excellent achievement of the Dharma preacher," it is abandoning the Dharma.
>
> When expressed with carelessness, since it degenerates daily activities (*spyod lam*) and morality, it is abandoning the Dharma.
>
> In brief, when expressing faults, saying "this and that for this Dharma preacher," it is abandoning the Dharma.

Further,

> Contempt for the Dharma preacher disparages the Buddha. That is abandoning the Dharma. That is deprecating the Saṅgha.
>
> One who disparages the Dharma preacher does not respect the Buddha.
>
> That is one who does not wish to see the Buddha.
>
> Saying unpleasant things to the Dharma preacher is completely letting go of the Buddha.

> It is like generating anger toward a bodhisattva who has generated the awakening mind.

Further,

> With regard to achieving the six perfections of awakening, it is said by these foolish people that bodhisattvas should train in the perfection of wisdom itself. If one thinks to discredit by stating, "What is the use of the remaining perfections?" [the Buddha has stated,] "When I was a king of Kāśi, was it useless to give flesh to a hawk for the sake of a dove?"[397]

Further,

> If the ignorant say, "Awakening is attained by one method alone, the method of emptiness," [the reply is that] "Those who state this are not purified in conduct." Thus you should train either in the practice of the indivisibility of causality and emptiness, the indivisibility of means and wisdom, the indivisibility of conventional and ultimate reality, or the indivisibility of suchness and pristine wisdom.

The text has been edited.

Appendix 1. Table of Texts

Source: *Byang chub lam gyi rim pa* (Leh, Ladakh: Thupten Tsering, 1973). Also in Dbyangs can lha mo et al., *Bka' gdams gsung 'bum* 91:21–202. The manuscript text of both these copies are found in Buddhist Digital Resource Center work number W1KG506. A printed text of the manuscript is also found in the *Jo bo rje dpal ldan a ti sha'i gsung 'bum*.

Chapter	English Title	Tibetan Title	BDRC W1KG506*	*Jo bo gsung 'bum*
1	Stages of the Path to Awakening	*Byang chub lam gyi rim pa*	1a–22a	428–64
2	Condensed Stages of the Path	*Lam rim mdor bsdus pa*	22a–b	464–65
	Structural Analysis of the Stages of the Path to Awakening	*Byang chub lam rim bsdus don*	22b–25a	465–70
3	General Meaning of the Stages of the Path	*Byang chub lam rim gyi spyi don*	22a–39a	471–98
	Citation of Two Sūtras	———		498–99

Chapter	English Title	Tibetan Title	BDRC W1KG506*	*Jo bo gsung 'bum*
	Instructions for Select Disciples	*Lkog chos*	39b–52a	499–526
4	Verses Requested by Upāli for Establishing Nonconceptual Thought and Recognizing the Buddha's Teaching	*Rnam rtog med pa sgrub pa dang sangs rgyas kyi bstan pa ngos 'dzin pa'i skor nye ba 'khor gyis zhus pa'i tshigs bcad 'ga'*	52a–52b	526–27
5	Pointing-Out Instructions in Sets of Five	*Ngo sprod lnga tshoms*	52b–65a	527–52
	Instruction to Lesser, Middling, and Superior Meditators	*Sgom chen che 'bring chung gsum la gdams pa*	65a	552
	Mantra for Overcoming Bad Dreams	*Rmi lam ngan pa zlog pa'i sngags*	65a	552
	Mantra for Overcoming Bad Omens	*Ltas ngan pa zlog pa'i sngags*	65a	552
	Mantra for Guarding against Infectious Disease	*Nad rims bsrung pa'i sngags*	65a	552
	Scripture Cited from the Ratnakuṭa Collection to Reverse Attachment to the View of Emptiness	*Stong pa nyid kyi lta ba la zhen pa zlog pa'i phyir du mdo sde dkon brtsegs las drangs pa'i lung*	65a–b	552
	Ten Aspects of the Buddha Taught from the *Dharmasamgītisūtra*	*Chos yang dag par sdud pa'i mdo las gsungs pa'i sangs rgyas rnam pa bcu*	65b	553

Chapter	English Title	Tibetan Title	BDRC W1KG506*	*Jo bo gsung 'bum*
6	Two Protection Wheels for Clearing Away Obstacles to the Stages of the Path	*Lam rim gegs sel gyi srung 'khor gnyis*	65b	—
	General Meaning of the Oral Instructions of the Stages of the Path	*Byang chub lam gyi rim pa'i man ngag gi spyi don*	66a–76a	553–74
	Refuting Those Who Say That an Explanation for the Ultimate Mind of Awakening Does Not Exist	*Don dam sems bskyed bshad pa med ces pa la dgag pa*	76b–77a	574–75
7	A Ritual for Generating the Awakening Mind	*Byang chub tu sems bskyed pa'i cho ga*	77a–85a	575–91
	Fourfold Four Distinctive Limbs of Five Fundamental Downfalls	*Smon pa'i rtsa ltung lnga la khyad par gyi yan lag bzhi bzhi sogs*	85b	591–92
	A Common Ritual of Taking Refuge	*Skyabs 'gro thun mong ba'i cho ga*	85b–86a	592–93
	One-Day Precepts	*Bsnyen gnas*	86a–b	593–94
	A Ritual for Establishing a Layperson	*Dge bsnyen du nye bar sgrub pa'i cho ga*	86b–87a	594–95

Chapter	English Title	Tibetan Title	BDRC W1KG506*	*Jo bo gsung 'bum*
8	Essence of the Bodhisattva Vows	*Byang chub sems dpa'i sdom pa'i snying po*	87a–90a	595–600
	A Citation from the *Sāgaramatisūtra* on the Benefit of the Upholder of Dharma	*Chos 'dzin pa'i phan yon blo gros rgya mtsho'i mdo las drangs pa*	90a	600
	Summary of Essence of the Vows	*Sdom pa'i snying po'i bsdus don*	90a–b	600–601
	A Method for Countermeasures to Downfalls	*Ltung ba phyir bcos pa'i thabs*	90b	601–2
	Ceasing to Count Good or Bad for Dharma as Cited from the *Sūtra Gathering All Fragments.*	*Chos la bzang ngan du rtsi ba la rnam par thar pa bsdus pa'i mdo'i lung drangs nas dgag pa*	90b–91a	602

Appendix 2. Table of Tibetan Transliteration

Ācārya Chakdum	A tsa ra Phyag rdum
Chakriwa	Lcags ri ba
Chapa Chökyi Sengé	Phya pa Chos kyi seng ge
Chekawa Yeshé Dorjé	'Chad ka ba Ye shes rdo rje
Chengawa Tsultrim Bar	Spyan snga ba Tshul khrims 'bar
Chim Jampaiyang	Mchims 'Jam pa'i dbyangs
Chiwo Lhepa Jangchup Ö	Spyi bo lhas pa Byang chub 'od
Dakpo Lhajé	Dags po lha rje
Dakpo Tashi Namgyal	Dags po Bkra shis rnam rgyal
Densathil	Gdan sa thil
Dergé	Sde dge
Dölpa Sherab Gyatso	Dol pa Shes rab rgya mtsho
Drakgyab	Brag rgyab
Drepung	'Bras spungs
Drigung Jikten Gönpo	'Bri gung 'Jig rten mgon po
Drigung Kagyü	'Bri gung Bka' brgyud
Drigung Sumgön	'Bri gung Gsum mgon
Drigung Thil	'Bri gung mthil
Drolungpa	Gro lung pa
Drom Sherab Meché	'Brom Shes rab me lce
Dromtön Gyalwai Jungné	'Brom ston Rgyal ba'i 'byung gnas
Dromtönpa	'Brom ston pa
Gampopa Sönam Rinchen	Sgam po pa Bsod nams rin chen
Gelukpa	Dge lugs pa
Geshé Ar Jangchup Yeshé	Dge bshes
Geshé Drepa	Dge bshes Sgre pa

Geshé Gangthang Karwa	Dge bshes sgang thang dkar ba
Geshé Gar	Dge bshes 'Gar
Geshé Gönpawa	Dge bshes Dgon pa ba
Geshé Langlungpa	Dge bshes Glang lung pa
Geshé Lhopa Könchok Pal	Dge bshes Lho pa Dkon mchog dpal
Geshé Lhundup Sopa	Dge bshes Lhun sgrub bzod pa
Geshé Thabkyé	Dge bshes Thabs mkhas
Geshé Tönpa (= Dromtönpa)	Dge bshes Ston pa
Gö Lotsāwa Shönu Pal	'Gos Lo tsā ba Gzhon nu dpal
Gön Ö Jowa	Dgon 'od 'jo ba
Gönpawa Wangchuk Gyaltsen	Dgon pa ba Dbang phyug rgyal mtshan
Gya Chakri Gongkawa Jangchup Pal	Rgya Lcags ri gong kha ba Byang chub dpal
Gya Chakriwa	Rgya Lcags ri ba
Gya Tsöndrü Sengé	Rgya Brtson 'grus seng ge
Gyayön Dak	Rgya yon bdag
Jang Tsakha	Byang tsha kha
Jangchup Ling	Byang chub gling
Jangchup Ö	Byang chub 'od
Jayulwa Shönu Ö	Bya yul ba Gzhon nu 'od
Jowojé	Jo bo rje
Kadampa	Bka' gdams pa
Kagyüpa	Bka' rgyud pa
Kamawa	Ka ma ba
Karmapa Mikyö Dorjé	Karma pa Mi bskyod rdo rje
Khamkom	Khams skom
Khampa Lungpa	Kham pa Lung pa
Khedrup Jé Gelek Palsang	Khas grub rje Dge legs dpal bzang
Khenchen Chökyab Sangpo	Mkhan chen Chos skyabs bzang po
Khenchen Namkha Gyaltsenpa	Mkhan chen Nam mkha' rgyal mtshan pa
Khön	'Khon
Khutön Tsöndrü Yungdrung	Khu ston Brtson 'grus g.yung drung
Khyungpo Naljor	Khyung po rnal 'byor

Kyebu Melha	Skyes bu me lha
Lama Shang	Bla ma zhang
Langri Thangpa Dorjé Sengé	Glang ri thang pa Rdo rje seng ge
Lechen Kunga Gyaltsen	Las chen Kun dga' rgyal mtshan
Lhatsun Jangchup Ö	Lha btsun Byang chub 'od
Lhodrak Namkha Gyaltsen	Lho brag Nam mkha' rgyal mtshan
Ma Gewai Lodrö	Ma Dge ba'i blo gros
Maldro	Mal gro
Milarepa	Mi la ras pa
Mokchok Rinchen Tsöndrü	Rmog lcog Rin chen brtson 'grus
Naktso Lotsāwa Tsultrim Gyalwa	Nag tsho Lo tsā ba Tshul khrims rgyal ba
Neusurpa Yeshé Bar	Sne'u zur pa Ye shes 'bar
Ngari	Mnga' ris
Ngok Lekpai Sherab	Rngog Legs pa'i shes rab
Ngok Loden Sherab	Rngog Blo ldan shes rab
Nyangral Nyima Öser	Myang ral Nyi ma 'od zer
Nyantso	Nyan tsho
Nyethang	Snye thang
Nyingma	Rnying ma
Nyukrumpa	Snyug rum pa
Nyukrumpa Tsöndrü Bar	Smyug rum pa Brtson 'grus 'bar
Paltsek	Dpal brtsegs
Patsab Nyima Drak	Spa tshab Nyi ma grags
Phakdru Kagyü	Phag gru Bka' brgyud
Phakmodrupa	Phag mo gru ba
Phenyul Gyal Lhakhang	'Phan yul gyal lha khang
Phuchungwa Shönu Gyaltsen	Phu chung ba Gzhon nu rgyal mtshan
Potowa Rinchen Sal	Po to ba Rin chen gsal
Radreng	Rwa sgreng, Ra sgreng, Ra sgyeng
Radreng Gomchen	Rwa sgreng Sgom chen
Rinchen Sangpo	Rin chen bzang po
Rongpa Chaksorpa	Rong pa Phyag sor pa
Sahor	Za hor

Sakya Paṇḍita Kunga Gyaltsen	Sa skya Paṇḍita Kun dga' rgyal mtshan
Sangphu Neuthok	Gsang phu Ne'u thog
Sangyé Öntön	Sangs rgyas dbon ston
Serlingpa	Gser gling pa
Shang Ö Jowa	Zhang 'od 'jo ba
Sharawa Yönten Drak	Sha ra ba Yon tan grags
Shawo Gangpa	Sha bo sgang pa
Shenyen Balpo	Bshes gnyen bal po
Sönam Lhai Wangpo	Bsod nams lha'i dbang po
Taklung Kagyü	Stag lung Bka' brgyud
Taklung Thangpa Tashi Pal	Stag lung thang pa Bkra shis dpal
Tholing	Mtho lding
Tsalpa Kagyü	Tshal pa Bka' brgyud
Tsalpa Kunga Dorjé	Tshal pa Kun dga' rdo rje
Tsaphung	Ttsa phung
Tsethang	Rtses thang
Tsongkhapa (Losang Drakpa)	Tsong kha pa Blo gzang grags pa
Ü	Dbus
Yeshé Dé	Ye shes sde

Notes

1. Previous translations of *Lamp* include Das 1893, Davidson 1995, Sonam Rinchen 1997, Sherburne 1983, Sherburne 2000, 1–20 and 328–45, Dalai Lama 2002 (trans. Ruth Sonam), and Apple 2019, 181–91.
2. The title *Bodhipathakrama*, as well as *Bodhipathapradīpa*, are back-translations of Sanskrit that have not been attested in currently available manuscripts.
3. See Ducher 2020 on the collections of manuscripts in Drepung Monastery; see Apple 2018, xii–xv, for an overview of the *Collected Works of the Kadampas* (*Bka' gdams pa gsung 'bum*).
4. See appendix 1. As discussed below, there is a slight distinction between the stages of the path to awakening (*byang chub lam gyi rim pa*) as a genre of literature and stages of the path (*lam rim*) as a system of practice and meditation.
5. See Apple 2019 on the life of Atiśa and the teachings he received in his youth.
6. *Ratnakaraṇḍodghāṭa*; *Dbu ma'i man ngag rin po che'i za ma tog kha phye ba*. Introduced and translated in Apple 2018, 63–113.
7. For an English translation of *Delivering the Mind from Cyclic Existence* (*Saṃsāramanoniryāṇīkāragīti*; *'Khor ba las yid nges par 'byung ba byed pa zhes bya ba'i glu*), see Sherburne 2000, 396–405. For a translation of *Explanation of the Ten Nonvirtuous Paths of Action* (*Daśākuśalakarmapathadeśanā*; *Mi dge ba bcu'i las kyi lam bstan pa*), see Sherburne 2000, 489–93. For a translation of *Analysis of Actions* (*Karmavibhaṅga*; *Las rnam par 'byed pa*), see Sherburne 2000, 494–517.
8. *Caryāsaṃgrahapradīpa*; *Spyod pa bsdus pa'i sgron me*; translated in Apple 2019, 159–63.
9. *Śaraṇagamanadeśana*; *Skyabs su 'gro ba bstan pa*.
10. **Mahāyānapathasādhanasaṃgraha*; *Theg chen sgrub thabs shin tu bsdus*.
11. **Mahāyānapathasādhanavarṇasaṃgraha*; *Theg pa chen po'i lam gyi sgrub thabs yi ger bsdus*.
12. See Apple 2019, 44, and Las chen kun dga' rgyal mtshan, *Bka' gdams kyi rnam par thar pa bka' gdams chos 'byung gsal ba'i sgron me*, 112.23–113.7. Also, Karmay 2007, 12; Karmay identifies the source of this statement as Dpal mang Dkon mchog rgyal mtshan (1764–1853), in *Byang chub lam gyi sgron me'i 'grel ba phul byung dgyes pa'i mchod sprin*, *Collected Works*, vol. 4, no. 1, 51–53.
13. *Lamp* is preserved in three lines of transmission: (1) the Madhyamaka section of xylograph Tengyur editions, (2) the *Jo bo'i chos chung*, and (3) paracanonical blockprints and manuscripts (Eimer 1982, 7).
14. Among these citations, nine quatrains of seven-syllable lines are preserved in extant Sanskrit works (Eimer 1982, 5). Nevertheless, Eimer argues that a Sanskrit reconstruction of *Lamp* is not possible.

15. Leh, Ladakh: Thupten Tsering. See Buddhist Digital Resource Center (BDRC) work no. W1KG506.
16. *Byang chub lam gyi rim pa*, 25a6: (*zhung la sa dpyad* [read: *sa bcad*] *dang* [/] *yig sna gnyis so *cho ga gsum* gdams ngag la bzhi* [/] *lkog chos* [/] *ngo sprod* [/] *gegs sel* [/] *cho ga'o* [/] *yig sna*). Note that terms between asterisks represent legible manuscript annotations.
17. A *rin chen spung shad* is a *shad* (vertical stroke) that follows a *tsheg bar* that starts a new line.
18. Tib. *las rgyu 'bras pa*. See Apple 2018, 350n101, Apple 2019, 80.
19. Cabezón and Dorjee (2019, 35) note that the practice of *upavasatha* (or *upavāsa*) was replaced by the twenty-four-hour "Mahāyāna fast" (*theg chen gso sbyong*) in Tibet.
20. On Atiśa's ordination and his advocacy of the Mahāsāṃghika ordination lineage, see Apple 2019, 15 and 61–62.
21. *Byang chub lam gyi rim pa*, folio 22a7: **sangs rgyas* byang chub *des 'gro bas* lam* [63.7] *gyi rim pa *bka' gdams gzhung par *** spyod phyogs su *** byed do *zhes bya ba dpal mar me mdzad ye shes gyis *'brom ston pa'i don du* mdzad pa sdzogs *spyod phyogs lam rim mo* so*. Three asterisks signify illegible notations.
22. *Byang chub lam rim gyi spyi don* (28b6–7): *byin rlabs til lo nas brgyud pa ni* [/] *na ra pas* [/] *rigs ngan rnal 'byor pa* [28b7] *des rje la'o* [/] *byams snying rje 'byong pa yang* [/] *gzhan gyis khyi mo la brgyab pas* [/] *jo bo yang ro tshor byung nas ltas pas skra lugs skad* [/] *bri ka ma la shi la'i paṇḍi ta lnga mya'i nang na mchog tu gyur pa des mdzad pa'o* [/] *des dgon pa ba *'dzed dbang phyug rgyal mtshan* la* [/] *des rgya lcags* [28b8] *ri gong kha ba la* [/] *des dgam po lha rje la* [/] *des phag mo gru ba la* [/].
23. 'Gos lo tsā ba, *Deb ther sngon po*, 316.8–9: *'brom la skyes bu gsum kyi khrid kyi gdams pa rnams kyang snye thang nyid du gnang.*
24. Las chen, *Bka' gdams chos 'byung gsal ba'i sgron me*, 14–15: *lta spyod zung 'brel du ston pa'i gdams pa'i rgyal po ni skyes bu gsum gyi lam gyi rim pa zhes grags pa de yin / 'di'i gzhung ni byang chub lam gyi sgron ma yin la / mngon par rtogs pa'i rgyan* [15.1] *gyi man ngag la brten pa'o / / lam gyi rim pa 'di jo bos dge bshes ston pa la lkog tu 'khrid par mdzad de / de yang dge bshes ston pas jo bo la khong gzhan la sngags kyi gdams pa gnang nas / dngos la lam gyi rim pa 'di gnang ba ji ltar lags zhus pas /* [15.5] *ngas khyod min pa gzhan la gtad sa ma rnyed pa yin zhes gsungs nas / man ngag 'di dge bshes ston pa la gtad de / khong bstan pa'i bdag po byin gyis brlabs pa yin / des na 'brom 'phrin las kyi khyab gdal che ba yang des yin no.*
25. Las chen, *Bka' gdams chos 'byung*, 5.
26. Las chen, *Bka' gdams chos 'byung*, 8: *sang rgyas dbon ston gyi zhal nas kyang / / des na rang cag bka' gdams pa / / tshogs su bshad pa lam rim yin /* [8.10] */ lkog tu 'khrid dang bsgom pa yang / / lam gyi rim pa kho na yin.*
27. Iuchi 2016, 84; folio 8b4: *bod gyi log par rtog pa mtha' dag gi gnyen por gzhung byang chub lam kyi sgron ma gsungs / de'i lkog chos su lam kyi rim pa gnang.*
28. Lo dgon pa Bsod nams lha'i dbang po (Tibetan only, Vetturini 2007, 2:224): *lam bstan rim gyi khyad par / bstan rim du gsungs pa ni / tshogs su 'chad na bstan pa'i rim pa / nyams len du dril ba lam gyi rim pa / gzhung du bkod pa byang chub lam gyi sgron ma ste / don gcig la ming gsum btags pa dang 'dra gsungs pa dang /...*
29. Jinpa 2006, 577n10.
30. Tsong kha pa, *Lam rim chen mo*, 812.17–20; Cutler and Newland 2002, 372 [misspelling of Kön-ba-wa (*dkon-pa-ba*) for Gönpawa (*dgon pa ba*)]; Sopa and Rochard 2017, 622.

31. Roesler, Holmes, and Jackson 2015, 25–26.
32. Las chen, *Bka' gdams chos 'byung*, 14–19.
33. *Be'u bum sngon po*, translation in Roesler, Holmes, and Jackson. 2015.
34. *Skyes bu gsum gyi lam gyi rim pa*. In Sha ra ba yon tan grags, *Dge ba'i bshes gnyen zhang sha ra ba yon tan grags kyis mdzad pa'i lam rim bzhugs so*.
35. That is, *Āryaśūra's Jātakamāla*, the *Udānavarga*, Asaṅga's *Bodhisattvabhūmi*, the *Mahāyānasūtrālaṃkāra*, and *Śāntideva's Bodhicaryāvatāra* and *Śikṣāsamuccaya*. See Jinpa 2008, 9 and 658–59n527; Apple 2018, 22.
36. On the latter two works, see Apple 2018.
37. See *Uttaratantra* commentary ad 8.33 (Skt.: Johnston et al. 1991, 27.17–18): *samāsata ime trividhāḥ satvāḥ sattvarāśau saṃvidyante / bhavābhilāṣiṇo vibhavābhilāṣiṇas tadubhayānabhilāṣiṇaś ca*. Tib. D 4024, vol. *phi*, 89a4–5: *mdor bsdu na sems can gyi tshogs na sems can gyi rnam pa 'di gsum yod de / srid pa 'dod pa dang / srid pa dang bral bar 'dod pa dang / de gnyis ka mngon par mi 'dod pa'o //*. English: "In brief, there are three kinds of sentient beings among the various groups: those who cling to conditioned existence, those who wish to be free from [conditioned existence], and those who do not cling to either [conditioned existence or freedom]" (i.e., Mahāyāna followers).
38. A brief question-and-answer text between Sharawa and Patsab Nyima Drak, the *Pa tshab lo tsha ba dang zhang sha ra ba chen po dang gnyis kyis dbu ma'i dri lan*, also does not make divisions of Madhyamaka into different schools, as the doxographic distinctions within Madhyamaka had yet to become well known in the early twelfth century.
39. Cf. Las chen, *Bka' gdams chos 'byung*, 463.11–12: *'di la thams cad mkhyen pa su ma ti kī rtis shar ba pa'i lam rim dang / be'u bum lta sogs pa bka' gdams gzhung pa nas brgyud pa'i chos mang du gsan no*. This passage represents a tradition from Tsongkhapa.
40. See Cutler and Newland 2002, 423n725.
41. Nyang ral, *Chos 'byung me tog snying po sbrang rtsi'i bcud*, 434.7–13: *khams pa lung pa dang / glang ri thang pa dang / rgya lcags ri gong kha ba dang / sha ra ba dang / sha po sgang pa dang / brag brgyab pa dang / nam 'bar ba dang / ja yul ba dang / sne zur ba dang / ka ma pa dang...*
42. Vetturini 2007, 2:151.
43. Las chen, *Bka' gdams chos 'byung*, 449.16–450.4.
44. 'Jam mgon kong sprul, *Gdams ngag mdzod*, vol. 4: *jo bo'i blo sbyong don bdun ma . . . jo bo rje / 'dzeng dbang phyug rgyal mtshan / pu to ba / rgya lcags ri ba / lha ri rtsa brgyad pa / dwags po lha rje / phag gru*. A myes zhabs, *Gsung 'bum*, vol. 2 (*kha*), 94b1: */ rten 'brel snying po'i khrid kyi brgyud pa . . . a ti sha 'brom ston pa rgyal ba'i 'byung gnas / pu to ba rin chen gsal / rgya ston lcags ri ba*. See also Jinpa 2006, 247 and 429.
45. Apple 2017, 5–13. The *Lta sgom chen mo* (642.18–20) colophon lists the following lineage: *brgyud pa ni / di paṃ ka ra shrī dz+nya na / rje lcag ri gung kha ba / mnyam med dwags po rin po / rje dus gsum mkhyen pa nas brgyud rim pa ltar las / mtshungs med chos kyi rje ma pham mgon po'i zhal snga nas / bdag gis zhus*.
46. The full title of the work is *A General Explanation of, and Framework of Understanding, the Two Realities*. See Apple 2018, 171–266, for a complete annotated English translation.
47. 'Gos lo tsā ba, *Deb ther sngon po*, 547.12: *bka' gdams kyi bstan pa'i rim pa'i bstan bcos kyang mjod / gdams ngag kyang mang du gsungs bas / 'di nas bka' phyag chu bo gnyis 'dres su grags te*. Also 660.5–7: *de yang rje sgam po ba de bka' gdams dang / rje btsun mi la gnyis ga'i lugs 'dzin pas bka' phyag chu bo gnyis 'dres su grags pa bzhin*.

48. Vetturini 2013, 139: *bya yul ba / rgya yon bdag / dge bshes sgre pa / smyug rum pa / rgya lcags ri gong kha ba dang lnga la bka' gdams kyi chos rnams cha tshang bar gsan.*
49. Sherpa 2004, 48–49; Sørensen 2007, 196 (text F, 9b5–10a2): *bya 'dul 'dzin la 'dul ba'i blab bya gsan / dgung lo nyi shu rtsa brgyad la 'gong ston khri nas dbu ru byang phyogs su byon / dge bshes snyug drum pa la lam rim gsan / zla ba brgyad bsten de phyin byang chub kyi sems dang 'bral ma myong gsungs / glang thang ba'i slob ma lcags ri gong kha ba byang chub dpal la / jo bo'i gdams ngag thams cad dang / rta mgrin lha nga dang / phyag rdo rsogs gsang sngags mang po dang / mgon po gri gug can gtso 'khor gyi dbang lung gsan pas / de'i nub mo zhal gzigs rgya yon bdag la lam rim gtso bor byas pa'i sgom zhus pas / sngar gyi bde gsal de chung du song.*
50. Sherpa 2004, 32 and 85; Vetturini 2013, 139.
51. 'Gos lo tsā ba, *Deb ther sngon po*, 542–43. English translation in Roerich 1976, 455–57, summarized in Brunnhölzl 2014, 190–92.
52. Sgam po pa, *Thar pa rin po che'i rgyan*, 295: *de la dang po dngos por 'dzin pa dgag pa ni / jo bo'i byang chub lam sgron du / yod pa skye bar rigs min te/ / med pa'ang nam mkha'i me tog bzhin / / zhes pa la sogs pa gtan chigs chen po rnams kyis dpyad nas gsungs te /* ***lam rim du gsung tsa na / dngos po'am dngos po 'dzin thams cad bdag gnyis su 'dus la / bdag gnyis po de rang bzhin gyis stong nyid yin par gsungs so.***
53. Lechen also claims that Atiśa's teachings were upheld by Gampopa and Phakmodrupa (Las chen, *Bka' gdams chos 'byung*, 47.12–48.1): *chos rje sgam po pa nas nye bar bzung ste dwags po'i bka' brgyud ches grags pas kyang / jo bo nas brgyud pa'i gdams pa nyid thugs nyams su bzhes / rje sgam po pa dang / 'gro mgon phag mo grub pas lam gyi rim pa'i bstan bcos kyang mdzad 'bri khung chos rje'i khyad chos su lta ba dang spyod pa' brgyud ba gnyis kar jo bo yab sras la brgyud par mdzad cing / sdom pa gsum la rim can du slob dgos pa dang / phyi nang gi khyad par skyabs 'gros 'byed pa dang / rtsa rlung la sogs pas las dang 'bras bu zab pa dang / spyod pa tshul khrims rin po cher bzhed pa sogs bka' gdams kyi zab chos thun mong ma yin pa'i khyad chos su mdzad cing / lho la yang pas chos bzhi'i bstan bcos brtsams pa yang / chos dang po gsum skyes bu gsum gyi lam rim du snang bas / jo bo'i man ngag nyid 'dzin pa yin no.*
54. Las chen, *Bka' gdams chos 'byung*, 231.4–6: *kha rag pa nas brgyud pa'i lam sgron gyi brgyud pa ni / kha rag pa / lho pa / dge bshes ar / des phag mo gru pa la brgyud pa'ang snang ngo.* Cf. Czaja 2013, 73n26.
55. Jackson 2019, 95–98.
56. Martin 2020; Czaja 2013, 77.
57. See Jackson 1996 and Roesler, Holmes, and Jackson 2015, 14–16, for an overview and outline of this work's content. In this work ('Phag mo gru pa, *Sangs rgyas bstan rim dang jo nang mdzad brgya*) Phakmodrupa mentions Atiśa sparingly (4b3, 31a6) and cites *Lamp* only twice (33a2, 33a7–33b1).
58. See Apple 2017, Apple 2018, and Jackson 2019, 96.
59. *General Meaning: des 'bri stag gnyis la / des khams skom la / des 'khon la / des bdag la'o.*
60. Sørensen and Hazod, 2007, 742.
61. Thuken 2009, 103.
62. Jinpa 2008, 661n551.
63. Thuken 2009, 103; Vetturini 2013, 24.
64. As E. Gene Smith (2001, 99) remarks, before speaking of a Sakya sect, "the religious practices . . . within the 'Khon family . . . [are] best referred to as the 'Khon-system Rnying ma pa."

65. Jackson 1985, 26; Jackson 1987, 27; Jackson 1994, 87; Stearns 2001, 167; Vetturini 2013, 37; Thuken 2009, 103.
66. Apple 2018, 24; Iuchi 2016, 60.
67. May 2012, 38–44.
68. Wylie 1977; Everding 2002, 110; Sørensen 2007, 156.
69. Schaeffer and van der Kuijp 2009, 6.
70. Wylie 1977, 108; Vitali 1996, 419n696; Everding 2002, 110–11; Sorensen 2007, 444–45.
71. McCleary and van der Kuijp 2010, 156.
72. Vitali 1996, 418; Vitali 2004, 140–42.
73. Apple 2014, 114.
74. Tsong kha pa, *Lam rim chen mo*, 812–13: *lam sgron gyi skyes bu gsum gyi spyi'i mtshan nyid ston pa tsam ma gtogs pa'i tshig rnams bla ba la bsams nas ma drangs par / lo tstsha ba chen po dang gro lung ba yab sras kyi lam rim gyi khog rnams la gzhi byas nas lam rim du ma nas gnad rnams bsdus te.* See translation in Cutler and Newland 2002, 372. See also pages 124, 139, and 150 of the excellent biography of Tsongkhapa by Thupten Jinpa (2019).
75. Las chen, *Bka' gdams chos 'byung*, 19.12–16: *lhag par rje'i zhal nas / dge bshes yin na be'u bum sngon po la lta dgos zhes bsngags par mdzad 'dug ste / be'u bum sngon po rtsa 'grel gnyis dang / de brten gzhir mdzad nas rje btsun tsong kha pa chen pos lam gyi rim pa'i 'khrid yig rgyas par mdzad de.* "Especially, the precious lord [Tsongkhapa] has recommended that 'If you are a geshé, you must pay attention to the *Blue Compendium*.' Thus, having made the root text of the *Blue Compendium* and its commentary a fundamental support, the foremost venerable great Tsongkhapa made his extensive lecture notes on the stages of the path." Cf. Jinpa 2013, 53.
76. Tsong kha pa, *Lam rim nyams mgur*. In *gsung 'bum*, vol. *kha*, 275–80. English translation in Thurman 2018, 59–65, and Jinpa 2022, 43–49.
77. Tsong kha pa, *Dri ba lhag bsal rab dkar*. In *gsung 'bum*, vol. *kha*, 308–30. See Jinpa 1999, Jinpa 2002, 21–36, and Jinpa 2019, 88–100, for analysis of this work.
78. On Shönu Pal's analytical and direct approaches to ultimate reality, see Mathes 2016.
79. Tsong kha pa, *Gsan yig*. In *gsung 'bum*, vol. *ka*, 226–27: "Lam rim teachings in the tradition of the Kadampa master Gönpawa: (1) Jowojé (Atiśa) [Dromtön?], (2) Gönpawa, (3) Neusurpa . . . (8) Khenchen Namkha Gyaltsenpa. The lineage for the *Lamp of the Path* treatise by Atiśa: (1) Jowojé, (2) [Drom]tönpa, (3) Potowa, (4) Sharawa, (5) Ja Chekhawa . . . (12) Khenchen Chökyab Sangpa." Cf. Jackson 2010, 167 and 245n345; Roesler, Holmes, and Jackson 2015, 25–26 and 637n64–66.
80. Las chen, *Bka' gdams chos 'byung*, 51.5–7: *phyis rje btsun tsong kha pa chen po yang pha rol tu phyin pa'i lam gyi gzhung shing jo bo'i man ngag skyes bu gsum gyi lam rim la brten par mdzad la.* "Later, the foremost venerable great Tsongkhapa relied upon the perfection-path treatises and the oral instructions of Lord [Atiśa], the stages of the path of the three types of individuals."
81. Bracketed numbers below are references to the section numbers in the translation.
82. *Bodhipathapradīpaḥ*, vv. 3–5: *gang zhig thabs ni gang dag gis / 'khor ba'i bde ba tsam dag la / rang nyid don du gnyer byed pa / de ni skyes bu tha mar shes* (v.3) // *srid pa'i bde la rgyab phyogs shing / sdig pa'i las las ldog bdag nyid / gang zhig rang zhi tsam don gnyer / skyes bu de ni 'bring zhes bya* (v.4) // *rang rgyud gtogs pa'i sdug bsngal gyis / gang zhig*

gzhan gi sdug bsngal kun / yang dag zad par kun nas 'dod / skyes bu de ni mchog yin no (v.5). English translation in Apple 2019, 182.

83. *Bodhimārgapradīpapañjikā*; *Byang chub lam gyi sgron ma'i dka' 'grel.*

84. *Bodhimārgapradīpapañjikā* (Sherburne 2000, 28): *dman pa de dang de'i thabs kyis rang gi rgyud du gtogs pa'i bde ba don du gnyer / 'bring po sdug bsngal ldog pa kho na'o bde min gang phyir de ni sdug bsngal gnas yin phyir // dam pa rang gi rgyud la yod pa'i sdug bsngal rnams kyis gzhan dag la ni bde ba dang / sdug bsngal dag gtan ldog kho na don gnyer gang phyir de yi sdug bsngal gyis de sdug bsngal phyir*. *Abhidharmakośabhāṣya* ad 3.93 (Pradhan 1975, 182): *hīnaḥ prārthayate svasantatigataṃ yais tair upāyaiḥ sukham / madhyo duḥkhanivṛttim eva na sukhaṃ duḥkhāspadaṃ tad yataḥ // śreṣṭhaḥ prārthayate svasantatigatair duḥkhaiḥ pareṣāṃ sukham / duḥkhātyantanivṛttim eva ca yatas tadduḥkhaduḥkhyeva saḥ*. Cf. Sherburne 2000, 29; Roesler 2009, 343–44; Engle 2009, 402–3n79.

85. *Bodhimārgapradīpapañjikā* (Sherburne 2000, 28): *theg pa chen po'i chos kyi snod yin pas so //.*

86. See Apple 2018, 159, on Atiśa's "system of inclination." For the systems of inclination in Buddhist thought, see Apple 2023.

87. The seven kinds of pratimokṣa vows are those taken and upheld by (1) a fully ordained monk (*bhikṣu*; *dge slong*), (2) a fully ordained nun (*bhikṣuṇī*; *dge slong ma*), (3) a novice monk (*śrāmanera*; *dge tshul*), (4) a novice nun (*śrāmanerikā*; *dge tshul ma*), (5) a female novice in training (*śikṣamāṇā*; *dge slob ma*), (6) a male lay practitioner (*upāsaka*; *dge bsnyen*), and (7) a female lay practitioner (*upāsikā*; *dge bsnyen ma*).

88. Sherburne 2000, 112–46.

89. Apple 2019, 80 and 123, and Apple 2018, 88–89.

90. One-day precepts (*upavāsa*; *bsnyen gnas*, literally "approximation") are a type of observance maintained by lay disciples who uphold eight precepts during the fortnightly *upoṣadha* (*gso sbyong*) ceremony. See discussion below in *Stages* §10.

91. Sherburne 2000, 121.

92. On *poṣadha* (*upoṣadha*; *gso sbyong*) as practiced in Burma, see Spiro 1972, 214–19.

93. *Bodhimārgapradīpapañjikā* (260a, Sherburne 2000, 120): *dge bsnyen ni rnam pa gnyis te 'dod pas log par g.yem pa spangs pa dang / rang gi chung ma yang spangs pa'o / / de gnyis ka'i thun mong gi bslab pa ni 'di lta ste / rtsa ba'i ltung bar gyur pa bzhi dang chang spangs pa'o.*

94. The eight inopportune moments, or unfavorable conditions (*aṣṭāv akṣaṇāḥ*; *mi khom pa brgyad*), are conditions in which there is no opportunity to hear and practice the Buddha's teachings. Nāgārjuna's *Suhṛllekha* provides a description: "To be born (1) addicted to perverse views, (2) an animal, (3) a hungry ghost, or (4) in hell, (5) in a place without the Victorious One's word, (6) a barbarian in a remote land, (7) dull-witted, deaf, and dumb, or (8) among the long-lived gods: these are eight unfavorable conditions. You have found leisure in their absence; make efforts to end rebirth." Skt.: *mithyādṛṣṭigrāhas tiryaktvaṃ pretatā prasūtir niraye / jinavacanānupalabdhiḥ pratyantamleccajanma jaḍamūkatvam //* (64) *anyatame dīrghāyuṣi devatve janma caiva cāṣṭābhir imam / varjitam akṣaṇadoṣair labdhvā kṣaṇam ārabhasva janmanivṛttyai //* (65) (Szántó 2021, 6). Tib.: *log par lta ba 'dzin dang dud 'gro dang / / yi dwags nyid dang dmyal bar skye ba dang / / rgyal ba'i bka' med pa dang mtha' 'khob tu / / kla klor skye dang glen zhing lkugs pa nyid /* (63) */ tshe ring lha nyid gang yang rung bar ni / skye ba*

zhes bgyi mi khom skyon brgyad po / / de dag dang bral khom pa rnyed nas ni / / skye ba bzlog pa'i slad du 'bad par mdzod / / (64). Cf. Engle 2009, 407n148.

95. See *Abhidharmakośa* and *Abhidharmakośabhāṣya* ad 3.58–59cd (Sangpo 2012, 2:1058–62).
96. Cf. *Abhidharmakośabhāṣya* ad 3.59cd (Sangpo 2012, 2:1229–30n751); Bayer 2010, 368.
97. *Yogācārabhūmi* (Bhattacharya 1957, 87.17–88.20): *pretāḥ puna samāsatas trividhā bahirbhojanapānakṛtāvaraṇā adhyātmaṃ bhojapānakṛtāvaraṇā bhojanapānakṛtāvaraṇāśca.*
98. On Atiśa's Middle Way mentalism and mere appearances, see discussions in *Jewels of the Middle Way* (Apple 2018), 40, 182–84, 207–11, 244, 246, and 258.
99. See *Stages* §165.
100. On nonanalytical cessation (*so sor brtags min 'gog pa*; *apratisamkhyānirodha*), see notes to §56.
101. See Apple 2008 on mainstream Buddhist stages of attainment, from stream enterer to arhatship.
102. See Sangpo 2012, 1:659n1030.
103. For Atiśa's support of the *ekayāna*, see Apple 2018, 132, 149–50, and 159, and Atiśa's *Sngags kyi don la 'jug pa*: *de yang sgyu 'phrul drwa ba las / / theg pa gsum gyi nges 'byung la / / theg pa gcig gi 'bras bur gnas / zhes gsung pa'i don gyis na / gsum ni rgyu yin la / gcig ni 'bras bu'i ngo bo nyid du btan pa yin no.*
104. See Apple 2008, 83, and references for the Mahāyāna soteriological theory of one ultimate vehicle.
105. *Lamp for the Path to Awakening* (Apple 2019, 183). See Apple 2022 for a full translation of the *Inquiry of Vīradatta* (*Vīradattaparipṛcchā*).
106. On Atiśa's method of "exchanging self and others" (*parātmaparivārtana*; *bdag dang gzhan du brje ba*), see Apple 2018, 78, 82, 92, 95–96, and 392n531.
107. *Lamp* (v. 22; Apple 2019, 184) and *Bodhimārgapradīpapañjikā* (Sherburne 2000, 165–69). See Zimmermann 2013 for an analysis of the chapter on conduct (*śīlapaṭala*) in the *Bodhisattvabhūmi*.
108. *Śikṣāsamuccaya*, Bendall 1971, 66–67 (Sanskrit); Bendall and Rouse 1971, 70–71 (English).
109. See Apple 2018, 77, 93, 162, 229, 230, and 366n291, for the four opponent powers in the works of Atiśa.
110. *Bodhimārgapradīpapañjikā*: *'dir don dam pa'i byang chub kyi sems bsgom pas / nyams su blang ba'i thabs ni bdag gis ma bris / bla ma yongs su mnyes par byas nas bla ma las zhu bar bya'o* (Sherburne 2000, 240).
111. See Atiśa's *Open Basket of Jewels* (translated in Apple 2018, 70–73 and 97).
112. Atiśa's outlines of mahāyoga (*rnal 'byor chen po*) and anuttarayoga (*rnal 'byor bla na med pa*) tantras are in Sherburne 2000, 286–87.
113. *Mūlāpattiṭīkā*, 192b7–193a1: *bla ma dang ni rdo rje 'dzin / / tha dad par ni mi brtag go.*
114. Cf. *Guhyasamājatantra*, 2.3–4: "Due to the sameness of the essencelessness of things, one's own mind—free of all entities, without aggregates (*skandha*), elements (*dhātu*), sense spheres (*āyatana*), and subject and object—[is] unproduced from the beginning, the very nature of emptiness (*śūnyatā*)." Matsunaga 1978, 10: *sarvabhāvavigataṃ skandhadhātvāyatana-grāhyagrāhakavarjitam / dharmanairātmyasamatayā svacittam ādyanutpannaṃ śūnyatābhāvam.*

115. *Bodhimārgapradīpapañjikā: shes rab gang yin zhe na / 'di ltar lhan gcig skyes pa'am / thos pa las 'byung ba 'am / bsam pa las 'byung ba 'am / bsgom pa las 'byung ba 'am* (Sherburne 2000, 226–28).
116. On Sunakṣatra, see Eimer and Tsering 1994 and Roesler, Holmes, and Jackson 2015, 43, 461–62, 639n16, and 698n225.
117. See Apple 2017, 17–18, for full citation and Tibetan sources. On pointing-out instructions (*ngo sprod*), see chapters 4 and 5 below.
118. See Apple 2019, 178, and Apple 2018, 41, 150–52, and 273–74, for examples of Atiśa's Middle Way instructions for "not seeing the mind."
119. See Almogi 2009, 278, and Yao 2007.
120. Atiśa discusses the three bodies according to Nāgārjuna in his *Open Basket of Jewels*. See Apple 2018, 100–102. On the three bodies of a buddha, cf. Buswell and Lopez 2014, 923.
121. On the multiple wisdoms of a buddha, see Almogi 2009, 114–18.
122. Harding 2011, 273n42.
123. Tsongkhapa states in his *Great Treatise on the Stages of the Path to Enlightenment*, "Former teachers have said that there is a precept that you practice going for refuge to the tathāgata of whichever directions you are going in. I have not seen a source for this" (translation Cutler and Newland 2000, 206; Tsong kha pa, *Lam rim chen mo*, 156: *phyogs gar 'gro yang de'i de bzhin gshegs pa la skyabs su 'gro ba la bslab ces pa'i bslab bya zhig gong ma rnams gsung ste khungs ma mthong ngo*). This statement provides evidence that Tsongkhapa did not view a manuscript of Atiśa's *Stages* himself but that he did receive an oral transmission of these teachings from his teachers. Geshe Sopa (Sopa and Patt 2004, 494–95) comments, "Tsongkhapa mentions another precept of refuge taught by some earlier teachers. Although he does not explicitly say that it is incorrect, he does say that he cannot find any valid scriptural source for the advice that, wherever you go, you should take refuge in the transcendent buddha of that direction. This refers to the five *tathāgatas* . . . traditionally arrayed with Amoghasiddhi in the north, Akṣobhya in the east, Ratnasambhava in the south, Amitābha in the west, and Vairocana in the center. According to the precept in question, when you go east, you should take refuge in Akṣobhya."
124. On the servant of Śrāvastī, see page 121 below.
125. Atiśa provides a different list of benefits in *A Teaching on Taking the Refuges* (*Śaraṇagacchāmideśa, Skyabs su 'gro ba'i bstan pa*) (Sherburne 2000, 430–37). Similar, but slightly different, lists of the benefits of taking refuge are found in the works of Gampopa (Roesler, Holmes, and Jackson 2015, 207), Dakpo Tashi Namgyal (Callahan 2019, 155), and Tsongkhapa (Cutler and Newland 2000, 203–5). Tsongkhapa, in his list (Tsong kha pa, *Lam rim chen mo*, 154), specifically enumerates them as eight "benefits as they appear in personal instructions" (*man ngag las 'byung ba'i phan yon*).
126. This list comprises the eight constituents to be abandoned for the vows of *upavāsa* discipline (*bsnyen gnas kyi sdom pa'i spang bya yan lag brgyad*). The vows of *upavāsa* discipline, or the "one-day precepts," are also known as the "fortnightly assembly with its eight constituents" (*aṣṭāṅgasamanvāgataṃ upavāsaṃ*; *yan lag brgyad pa'i gso sbyong*). See under "Supplementary Material" in chapter 7 below.
127. In Buddhist monastic law the four root downfalls are known as *defeats* (*pārājika*; *pham pa*) and may entail automatic expulsion from the Saṅgha (Buswell and Lopez 2014,

621). However, not all Buddhist monastic law codes enforce expulsion in the same manner; see Clarke 2009.

128. On these eight places, or unfortunate conditions, see note 94 above.
129. The analogy of the turtle is found in *Bodhicaryāvatāra* 4.20 and numerous other traditional sources, such as the *Saccasaṃyutta* of the Saṃyutta Nikāya (see Allon 2007).
130. See Śāntideva's *Bodhicaryāvatāra* 7.14 (Crosby and Skilton 1995, 68): "Now that you have met with the boat of human life, cross over the mighty river of suffering. Fool, there is no time to sleep! It is hard to catch this boat again."
131. Compare dimensions in *Abhidharmakośa* 3.58 (Sangpo 2012, 2:1058).
132. Eight hot hells (*aṣṭa-uṣṇanaraka*) are listed in *Abhidharmakośa* 3.58 (Sangpo 2012, 2:1058). The initial listing is in the *Abhidharmakośabhāṣya* (Sangpo 2012, 2:936).
133. Cf. *Abhidharmakośa* 3.59cd (Sangpo 2012, 2:1061).
134. On the adjoining hells (*utsada*), see *Abhidharmakośa* 3.59a–c (Sangpo 2012, 2:1059–60 and 1226–28nn732–40).
135. Occasional hell (*pratyekanaraka*; *nyi tshe*), Edgerton 1953, 378b, and *Abhidharmakośabhāṣya* ad 3.59a–c (Sangpo 2012, 2:1059–60 and 1229–30).
136. See *Abhidharmakośa* 3.82 (Sangpo 2012, 2:1082).
137. Cf. The measure of lifespan of the cold hells in *Abhidharmakośa* 3.84. See Sangpo 2012, 2:1083, and also Chim Jampaiyang 2018, 486–87.
138. Compare *Abhidharmakośabhāṣya* (Sangpo 2012, 2:1062).
139. This is one of the three divisions of hungry ghosts (*preta*; *yi dwags*): those whose obstruction is external (*sgrib pa phyi na yod pa*), those whose obstruction is internal (*sgrib pa nang na yod pa*), and those whose obstructions are both external and internal (*sgrib pa phyi nang gnyis ka yod pa*).
140. Compare *Abhidharmakośa* 3.9d (Sangpo 2012, 2:956) and 3.83c (Sangpo 2012, 2:1083).
141. See *Abhidharmakośa* 3.83 (Sangpo 2012, 2:1083).
142. *Abhidharmakośabhāṣya* ad 3.83bd (Sangpo 2012, 2:1083).
143. Cf. *Abhidharmakośabhāṣya* ad 4.85ab (Sangpo 2012, 2:1433–34).
144. Atiśa will discuss in the following sections "the effect of actions similar to the cause" (*byed pa rgyu mthun gyi 'bras bu*) and "the effect of experiences similar to the cause" (*myong ba rgyu mthun gyi 'bras bu*). These effects are two types of correlative effect (*niṣyandaphala*) or "effect similar to the cause" (*rgyu mthun pa'i bras bu*). Atiśa also discusses "correlative effect" and "retributive effect" (*rnam smin*) in his works on Madhyamaka; see Apple 2018, 232–42. See Bayer 2010, 341n120 and 343n131, on *niṣyandaphala* in Abhidharma works and later Tibetan sources.
145. On the dominant result (*adhipataphala*) of negative actions, cf. *Abhidharmakośabhāṣya* ad 2.56b (Sangpo 2012, 1:650); *Abhidharmasamuccayavyākhyā* (Bayer 2010, 354–55n167). See also *Abhidharmakośabhāṣya* ad 4.85ab (Sangpo 2012, 2:1434).
146. The analogy of leather covering the ground is found in the "Guarding Awareness" (*saṃprajanyarakṣaṇaḥ*) chapter of Śāntideva's *Bodhicaryāvatāra* (5.13–14), which states, "Where is there hide to cover the whole world? The wide world can be covered with hide enough for a pair of shoes alone. In the same way, since I cannot control external events, I will control my own mind. What concern is it of mine whether other things are controlled?" (translation Crosby and Skilton 1995, 35).
147. On nonanalytical cessation (*so sor brtags min 'gog pa*; *apratisamkhyānirodha*), see *Abhidharmakośa* 1.6 (Sangpo 2012, 1:209–11) and 2.55cd (Sangpo 2012, 1:639–40); *Abhidharmakośabhāṣya* ad 2.36cd (Sangpo 2012, 1:538); Cox 1995, 102n25 and

240n5; and Kramer 2012. For other remarks by Atiśa on this cessation, see Apple 2018, 224–25.

148. The following sections presume an understanding of Atiśa's mere-appearance Madhyamaka within the context of his stages of the path system. In Atiśa's Madhyamaka, conventional realities are classified as either mistaken or correct when viewed from different perspectives—that is, in relation to the cognitive understanding of ordinary individuals or to the realizations of those who have reached the path of vision (*darśanamārga*). Within this framework of perspectives that shift as one progresses along the path, mere appearances dependently arise according to the principle of cause and effect as imputed by the mind. Atiśa repeatedly stresses in his works that appearances from causes and effects are perceived as real at the level of conventional reality until reaching the path of vision (Apple 2018, 272). Upon directly perceiving reality in the path of vision, the bonds of karma loosen, as karma does not exist, the ripening of karma does not exist, the experiencer of karma does not exist, and the agent who accumulates karma does not exist. However, as long as the cause and effect of mistaken perception is not refuted, cause and effect manifests as true from the perspective of mere deluded perception (Apple 2018, 230). The mode of relating to cause and effect as real occurs as an experiential continuum of compatible effects until reaching buddhahood (Apple 2018, 232). For Atiśa, the twelve links of dependent arising, the cause and effect of saṃsāra, are established only from the mental continuum. External objects are not established, they are not inherently real, as both appearances and the mind are dependent arisings (Apple 2018, 208). In this way, "saṃsāra appears as cause and effect as enhanced by the power of mental afflictions from the mind through the accumulation of causes and conditions in the presence of the mind. Nirvāṇa appears as cause and effect through purification as enhanced by the uncontaminated virtuous qualities of one's own mind" (Apple 2018, 209). In the context of a continuum of dependent arising, Atiśa provisionally accepts the seed/sprout metaphor for the functioning of karma along the lines of the *Śālistambasūtra* (Reat 1993; Schoening 1995) and the Madhyamaka works of Candrakīrti (Apple 2018, 353). Atiśa does not accept Yogācāra models of this metaphor, as he employs the seed/sprout example to refute Yogācāra proponents and to illustrate how things are dependent arisings that lack any intrinsic essence (Apple 2018, 32–33). On the seed metaphor in Abhidharma and Yogācāra, see Bayer 2010, 339. On Atiśa's understanding of a continuum, see Apple 2018, 207–14.

149. In this section Atiśa discusses various types of accumulated action (*bsag pa'i las*; *karmopacita*). The three factors required for karmic action to be accumulated are the preparation (*sbyor*; *maula*), the actual action (*dngos*; *prayoga*), and the conclusion (*rjes*; *pṛṣṭha*). On accumulated actions, see *Abhidharmakośabhāṣya* ad 4.120 (Sangpo 2012, 2:1474–75). In addition to accumulated actions, Atiśa mentions unaccumulated actions (*byas la ma bsag*), actions neither performed nor accumulated (*ma byas ma bsags*), and accumulated actions not performed (*ma byas bsags pa*). These categories are discussed in Asaṅga's *Viniścayasaṃgrahaṇī* (D 4038, *zhi*:139a–b). Compare with Chim Jampaiyang 2018, 699–702. For a contemporary Tibetan Buddhist commentary on these categories, see Sopa 2005, 31–33 ("actions not performed"), 114–15 ("unaccumulated"), and 292–303 ("accumulation").

150. On projecting (*ākṣepaka*; *'phen pa*) and completing (*paripūraka*; *yongs su rdzogs par byed pa*) karma, see *Abhidharmakośabhāṣya* ad 4.95 (Sangpo 2012, 2:1445–46), and

for these types of karma in the *Abhidharmasamuccaya*, see Bayer 2010, 167–69 and 356–60. See also Chim Jampaiyang 2018, 596–98 and 651–53, and Sopa 2005, 109–12.

151. See Chim Jampaiyang 2018, 595–99, on karma that is definitely experienced. On motivation (*kun slong pa*; *samutthāna*), see *Abhidharmakośabhāṣya* ad 4.8b–4.10d (Sangpo, 2012, 2:1315–20) and Chim Jampaiyang 2018, 534–38. See Chim Jampaiyang 2018, 652, for comparable examples of the mixture of consummated and projected types of karma.

152. On Atiśa's understanding of all things as one's mind, see Apple 2018, 273–74 and 406n65; on the differences between Atiśa's Madhyamaka and Yogācāra understanding of mind, see Apple 2018, 67–68 and 78; and for Atiśa's discussions on the nature of mind, see Apple 2018, 208–14, 228, 249, and 258–62.

153. The eight worldly perceptions of this lifetime are synonymous with the eight worldly concerns (*aṣṭalokadharma*), the fixation of ordinary individuals with loss (*alābha*) and gain (*lābha*), suffering (*duḥkha*) and pleasure (*sukha*), blame (*nindā*) and praise (*praśaṃsā*), and disrepute (*ayaśas*) and fame (*yaśas*).

154. The five divisions of the downfalls that occur in the Vinaya (*ltung ba sde lnga*; *pañcāpattinikāya*) include defeats (*pham pa*; *pārājika*), saṅgha stigmata (*dge 'dun lhag ma*; *saṃghāvaśeṣa*), transgressions (*ltung byed*; *pāyantikā*), confessable offenses (*sor bshags*; *pratideśanīya*), and misconduct (*nyes byas*; *duṣkṛta*). See "The Chapter on Going Forth" (*Pravrajyāvastu*) from the *Chapters on Monastic Discipline* (*Vinaya-vastu*) (Miller et al. 2023).

155. In the following sections Atiśa describes eight and three types of human suffering. In general, the eight types of human suffering are (1) birth, (2) aging, (3) sickness, (4) death, (5) suffering of encountering what is unpleasant, (6) the suffering of separation from what is pleasant, (7) the suffering of not getting what one wants, and (8) the suffering of the five appropriated aggregates. The three types of suffering are the suffering of suffering, suffering of change, and suffering of conditioned existence.

156. This section is based on Nāgārjuna's *Pratītyasamutpādahṛdaya*. See Apple 2018, 215 and 400n597; Apple 2019, 146–48.

157. The single-session path of application (*sbyor lam stan gcig*) is the ability to generate continuously in one meditative sitting (*stan gcig pa*; *ekāsanika*) both the path of preparation (*prayogamārga*) and the path of vision (*darśanamārga*). See Apple 2008, 115.

158. This section mentions afflictions (*nyon mongs*) and seminal aspects (*sa bon cha*) of the afflictions in regards to the attainment of arhatship. Atiśa appears to be provisionally following Vasubandhu (*Abhidharmakośabhāṣyam* 63.19–23 ad 2.36d; Sangpo 2012, 1:542) and Yaśomitra at this stage of the path. Vasubandhu states that when "seeds" (*bīja*) are eradicated, afflictions will no longer occur. In his subcommentary to the *Abhidharmakośabhāṣyam*, Yaśomitra explains that "seeds" are only nominally existing entities (*prajñaptisat*). Atiśa does not discuss any other factors in this section such as maturation factors (*rnam smin gyi cha*) related to the storehouse consciousness (*ālayavijñāna*) that are found in the consciousness models of Yogācāra thinkers.

159. See chapter 3 commentary and notes on §107 on the Siṃhala Island story and its numerous sources and variations.

160. The threefold existence (*srid gsum*; *tribhava*), or three states of existence, that together comprise saṃsāra are the three realms (*khams gsum*; *tridhātu*): the realm of sensory desires (*kāmadhātu*), the form realm (*rūpadhātu*), and the formless realm (*ārūpyadhātu*). See Apple 2008 on the attainments of stream enterer to arhat.

161. See Atiśa's *Cittotpādasaṃvaravidhikrama* (*Ritual for Generating the Awakening Mind and for the Bodhisattva Vow*). The corresponding excerpt of the ritual reads (Sherburne 2000, 543), "Listen, Child of Good Family. Do you aspire to rescue the unrescued, liberate the unliberated, comfort the uncomforted, cause those who have not yet reached *parinirvāṇa* to attain *parinirvāṇa*, and continue the lineage of the Buddhas? For that you must be firm in generating the awakening mind, and firm in the obligation." This is also mentioned in *Śāntarakṣita*'s *Saṃvaraviṃśakavṛtti* (*Commentary on the Twenty Vows* [*of a Bodhisattva*]; Tatz 1978, 269) in relation to the ceremony to take the bodhisattva vow. See Nattier 2005, 148–51, on the early Mahāyāna Buddhist development of these four vows.

162. The four ways of gathering disciples (*catvāri saṃgrahavastūni*; *bsdu ba'i dngos po bzhi*) are generosity, pleasing speech, beneficial conduct, and consistency between your words and deeds.

163. The standard set of six perfections in Mahāyāna sūtras are generosity (*dāna*), morality (*śīla*), patience (*kṣānti*), vigor (*vīrya*), concentration (*dhyāna*), and wisdom (*prajñā*). On the perfections in Buddhist literature, see Apple 2016b.

164. Cf. Apple 2018, 184; *Bodhimārgapradīpapañjikā* (Sherburne 2000, 164–65).

165. The five heinous acts, also known as "acts that brings immediate retribution" (*mtshams med pa'i las*; *ānantaryakarman*), are evil deeds that lead to the karmic retribution of immediate rebirth in the lowest hell of Avīci. The five heinous acts include killing one's father, mother, or an arhat, spilling the blood of a buddha, and creating a schism in the monastic order. Cf. *Abhidharmakośabhāṣya* ad 4.96 (Sangpo 2012, 2:1448). See Silk 2007 for a detailed study of these acts.

166. As Atiśa instructs in his *Extensive Commentary on the Root Downfalls* (*Mūlāpattiṭīkā*), 192b7–193a1: "Do not regard the guru as separate from Vajradhara."

167. Cf. *A General Explanation of the Two Realities* (Apple 2018, 219–20).

168. The six modes of consciousness (*ṣaḍ vijñānakāyāḥ*) are eye (*mig*, *cakṣu*), ear (*rna ba*, *śrota*), nose (*rna ba*, *ghrāṇa*), tongue (*lce*, *jihvā*), body (*lus*, *kāya*), and mind (*yid*, *manas*).

169. Compare similar statements of Atiśa's on "not seeing the mind" in Apple 2018, 250–52, and Apple 2019, 178.

170. A scribal note to the *Stages* manuscript (19a4) on the "union with the four times" (*dus bzhi mnyam par sbyor ba*) indicates that unifying the times of the flickering (*'gyus pa*) of thought, mindfulness (*dran pa*), emptiness, and dissolution (*grol ba*) synchronically purifies the four times.

171. On translation of the term *rang snang*, see https://www.nalandatranslation.org/choosing-the-right-word/right-or-rang/.

172. The four daily activities (*spyod lam rnam bzhi*) are walking (*'chags pa*), standing (*'greng ba*), sitting (*'dug pa*), and sleeping (*nyal ba*). See Callahan 2019, 646.

173. *Stages* in section 3 mentions that each of the three types of individuals may possess four qualities: practices, meditation objects, a reversal of tendencies, and a result.

174. Thus the Kadampa commentator employs a fourfold connected purpose (*dgos 'brel bzhi*). Buddhist and non-Buddhist commentaries often use four requisites stated at the beginning of work, the *anubandhacatuṣṭaya*. In Buddhist exegesis, the set of terms used is called a *purpose connection* (*dgos 'brel*), a term found in Indian and Tibetan commentaries (Schoening 1995, 33). The purpose connection often comprises a set of five terms: *purpose* (*dgos pa*; *prayojana*), *connection* (*'brel pa*; *sambandha*), *text* (*rjod pa*; *abhidhāna*), *subject matter* (*brjod par bya ba*; *abhidheya*), and *purpose of the pur-*

pose (*dgos pa'i dgos pa*; *prayojanaprayojana*). See Apple 2018, 303, for another Kadampa commentary's use of these terms. On purpose connection in Buddhist commentaries, see Broido 1983, Schoening 1995, 32–45, Schoening 1996, 117–20, Manevskaia 2008, Nance 2012, 105–20, MacDonald 2015, 10–11 and 351–55, and van der Kuijp 2020, 7–8.

175. On the *Guhyagarbhatantra*, see Martin 1987, Wangchuk 2002, and van der Kuijp 2018.

176. Cf. *Mañjuśrīnāmasaṃgīti* (Davidson 1981, 67): *sarvaśāstraviśārado vāgmī ca bhaviṣyati*. Note that the author cites the text title as *mtshan brjod phan yon*.

177. *Pitāputrasamāgamasūtra*. The Sanskrit is found in Śāntideva's *Śikṣāsamuccaya* (Bendall 1971, 256): *etāvaccaitat jñeyam / yaduta saṃvṛtiḥ paramārthaśca*; English is in Bendall and Rouse 1971, 236; it is also found in Prajñākaramati's *Bodhicaryāvatārapañjikā* (Vaidya 1960a, 177). See Mimaki 1982, 138–40.

178. Cited as *Lha'i bus zhus pa'i mdo*. Cabezón 2013, 59n15, locates this quote in Vasubandhu's *Vyākhyāyukti*. It is not found in the *Suvikrāntadevaputraparipṛcchā*.

179. See *Aṣṭasāhasrikāprajnāpāramitā*, chap. 1: *sarvākārajñatācaryā prathamaḥ parivartaḥ*.

180. On this section of the *Heart Sūtra*, see Lopez 1988, 19 and 49–56.

181. "Twelve sets of discourses" (*mdo sde bcu gnyis*) is an older Tibetan expression (Stein 2010, 48) for the "twelve branches of the scriptures" (*gsung rab yan lag bcu gnyis*; *dvādaśāṅgapravacana*), a category based on Sanskrit Buddhist sources. The twelve are comprised of discourses (*sūtra*; *mdo sde*); aphorisms in mixed prose and verse (*geya*; *dbyangs bsnyad*); prophetic declarations (*vyākaraṇa*; *lung bstan*); verses (*gāthā*; *tshig bcad*); utterances or meaningful expressions (*udāna*; *ched brjod*); frame stories (*nidāna*; *gleng gzhi*); extensive teachings (*mahāvaipulya*; *shin tu rgyas pa*); tales of past lives (*jataka*; *skyes rabs*); miraculous events (*adbhutadharma*; *rmad du byung*); narratives (*avadāna*; *rtogs brjod*); fables (*itivṛttaka*; *de lta bu byung ba*); and instructions (*upadeśa*; *gtab phab*). Cf. Cabezón 2013, 78–79, and Buswell and Lopez 2014, 276.

182. The four seals (*phyag rgya bzhi*; *caturmudrā*) or the seals of the doctrine (*dharmamudrā* or *dharma-uddāna* in Sanskrit) are mentioned in the *Ekottara-āgama* and the *Sāgaranāgarājaparipṛcchā* (D 155), among other texts. See Mizuno and Sekimori 1996, 121–34, and Buswell and Lopez 2014, 171. See also Apple 2018, 128, 141, and 377n411, for discussion in other Kadam commentaries.

183. *Madhyāntavibhāgaṭīkā*: *nyon mongs dgra rnams ma lus 'chos pa dang / ngan 'gro srid las skyob pa gang yin pa / 'chos skyob yon tan phyir na bstan bcos te / gnyis po 'di dag gzhan gyi lugs la med* (190b1–2); Sanskrit: *yac chāsti ca kleśaripūn aśeṣān saṃtrāyate durgatito bhavāc ca / tac chāsanāt trāṇa guṇāc ca śāstram etad dvayaṃ cānyamateṣu nāsti* (Pandeya 1999, 4). See also Apple 2008, 197n2, and MacDonald 2015, 2:14, on the etymology of *śāstra*.

184. See Apple 2018, 13 and 66, on the Tibetan genre classification known as the "six collections of Madhyamaka reasonings" (*dbu ma rigs tshogs drug*).

185. The Tibetan term *spyod phyogs* may be translated as "domain of practice," "concern with conduct," or even "performance class." The term is mentioned in numerous colophons throughout the *Stages* manuscript and signifies instructions, meditations, and rituals based on texts associated with Atiśa's *stages of the path* system. In early Kadam scholasticism based at the monastery of Sangphu Neuthok, the term signifies practices derived from the *Bodhisattvacaryāvatāra* and *Śikṣāsamuccaya* literature (Nishizawa 2014, 348).

186. This verse is attributed to Asaṅga's *Yogācārabhūmi* by Khedrup Jé Gelek Palsang (see

Lessing and Wayman 1968, 70–71). I have not been able to trace this verse in the extant version of the *Yogācārabhūmi*. Khedrup Jé identifies the three genuine treatises to be adhered to among the nine texts as those treatises that are (3) meaningful, (6) eliminate suffering, (9) devoted to accomplishment.

187. *Mahāyānasūtrālaṃkāra* 17.10: *mitraṃ śrayed dāntaśamopaśāntaṃ guṇādhikaṃ sodyamam āgamāḍhyaṃ / prabuddhatatvaṃ vacas ābhyupetaṃ kṛpātmakaṃ kheda-vivarjitaṃ ca*. Translation Schoening 1995. Compare Maitreyanātha/Asaṅga and Vasubandhu 2004, 224.

188. See Bajetta 2019, 149. Cited from **Sarvadharmacaryopadeśābhisamayatantra*. See also Wangchuk 2016.

189. This discourse is also known the *Great Vehicle Discourse Repudiating Those Who Violate the Discipline, the Buddha's Collected Teachings* (*Sangs rgyas kyi sde snod tshul khrims 'chal pa tshar gcod pa zhes bya ba theg pa chen po'i mdo, Buddhapiṭakaduḥśīlanigraha-nāmamahāyānasūtra*, D 220) according to the Peking colophon (P 886). The cited passage is not found in the present Kangyur editions.

190. The citation of the *Bodhisattvapratimokṣacatuṣkanirhārasūtra* (D 248) is from the *Śikṣāsamuccaya* (Bendall 1971, 144.11–15): *yaś ca śāriputra gṛhī bodhi-satvo gaṅgānadīvālikāsamāni buddhakṣetrāṇi saptaratnapratipūrṇāni kṛtvā tathāgatebhyo 'rhadbhyaḥ samyaksaṃbuddhebhyo dānaṃ dadyād / yaś ca śāriputra pravrajyāparyāpanno bodhisatva ekāṃ catuṣpadikāṃ gāthāṃ prakāśayed ayam eva tato bahutaraṃ puṇyaṃ prasavati / na śāriputra tathāgatena pravrajitasyāmiṣadānam anujñātaṃ //*. Tsongkhapa also cites the passage in his *Lam rim chen mo*, 372.

191. *Jatakamālā* (Vaidya 1959, 223): *dīpaḥ śrutaṃ mohatamaḥpramāthī caurādyahāryaṃ paramaṃ dhanaṃ ca / saṃmohaśatruvyathanāya śastraṃ nayopadeṣṭā paramaśca mantrī // 31.32 // āpadgatasyāpyavikāri mitramapīḍanīśokarujaścikitsā / balaṃ mahaddoṣabalāvamardi paraṃ nidhānaṃ yaśasaḥ śriyaśca // 31.33 // satsaṃgame prābhṛtaśībharasya sabhāsu vidvajjanarañjanasya / parapravādadyutibhāskarasya spardhāvatāṃkīrtimadāpahasya//31.34//prasannanetrānanavarṇarāgairasaṃskṛtair-apyatiharṣalabdhaiḥ / saṃrādnanavyagrakarāgradeśairvikhyāpyamānātiśayakramasya // 31.35*. Compare Khoroche 2006, 228, and Butön Rinchen Drup 2013, 12–13.

192. The citation is from the *Sarvapuṇyasamuccayasamādhi* (D 134, 92b2–4) with slight differences: *de ci'i phyir zhe na / rigs kyi bu 'di ltar thos pa dang ldan na shes rab skye bar 'gyur ro / / shes rab dang ldan na nyon mongs pa zhi bar 'gyur ro / / nyon mongs pa med na bdud kyis glags mi rnyed do / thos pa dang ldan na rtog par 'gyur ro / / rtog pa yod na tshul bzhin du chos yongs su tshol bar 'gyur ro / / tshul bzhin du chos yongs su tshol ba la brtson na bdud sdig can gyis glags mi rnyed do / / thos pa dang ldan na log par lta ba dang bral bar 'gyur la yang dag pa'i lta ba'ang skyed par 'gyur ro / / yang dag par zhugs na bdud kyis glags mi rnyed do / / yang dag par zhugs na don la nye bar rtog pa dang gnod pa dang 'bral bar 'gyur ro /*. The first portion is found in the *Śikṣāsamuccaya* by Śāntideva and is cited as the *Inquiry of Nārāyaṇa* (*sred med kyi bus zhus pa, nārāyaṇaparipṛcchā*): *tathā hi kulaputrāḥ śrutavataḥ prajñāgamo bhavati / prajñāvataḥ kleśapraśamo bhavati / niḥkleśasya māro 'vatāraṃ na labhate / /* (Bendall 1971, 189.7–8; English translation in Goodman 2016, 186).

193. This citation is a paraphrase from the *Sarvapuṇyasamuccayasamādhi* (D 134, 97a) with differences: *dri ma med pa'i gzi brjid gsum po 'di dag ni bsod nams nye bar rton pa dang / bsod nams kyi tshogs dang / bsod nams 'byung ba dang / bsod nams rgyas pa dang / bsod nams kyi rgyu 'thun pa dang / bsod nams mi zad pa dang / bsod nams bsam gyis*

mi khyab pa dang / bsod nams rgya mtsho yin te / de la gnas pa'i byang chub sems dpa' sems dpa' chen po dag gi bsod nams rnams kyi mtha' 'am tshad ni rtogs par mi nus so / / dri ma med pa'i gzi brjid rgya mtsho chen po'i thigs pa rnams kyi tshad dang mtha' ni rtogs par nus kyi byang chub sems dpa' sems dpa'chen po rnams kyi sbyin pa'i tshogs dang / tshul khrims kyi tshogs dang / thos pa'i tshogs bsags pa'i bsod nams kyi phung po'i shad dang mtha' ni rtogs par mi nus so / / dri ma med pa'i gzi brjid stong gsum gyi stong chen po'i 'jig rten gyi khams na sa la ri dang / shing ljon pa dang / nags tshal dang / rtswa yod pa thams cad ni srang tshad kyis tshad dang mtha' rtogs pa'am shes par nus kyi byang chub sems dpa' sems dpa' chen po rnams kyi sbyin pa'i tshogs dang / tshul khrims kyi tshogs dang / thos pa'i tshogs bsags pa'i bsod nams kyi phung po ni tshad gzung bar mi nus so zhes nga smra'o /.

194. The verse is found twice in the *Bodhisattvapiṭaka* (Pagel 1995, 341 and 344).
195. *Udānavarga* [22.4b–22.6]: *tathaiveha naro nityaṃ jñānavān api yo bhavet / aśrutvā na vijānāti dharmān kalyāṇapāpakān* [22.4] *pradīpena tu rūpāṇi cakṣuṣmān paśyate yathā / evaṃ śrutvā vijānāti dharmān kalyāṇapāpakān* [22.5] [Kadampa Tibetan 22.5d reads *thos pas* rather than canonical *chos pas*] *śrutvā dharmān vijānāti śrutvā pāpaṃ na sevate / śrutvā hy anarthaṃ varjayate śrutvā prāpnoti nirvṛtim.* [22.6] [Citation missing 22.6b.] See also translation in Rockhill 1892, 94; Bernhard 1965.
196. See Apple 2019, 14, for this episode in Atiśa's biography.
197. On Atiśa's rebirth in Tuṣita, see Apple 2018, 18, and Apple 2019, 75.
198. On this episode in Atiśa's biography, see Apple 2019, 21.
199. See above: "All conditioned things are impermanent. All contaminated things are suffering. All things lack essence. All nirvāṇas are peaceful."
200. The threefold training in morality (*śīla*), meditation (*samādhi*), and wisdom (*prajñā*).
201. The Kadampa commentator mentions four purposes for including a Sanskrit title. This commentary may be one of the earliest extant Tibetan commentaries to briefly discuss this literary practice. In the Tibetan assimilation of Indian Buddhism and translation of Sanskrit works, a Sanskrit title would be given along with the title in Tibetan. The Tibetans placed great importance in retaining an original Sanskrit title of an Indian Buddhist text when translating a work into Tibetan Buddhist literature. The beginnings of this literary practice are difficult to trace, but Kadampa sources claim that the necessity of a Sanskrit title goes back to the imperial period in the seventh and eighth centuries (see Apple 2018, 140). Among the purposes listed, the commentator mentions "establishing predispositions for the Sanskrit language." Although several centuries later from the current commentary, the First Dalai Lama, Gendun Drub (1391–1474), in his commentary to the *Abhidharmakośa*, says that "we need to place subtle propensities [in order to acquire] good Sanskrit [in future lives]. Since all the Buddhas of the three times, having become enlightened, teach the Dharma in Sanskrit, now, by merely assimilating this much, by this propensity, in the future our understanding of the language will come naturally" (Patt 1993, 280). For further analysis of this Tibetan literary practice, see Almogi 2005, 52–54.
202. See Apple 2008 and Apple 2013 on the metaphor of the stairway in Buddhist soteriology.
203. Nāgārjuna, *Pañcakrama*, 2.2: *ji ltar chu la chu bzhag dang / / ji ltar mar la mar bzhin du / / rang gis rang gi ye shes ni / / legs mthong gang yin 'dir phyag yin*. Skt.: *yathā jalaṃ jale nyastaṃ ghṛtaṃ caiva yathā ghṛte / svakīyaṃ ca svayaṃ paśyej jñānaṃ yatreha vandanā* (Mimaki and Tomabechi 1994, 15).

204. The text implies that the act of prostration signifies that one understands, or perceives, that the other person being prostrated to, a teacher, has noble qualities.
205. I have not been able to trace the *Piled Up Stūpas Tantra* (*mchod rten brtsegs pa'i rgyud*) as extant.
206. Cf. Sanskrit preserved in Sferra 2000, 76.17–18: *gurur buddho gurur dharmo guruḥ saṅghas tathaiva ca / gurur vajradharaḥ śrīmān gurur evātra kāraṇam*. Sferra notes: "This stanza is also quoted in the *Abhisamayamañjarī* (Dhīḥ XIII, p. 154). The first half of the verse is very similar to JS I, 24ab (*gurur buddha bhaved dharmaḥ saṅghaś cāpi sa eva hi*)." See also Sferra 2003, 63n12, for other sources.
207. *Samājasarvavidyāsūtra* (i.e., *Dgongs 'dus*, 260a2–3): *bskal pa 'bum gyi sangs rgyas pas / / slob dpon gnyan par shes par bya / / ci phyir bskal pa'i sangs rgyas rnams / / slob dpon dag la brten nas byung.*
208. Although the meaning of the statement is not explicitly clear, in some forms of esoteric Buddhist practice in Tibet, Vajrasattva may be placed in the eastern section of a maṇḍala and associated with the qualities of equanimity. The statement may therefore imply that the Kashmiri king held steadfast with equanimity even while being slaughtered to bits.
209. See *Damamūkonāmasūtra*, 357b–359b. "Joy, The Brahmin's Wife": *Bram ze mo bde ba'i le'u* (trans. in Frye 1981, 140–41).
210. Frame story from the *Sarvadurgatipariśodhanatantra*; see Bjerken 2005.
211. The Kadam commentator cites the title of the text as the *Candrapradīpasūtra*, a common title in India for the *Samādhirājasūtra*, which as Gómez and Silk (1989, 15) note may be an allusion to the bodhisattva Candraprabha, the main interlocutor of the scripture. On the titles of this scripture, see also Brunnhölzl 2014, 48–49 and 988n46.
212. *Śraddhābalādhānāvatāramudrā*. Citation not located in Dergé Kangyur. Evidently this is a sūtra quoted in Atiśa's *Mahāsūtrasamuccaya* but with the shorter title *Dad pa'i stobs bskyed pa'i mdo*.
213. See Alexander Csoma de Kőrös Translation Group 2023 for full English translation of the sūtra.
214. Citation slightly differs from canonical version. Tib. *gang dag stong chen sems can de dag kun / / byang chub phyir ni rab tu zhugs gyur cing / / ma zhum sems kyis bskal pa rdzogs par ni / / bu dang chung ma'i sbyin pa byas pa bas / / gang gis byang chub phyir ni sems bskyed nas / / de bzhin gshegs pa'i rjes su bslab pa dang / / rab 'byung sems kyis gom pa gcig bor ba / / de ni de bas bsod nams khyad par 'phags*. Several lines later: *rab 'byung de bzhin gshegs pa thams cad kyis / / rab tu bstod cing bsngags la bkur ba ste / / gang zhig sangs rgyas kun la mchod 'dod pa / / rgyal ba'i bstan la rab 'byung gzung bar gyis / / gang zhig khyim gnas rin chen khyim brgyan pa'i / / gang gā'i bye snyed sangs rgyas zhing byin dang / / gang zhig rab 'byung nyin dang mtshan gcig tu / / mi rtag sdug bsngal bdag med sems byed na / / gang zhig rab 'byung bag yod gyur ba yi / / byang chub sems' byang chub nye ba dang / / bdud kyi dkyil 'khor shin du bcom byas shing / / dge ba'i phyogs kyang mi 'grib 'phel ba yin / / rab 'byung de ni lam ngan spangs pa dang / / lam gyi rjes 'thun 'phags pa'i skye bos bstod / / de ni dge ba chud za ma yin zhing / / de ni yongs su 'dzin pa spangs pa yin / / khyim las grol ba nyon mongs mi 'phel zhing / / nyon mongs rnam grol bdud kyi 'ching ba med / / rnam grol sems ni byang chub spyad pa spyod / / spyod pa dag pas byang chub rnyed mi dka'* (*Mahāpratihāryopadeśa*, 53b).
215. *Ratnarāśisūtra* (see Silk 1994, 699–702). Also cited in Nāgārjuna's *Sūtrasamuccaya*, 216a. Note *mi phod pa nas rgyu'i bar du yang mi bzod* may correlate with *yāvad upaniṣadam api nopaiti*.

216. The citation is close to *Samādhirājasūtra*, 16a: *gang dag khyim gyi dbus na 'dug bzhin du / / byang chub dam pa mchog 'di thob pa ni / / de 'dra 'i sangs rgyas gang yang sngon ma byung / / ma byon pa dang da ltar bzhugs p'ang med / / rgyal srid mchil ma bzhin du rab spangs la / / dben pa 'dod pas dgon par gnas par gyis / / nyon mongs rab spangs bdud kyang rnam bcom na / / byang chub rdul med 'dus ma byas pa rtogs*; translation in Roberts 2022, §5.24.
217. Slight difference with canonical version. *Gośṛṅgavyākaraṇa*, 380: *'jig rten na rab tu byung bas thob pa ma gtogs par khyim pa'i cha lugs kyis dgra bcom pa'am / rang sangs rgyas sam / bla na med pa'i byang chub thob pa ni sus kyang ma thos ma mthong ngo*
218. *Mahāpratihāryanirdeśa*, 48b2: *gang dag sngon chad byung ba'i sangs rgyas dang / / gang dag ma byon byung dang bzhugs pa rnams / / de dag skyon mang khab ni ma spangs par / / bla med byang chub zhi ba thob pa med.*
219. *Vinayavastu*, *ka*:70a, and *Vinayakṣudrakavastu*, *tha*:160b1: *bcom ldan 'das de bzhin gshegs pa dgra bcom pa yang dag par rdzogs pa'i sangs rgyas shākya thub pa / shākya'i seng ge / shākya'i rgyal po gtso bo de rab tu byung ba'i rjes su bdag rab tu 'byung ste / khyim pa'i rtags spong ngo / / rab tu byung ba'i rtags yang dag par len to.*
220. *Śrīmālādevīsiṃhanādasūtra*. Translation based on Wayman 1990, 80.
221. The Kadampa author is citing the underlined portion from the *Bhaiṣajyaguru-vaiḍūryaprabhasūtra* as it appears in the *Śikṣāsamuccaya*: *evaṃ śikṣamāṇaḥ śāriputra bodhisatvo mahāsatvaḥ sarvasyāṃ jātau pravrajaty utpādād vā tathāgatānām anutpādād vāvaśyaṃ gṛhāvāsān niṣkrāmati / tat kasya hetoḥ / paramo hy ayaṃ śāriputra lābho yad uta gṛhāvāsān niṣkramaṇam iti* (Bendall 1971, 14.17–20). The Tibetan in Dergé (11a) reads: *sha ri'i bu de ltar bslabs na byang chub sems dpa' sems dpa' chen po tshe rabs thams cad du rab tu 'byung ste / de bzhin gshegs pa byung yang rung ma byung yang rung / gdon mi za bar khyim gyi gnas nas 'byung ngo / / de ci'i phyir zhe na / sha ri'i bu 'di ltar khyim gyi gnas nas mngon par 'byung ba 'di ni byang chub sems dpa' rnams kyi rnyed pa'i mchog go*. See also Goodman 2016, 17.
222. Cited from the *Bodhisattvabhūmi*; see Engle 2016, 240, section on the morality of restraint (I.10.2.1).
223. *Śrīmālādevīsiṃhanādasūtra*, D 92, 263b. Translation based on Wayman 1990, 80.
224. Citation from *Vajraśekharatantra* (D 480, 199b3) with slight differences: *lha gzhan 'dod pa brtson mi bya / / dkon mchog gsum la dad bya ste / / de gzhol ba la brtson par bya / / srog gcod rku dang 'khrig pa dang / / dang myos byed rnam par spang / / khyim pa'i sdom pa la gnas nas / / de tshe rig pa'i rgyal po bsgrub / / gal te de ni rab byung gyur / / sdom pa gsum la yang dag gnas / / so sor thar dang byang chub sems / / rig 'dzin sdom pa mchog yin no / .*
225. Also in the *Yamārikṛṣṇakarmasarvacakrasiddhakaranāmatantrarājā*, 355.
226. *Poṣadhaṃ dīyate prathamaṃ / tad anu śikṣāpadaṃ daśaṃ / / vaibhāṣyaṃ tatra deśeta / sūtrāntaṃ vai punas tathā* (*Hevajratantra* II.viii.9–10; Skt.: Snellgrove 2010, 90–91; English: Snellgrove 2010, 116).
227. *Samādhirājasūtra*, 16a. In Roberts 2022, §5.23 and §5.25.
228. *Gośṛṅgavyākaraṇa*, 226a: *de ci'i phyir zhe na / sangs rgyas gang gā'i klung gi bye ma snyed thams cad kyang sngar khyim gyi gnas spangs te rab tu byung nas spyod lam de nyid kyis byang chub chen po brnyes so / / nga yang pha rol tu phyin pa drug yongs su rdzogs te / sa bcu brnyes nas srid pa tha ma'i tshe na ma phyed na rgyal po'i khab nas byung ste nags tshal du gshegs so.*
229. Note that Atiśa's root text reads "sorceress spirits on a demonic island." The following two sections are summaries drawn from the miraculous tale (*avadāna*) of Siṃhala,

a caravan leader who with his crew becomes shipwrecked on an island inhabited by female demonesses and is rescued by the bodhisattva Avalokiteśvara in the form of a horse named Balāhakāśvarājā (*rta'i rgyal po sprin gyi shugs can*). The story is found in numerous traditional literary sources and is represented in ancient Buddhist works of art. See Lewis 1995 for an overview and Appleton 2007 for further analysis and story variations.

230. Note that the commentary does match the exact words of the root text at this point.

231. Cf. *Daśacakrakṣitigarbhasūtra* (283b): *de bzhin du sems can gang theg pa gnyis kyi chos la nan tan ma byas par theg pa chen po ston na gnyis ka nyams shing 'khyams par 'gyur ro.*

232. *Mahāyānasūtrālaṃkāra* 4.2: *cittotpādo 'dhimokṣo 'sau śuddhādhyāśayiko 'paraḥ / vaipākyo bhūmiṣu matas tathāvaraṇavarjitaḥ.* See Maitreyanātha/Asaṅga and Vasubandhu 2004, 32.

233. *Abhisamayālaṃkāra* 1.19–20: *bhūhemacandrajvalanari nidhiratnākarārṇavaiḥ / vajrācalauạdhimitraiś cintāmaṇyarkagītibhiḥ / nṛpagañjamahāmārgayānaprasravaṇo dakaiḥ / ānandoktinadīmeghair dvāviṃśatividhaḥ sa c'iti.*

234. *Bodhicaryāvatāra* 1.15: *tad bodhicittaṃ dvividhaṃ vijñātavyaṃ samāsataḥ / bodhipraṇidhicittaṃ ca bodhiprasthānam eva ca.*

235. *Bodhicittam utpādayed vaivṛtisaṃvṛtirūpakaṃ* (*Hevajratantra* II.iv; Skt.: Snellgrove 2010, 66; English: Snellgrove 2010, 104).

236. *Saṃvṛtaṃ kundasaṃkāśaṃ vivṛtaṃ sukharūpiṇaṃ* (*Hevajratantra* II.iv; Skt.: Snellgrove 2010, 66; English: Snellgrove 2010, 104).

237. *Bde ba bdag med tshul can nyid / de yi bde ba phyag rgya che* (*Hevajratantra* II.iv; underlined Tibetan differs in Snellgrove 2010, 67). Skt.: *sukhaṃ nairātmyarūpiṇaṃ / tasya saukhyaṃ mahāmudrā* (Snellgrove 2010, 66). Cf. Snellgrove 2010, 104.

238. *Nirvṛti bodhicittaṃ tu vivṛtisaṃvṛtirūpakaṃ* (*Hevajratantra* II.iv; Snellgrove 2010, 66).

239. *Dharmadhātusvabhāvaś ca prajñayaivopabhujyate // saiva sahajarūpā tu mahāsukhā divyayoginī* (*Hevajratantra* II.iv; Skt.: Snellgrove 2010, 68; English: Snellgrove 2010, 105).

240. *Bodhisattvabhūmi*; see Engle 2016, 240; section on the morality of restraint [I.10.2.1].

241. *Pratimokṣa damatyāgaḥ śikṣānikṣepaṇāc cyuteḥ / ubhayavyañjanotpatter mūlacchedān niśā'tyayāt* (*Abhidharmakośa* 4.38; Pradhan 1975, 222). See Sangpo 2012, 2:1363; Rhoton 2002, 41; Sobisch 2002. The *Abhidharmakośabhāṣyam* clarifies that "through the arrival of the end of the night" applies to the restraint of the practitioners of the fast (*upavāsa*) (Sangpo 2012, 2:1364).

242. On "upwardly progressing good qualities (*yon tan yar ldan*)," see Sobisch 2002, s.v. *yon tan yar ldan.*

243. *Sarvabuddhamahārahasyopāyakauśalyasūtra.* See the discussion below on enumerating the root downfalls.

244. In general, mindfulness (*dran pa*; *smṛti*) includes familiarization (*'dris pa'i dngos po*; *samstute vastuni*), nondistraction (*mi g.yeng ba*; *avikṣipta*), and nonforgetfulness (*brjed pa med pa*; *asaṃpramoṣa*).

245. The Kadampa author provides a paraphrased citation from the *Śikṣāsamuccaya*: *yathoktam āryacandrapradīpasūtre / yāvanta dharmāḥ kuśalāḥ prakīrtitāḥ / śīla śrutaṃ tyāgu tathaiva kṣāntiḥ / sarveṣu mūlaṃ hy ayam apramādo / nidhānalambhaḥ sugatena deśita / / iti // ko 'yam apramādo nāma / iṣṭavighātāniṣṭāgamaśaṅkāpūrvakaṃ pratikāratātparyaṃ / tad yathā tīvrakopaprasādasya rājño bhaiṣajyatailaparipūrṇa-*

bhājanaṃ gṛhītvā picchilasaṃkrameṇa bhṛtyasya gacchataḥ (Bendall 1971, 356). *Zla ba sgron ma'i mdo las ji skad du / tshul khrims thos dang gtong dang de bzhin bzod / / dge ba'i chos su brjod pa ji snyed pa / / kun gyi rtsa ba bag yod 'di yin te / / gter 'thob byed ces bde bar gshegs pas bstan / / zhes gsungs pa bzhin no / bag yod pa zhes bya ba 'di ji lta bu zhe na / 'dod pa las nyams pa dang mi 'dod pa byung bar dogs pa sngon du 'gro bas gzob pa lhur len pa ste / 'di lta ste / dper na rgyal po drag po khro zhing mgu dka' ba'i bran sman gyi 'bru mar gyis gang ba'i snod thogs te / stegs 'drod pa la 'gro bas bya ba bzhin no* (*Śikṣāsamuccaya*, 191b). See Goodman 2016, 330, for English translation. On other examples of attentiveness with vessels filled with oil, see *Telapatta Jātaka* (*Jātaka*, 1:393) in Fausbøll 1962–64, *Bodhicaryāvatāra* 7.70, and Lang 2003, 43–44.

246. The Kadampa author provides a paraphrased citation from the *Śikṣāsamuccaya*: *āryatathāgataguhyasūtre / tatra katamo 'pramādo / yad indriyasaṃvaraḥ / sa cakṣuṣā rūpāṇi dṛṣṭvā na nimittagrāhī bhavati / nānuvyañjanagrāhī / evaṃ yāvan manasā dharmān vijñāya na nimittagrāhī bhavati* (Bendall 1971, 357). *De bzhin gshegs pa'i gsang ba'i mdo las gsungs te / de la bag yod pa gang zhe na / gang 'di dbang po sdom pa'o / / de mig gis gzugs rnams mthong na mtshan mar mi 'dzin cing mngon rtags su mi 'dzin pa nas / yid kyis chos rnams rnam par shes na mtshan mar mi 'dzin cing mngon rtags su mi 'dzin pa yin te / chos rnams kyi ro myang ba dang nyes dmigs dang 'byung ba yang yang dag pa ji lta ba bzhin du rab tu shes pa ste / 'di ni bag yod pa zhes bya'o* (*Śikṣāsamuccaya*, 191b).

247. Embarassment (*lajjā*; *'dzem pa*) and shame (*hrīḥ*; *ngo tsha ba*); see Engle 2009, 468n126, on the translation of these terms.

248. *Daśacakrakṣitigarbhasūtra*, 294: *khyod 'di ltar 'dzem pa dang / ngo tsha bas so sor bshags pa legs so / / nga'i bstan pa la ma nyams pa'i skyes bu dam pa gnyis yod de / gcig ni rang bzhin gyis yongs su dag cing thog ma nas nyes pa mi byed pa'o / / gcig ni nyes pa byas su zin kyang 'dzem pa dang / ngo tsha bas so sor 'chags pa ste / skyes bu dam pa 'di gnyis ni nga'i chos la shin tu 'dun pa rnam par dag pa zhes bya'o.*

249. *Caturdharmanirdeśasūtra*, 59b1–2. The Kadampa author cites a slightly different order of the four qualities: *byams pa byang chub sems dpa' sems dpa' chen po chos bzhi dang ldan na sdig pa byas shing bsags pa zil gyis non par 'gyur ro / / bzhi gang zhe na / 'di lta ste / rnam par sun 'byin pa kun tu spyod pa dang / gnyen po kun tu spyod pa dang / sor chud par byed pa'i stobs dang / rten gyi stobs so.* See Vinītā 2010, 1:396–97, for a Sanskrit edition of this sūtra and comparative annotation with Sanskrit, Tibetan, and Chinese sources.

250. *Sarvabuddhamahārahasyopāyakauśalyasūtra*. See Tatz 1994.

251. *Sarvabuddhamahārahasyopāyakauśalyasūtra*, 37. See Chang 1983, 433ff.; Tatz 1994, 34, "The Story of Jyotis."

252. Also from the *Skillful Means of the Great Secret Sūtra*, the story of the bodhisattva ship captain involves the skillful means of taking life with a compassionate intention; see Chang 1983, 456, and Tatz 1994, 73–74.

253. *Saṃvaraviṃśakavṛtti*. See Tatz 1978, 277.

254. The opponent in this commentary is claiming that the *Ākāśagarbhasūtra* listing of the vows as found in Śāntideva's *Śikṣāsamuccaya* should be applied in the enumeration of bodhisattva downfalls (See Goodman 2016, 63–68). Atiśa provides his enumeration of bodhisattva downfalls in the following paragraphs. The Sanskrit for the citation reads: *yathā tāvad ākāśagarbhasūtre / pañcemāḥ kulaputra kṣatriyasya mūrddhābhiṣiktasya mūlāpattayaḥ / yābhir mūlāpattibhiḥ kṣatriyo*

mūrddhābhiṣiktaḥ sarvāṇi pūrvāvaropitāni kuśalamūlāni jhāṣayati / vastupatitaḥ pārājikaḥ sarvadevamanuṣyamukhebhyo 'pāyagāmī bhavati (*Śikṣāsamuccaya*, Bendall 1971, 59.10–13). Tib. (38b): *re zhig 'phags pa nam mkha'i snying po'i mdo las / rigs kyi bu rgyal po rgyal rigs spyi bo nas dbang bskur ba'i rtsa ba'i ltung ba lnga ste / rtsa ba'i ltung ba de dag gis rgyal rigs spyi bo nas dbang bskur ba dge ba'i rtsa ba sngon bskyed pa thams cad thal bar rlog ste / pham par gyur cing lha dang mi'i bde ba'i gnas thams cad las lhung nas ngan song du 'gro bar 'gyur ro*. Śāntideva also refers to the list of *Ākāśagarbhasūtra* transgressions in *Bodhisattvacaryāvatāra* 5.104. See also Apple 2018, 88–89, for Atiśa's remarks on this topic.

255. *Dpang skong phyag brgya pa*, 5a: *phung po dang / khams dang / skye mched kyis ma zin pa'i chos bdag med pa dang mnyam pa / thog ma nas ma skyes pa / stong pa nyid kyi rang bzhin gyis byang chub kyi sems bskyed pa ltar bdag ming 'di zhes bgyi bas kyang / dus 'di nas nam byang chub kyi snying po la mchis kyi bar du byang chub tu sems bskyed par bgyi'o*.
256. *Anutpannāniruddhān sarvadharmān avabhotsya* (*Śikṣāsamuccaya*; Bendall 1971, 18). English in Goodman 2016, 21.
257. *Bodhicittam utpādayed vaivṛtisaṃvṛtirūpakaṃ* (*Hevajratantra* II.iv; Snellgrove 2010, 66). English in Snellgrove 2010, 104.
258. *Sarvabhāvavigataṃ skandhadhātvāyatana-grāhyagrāhakavarjitam / dharmanairātmyasamatayā svacittam ādyanutpannaṃ śūnyatābhāvam* (*Guhyasamājatantra* 2.3–4; Matsunaga 1978, 10); for Tibetan, see Fremantle 1971, 93.
259. *De nas gnyis su med pa'i bdag nyid chen pos ye nas sangs rgyas pa'i sems ye shes su bskyed pa 'di gsungs so* (*Guhyagarbhatattvaviniścaya*, 112a; Almogi 2009, 191n8).
260. *Don dam pa dang kun rdzob kyi byang chub kyi sems ye shes su bskyed pa'i le'u ste gnyis pa'o* (*Guhyagarbhatattvaviniścaya*, 112).
261. *Shes rab snying po las / gzugs stong pa'o / / stong pa nyid gzugs so / / gzugs las kyang stong pa nyid gzhan ma yin / stong pa nyid las kyang gzugs gzhan ma yin no* (Silk 1994, 120). *Rūpaṃ śūnyatā śūnyataiva rūpaṃ rūpan na pṛthak śūnyatā śūnyatāyā na pṛthak rūpaṃ* (*Prajñāpāramitāhṛdaya*; see also Conze 1948, 35).
262. *Yod dang med pa 'di gnyis med pa'i chos yin te* (*Prajñāpāramitāsaṃcayagāthā* 1.13c, 2b; Yuyama 1976, 160). Skt.: *vidyā avidya ubhi ete asanta dharmā* (Yuyama 1976, 10).
263. *Bcom ldan 'das rnal 'byor spyod pa gang 'dod chags dang / zhe sdang dang / gti mug las gud du stong pa nyid tshol ba de ni rnal 'byor la mi spyod pa lags te / rnal 'byor ma lags pa'o / / de ci'i slad du zhe na / bcom ldan 'das 'dod chags dang / zhe sdang dang / gti mug las gud du stong pa nyid btsal bar bgyi ba ma mchis te / bcom ldan 'das 'dod chags dang / zhe sdang dang / gti mug nyid stong pa lags so* (*Acintyabuddhaviṣayanirdeśasūtra*, 268b).
264. *Pañcakāyātmako buddhaḥ pañcajñānātmako vibhuḥ* (*Mañjuśrīnāmasaṃgīti*, 59ab; Davidson 1981, 26).
265. This list differs from that noted by Davidson (1981, 26n73) as *svabhāvikakāya*, *saṃbhogakāya*, *nirmāṇakāya*, *dharmakāya*, and *jñānakāya*—that is, nature body, enjoyment body, emanation body, Dharma body, and wisdom body.
266. The manuscript lists *kun rdzob kyi ye shes* which I have translate as "conventional wisdom." Most sources list the wisdom of discernment (*pratyavekṣanajñāna*; *so sor rtog pa'i ye shes*) for this wisdom.
267. See Dorje 1987, 461–62.
268. *Guhyagarbhatantra* 6.12–16 (Dorje 1987, 628–29). See also Sur 2015, 218–19.

269. *Guhyagarbhatantra* 3.17. Dorje 1987, 461–62.
270. *Guhyagarbhatantra*, chap. 3. Dorje 1987, 461. Note also the mention of "four times" that follows.
271. *Tathāgatācintyaguhyanirdeśasūtra*. See Krobath 2011, 52, for Tibetan citation of Ye she sde's *Lta ba'i khyad par*; for German translation, see Krobath 2011, 91–92.
272. *Anantamukhaviśodhananirdeśasūtra*, 81a.
273. In this passage I have translated *kāraṇa* ([supreme] cause) as "creator." See Nanjio 1923, 217.3–9, for the Sanskrit citation of the *Laṅkāvatārasūtra* as compared to the Kadam manuscript citation (bracketed portions differ): *bhagavān āha na mahāmate tathāgato nityo nānityaḥ / [tatkasya hetoḥ yad uta ubhayadoṣaprasaṅgāt / ubhayathā hi mahāmate doṣaprasaṅgaḥ syāt /] nitye sati kāraṇaprasaṅgaḥ syāt / nityāni hi mahāmate sarvatīrthakarāṇāṃ kāraṇāny akṛtakāni ca / ato na nityas tathāgato 'kṛtakanityatvāt / anitya sati kṛtakaprasaṅgaḥ syāt*. Tibetan (141a6–7): *blo gros chen po de bzhin gshegs pa ni rtag pa'ang ma yin / mi rtag pa'ang ma yin no / [de ci'i phyir zhe na / 'di lta ste / gnyi gar yang nyes par 'gyur ba'i phyir ro / / blo gros chen po gnyi gar yang nyes par 'gyur ba ni rtag tu zin na ni rgyur 'gyur ro / /] blo gros chen po mu stegs byed thams cad kyi rgyu rnams ni ma byas pa rtag pa ste / de bas nam byas pa rtag pa'i phyir de bzhin gshegs pa ni rtag pa'ang ma yin no / / mi rtag na ni byas pa mi rtag par 'gyur ro*. Also Nanjio 1923, 218–19: *yāvan mahāmate vāgvikalpaḥ pravartate, tāvan nityānityadoṣaḥ prasajyate / vikalpabuddhikṣayān mahāmate nityānityagrāho nivāryate bālānāṃ na tu viviktadṛṣṭibuddhikṣayāt.*
274. This citation of *Suvarṇaprabhāsasūtra* follows the *Lta ba'i khyad par* of Ye shes sde. The canonical version strongly diverges from the citation. See Krobath 2011, 93–94.
275. Cf. *Mahāyānasūtrālaṃkāra* 9.66: *teṣu ca triṣu kāyeṣu yathākramaṃ trividhā nityatā veditavyā yena nityakāyās tathāgatā ucyante / prakṛtyā nityatā svābhāvikasya svabhāvena nityatvāt / asraṃsanena sāṃbhogikasya dharmasaṃbhāgo vicchedāt / prabandhena nairmāṇikasyāntarvyaye punaḥ punar nirmāṇadarśanāt*. Tibetan: *sku gsum po de dag la go rims bzhin du gang gis na de bzhin gshegs pa rnams sku rtag pa'o zhes brjod pa rtag pa nyid rnam pa gsum du rig par bye ste / ngo bo nyid kyi sku ni rang bzhin gyis rtag pa'i phyir rang bzhin gyi rag pa nyid do / / longs spyod rdzogs pa'i sku ni rgyun mi 'chad pas te / chos la longs spyod rdzogs pa rgyun mi 'chad pa'i phyir ro / / sprul pa'i sku ni rgyun gyis te || mi snang bar byas nas yang dang yang du sprul pa kun tu ston pa'i phyir ro*. See Maitreyanātha/Asaṅga and Vasubandhu 2004, 97–98.
276. *Dharmatāsvabhāvaśūnyatācalapratisarvālokasūtra*, 171: *smon lam dang thugs rje'i byin gyi rlabs kyis 'khor rnams kyi so so'i mos pa dang bsam pa ji lta ba bzhin du gsung sgrogs bar snang ste / bcom ldan 'das ni bdag la chos ston te / gzhan dag la ni ma yin no snyam mo / / de'ang 'khor phal po che de dag las kyang kha cig gis ni ji ltar snang ba bzhin du yod pa'i chos ston to snyam ste / de la nges par 'dzin cing rtog par byed do / / kha cig gis ni chos thams cad sems tsam las ma gtogs par gzhan med pa'i chos ston te snyam ste / de la nges par 'dzin cing rtog par byed do / / kha cig gis ni sems nyid kyang ma skyes pa yin par bdag cag la chos ston to snyam ste / de la nges par 'dzin cing rtog par byed do / / kha cig gis ni chos thams cad sgyu ma bzhin du snang zhing sgyu ma bzhin du ma grub pa'i chos ston to snyam ste / de la nges par 'dzin cing rtog par byed do / / kha cig gis ni chos thams cad rang bzhin gyis ma skyes pa / ngo bo nyid kyis mi gnas pa / las dang bya ba'i mtha' thams cad dang bral ba rtog pa dang rtog pa'i yul las 'das pa / thog ma med pa'i dus nas spros pa rnam par dag pa'i chos ston to snyam ste / de la nges par 'dzin cing rtog par byed do*. Atiśa lists

this discourse among those to be studied in his *Bodhimārgapradīpapañjikā* (Sherburne 2000, 258–59). On the development of this discourse in Tibetan Buddhist history, see Kobayashi 2018.

277. Citation not found in *Sāgaramatisūtra* but located in *Daśacakrakṣitigarbhasūtra*, 141b: *gzhan yang mtshams med pa'i kha na ma tho ba chen po'i las dang nye ba rnam pa bzhi yod de / bzhi gang zhe na / mi dge ba'i sems kyis rang sangs rgyas bsad pa ste / de yang srog gcod pa'i nang na kha na ma tho ba chen po'i las yin te nyes pa'i rtsa ba yin no / / dgra bcom pa'i dge slong ma la mi tshangs par spyod pa ste / 'dod pas log par g.yem pa'i nang na kha na ma tho ba chen po'i las yin pas nyes pa'i rtsa ba yin no / / dad pas byin pa'i dkon mchog gsum gyi dkor nor la spyod pa ste/ ma byin par len pa'i na nga na kha na ma tho ba chen po'i las yin pas nyes pa'i rtsa ba yin no*. The five heinous acts, also known as "acts that brings immediate retribution" (*mtshams med pa'i las*; *ānantaryakarman*), are evil deeds that lead to the karmic retribution of immediate rebirth in the lowest hell, Avīci. The five heinous acts include killing one's father, mother, or an arhat, spilling the blood of a buddha, and creating a schism in the monastic order.

278. *Pūrṇaparipṛcchāsūtra*, 205a: *gang po de bzhin gshegs pa ni rtag par 'di lta bu'i rdzu 'phrul gyi mthu dang ldan pa rgyun chad pa med pa yin na deng nyan thos rnams ni de bzhin gshegs pa 'di 'ba' zhig tu bzhugs nas chos 'chad par mthong ste / da ni yang dag par na phyogs bcu'i 'jig rten gyi khams gang gā'i klung gi bye ma snyed kun du rgyun chad pa med par sangs rgyas kyi mdzad pa mdzad cing phyogs bcu'i 'jig rten gyi khams kun tu de bzhin du chos ston par mdzad de.*

279. After the life of Atiśa, a number of Kadam teaching lineages become organized into either texts (*gzhung*), instructions (*gdams ngag*), or oral instructions (*man ngag*) and were associated with the direct disciples of Dromtönpa Gyalwai Jungné—Potowa Rinchen Sal, Chengawa Tsultrim Bar, and Phuchungwa Shönu Gyaltsen (1031–1106). While these disciples are not directly associated with the *Stages* manuscript, reference is made in the *Stages* manuscript to the above classifications of Kadam teachings. The extant historical sources indicate that these classifications developed and solidified over time. For example, Nyang ral (2010, 434) mentions in the twelfth century that the disciples of Potowa are renowned as followers of the texts (*gzhung pa ba*) while Chengawa's disciples are followers of the oral instrution (*man ngag pa*). Writing centuries later, Las chen (2003, 9) states, "Nowadays, the Kadam teachings are well known in two aspects, texts (*gzhung*) and instructions (*gdams ngag*), and if you further classify them into three, oral instructions (*man ngag*)" (*ding sang bka' gdams kyi chos yongs su grags pa la rnam pa gnyis te / gzhung dang / gdams ngag yang na man ngag dang gsum du dbye'o /*). See also Jinpa 2008, 8–10, Thuken 2009, 100, and Buswell and Lopez 2014, 123, on the classification of Kadam teaching lineages.

280. This is the *Sādhana of One Hundred Syllables* (*Yi ge brgya'i sgrub thabs*) in *Jo bo rje dpal ldan a ti sha'i gsung 'bum*, 2:934–35.

281. Compare with Kagyü-based accounts in Brown 2006, 331, 400–401; Callahan 2019, 240, 248–49, 278.

282. Compare with Kagyü-based accounts in Brown 2006, 262–64; Callahan 2019, 337–38.

283. **Sems mi bzung bar* mkhas pa ba glang skyong* [21b4] *bzhin dran pas bzung*** / mi spro mi bsdu rang sar bzhag pas *rmongs rnam rtog sdug bsngal las* grol* (*Byang chub lam gyi rim pa*, §170).

284. See *Stages* §13 and note.

285. Similar to citation in *General Meaning*, ad 31a; see page 122 in chapter 3.

286. *Kṣaṇasampad iyaṃ sudurlabhā* (*Bodhicaryāvatāra* 1.4a). The Kadam citation matches the canonical Tibetan: *Dal 'byor 'di ni rnyed par shin tu dka'.*

287. *Mānuṣyaṃ nāvam āsādya tara duḥkhamahānadīm / mūḍha kālo na nidrāyā iyaṃ naur durlabhā punaḥ* (*Bodhicaryāvatāra* 7.14). The Kadam citation matches the canonical Tibetan: *mi yi gru la brten nas su / / sdug bsngal chu bo che las sgrol / / gru 'di phyi nas rnyed dka' bas / / rmongs pa dus su gnyid ma log.*

288. See page 50 § 21 above.

289. *Na praṇaśyanti karmāṇi kalpakoṭiśatair api / sāmagrīṃ prāpya kālaṃ ca phalanti khalu dehināṃ.* Cited from *Dhanapālakavaineyasūtra*, published in Vinītā 2010, 692. Translation based on Kragh 2003, 223n379. See also Rotman 2008, 116. Note that Atiśa recommends consulting the *Smṛtyupasthānasūtra* for understanding cause and effect in his *Karmavibhaṅga* (see Sherburne 2000, 514).

290. *Śrīguptasūtra*, 283b6, where this is set as two stanzas. For context in translation, see §1.130–31 in Liljenberg and Pagel 2021.

291. The eighteen hell realms include eight hot hells, eight cold hells, the neighboring or adjoining hells (*utsada*), and occasional hells (*prādeśika*). See §§36–39 in chapter 3 above for Tibetan and Sanskrit names and other details of the hells mentioned below.

292. In this opaque reference, apparently someone seeking a horse from the Jang Tsakha region northwest of Lhasa only receives a whip from a person in the southern region of Tibet.

293. Note that the manuscript seems to be missing several sentences at this point.

294. Nāgārjuna, *Letter to a Friend* (*Suhṛllekha*), v. 68cd. This is slightly different from the canonical version: "A heap of all the bones each being has left would reach to Meru's top or even higher. To count one's mother's lineage with pills the size of berries, the earth would not suffice." Skt.: *ekaikasyātītā bhaveyur ātmāsthiparvatā merusamāḥ / jananīparamparāsu ca badarāsthinibhair gulair na bhūḥ samprabhavat* (v. 69) (Szántó 2021, 6). Tib.: *Re re'i bdag nyid rus pa'i phung po ni / / lhun po mnyam pa snyed cig 'das gyur te / / ma yi thug mtha' rgya shug tshig gu tsam / / ril bur bgrangs kyang sa yis lang mi 'gyur* (v. 68) (Klong-chen ye-shes-rdo-rje 2005, 52).

295. A *sa dgra*, literally "enemy of the earth," refers to hostile spirits or geomantic space that is unsuitable and inauspicious in Tibetan cultural topography.

296. This is usually known as the sevenfold posture of Vairocana (*rnam snang chos bdun*): *rkang pa skyil krung / lag pa mnyam gzhag sgal tshigs drang po bsrang ba / mgrin pa cung zad gug pa / dpung pa rgod gshog ltar brgyang ba / mig sna rtser phab pa / lce rtse ya rkan la sbyar ba ste bdun no /* ("Crossed legs, hands in fists or right over left or on knees, shoulders raised and slightly forward, spine straight, chin tucked slightly toward throat, tongue tip touching palate, eyes unblinking and unwavering twelve finger-breadths from tip of nose"). See Buswell and Lopez 2014, 1078–79.

297. This resembles the mahāsiddha Tīlopa's special instructions (*upadeśa*) on coemergent union (*sahajayoga*). See Draszcyk 2015, 84.

298. The four daily activities (*spyod lam rnam bzhi*) are walking (*'chags pa*), standing (*'greng ba*), sitting (*'dug pa*), and sleeping (*nyal ba*). See Callahan 2019, 646. The sense here is that one should go about one's daily activities while sustaining the awareness of things as like illusions or dreams.

299. The absorption of cessation (*'gog pa'i snyoms par 'jug pa* ≈ *nirodhasamāpatti*) is considered a high-level attainment in mainstream forms of Buddhism that temporarily

ceases physical and mental activity. On the general Abhidharma understanding of this absorption, see Apple 2008, 136,164, 211n55, and 215n5. The Vaibhāṣika posits this absorption among fourteen conditioned forces dissociated from thought (*cittaviprayuktasaṃskāra*); see Apple 2018, 377n416. See also *Abhidharmakośabhāṣya* ad 2.42 (Sangpo 2012, 1:561–75). The nature of the absorption of cessation, and how one reverts back to consciousness, is frequently discussed and debated in Abhidharma literature among Vaibhāṣika, Sarvāstivāda, and Yogācāra advocates. Atiśa, instructing on sustaining awareness mindfully free from elaborations in the Great Middle Way, may be associating the desire to suppress conceptual thought with the absorption of cessation to illustrate an extreme of annihilationism among those who advocate the practice of the absorption of cessation. Atiśa's sustaining union of awareness instructions may be compared with integrating thoughts into the path as found in *Stages* (see chap. 1, §170–72) as well as Atiśa's instructions on coemergent union (*lhan cig skyes sbyor*) (Apple 2017, 29). The practice of integrating thoughts into the path also occurs in Kagyü traditions of mahāmudrā instruction (see, e.g., Callahan 2019, 342–45, 404–6, 407–90).

300. The following line mentioning fleeting movement, mindfulness, emptiness, and being free explains Atiśa's synchronization with the fourth time. For other Tibetan accounts, see Almogi 2009, 278: "The transcendence of present, past, and future—that is, atemporality—is often described in the rNying-ma literature as the 'fourth time' (*dus bzhi pa*)."

301. *Stong pa nyid la stong mi lta / / stong las gud na stong mi lta / / de lta bur ni gang lta ba / / stong pa mthong ba zhes bya'o* (*Varmavyūhanirdeśa*, D 51, 184a).

302. See the section "The cultivation of insight" above on page 164.

303. Tib. *gsung yan lag drug cu*. This is usually given as *gsung dbyangs yan lag drug chu*, "sixty aspects of melodious speech."

304. Sanskrit: (50) *sūsukhita sada te nara loke / yehi acintiya ñāt' imi dharmāḥ / na ca dharma-adharma-vikalpo / cittapapañcavibhāvita sarvi* (51) *bhāva abhāva vibhāvayi jñānāṃ sarvam acintiya sarvam abhūtaṃ / ye puna cittavaśānuga bālās / te dukhitā bhavakoṭiśateṣu /* [52 not extant] (53) *yo 'pi ca cintayi śūnyaka dharmān / so 'pi kumārgapapannaku bālaḥ / akṣarakīrtita śūnyaka dharmāḥ / te ca anakṣara akṣara-uktāḥ* (54) *śāntapaśānta yo cintayi dharmān / so 'pi cittu na jātu na bhūtaḥ / cittavitarkaṇa sarvi papañcāḥ / tasma acintiya budhyatha dharmān* [55 not extant]; (*Upālipariprcchāsūtra*, Python 1973, 56–57). Tibetan: (50) *gang dag bsam pas chos rnams 'di shes pa'i / / mi rnams de dag rtag du bde ba yin / / chos dang chos min rnam rtog med pa ste / / thams cad sems kyis spros pas phye ba yin* (51) */ thams cad bsam yas thams cad 'byung min pas / / dngos dang dngos med shes pa rnam par bshig / byis pa gang dag sems kyi dbang song bas / / de dag srid pa bye ba brgyar sdug bsngal* (52) *dge slong gang dag bsam yas yod min pa'i / / sangs rgyas mi mchog de sems tshul bzhin min / / rtog pa'i dbang gis sangs rgyas rnam par brtags / / rtog pa de yang nam yang 'byung ma yin /* (53) *gang dag chos rnams stong la sems byed pa'i / / byis pa de dag lam ngan zhugs pa yin / / chos rnams stong pa yi ges brjod pa ni / de dag yi ge med par yi ger bstan /* (54) *gang dag zhi zhing rab zhi'i chos sems pa'i / / sems pa de yang nam yang 'byung ma yin / / spros kun sems kyi rnam par rtog yin te / / de phyir chos rnams bsams pas rtogs par gyis /* (55ab) *chos 'di thams cad sems med sems pa'ang med / / ji srid mi sems de nyid stong pa yin / /*.

305. See Germano 1994; Achard 1999, 58, 176, 197n172; Achard 2002, 45; Achard 2004.

306. *Dpal ldan bla ma rmog cog pa chen po'i rnam par thar pa* (15a1–6; 391.1–6): *jo bo nas*

brgyud pa'i dang / mi la'i rnams tshar bar mdzad / dpe rnams dge bshes gar la yod kyis khong la zhus gsungs / de nas dge bshes gar la dar yug gcig phul nas / phyag dpe rnams ma lus par zhus pas / jo bo khyed chos la nan tan byed pa chos dang mthun pa gcig 'dug pas dpe rnams btang gis . . . gzhang yang ngo sprod kyi gdams pa mang du zhus so / / bla ma rang gis mdzad pa'i go cha rnam gnyis dang / ngo sprod lnga dang / tshig rkang brgyad pa dang / sku gsum lam 'khyer la sogs pa'i mahā mu tra'i gdams pa rnams ma lus par gnang nas. See also Apple 2017, 25.

307. Compare with Kagyü manuals in Brown 2006 (262–64, 331, 400–401); Callahan 2019 (240, 242, 248–49, 270, 278, 337–38); Roberts 2011 (87); Trungam 2004 (175). Seel also *Stages* manuscript fols. 54a, 60a, 60b.

308. Cf. *Prajñāpāramitāsaṃcayagāthā*, 20.10cd (Yuyama 1976, Skt. 78: *tāvan na tāṃ paramaśūnyata prāpuṇoti yāvan na te kuśalamūla bhavanti pūrṇāḥ*, Tib. 177: *de dag dge ba'i rtsa ba ji srid ma rdzogs pa / / de srid stong nyid dam pa de ni thob mi byed*). Differs slightly from canonical Tibetan. English in Conze 1973, 46.

309. Phrase missing from the manuscript.

310. Compare Brunnhölzl 2004, 867n211, regarding the four pitfalls to be avoided in advanced mahāmudrā meditation (*stong nyid shor sa bzhi*): "Grasping at it as the fundamental nature of knowable objects (*shes bya'i gshis la shor ba*), deviating from emptiness through sealing things and experiences as empty (*rgyas 'debs su shor ba*), deviating from emptiness through taking it as the remedy that annihilates the afflictions (*gnyen por shor ba*), and deviating from emptiness through taking meditation on emptiness as the only path that leads to the later attainment of Buddhahood (*lam du shor ba*)."

311. The words between the two asterisks indicate writing under the line in the manuscript at 59a7.

312. In this passage meditative experience is described to be like smoke (*du ba*; *dhūma*), mirage (*smig rgyu*; *marīcika*), fireflies (*me khyer*; *khadyota*), multicolored drops (*thig le kha dog sna tshogs pa*), and pure space (*nam mkha' rnam par dag pa*). This list is similar to what is found in the section "Meditative appearance" in chapter 4 (see page 171). Atiśa describes these signs as "the appearance of one's own mind at the time of abiding in nonconceptual meditative stabilization." Signs of meditative experience have been elucidated in Indian religious literature since at least the *Upaṇisads* (e.g., *Śvetāśvatara Upaniṣad* 2.9.11, Olivelle 1996, 256). Signs (*nimitta*; *mtshan ma*) in the context of Buddhism are often a type of image that appears to the mind after cultivating a certain level of concentration (*samādhi*) (Buswell and Lopez 2014, 585–86). Signs of meditative experience in advanced yogas are found in a number of esoteric Buddhist scriptures, such as the five signs (mirage, smoke, fireflies, lamp, and a cloudless sky) listed in the *Guhyasamājatantra* (Matsunaga 1978, 124, 18.150c–151d) and the ten signs listed in the the *Kālacakratantra* (5.115), the first four like the *Guhyasamājatantra* but beginning with smoke, then (5) a flash of flame (*jvāla*; *'bar ba*), (6) the moon (*candra*; *zla ba*), (7) the sun (*arka*; *nyi ma*), (8) darkness (*tamaḥ*; *mun can*), (9) a flash of lightning (*paramakalā*; *cha shas*), and (10) an iridescent sphere (*mahābindu*; *thig le che*) or the universal form of clear light (*viśvabimbaṃ prabhāsvara*; *'od gsal sna tshogs gzugs*). For an overview of these signs in Indian esoteric Buddhist literature, see Sferra 2000, 22–28, and Orofino 2022. Atiśa's list resembles the *Guhyasamājatantra* in that it is comprised of five components but is similar to a *Kālacakra*-based tradition list in that his list begins with smoke (*dhūma*) and includes various-colored drops (*thig le kha dog sna tshogs pa*) and pure space (*nam mkha' rnam par dag pa*). Atiśa's list

beginning with smoke is significant in that *Kālacakra*-influenced traditions such as the *Vimalaprabhā* state that the "path of mahāmudrā meditation begins with smoke and so forth" (*mahāmudrābhāvanāmārgo dhūmādikaḥ*; Upādhyāya 1986, 19). Along these lines, an extensive commentary (*pañjikā*) called *Marmakalikā* by Vīryaśrīmitrapāda on Śūnyasamādhipāda's *Tattvajñānasaṃsiddhi*, a sādhana of Vajravārāhī, details in its third chapter on meditation (*bhāvanāvidhi* ad verses 13–15) the occurrence of five signs by synthesizing verses from the *Kālacakratantra* and *Ḍākinīvajrapañjaratantra* in its exegesis (D 1585, 93a–94a). This approach to harmonizing the list of ten signs in the *Kālacakra* to a list of five with other tantras may be what is reflected in Atiśa's peculiar list of signs. See Khedrup Norsang Gyatso 2004, 430–54, for a discussion of the signs of meditative accomplishment and their appearance in Indian Buddhist tantras along with their commentaries in relation to the exegesis of the *Kālacakratantra*.

313. These activities correspond to the four activities (*caturkarman*; *las bzhi*) presented in esoteric Buddhist literature that classify ritual events in terms of these functions that are often correlated with colors and directions. In this manner, (1) pacifying (*śāntika*; *zhi ba*) rites are white and and performed facing north, (2) increasing (*pauṣṭika*; *rgyas pa*) are yellow and performed facing east; (3) magnetizing (*vaśīkaraṇa*; *dbang ba*) are red and performed facing west, (4) destroying (*abhicāra*; *drag po*) are black and performed facing south.

314. Skt.: *dhṛtimān*; Tib.: *mi dga' ba med pa*. See Engle 2016, 15.

315. Translated according to manuscript citation. Close to Dergé Kangyur version with a few variants. Cf. *Kāśyapaparivartasūtra* (Pāsādika 2015, 46): *kāśyapa sumerumātrā pudgaladṛṣṭir āśritā na tv evādhimānikasya śūnyatādṛṣṭim ālīnā / tat kasmād dheto pudgaladṛṣṭigatānāṃ kāśyapa śūnyatā niḥsaraṇaṃ / śūnyatādṛṣṭi puna kāśyapa kena niḥsariṣyaṃti*. Tib. *'od srung gang zag tu lta ba ri rab tsam la gnas pa sla'i / / mngon pa'i nga rgyal can stong pa nyid du lta ba ni de lta ma yin no / / de ci'i phyir zhe na / 'od srung lta bar gyur pa thams cad las 'byung ba ni stong pa nyid yin / / 'od srung gang stong pa nyid kho nar lta ba de ni gsor mi rung ngo zhes ngas bshad do* (*Kāśyapaparivartasūtra*, §64; D 87, 132b). This verse is also cited in the *Uttaratantra* (ad 1.32; see Brunnhölzl 2014, 359), *Catuḥśatakavṛtti*, *Madhyāntavibhāgaśāstra*, and *Prasannapadā* (Pāsādika 2015, 5).

316. Cf. *Dharmasaṃgītisūtra*: *rigs kyi bu byang chub sems dpas chos kyi tshul la 'jug pa bcus sangs rgyas khong du chud par bya ste / bcu gang zhe na / 'di lta ste / rgyu 'thun pa'i sangs rgyas dang / rnam par smin pa las byung ba'i sangs rgyas dang / ting nge 'dzin gyi sangs rgyas dang / smon lam gyi sangs rgyas dang / sems kyi sangs rgyas dang / ngo bo nyid kyi sangs rgyas dang / longs spyod rdzogs pa'i sangs rgyas dang / sprul pa'i sangs rgyas dang / btags pa'i sangs rgyas dang / mdun du gzhag pa'i sangs rgyas so* (D 238, 10a).

317. Czaja 2019, 293; see also McGrath 2017, 63, 255.

318. Beyer 1978, 284.

319. The text here matches the citation of the same passage in Atiśa's brief song the *Saṃsāramanoniryāṇikāranāmasaṃgīti*.

320. The generation stage of the deity (*yi dam gyi bskyed rim*) refers to tantric practice where a practitioner transforms their ordinary identity into that of a deity constituted by awakened wisdom and compasssion. The wrathful approach (*khro bo'i bsnyen pa*) is a form of approach practice (*bsnyen pa*; *sevā*) that focuses on wrathful (*krodha*) Buddhist deities.

321. I am not aware of the source or exact significance of this simile.

322. *Ra dug, zim pa* (*Polyanthum aconite*).
323. *Thar nu* (*Euphorbia wallichii*).
324. I am not aware of the source or the exact significance of "white mouse in a pile of yak hair" (*byi ba dkar mo sbra phung*).
325. I am not aware of the exact significance of the reference to a "yellow pit" (*dong ser po*) here.
326. *Bodhicaryāvatāra* 6.72cd (Tibetan translation by Sumatikīrti and Ngok Loden Sherab, Tengyur D 3871, 17b2): *gal te mi yi sdug bsngal gyis / / dmyal ba bral na cis ma legs*. Underlined portions of Kadam manuscript differ from canonical *mi yi sdug bsngal chung ngu yis / / dmyal ba bral na tsam ma legs*. Sanskrit: *manuṣyaduḥkhair narakān muktaś cet kim abhadrakam*.
327. According to Shirshova 2018, 256, Tibetan medicine understands the "seventh vertebra" (*tshigs pa bdun pa*) to be a secret point, connected to the heart, that may indicate an overly strong heartbeat.
328. *Tha snyad tshig gi yon tan*. The Tibetan author is implying here that "conventional words *without application of the meaning* do not have virtue"—in other words, to understanding the meaning of words properly, one must follow the special instructions and their meaning.
329. *Bodhicittam utpādayed vaivṛtisaṃvṛtirūpakaṃ* (*Hevajratantra* II.iv.29cd; Skt.: Snellgrove 2010, 66; English: Snellgrove 2010, 104).
330. *Saṃvṛtaṃ kundasaṃkāśaṃ viṿrtaṃ sukharūpiṇaṃ* (*Hevajratantra* II.iv.30; Skt.: Snellgrove 2010, 66; English: Snellgrove 2010, 104).
331. *Sukhaṃ nairātmyarūpiṇaṃ / tasya saukhyaṃ mahāmudrā* (*Hevajratantra* II.iv.40; Skt.: Snellgrove 2010, 66); Tib. *Bde ba bdag med tshul can nyid / de yi bde ba phyag rgya che* (underlined text differs from Sanskrit; Snellgrove 2010, 67; cf. English: Snellgrove 2010, 104).
332. *Nirvṛti bodhicittaṃ tu vivṛtisaṃvṛtirūpakaṃ* (*Hevajratantra* II.iv.35ab; Skt.: Snellgrove 2010, 66; English: Snellgrove 2010, 104).
333. *Dharmadhātusvabhāvaś ca prajñayaivopabhujyate //* (44cd) *saiva sahajarūpā tu mahāsukhā divyayoginī* (45ab) (*Hevajratantra* II.iv; Skt.: Snellgrove 2010, 68; English: Snellgrove 2010, 105).
334. *De nas gnyis su med pa'i bdag nyid chen pos ye nas sangs rgyas pa'i sems ye shes su bskyed pa 'di gsungs so* (*Guhyagarbhatattvaviniścaya*, 112a; English: Almogi 2009, 191n8).
335. Cf. *Guhyagarbhatattvaviniścaya*, 112b: *gsang ba'i snying po de kho na nyid nges pa las don dam pa dang kun rdzob kyi byang chub kyi sems ye shes su bskyed pa'i le'u ste gnyis pa'o*.
336. Cf. citation in Śāntideva's *Śikṣāsamuccaya*: *anutpannāniruddhān sarvadharmān avabhotsya ity evaṃ cittam utpādya nāntarā dṛṣṭigateṣu prapatati, idaṃ devaputra caturtham ānantaryam* (Skt.: Bendall 1971, 18; English: Goodman 2016, 21).
337. Compare the Kangyur text *Dpang skong phyag brgya pa* (D 267), 5a: *dus 'di nas nam byang chub kyi snying po la mchis kyi bar du dkon mchog gsum la skyabs su mchi ste / bdag nyid lus dbul gyis thugs rje chen po dang ldan pa rnams kyis so so nas rtag tu bzhes shig / ji ltar na dus gsum gyi sangs rgyas dang / byang chub sems dpa' dngos po thams cad dang bral ba / phung po dang / khams dang / skye mched kyis ma zin pa'i chos bdag med pa dang mnyam pa / thog ma nas ma skyes pa / stong pa nyid kyi rang bzhin gyis byang chub kyi sems bskyed pa ltar bdag ming 'di zhes bgyi bas kyang / dus 'di nas nam byang chub kyi snying po la mchis kyi bar du byang chub tu sems bskyed par bgyi'o / / byang chub*

kyi sems ni nam gzhar yang mi stor zhing dge ba'i bshes gnyen dam pa de dang nam yang mi 'bral bar shog shig.

338. *Abhidharmasamuccaya*, Boin-Webb 2001, 121–22.
339. *Abhidharmasamuccaya*, Boin-Webb 2001, 123–24.
340. *Abhidharmasamuccaya*, Boin-Webb 2001, 124.
341. Sherburne 2000, 69–110.
342. See *Stages*, sections 79, 109, 113, 116, 117, 118, 119, 120, 125, 129, 131, 133, 146, 147, 149, 164, and 166.
343. *Cittotpādasaṃvaravidhikrama*. See Sherburne 2000 for Tibetan and English translations.
344. For the brief ritual and advice to consult other works, see Sherburne 2000, 71–73.
345. See Apple 2014b for an introduction and translation of the *Inquiry of Avalokiteśvara on the Seven Qualities* (*Avalokiteśvaraparipṛcchāsaptadharmakasūtra*) along with a discussion of Atiśa's citations of the sūtra.
346. The other four listed in the text are (b) abandoning the four negative qualities and training in the wholesome qualities, (c) training in the beneficial qualities of the awakening mind, (d) training in purifying the awakening mind, and (e) earnestly training in the effort to accrue the two accumulations.
347. See Rhoton 2002, 81, for *A Clear Differentiation of the Three Codes* (*Sdom gsum rab dbye*) and Roesler, Holmes, and Jackson 2015, 401–5, on *Clarifiying the Sage's Intent* (*Thub pa'i dgongs pa rab tu gsal ba*).
348. Wangchuk 2007, 169–94.
349. Sha ra ba yon tan grags, *Dge ba'i bshes gnyen zhang sha ra ba yon tan grags kyis mdzad pa'i lam rim bzhugs so*, 161–68.
350. Translation Jinpa 2006, 327. The Kadam text cites the sources as *Secret Night Sūtra* (*Mtshan mo gsang ba'i mdo*) but the source is *Good Signs Sūtra* (*Bhadrakāratrisūtra*, D 313), 162–63: *Sang tsam shi yang su shes kyis / / de ring nyid du brtun te bya / / 'chi bdag sde chen de dang ni / / bdag tu bshes pa ma yin no*. Kangyur version differs from the Kadam manuscript.
351. *Hevajratantra* II.iv: *bodhicittam utpādayed vaivṛtisaṃvṛtirūpakaṃ* (*Hevajratantra*, Skt.: Snellgrove 2010, 66; English: Snellgrove 2010, 104).
352. See Skilling and Saerji 2014 on Tathāgata Yaśas (no. 17), Tathāgata Flaming One (*arciṣmant*; *'od 'phro can*) (no. 24), Tathāgata Duṣpradharṣa (no. 39), and Maitreya in the *pūrvapraṇidhāna*s of the last major section of the *Fortunate Eon Sūtra* (*Bhadrakaplikasūtra*). The numbers in brackets refer to the sequence number of each Buddha as enumerated in the *Bhadrakaplikasūtra*.
353. See Crosby and Skilton 1995, 10. The seven-limbed practice consists of prostrating to the Three Jewels, confessing negative actions, making offering, rejoicing in the virtue of others, requesting to turn the wheel of Dharma, beseeching to not pass into nirvāṇa, and dedicating the merit to the enlightenment of all sentient beings.
354. The Kadam author has left out the "beseeching (*ādhyeṣaṇa*) to not pass into nirvāṇa" limb (*mya ngan las mi 'da' bar gsol ba gdab pa'i yan lag*) of the prayer. Cf. citation in Śāntideva's *Śikṣāsamuccaya*: *sakaladuṣkhitajanaparitrāṇadhuram avavoḍhuṃ tena van danapūjanapāpadeśanapuṇyânumodanabuddhâdhyeṣaṇa-yācanabodhipariṇāmanaṃ kṛtvā* (Skt.: Bendall 1971, 13; see also English translation in Goodman 2016, 16).
355. Read: *ta la bdun srid du 'phags nas*. See Matsumura 2011 on the prophecy of Dīpaṃkara.
356. *Ratnolkādhāraṇī*, 63b: *rgyal dang rgyal ba'i chos la dad gyur cing / / sangs rgyas sras kyi*

spyod la dad byed la / / byang chub bla na med la dad gyur nas / / skyes bu chen po rnams kyi sems skye'o. Differences from the Kadam manuscript are underlined.

357. Compare with *Stages* §8.

358. The Kadampa citation differs significantly from the canonical version of the *Vajra Rosary Tantra* (*Vajramālāvyākhyātantra*), 2.26–27 (Kittay with Jamspal 2020, 125). It demonstrates a tradition of esoteric monastic domestication.

359. Cf. *Gaṇḍavyūhasūtra*: *bodhicittaṃ hi kulaputra bījabhūtaṃ sarvabuddhadharmāṇām / kṣetrabhūtaṃ sarvajagacchukladharmavirohaṇatayā dharaṇibhūtaṃ sarvalokapratiśaraṇatayā . . . pitṛbhūtaṃ sarvabodhisattvārakṣaṇatayā . . . vaiśravaṇabhūtaṃ sarvadāridryasamucchedanatayā . . . cintāmaṇirājabhūtaṃ sarvārthasaṃsādhanatayā . . . iti hi kulaputra bodhisattvaścānyaiścāpramāṇairguṇaviśeṣaiḥ samanvāgataḥ* (Vaidya 1960b, 396–98).

360. *Bodhicaryāvatāra* 1.9: *bhavacārakabandhano varākaḥ sugatānāṃ suta ucyate kṣaṇena / sanarāmaralokavandanīyo bhavati smodita eva bodhicitte* // 1.10: *aśucipratimām imāṃ gṛhītvā jinaratnapratimāṃ karoty anarghām / rasajātam atīva vedhanīyaṃ sudṛḍhaṃ gṛhṇata bodhicittasaṃjñam*. English: Crosby and Skilton 1995, 5–6; Tibetan Dunhuang (Saito 1993) 10,8–11, Stein.628 ka 1a6–7; Tengyur 2a5–2b1. Tibetan of Kadampa manuscript follows Dunhuang Tibetan in verse 10 (Tibetan Dunhuang (Saito 1993) 10,12–15, Stein.628 ka 1a7–8; Tengyur 2b1): *gser sgyur rtsi'i rnam pa mchog lta bur / / myi gtsang lus 'di blangs nas rgyal ba'i sku / / rin cen rin thang myed par sgyur bas na / / byang cub sems shes bya ba rab* (var. *legs*) *brtan zung*.

361. *Bodhicaryāvatāra* 1.12: *kadalīva phalaṃ vihāya yāti kṣayam anyat kuśalaṃ hi sarvam eva / satataṃ phalati kṣayaṃ na yāti prasavaty eva tu bodhicittavṛkṣaḥ*. English: Crosby and Skilton 1995, 6; Tibetan Dunhuang (Saito 1993) 10.20–23, Stein.628 ka 1b1; Tengyur 2b2–3.

362. See Lamotte 1998, 176–77, for this episode in the *Śūraṅgamasamādhisūtra*.

363. *Yuktiṣaṣṭikā* v. 12. Kadam text differs from Tengyur (Scherrer-Schaub 1991, 47–48) and other Kadam works attributed to Atiśa (Apple 2019b, 238), cited from the Candrakīrti's *Yuktiṣaṣṭikāvṛtti* with differences: *shin tu* {Tengyur *du*} *phra ba'i dngos rnams la* {*la yang*} / / *gang gis chad par* {*skye bar*} *rnam brtags pa / / rnam par mi mkhas de yis ni / / rkyen las byung ba'i don ma mthong*. See Loizzo 2007, 158–59 and 283.

364. *Bodhicaryāvatāra* 5.7cd–5.8ab: *taptāyaḥkuṭṭimaṃ kena kuto jātāś ca tāḥ striyaḥ / pāpacittasamudbhūtaṃ tattatsarvaṃ jagau muniḥ*. English translation in Crosby and Skilton 1995, 34; Tengyur, 10b1–2.

365. *Bodhicaryāvatāra* 3.25: *adya me saphalaṃ janma sulabdho mānuṣo bhavaḥ / adya buddhakule jāto buddhaputro 'smi sāmpratam*. English translation in Crosby and Skilton 1995, 22; Tengyur, 7b3–4. The Kadam text differs from the Tengyur edition as follows: *'di ltar* {Tengyur: *deng du*} *bdag tshe 'bras bu ldan* {*yod*} / / *mi yi srid pa legs par thob / / de ring sangs rgyas rigs su skyes / / sangs rgyas sras su* {*su da*} *gyur to*.

366. Quoted in *Kāśyapaparivarta*: *yathāpi rājña pṛthivīśvarasya putro bhavel lakṣaṇacitritāṅgaṃ dṛṣṭvā eva taṃ jātamātraṃ kumāraṃ sakoṭṭa rājā praṇamaṃti paurāḥ utpannamātre tatha bodhisatve sallakṣaṇaṃ taṃ jinarājaputraṃ lokas sadevo 'pi namaskaronti prasannacittaṃ bahumānapūrvam* (*Kāśyapaparivarta*, §86; English: Pāsādika 2015, 148).

367. *Bodhicaryāvatāra* 1.17: *bodhipraṇidhicittasya saṃsāre 'pi phalaṃ mahat / na tv avicchinnapuṇyatvaṃ yathā prasthāna cetasaḥ*. Crosby and Skilton 1995, 6; Tengyur, 2b6.

368. *Bodhicaryāvatāra* 1.18d: *cittam anivartyena cetasā* / 1.19: *bodhipraṇidhicittasya saṃsāre*

'pi phalaṃ mahat / na tv avicchinnapuṇyatvaṃ yathā prasthāna cetasaḥ. Crosby and Skilton 1995, 6–7; Tengyur, 2b7.

369. *Bodhisattvasaṃvaraviṃśaka*, verse 1 (Tatz 1985, 27).
370. Abbreviated title for *Sāgaramatiparipṛcchāsūtra*; cf. *Śikṣāsamuccaya* (Bendall 1971, 313) and works of Atiśa (Sherburne 2000).
371. *Vīradattaparipṛcchā*. See Tibetan critical edition, section 14, verse 7 (Apple 2020, 110): *byang chub sems kyi bsod nams gang / / de la gal te gzugs mchis na / / nam ka' khams ni kun gang ste / / de ni de bas lhag par 'gyur*. Cited by Atiśa in *Lamp for the Path to Awakening* (Apple 2019, 183). See Apple 2022 for a complete translation of this sūtra.
372. The underlying meaning of "three equalizations" (*snyoms pa gsum*) and "four certainties" (*nges pa bzhi*) is not clear. On this point of the four certainties or definitenesses (*nges pa zhi*), see Almogi's (2009, 242n19) contrastive discussion of the *five definitenesses* (*nges pa lnga*), "which are the five attributes of the *saṃbhogakāya*, namely, a definite teacher (*ston pa*), definite doctrine (*bstan pa or chos*), definite retinue (*'khor*), definite place (*gnas*), and definite time (*dus*)."
373. This is close to Śāntarakṣita's *Saṃvaraviṃśakavṛtti* (Tatz 1978, 553).
374. *Bodhisattvasaṃvaraviṃśaka*, v. 3 (Tatz 1985, 27).
375. The four fundamental downfalls (*rtsa ba'i ltung ba bzhi*) are killing, stealing, lying, and sexual misconduct. The eleven friends (*grogs bcu gcig*) most likely refers to eleven instructions on points of discipline (*gdams ngag bcu gcig*) given by a ceremonial master to new monks on protecting and training in the vows. The eleven instructions include: (1) instruction on right lifestyle, (2) instruction on right morality, (3) instruction on the four duties of a monk, (4) instruction on favorable conditions for the training, (5) instruction on example, (6) first instruction on right outlook, (7) second instruction on right outlook, (8) actual instruction on the right outlook, (9) instuction on post-ordination concerns, (10) instructions on training, and (11) instruction on the root of all discipline. See Kong-sprul Blo-gros-mtha'-yas 1998, 369n74, for details and sources.
376. Cf. citation in Śāntideva's *Śikṣāsamuccaya*: *yathoktam āryakṣitigarbhasūtre / ebhir daśabhiḥ kuśalaiḥ karmapathair buddhatvaṃ / na punar yo 'ntaśaikam api yāvajjīvaṃ kuśalaṃ karmapathaṃ na rakṣati atha ca punar evaṃ vadati / ahaṃ mahāyāniko 'haṃ cānuttarāṃ samyaksaṃbodhiṃ paryeṣāmīti / sa pudgalaḥ paramakuhako mahāmṛṣāvādikaḥ sarveṣāṃ buddhānāṃ bhagavatāṃ purato visaṃvādako lokasyocchedavādī sa mūḍhaḥ kālaṃ kurute vinipātagāmī bhavatīti*. Skt.: Bendall 1971, 13; see also English translation in Goodman 2016, 15.
377. Only the second half of the verse is preserved in the Kangyur edition of the *Prajñāpāramitāsaṃcayagāthā*. Skt.: *anupāya prajñāvikalo pati śrāvakatve* (Yuyama 1976, 62). Tib.: *thabs med shes rab bral ba nyan thos nyid du ltung* (Yuyama 1976, 174). Translation adapted from Conze 1973, 309–11.
378. This resembles a discussion in *Gayāśīrṣasūtra*, 289a. However, the citation closely follows the section in Atiśa's *Bodhipathapradīpa*; cf. Eimer 1978, 126: *thabs dang bral ba'i shes rab dang / / shes rab bral ba'i thabs dang kyang / / gang phyir 'ching ba zhes gsungs pa / / de phyir gnyis ka spang mi bya*.
379. Cf. *Dohākoṣa*, attributed to Saraha, 71b. The Kadam citation is underlined, with differences in bold: *snying rje dang bral stong pa nyid zhugs gang / / des ni lam mchog rnyed* ***par mi 'gyur*** */ 'on te snying rje 'ba' zhig bsgoms na yang / / 'khor ba 'dir gnas thar pa*

thob mi 'gyur / / gang gis gnyis po sbyor bar nus pa des / / 'khor **bar** *mi gnas mya ngan 'das mi gnas*. See also Jackson 2004, 61.

380. Sferra 2000, 76.17–18: *gurur buddho gurur dharmo guruḥ saṅghas tathaiva ca / gurur vajradharaḥ śrīmān gurur evātra kāraṇam*. Sferra notes, "This stanza is also quoted in the *Abhisamayamañjarī* (*Dhiḥ* XIII, 154). The first half of the verse is very similar to JS I, 24ab (*gurur buddha bhaved dharmaḥ saṅghaś cāpi sa eva hi*)."

381. *Dgongs pa 'dus pa'i mdo* (D 829), 260a2–3. See Cabezón 2013, 64n16.

382. *Sarvabhāvavigataṃ skandhadhātvāyatana-grāhyagrāhakavarjitam / dharmanairātmyasamatayā svacittam ādyanutpannaṃ śūnyatābhāvam*. *Guhyasamājatantra*, 2.3–4 (Matsunaga 1978, 10); Tibetan in Fremantle 1971, 93.

383. Cited from *Guhyagarbhatantra*, 200a: *sangs rgyas nyid* {Kadam, *rang gi sems*} *las gzhan pa'i chos / / sangs rgyas nyid kyis mi rnyed do*.

384. *Guhyagarbhatantra*, 222a: *dus bzhi phyogs bcu gang nas kyang / / rdzogs pa'i sangs rgyas rnyed mi 'gyur / / sems nyid rdzogs pa'i sangs rgyas te / / sangs rgyas gzhan du ma tshol cig*.

385. *Stages*, §131.

386. These names are given according to how they appear in the *Stages* manuscript, and the Tibetan transcription in brackets is from notes inscribed in the manuscript by an unknown Tibetan editor. See the introduction to this chapter on this list of names. Some of the Sanskrit names as they appear in the manuscript do not exactly correlate to Tibetan equivalents. For example, "Ratnamabhapa" does not correlate to *rin chen dga' pa*, and Shvararāja could be emended to Īśvaradhvaja (*dbang phyug rgyal mtshan*).

387. *Mahāyānottaratantraśāstra*, verses 149–50. Kadampa citation differs from the Tengyur edition: *gter dang 'bras bu'i shing bzhin du / / rigs 'di gnyis su shes bya ste /* {Tengyur: *rigs de rnam gnyis shes bya ste*} */ thog med rang bzhin gnas pa dang / / yang dag blang ba mchog nyid do / / rigs 'di gnyis la* {*las*} *sangs rgyas kyi / / sku gsum thob par 'dod pa ste* {*yin*} */ / dang po yi ni* {*po'i sku ni*} *dang po ste / / gnyis pa yi* {*yis*} *ni phyi ma gnyis* (*Mahāyānottaratantraśāstra*, 61b). See translation in Holmes 1985, 66–68, and Takasaki 1966, 288. Skt.: *Gotraṃ tad dvividhaṃ jñeyaṃ nidhānaphalavṛkṣavat / anādiprakṛtisthaṃ ca samudānītam uttaram //* (149) */ buddhakāyatrayāvāptir asmād gotradvayān matā / prathamāt prathamaḥ kāyo dvitīyād dvau tu paścimau* (150) (Johnston et al. 1991, 71–72). These verses may represent an early translation by Atiśa and Naktso (compare Kano 2016b, 329n191). On the translation of Atiśa and Naktso, see Kano 2016b, 156–63.

388. Compare these subsequent practices with *Stages* §8.

389. See Lamotte 1949, 816, footnote: "The classical formula (e.g., Aṅguttara, IV, p. 248; Mahāvyutpatti. no. 8505) is: *surāmaireyamadyapramādasthānavirati*, i.e., renouncing fermented rice drink (*surā*) and the fermented drink of ingredients (*maireya*) when they are still intoxicating (*madya*); because they are the cause of all failings (*pramādasthāna*)." Cf. *Abhidharmakośabhāṣya* ad 4.34cd (Sangpo 2012, 2:1355).

390. I have retained the spelling *bodhisatva* when refering to the title of this composition as it appears in the *Stages* manuscript. On the spelling *bodhisatva* in Buddhist manuscripts and inscriptions, see Bhattacharya 2010.

391. See Apple 2018, 140, for an example of this practice explained in a Kadampa commentary. See Roesler 2018 on this cultural practice and Halkias 2014 for an overview in Tibetan Buddhist history.

392. Zimmermann 2013, 873.

393. *Open Basket of Jewels* (Apple 2018, 87) and *Lamp* v. 22 (Apple 2019, 184), *Bodhimārgapradīpapañjikā* (Sherburne 2000, 165–69).
394. Abbreviated title for *Sāgaramatiparipṛcchāsūtra*; cf. *Śikṣāsamuccaya* (Bendall 1971, 313) and works of Atiśa (Sherburne 2000).
395. *Sāgaramatiparipṛcchāsūtra*, 51b: *de bzhin gshegs pa'i dam pa'i chos 'dzin pa / / dran ldan blo gros ldan zhing blo ldan 'gyur / / shes rab rgya chen kun nas ye shes ldan / / mkhas pa bag chags bcas pa'i nyon mongs spong / / de bzhin gshegs pa'i dam pa'i chos 'dzin pa / / de la bdud kyi skyon chags rnyed mi 'gyur / / de la 'gyod dang de bzhin dogs pa med / / de la bcings med sgrib pa cung zad med / / de bzhin gshegs pa'i dam pa'i chos 'dzin pa / / zhing stong dag tu nam yang mi skye ste / / skye ba kun tu de ni rgyal ba mthong / / mthong nas de la dad pa rab tu 'thob / / de bzhin gshegs pa'i dam pa'i chos 'dzin pa / / chos kyi bdag nyid chen po skye dran 'gyur / / yang dang yang du rab tu 'byung ba 'thob / / spyod pa yongs dag sgrub pa snying por byed / / de bzhin gshegs pa'i dam pa'i chos 'dzin pa / / tshul khrims thos pas 'phags pa'i chos spyod pa / / mkhas pa mngon shes lnga la myur du reg / ma smad bsam gtan rnam par thar pa 'thob / / de bzhin gshegs pa'i dam pa'i chos 'dzin pa / / de ni zab chos rtogs par khong du chud / / sangs rgyas spyod yul stong nyid the tshom med / / sems can bdag med par yang mos par 'gyur / / de bzhin gshegs pa'i dam pa'i chos 'dzin pa / / de ni so so yang dag rig pa 'thob / / 'jigs med shes rab rno zhing chags med dag / de ni srog chags kun gyi the tshom gcod / / de bzhin gshegs pa'i dam pa'i chos 'dzin pa / / mkhas pa de ni gzungs rnams 'thob par 'gyur / / bskal pa brgyar yang gang thos chud mi za / / spobs dang ldan zhing chags pa med par 'gyur / / de bzhin gshegs pa'i dam pa'i chos 'dzin pa / de la mkhas pa rtag tu dga' bar 'gyur / / lha dang lha min mi ci'i yid du 'ong / / de la sangs rgyas bu gcig bzhin* [52a] *du bstod / / de bzhin gshegs pa'i dam pa'i chos 'dzin pa / / brgya byin tshangs pa de bzhin 'jig rten skyong / / 'khor los sgyur dang mi yi rgyal por 'gyur / / bde dang yid bde byang chub de 'tshang rgya.*
396. See Tatz 1978, 281, "treatment for middling defilement."
397. This story is a variant on the famous *jātaka* tale in which the Buddha in his past life as King Śibi offers his own flesh to a hawk as ransom for the life of a dove.

Bibliography

Canonical Texts (Kangyur and Tengyur)

Abhidharmakośabhāṣya by Vasubandhu. *Commentary on the Treasury of Higher Knowledge. Chos mngon pa'i mdzod kyi bshad pa.* Tengyur Dergé 4090, Mngon pa, *ku*: 26–258, and *khu*: 1–95. Sanskrit in Pradhan 1975. French translation in La Vallée Poussin 1923–31. English translation in Sangpo 2012.

Abhidharmakośa by Vasubandhu. *Treasury of Higher Knowledge. Chos mngon pa'i mdzod.* Tengyur Dergé 4089, Mngon pa, *ku*: 1–25. Sanskrit in Pradhan 1975. French translation in La Vallée Poussin 1923–31. English translation in Sangpo 2012.

Abhidharmasamuccaya by Asaṅga. *Compendium of Higher Knowledge. Chos mngon pa kun las btus pa.* Tengyur Dergé 4049, Sems tsam, *ri*: 44–120.

Abhisamayālaṃkāra by Maitreya. *Ornament for Clear Realization. Mngon par rtogs pa'i rgyan.* Tengyur Dergé 3786, Shes phyin, *ka*: 1–13. Edition in Stcherbatsky and Obermiller 1929.

Abhisamayavibhaṅga by Dīpaṃkaraśrījñāna (Atiśa). *Analysis of Realization. Mngon par rtogs pa rnam par 'byed pa.* Tengyur Dergé 1490, Rgyud, *zha*: 186–202.

Acintyabuddhaviṣayanirdeśasūtra. Teaching on the Inconceivable Properties of the Buddhas Sūtra. Sangs rgyas kyi yul bsam gyis mi khyab pa'i mdo. Kangyur Dergé 79, Dkon brtsegs, *ca*: 266–84.

Akṣayamatinirdeśasūtra. Teaching of Akṣayamati. Blo gros mi zad pas bstan pa'i mdo. Kangyur Dergé 175, Mdo, *ma*: 79–174. English translation in Braarvig 1993.

Anantamukhapariśodhananirdeśaparivarta. Limitless Doorways Sūtra. Sgo mtha' yas pa rnam par sbyong ba bstan pa'i le'u. Kangyur Dergé 46, Dkon brtsegs, *ka*: 45–99.

Aṣṭasāhasrikāprajñāpāramitā. Perfection of Wisdom in Eight Thousand Lines. 'Phags pa shes rab kyi pha rol tu phyin pa brgyad stong pa. Kangyur Dergé 12, Brgyad stong, *ka*: 1–286. Sanskrit in Wogihara 1932–35.

Avalokiteśvaraparipṛcchāsaptadharmakasūtra. Inquiry of Avalokiteśvara on the Seven Qualities. 'Phags pa spyan ras gzigs dbang phyug gis zhus pa chos bdun pa'i mdo. Kangyur Dergé 150, Mdo, *pa*: 331a2–b5.

Bhadrakalpikasūtra. Fortunate Eon Sūtra. Bskal pa bzang po'i mdo. Kangyur Dergé 45, *ka*: 1–340.

Bhadrakāratrisūtra. Good Signs Sūtra. Mtshan mo bzang po'i mdo. Kangyur Dergé 313, Mdo, *sa*: 161–63.

Bodhicaryāvatāra by Śāntideva. *Introduction to the Practice of Awakening. Byang chub sems dpa'i spyod pa la 'jug pa.* Tengyur Dergé 3871, Dbu ma, *la*: 1–40. Sanskrit edition in Vaidya 1960. English translation in Crosby and Skilton 1995.

Bodhimārgapradīpapañjikā by Dīpaṃkaraśrījñāna (Atiśa). *Commentary on the Difficult Points of the Lamp for the Path to Awakening. Byang chub lam gyi sgron ma'i dka' 'grel.* Tengyur Dergé 3948, Dbu ma, *khi*: 241–93. In Sherburne 2000.

Bodhipathapradīpa by Dīpaṃkaraśrījñāna (Atiśa). *Lamp for the Path to Awakening. Byang chub lam gyi sgron ma.* Tengyur Dergé 3947, Dbu ma, *khi*: 238–41. In Eimer 1978 and Sherburne 2000. English translation in Apple 2019, 181–91.

Bodhisattvabhūmi by Asaṅga. *Bodhisattva Levels. Byang chub sems dpa'i sa.* Tengyur Dergé 4037, Sems tsam, *wi*: 1–213. Sanskrit edition in Dutt 1966. English translation in Engle 2016.

Bodhisattvapiṭakasūtra. Bodhisattva's Scriptural Collection Sūtra. Byang chub sems dpa'i sde snod kyi mdo. Kangyur Dergé 56, Dkon brtsegs, *kha*: 255–94, *ga*: 1–205. In Pagel 1995.

Bodhisattvapratimokṣacatuṣkanirhārasūtra. Bodhisattvas' Prātimokṣa: Accomplishing the Sets of Four Qualities. Byang chub sems dpa'i so sor thar pa chos bzhi sgrub pa. Kangyur Dergé 248, Mdo sde, *za*: 46–59.

Bodhisattvasaṃvaraviṃśaka by Candragomin. *Twenty Verses on the Bodhisattva Vow. Byang chub sems dpa'i sdom pa nyi shu pa.* Tengyur Dergé 4081, Sems tsam, *hi*: 166–67. In Tatz 1985.

Caryāsaṅgrahapradīpa by Dīpaṃkaraśrījñāna (Atiśa). *Lamp for the Summary of Conduct. Spyod pa bsdus pa'i sgron ma.* Tengyur Dergé 3960 (also 4466), Dbu ma, *khi*: 312–13. English translation in Apple 2019, 159–63.

Caturdharmanirdeśasūtra. Teaching on the Four Qualities Sūtra. Chos bzhi bstan pa'i mdo. Kangyur Dergé 249, Mdo, *za*: 59.

Cittotpādasaṃvaravidhikrama by Dīpaṃkaraśrījñāna (Atiśa). *A Ritual for Generating the Awakening Mind and for the Bodhisattva Vow. Sems bskyed pa dang sdom pa'i cho ga'i rim pa.* Tengyur Dergé 3969 (also 4490), Dbu ma, *gi*: 245–48. English in Sherburne 2000, 536–51.

Damamūkosūtra. Sūtra of the Wise and Foolish. Mdzangs blun gyi mdo. Kangyur Dergé 341, Mdo, *a*: 129–298. In Frye 1981.

Daśacakrakṣitigarbhasūtra. Ten Wheels of Kṣitigarbha Sūtra. Sa'i snying po'i 'khor lo bcu pa mdo. Kangyur Dergé 239, Mdo, *zha*: 100–241.

Daśākuśalakarmapathadeśanā by Dīpaṃkaraśrījñāna (Atiśa). *Explanation of the Ten Non-virtuous Paths of Action. Mi dge ba bcu'i las kyi lam bstan pa.* Tengyur Dergé 3958 (also 4483), Dbu ma, *khi*: 306–7. English translation in Sherburne 2000.

Dharmasaṃgītisūtra. Perfect Gathering of Qualities Sūtra. Chos yang dag par sdud pa'i mdo. Kangyur Dergé 238, Mdo, *zha*: 1–99.

Dharmatāsvabhāvaśūnyatācalapratisarvālokasūtra. Sūtra Illuminating Appearance of All Things Distinctly without Their Departing from Their Essential Nature, Emptiness. Chos nyid rang gi ngo bo stong pa nyid las mi g.yo bar tha dad par thams cad la snang ba'i mdo. Kangyur Dergé 128, Mdo, *da*: 171–74.

Dohākoṣa by Saraha. *Treasury of Dohās. Do ha mdzod kyi glu.* Tengyur Dergé 2224, Rgyud, *wi*: 70–77.

Dpang skong phyag brgya pa. Calling Witness with a Hundred Prostrations. Kangyur Dergé 267, Mdo, *ya*: 1–5.

Gaṇḍavyūhasūtra. Stem Array Sūtra. Sdong po bkod pa'i mdo. Final chapter of the *Avataṃsakasūtra.* Kangyur Dergé 44, Phal chen, *ka*, *kha*, *ga*, and *a*. Sanskrit edition in Vaidya 1960b.

Gayāśīrṣasūtra. Gayāśīrṣa Hill Sūtra. Ga yā mgo'i ri'i mdo. Kangyur Dergé 109, Mdo, *ca*: 285–92.

Gośṛṅgavyākaraṇa. Prophecy on Mount Gośṛṅga. Glang ru lung bstan pa. Kangyur Dergé 357, Mdo, *a*: 220–32.

Guhyagarbhatantra. Gsang ba'i snying po'i rgyud. Kangyur Dergé 834, Rnying rgyud, *kha*: 198–298.

Guhyagarbhatattvaviniścaya. Secret Nucleus Definitive with Respect to the Real. Gsang ba'i snying po de kho na nyid rnam par nges pa. Kangyur Dergé 832, Rnying rgyud, *kha*: 110–32.

Guhyasamājatantra. Gsang ba 'dus pa'i rgyud. Kangyur Dergé 442, Rgyud, *ca*: 90–148. Sanskrit edition in Matsunaga 1978.

Hevajratantra. Kye'i rdo rje rgyud. Kangyur Dergé 417, Rgyud, *nga*: 1–13. See Snellgrove 2010.

Jātakamālā by Āryaśūra. *Birth Stories of the Buddha. Skyes pa'i rabs kyi rgyud.* Tengyur Dergé 4150, Skyes rab, *hu*: 1–135. Sanskrit in Vaidya 1959. English translation in Khoroche 2006.

Karmavibhaṅga by Dīpaṃkaraśrījñāna (Atiśa). *Analysis of Actions. Las rnam par 'byed.* Tengyur Dergé 3959 (also 4484), Dbu ma, *khi*: 308–12. English translation in Sherburne 2000.

Kāśyapaparivarta. Kāśyapa Chapter. 'Od srung gi le'u. Kangyur Dergé 87, Dkon brtsegs, *cha*: 119–51. Romanized text and facsimiles in Vorobyova-Desyatovskaya 2002. English translation in Pāsādika 2015.

Lalitavistarasūtra. Play in Full. Rgya cher rol pa'i mdo. Kangyur Dergé 95, Mdo, *kha*: 1–216. Sanskrit edition in Vaidya 1958.

Laṅkāvatārasūtra. Descent into Laṅkā Sūtra. Lang kar gshegs pa'i mdo. Kangyur Dergé 107, Mdo, *ca*: 56–191. Sanskrit edition in Nanjio 1923. English translation in Suzuki 1932.

Madhyamakopadeśa by Dīpaṃkaraśrījñāna (Atiśa). *Special Instructions on the Middle Way. Dbu ma'i man ngag.* Tengyur Dergé 3929 (also 4468), Dbu ma, *ki*: 95–96. English translation in Apple 2018.

Madhyāntavibhāga of Maitreyanātha. *Clear Differentiation of the Middle Beyond Extremes. Dbus dang mtha' rnam par 'byed pa.* Tengyur Dergé 4021, Sems tsam, *phi*: 40–45. Sanskrit in Pandeya 1999.

Madhyāntavibhāgaṭīkā of Sthiramati. *Commentary on the Middle Beyond Extremes. Dbus dang mtha' rnam par 'byed pa'i 'grel bshad.* Tengyur Dergé 4032, Sems tsam, *bi*: 189–318. Sanskrit in Pandeya 1999.

Mahāpratihāryanirdeśa. Teaching of the Great Magical Display. Cho 'phrul chen po bstan pa. Kangyur Dergé 66, Dkon brtseg, *ca*: 36–67.

Mahāyānasūtrālaṃkāra by Maitreya. *Ornament of Mahāyāna Sūtras. Theg pa chen po mdo sde'i rgyan.* Tengyur Dergé 4020, Sems tsam, *phi*: 1–39. Sanskrit in Lévi 1907. English in Maitreyanātha/Asaṅga and Vasubandhu 2004.

Mahāyānottaratantraśāstra by Maitreya. *Treatise on the Higher Teaching of the Great Vehicle. Theg pa chen po rgyud bla ma'i bstan bcos.* Tengyur Dergé 4024, Sems tsam, *phi*: 54–73. English translation and Sanskrit text in Johnston et al. 1991.

Mañjuśrīnāmasaṃgīti. Recitation of the Names of Mañjuśrī. 'Jam dpal gyi mtshan yang dag par brjod pa. Kangyur Dergé 360, Rgyud, *ka*: 1–13. English translation and Sanskrit text in Davidson 1981.

Marmakalikāpañjikā-nāma Tattvajñānasaṃsiddhipañjikā by Vīraśrīmitra. An Extensive

Commentary on the Perfect Attainment of the Gnosis of Suchness called "An Explanation of Suchness. *De kho na nyid ye shes yang dag par grub pa'i rgya cher 'grel pa de kho na nyid bshad pa.* Tengyur Dergé 1585, *'a*, 68–102.

Mūlamadhyamaka by Nāgārjuna. *Fundamental Verses on the Middle Way. Dbu ma rtsa ba'i shes rab.* Tengyur Dergé 3824, Dbu ma, *tsa*: 1–19. Sanskrit in La Vallée Poussin 1903–13. English translation in Katsura and Siderits 2013.

Mūlāpattiṭīkā by Dīpaṃkaraśrījñāna (Atiśa). *Extensive Commentary on the Root Downfalls. Rtsa ba'i ltung ba'i rgya cher 'grel pa.* Tengyur Dergé 2487, Rgyud, *zi*: 192–97.

Nandapravrajyāsūtra. Nanda's Ordination Sūtra. Dga' bo rab tu byung ba'i mdo. Kangyur Dergé 328, Mdo sde, *sa*: 254–57.

Pañcakrama by Nāgārjuna. *Five Stages. Rim pa lnga pa.* Tengyur Dergé 1802, Rgyud, *ngi*: 45–57. Sanskrit and Tibetan in Mimaki and Tomabechi 1994.

Pitāputrasamāgamana. Meeting of Father and Son. Yab dang sras mjal ba'i mdo. Kangyur Dergé 60, Dkon brtsegs, *nga*: 1–168.

Prajñāpāramitāhṛdaya. Essence of the Perfection of Wisdom (Heart Sūtra). Bcom ldan 'das ma shes rab kyi pha rol tu phyin pa'i snying po. Kangyur Dergé 21 (also 531), Shes rab sna tshogs, *ka*: 144–46. See Lopez 1988.

Prajñāpāramitāsaṃcayagāthā, a.k.a. *Ratnaguṇasaṃcayagāthā. Verses That Summarize the Perfection of Wisdom. Shes rab kyi pha rol tu phyin pa sdud pa tshigs su bcad pa.* Kangyur Dergé 13, Shes rab sna tshogs, *ka*: 1–19. See Obermiller 1937 and Yuyama 1976.

Prajñāpāramitopadeśa by Ratnākaraśānti. *Special Instructions on the Perfection of Wisdom. Shes rab kyi pha rol tu phyin pa'i man ngag.* Tengyur Dergé 4079, Sems tsam, *hi*: 133–62.

Pratītyasamutpādahṛdaya by Nāgārjuna. *Verses on the Essence of Dependent Origination. Rten cing 'brel bar 'byung ba'i snying po.* Tengyur Dergé 3836 (also 4553), Dbu ma, *tsa*: 146.

Pūrṇaparipṛcchāsūtra. Inquiry of Pūrṇa Sūtra. Gang pos zhus pa'i mdo. Kangyur Dergé 61, Dkon brtsegs, *nga*: 168–227.

Ratnakaraṇḍodghāṭanāmamadhyamakopadeśa by Dīpaṃkaraśrījñāna (Atiśa). *Open Basket of Jewels: Special Instructions on the Middle Way. Dbu ma'i man ngag rin po che'i za ma tog kha phye ba.* Tengyur Dergé 3930, Dbu ma, *ki*: 96–116. English translation in Apple 2018.

Ratnarāśisūtra. Mass of Jewels Sūtra. Rin po che'i phung po'i mdo. Kangyur Dergé 88, Dkon brtsegs, *cha*: 152–75.

Ratnolkādhāraṇī. Jewel Torch Dhāraṇī. Dkon mchog ta la la'i gzungs gyi mdo. Kangyur Dergé 145 (also 847), Mdo, *pa*: 34–82.

Sāgaramatiparipṛcchāsūtra. Inquiry of Sāgaramati Sūtra. Blo gros rgya mtshos zhus pa'i mdo. Kangyur Dergé 152, Mdo, *pha*: 1–115.

Śālistambasūtra. Rice Sprout Sūtra. Sa lu ljang pa'i mdo. Kangyur Dergé 210, Mdo, *tsha*: 116–23. Tibetan edition and English translation in Reat 1993. Indian commentaries in Schoening 1995.

Samājasarvavidyāsūtra. Sūtra That Gathers All Intentions. Dgongs pa 'dus pa'i mdo. Kangyur Dergé 829, Rnying rgyud, *ka*: 86–290.

Saṃsāramanoniryāṇikāranāmasaṅgīti by Dīpaṃkaraśrījñāna (Atiśa). *A Song Called "Bringing About the Definite Liberation of the Mind from Saṃsāra." 'Khor ba las yid nges par 'byung bar byed pa zhes bya ba'i glu.* Tengyur Dergé 2313 (also 4473), Rgyud, *zhi*: 253–54. English translation in Sherburne 2000, 396–405.

Saṃvaraviṃśakavṛtti by Śāntarakṣita. *Commentary on The Twenty Vows [of a Bodhisattva].*

Sdom pa nyi shu pa'i 'grel pa. Tengyur Dergé 4082, Sems tsam, *hi*: 167–84. English translation in Tatz 1978.

Sarvabuddhamahārahasyopāyakauśalya. Skillful Means of the Great Secret (a.k.a. *Jñānotta rabodhisattvaparipṛcchāparivarta. Chapter of the Bodhisattva Jñānottara's Questions*). *Sangs rgyas thams cad kyi gsang chen thabs la mkhas pa byang chub sems dpa' ye shes dam pas zhus pa'i le'u gyi mdo.* Kangyur Dergé 82, Dkon brtsegs, *cha*: 30–70. See Tatz 1994.

Sarvadurgatipariśodhanatantra. De bzhin gshegs pa dgra bcom pa yang dag par rdzogs pa'i sangs rgyas ngan song thams cad yongs su sbyong ba gzi brjid kyi rgyal po'i brtag pa zhes bya ba. Kangyur Dergé 483, Rgyud, *ta*: 58–96.

Sarvapuṇyasamuccayasamādhisūtra. Samādhi That Gathers All Merit Sūtra. Bsod nams thams cad sdud pa'i ting nge 'dzin gyi mdo. Kangyur Dergé 134, Mdo, *na*: 70–121.

Sarvavaidalyasaṃgrahasūtra. Sūtra Gathering All Fragments. Rnam par 'thag pa thams cad bsdus pa'i mdo. Kangyur Dergé 227, Mdo, *dza*: 177–88.

Satyadvayāvatāra by Dīpaṃkaraśrījñāna (Atiśa). *Entry to the Two Realities. Bden pa gnyis la 'jug pa.* Tengyur Dergé 3902 (also 4467), Dbu ma, *a*: 72–73. See also Sherburne 2000, 352–59. English translation in Apple 2018 and Apple 2019.

Śikṣāsamuccaya by Śāntideva. *Compendium of Training. Bslab pa kun las btus pa.* Tengyur Dergé 3940, Dbu ma, *khi*: 3–194. Sanskrit edition in Bendall 1971; English translations in Bendall and Rouse 1971 and Goodman 2016.

Śrīguptasūtra. Sūtra of [the Householder] Śrīgupta. Dpal sbas gyi mdo. Kangyur Dergé, Mdo, *tsha*: 269–84.

Śrīmālādevīsiṃhanādasūtra. Lion's Roar of Queen Śrīmālā Sūtra. Lha mo dpal phreng gi seng ge'i sgra mdo. Kangyur Dergé 92, Dkon brtsegs, *cha*: 255–77.

Suhṛllekha by Nāgārjuna. *Letter to a Friend. Bshes pa'i spring yig.* Tengyur Dergé 4496, Dbu ma, *nge*: 40–46.

Śūnyatāsaptati by Nāgārjuna. *Seventy Stanzas on Emptiness. Stong pa nyid bdun cu pa.* Tengyur Dergé 3827, Dbu ma, *tsa*: 24–27.

Śūraṅgamasamādhisūtra. Samādhi of Heroic Progress Sūtra. Dpa' bar 'gro ba'i ting nge 'dzin gyi mdo. Kangyur Dergé 132, Mdo, *da*: 253–316. English translation in Lamotte 1998.

Sūtrasamuccaya by Nagārjuna. *Compendium of Sūtra. Mdo kun las btus pa.* Tengyur Dergé 3934, Dbu ma, *ki*: 148–215. Tibetan edition in Pāsādika 1989. English translation in Pāsādika 1978–82.

Suvarṇaprabhāsasūtra. Golden Light Sūtra. Gser 'od dam pa'i mdo. Kangyur Dergé 557, Rgyud, *pha*: 1–62. Sanskrit text with English introduction in Bagchi 1967.

Tathāgatācintyaguhyanirdeśasūtra. The Teaching on the Unfathomable Secrets of the Tathāgatas. De bzhin gshegs pa'i gsang ba bsam gyis mi khyab pa bstan pa'i mdo. Kangyur Dergé 47, Dkon brtsegs, *ka*: 100–203.

Udānavarga. Collection of Purposeful Sayings. Ched du brjod pa'i rtsoms. Dergé Kangyur 326, Mdo, *sa*: 209–53. Sanskrit edition in Bernhard 1965.

Upāliparipṛcchāsūtra. Vinayaviniścayopāliparipṛcchāsūtra. Ascertaining the Vinaya: The Questions of Upāli Sūtra. 'Dul ba rnam par gtan la dbab pa nye bar 'khor gyis zhus pa'i mdo. Kangyur Dergé 68, Dkon brtsegs, *ca*: 115–31.

Uttaratantra by Maitreya. *Higher Teaching.* See under *Mahāyānottaratantraśāstra.*

Vairocanābhisambodhi. Complete Enlightenment of Vairocana Tantra. Rnam par snang mdzad mngon par rdzogs par byang chub pa'i rgyud. Kangyur Dergé 494, Rgyud, *tha*: 151–260.

Vajrapañjaratantra. Indestructible Tent Tantra. Ḍākinīvajrapañjara-mahātantrarājakalpa

(*'Phags pa mkha' 'gro ma rdo rje gur zhes bya ba'i rgyud kyi rgyal po chen po'i brtag pa*). Kangyur Dergé 419, Dergé Kangyur, *nga*, 30–65. Tr. by Gayadhara and Shākya ye shes.

Vajraśekharatantra. *Vajra Pinnacle Tantra*. *Gsang ba rnal 'byor chen po'i rgyud rdo rje rtse mo*. Kangyur Dergé 480, Rgyud, *nya*: 142–274.

Varmavyūhanirdeśasūtra. *Teaching of the Armor Array Sūtra*. *Go cha'i bkod pa bstan pa'i mdo*. Kangyur Dergé 51, Dkon brtsegs, *kha*: 70–140.

Vinayakṣudrakavastu. *Finer Points of Discipline*. *'Dul ba phran tshegs kyi gzhi*. Kangyur Dergé 6, 'Dul ba, *tha–da*.

Vinayavastu. *Chapters on Monastic Discipline*. *'Dul ba gzhi*. Kangyur Dergé 1, *ka, kha, ga,* and *nga*. Partial English translation in Miller 2023.

Viniścayasaṃgrahaṇī by Asaṅga. *Compendium of Determinations*. *Rnam par gtan la dbab pa bsdu ba*. Tengyur Dergé 4038, Sems tsam, *zhi*: 1–289 and *zu*: 1–127.

Vīradattagṛhapatiparipṛcchāsūtra. *Questions of Vīradatta Sūtra*. *Khyim bdag dpas byin gyis zhus pa'i mdo*. Kangyur Dergé 72, Dkon brtsegs, *ca*: 194–204. English translation in Apple 2022.

Yamārikṛṣṇakarmasarvacakrasiddhakara. *Cycle Accomplishing All the Actions of Black Yamāri*. *Gshin rje'i gshed dgra nag po'i 'khor lo las thams cad grub par byed pa*. Tengyur Dergé 473, Rgyud, *ja*: 175–85.

Yogācārabhūmi by Asaṅga. *Levels of Spiritual Practice*. *Rnal 'byor spyod pa'i sa*. Tengyur Dergé 4035, Sems tsam, *tshi*: 1–283. Sanskrit edition in Bhattacarya 1957.

Yuktiṣaṣṭikā by Nāgārjuna. *Rigs pa drug cu pa*. Tengyur Dergé 3825, Dbu ma, *tsa*: 20–22. See Scherrer-Schaub 1991.

Yuktiṣāṣṭikāvṛtti by Candrakīrti. *Sixty Stanzas of Reasoning*. *Rigs pa drug cu pa'i 'grel pa*. Tengyur Dergé 3864, Dbu ma, *ya*: 1–30. See Scherrer-Schaub 1991.

Tibetan Sources

A myes zhabs Ngag dbang kun dga' bsod nams (1597–1659). *Gsung 'bum: Chos kyi rje dpal ldan bla ma dam pa rnams las dam pa'i chos ji ltar thos tshul legs par bshad pa zab rgyas chos kun gsal ba'i nyin byed ces bya ba las khyab bdag 'khor lo'i mgon po rgyal ba mus pa chen po rdo rje 'chang sangs rgyas rgyal mtshan gyis rjes su bzung ba'i tshul gyi sar ga*. *Gsung 'bum ngag dbang kun dga' bsod nams*, 2: 7–252. Sa skya rgyal yongs gsung rab slob gnyer khang, 2000.

Atiśa Dīpaṃkaraśrījñāna. *Lta sgom 'breng po* [sic: *'bring po*]. In *Gsung 'bum / a ti sha*, 657–62. Beijing: Krung go'i bod rig pa dpe skrun khang, 2006.

———. *Lta sgom chen mo*. In *Gsung 'bum / a ti sha*, 628–42. Beijing: Krung go'i bod rig pa dpe skrun khang, 2006.

———. *Lta sgom chung ngu*. In *Gsung 'bum / a ti sha*, 653–56. Beijing: Krung go'i bod rig pa dpe skrun khang, 2006

Bka' gdams gsung 'bum. See under Dbyangs can lha mo et al.

Byang chub lam gyi rim pa. *Writings of Lord Atiśa on the Theory and Practice of the Graduated Path*. Leh, Ladakh: Thupten Tsering, 1973.

Byang chub lam gyi rim pa (*Bodhipathakrama*). *Stages of the Path to Awakening*. In *Byang chub lam gyi rim pa*, 21–63.7; *Bka' gdams gsung 'bum phyogs bsgrigs glegs bam go gcig*, 21–202. Dpal brtsegs bod yig dpe rnying zhib 'jug khang, 2015.

Byang chub lam rim gyi spyi don. In *Byang chub lam gyi rim pa*, 55–83. Leh, Ladakh: Thupten Tsering, 1973.

Dbyangs can lha mo et al., eds. *Bka' gdams gsung 'bum phyogs bsgrigs bzhugs so*. 120 vols. Chengdu: Si-khron Dpe-skrun Tshogs-pa, Si-khron mi-rigs dpe skrun-khang, 2006–15.

Dpal ldan bla ma rmog cog pa chen po'i rnam par thar pa. In *Sa skya pa dang sa skya pa ma yin pa'i bla ma kha shas kyi rnam thar*. 3 vols. Kathmandu: Sa skya rgyal yongs gsung rab slob gnyer khang.

Dpal mang Dkon mchog rgyal mtshan (1764–1853). *Byang chub lam gyi sgron me'i 'grel ba phul byung dgyes pa'i mchod sprin*. In *Collected Works*, 4:1. New Delhi: Gyalten Gelek Namgyal, 1974.

'Gos lo tsā ba Gzhon nu dpal (1392–1481). *Deb ther sngon po*. 2 vols. Edited by Dung dkar blo bzang 'phrin las. Chengdu: Si khron mi rigs dpe skrun khang, 1984. Translation in Roerich 1979.

'Jam mgon kong sprul Blo gros mtha' yas (1813–99). *Gdams ngag mdzod*. 18 vols. Delhi: Shechen Publications, 1999.

Jo bo rje dpal ldan a ti sha'i gsung 'bum. Works Attributed to Atiśa and His Early Disciples. Compiled by Dpal brtsegs bod yig dpe rnying zhib 'jug khang. Bka' gdams dpe dkon gces btus. Zi ling: Krung go'i bod rig pa dpe skrun khang, 2006.

Lam rim mdor bsdus pa. In *Byang chub lam gyi rim pa*, 63.7–64.2. Also in *Bka' gdams gsung 'bum phyogs bsgrigs glegs bam go gcig*, 21–202. Khreng tu'u: Dpal brtsegs bod yig dpe rnying zhib 'jug khang, 2015.

Las chen Kun dga' rgyal mtshan (1432–1506). *Bka' gdams kyi rnam par thar pa bka' gdams chos 'byung gsal ba'i sgron me*. Lhasa: Bod ljongs mi dmangs dpe skrun khang, 2003.

Lkog chos (*Instructions for Select Disciples*). In *Byang chub lam gyi rim pa*, 39–52 (77–103). Leh, Ladakh: Thupten Tsering, 1973. Also in *Jo bo rje dpal ldan a ti sha'i gsum 'bum*, 2:499–526.

Ngo sprod lnga tshoms (*Pointing-Out Instructions in Sets of Five*). In *Byang chub lam gyi rim pa*, 104–29. Leh, Ladakh: Thupten Tsering, 1973. Also in *Jo bo rje dpal ldan a ti sha'i gsung 'bum*, 2:527–52.

Nyang ral Nyi ma 'od zer (1124–92). *Chos 'byung me tog snying po sbrang rtsi'i bcud*. Lhasa: Bod rjongs bod yig dpe snying skrung khang, 2010.

'Phag mo gru pa Rdo rje rgyal po (1110–70). *Sangs rgyas bstan rim dang jo nang mdzad brgya*. Bir, H.P.: Zogyam and Pema Lodoe, 1977.

Sgam po pa Bsod nams rin chen (1079–1153). *Dam chos yid bzhin nor bu thar pa rin po che'i rgyan*. Kathmandu: Gam-po-pa Library, 2003.

Sha ra ba Yon tan grags (1070–1141). *Dge ba'i bshes gnyen zhang sha ra ba yon tan grags kyis mdzad pa'i lam rim bzhugs so*. Ser gtsug nang bstan dpe rnying 'tshol bsdu phyogs sgrig khang nas bsgrigs, 2014. BDR: W4C257131.

———. *Pa tshab lo tstsha ba dang zhang sha ra ba chen po dang gnyis kyis dbu ma'i dri lan bzhugs sho*. In *Byams pa sgom lugs sogs sha ra ba dang 'brel ba'i bka' gdams pa'i gsung chos tshan 'ga'*, images 21–30. BDR: W3CN18532.

Tshul khrims rin chen, Zhu chen (1697–1774). Bstan 'gyur (sde dge). Tibetan Buddhist Resource Center W23703. 213 vols. Delhi: Delhi Karmapae Choedhey, Gyalwae Sungrab Partun khang, 1982–85.

Tsong kha pa Blo bzang grags pa (1357–1419). *Lam rim chen mo. Mnyam med Tsong kha pa chen pos mdzad pa'i byang chub lam rim che ba*. Kokonor, Tibet: Mtsho ngon mi rigs dpe skrun khang, 1985.

———. *Rje tsong kha pa chen po'i gsung 'bum.* 18 vols. Beijing: Krung go'i bod rig pa dpe skrun khang, 2012.

Secondary Sources

Achard, Jean-Luc. 1999. *L'Essence Perlée du Secret Recherches Philologiques et Historiques sur l'Origine de la Grande Perfection dans la Tradition "rNying ma pa".* Turnhout: Brepols Publishers.

———. 2002. "La base et ses sept interpretations dans la tradition rdzogs chen." *Revue d'Études Tibétaines* 1: 44–61.

———. 2004. *Bon po Hidden Treasures: A Catalogue of gTer ston bDe chen gling pa's Collected Revelations.* Leiden: Brill.

Alexander Csoma de Kőrös Translation Group. 2023. *The Sūtra of Nanda's Going Forth (Nandapravrajyāsūtra, Toh 328).* 84000: Translating the Words of the Buddha. https://read.84000.co/translation/toh328.html.

Allon, Mark. 2007. "A Gāndhāri Version of the Simile of the Turtle and the Hole in the Yoke." *Journal of the Pali Text Society* 29: 229–62.

Almogi, Orna. 2005. "Analysing Tibetan Titles: Towards a Genre-Based Classification of Tibetan Literature." *Cahiers d'Extrême-Asie* 15: 27–58.

———. 2009. *Rong-Zom-Pa's Discourses on Buddhology: A Study of Various Conceptions of Buddhahood in Indian Sources with Special Reference to the Controversy Surrounding the Existence of Gnosis (Jñāna: Ye Shes) as Presented by the Eleventh-Century Tibetan Scholar Rong-Zom Chos-Kyi-Bzang-Po.* Tokyo: International Institute for Buddhist Studies of the International College for Postgraduate Buddhist Studies.

Apple, James B. 2008. *Stairway to Nirvāṇa: A Study of the Twenty Saṃghas Based on the Works of Tsong kha pa.* Albany: State University of New York Press.

———. 2010. "Atiśa's Open Basket of Jewels: A Middle Way Vision in Late Phase Indian Vajrayāna." *Indian International Journal of Buddhist Studies* 11: 117–98.

———. 2013a. "An Early Tibetan Commentary on Atiśa's *Satyadvayāvatāra.*" *Journal of Indian Philosophy* 41: 263–329.

———. 2013b. *A Stairway Taken by the Lucid: Tsong kha pa's Study of Noble Beings.* New Delhi: Aditya Prakashan.

———. 2014a. "Buddhism in Tibetan History." In *Blackwell Companion to East and Inner Asian Buddhism,* edited by Mario Poceski, 104–23. Oxford: Blackwell Publishing.

———. 2014b. *Inquiry of Avalokiteśvara on the Seven Qualities Sūtra: Avalokiteśvaraparipṛcchāsaptadharmakanāmamahāyānasūtra* (Toh 150). 84000: Translating the Words of the Buddha. https://read.84000.co/translation/toh150.html.

———. 2015a. "A Study and Translation of Atiśa's Madhyamakopadésa with Indian and Tibetan Commentaries." *Acta Tibetica et Buddhica* 7: 1–82.

———. 2015b. "Candrakīrti and the Lotus Sūtra." *Bulletin of the Institute of Oriental Philosophy* 31.1: 97–122.

———. 2016a. "An Early Bka'-gdams-pa Madhyamaka Work Attributed to Atiśa Dīpaṃkaraśrījñāna." *Journal of Indian Philosophy* 44: 619–725.

———. 2016b. "Perfections (Six and Ten) of Bodhisattvas in Buddhist Literature." *Oxford Research Encyclopedia of Religion.* https://doi.org/10.1093/acrefore/9780199340378.013.193

———. 2017. "Atiśa's Teachings on Mahāmudrā." *Indian International Journal of Buddhist Studies* 18: 1–42.

———. 2018. *Jewels of the Middle Way: The Madhyamaka Legacy of Atiśa and His Early Tibetan Followers*. Somerville, MA: Wisdom Publications.

———. 2019. *Atiśa Dīpaṃkara: Illuminator of the Awakened Mind*. Boulder, CO: Shambhala.

———. 2020. "Diplomatic Edition of the Dunhuang Tibetan Version of the *Vīradattaparipṛcchā* (*dpa' sbyin gyis zhus pa*)." *Annual Report of The International Research Institute for Advanced Buddhology at Soka University* 23: 89–115.

———. 2022. *The Questions of the Householder Vīradatta* (*Vīradattagṛhapatiparipṛcchā, Toh 72*). 84000: Translating the Words of the Buddha. https://read.84000.co/translation/toh72.html.

———. 2023. "The Tilting Stream of Dharma Metaphor in Mahāyāna Buddhist Exegesis." *Journal of Oriental Studies* 32: 207–27.

Appleton, Naomi. 2007. "The Story of the Horse-King and the Merchant Siṃhala in Buddhist Texts." *Buddhist Studies Review* 23.2: 187–201.

Bagchi, S., ed. 1967. *Suvarṇaprabhāsasūtra*. Darbhanga, India: Mithila Institute.

Bajetta, Nicola. 2019. *The Clear Realisation of the Quintessential Instructions on All Dharma Practices: A Critical Edition and Annotated Translation of the* *Sarvadharmacaryopadeśābhisamayatantra *(Chos spyod thams cad kyi man ngag mngon par rtogs pa'i rgyud) Based on Two Unpublished Manuscripts from the 'Bras-spungs-gnas-bcu-lha-khang*. Hamburg: Department of Indian and Tibetan Studies, Universität Hamburg.

Barron, Richard, trans. 2011. *The Treasury of Knowledge, Journey and Goal: An Analysis of the Spiritual Paths and Levels to Be Traversed and the Consummate Fruition State*. Ithaca, NY: Snow Lion Publications.

Bayer, Achim. 2010. *The Theory of Karman in the Abhidharmasamuccaya*. Tokyo: International Institute for Buddhist Studies of the International College for Postgraduate Buddhist Studies.

Bendall, Cecil, ed. 1903 and 1904. *Subhāṣita-Saṃgraha. Le Muséon* vol. 4 (1903): 375–402; vol. 5 (1904): 1–46, 245–74. Louvain, Belgium: J. B. Istas.

———. 1971. *Çikshāsamuccaya: A Compendium of Buddhistic Teaching*. Bibliotheca Buddhica 1. St. Petersburg, Russia: 1897–1902. Reprint, Delhi: Motilal Banarsidass.

Bendall, C., and W. H. D. Rouse, eds. 1971. *Śikṣā Samuccaya: A Compendium of Buddhist Doctrine*. London: J. Murray, 1922. Reprint, Delhi: Motilal Banarsidass.

Bentor, Yael. 2002. "Fourfold Meditations: Outer, Inner, Secret and Suchness." In *Religion and Secular Culture in Tibet*, edited by H. Blezer, 41–55. Leiden: E. J. Brill.

———. 2003. "The Content of Stūpas and Images and the Indo-Tibetan Concept of Relics." *The Tibet Journal* 28.1–2: 21–48.

Bernhard, Franz. 1965. *Udānavarga, Sanskrittexte aus den Turfanfunden X*. Göttingen: Vandenhoeck and Ruprecht.

Beyer, Stephan. 1978. *The Cult of Tārā: Magic and Ritual in Tibet*. Berkeley: University of California Press.

Bhattacarya, Vidhushekhara, ed. 1957. *The Yogācārabhūmi of Ācārya Asaṅga, Part One*. Calcutta: University of Calcutta.

Bhattacharya, Gouriswar. 2010. "How to Justify the Spelling of the Buddhist Hybrid Sanskrit Term Bodhisatva?" In *From Turfan to Ajanta: Festschrift for Dieter Schlingloff on the Occasion of his Eightieth Birthday*, edited by Eli Franco and Monika Zin, 2:35–50. Rupandehi: Lumbini International Research Institute.

Bjerken, Zeff. 2005. "On Maṇḍalas, Monarchs, and Mortuary Magic: Siting the *Sarvadurgatipariśodhana Tantra* in Tibet." *Journal of the American Academy of Religion*, 73.3 (Sept.): 813–41.

Braarvig, Jens. 1993. *Akṣayamatinirdeśasūtra*. 2 vols. Oslo: Solum Forlag.

Braarvig, Jens, et al., eds. 2006. *Buddhist Manuscripts, vol. 3: Manuscripts in the Schøyen Collection*. Oslo: Hermes.

Broido, M. 1983. "A Note on dgos-'brel." *Journal of the Tibet Society* 3: 5–19.

———. 1984. "Padma Dkar-po on Tantra as Ground, Path, and Goal." *Journal of the Tibet Society* 4: 5–46.

———. 1985. "Padma Dkar-po on Integration as Ground, Path, and Goal." *Journal of the Tibet Society* 5: 5–54.

Brown, Daniel P. 2006. *Pointing Out the Great Way: The Stages of Meditation in the Mahāmudrā Tradition*. Boston: Wisdom Publications.

Brunnhölzl, Karl. 2004. *The Center of the Sunlit Sky: Madhyamaka in the Kagyü Tradition*. Ithaca, NY: Snow Lion Publications.

———. 2014. *When the Clouds Part: The Uttaratantra and Its Meditative Tradition as a Bridge Between Sutra and Tantra*. Ithaca, NY: Snow Lion Publications.

Buswell, Robert E., and Donald S. Lopez Jr. 2014. *The Princeton Dictionary of Buddhism*. Princeton, NJ: Princeton University Press.

Butön Rinchen Drup. 2013. *Butön's History of Buddhism in India and Its Spread to Tibet: A Treasury of Priceless Scripture*. Translated by Lisa Stein and Ngawang Zangpo. The Tsadra Foundation Series. Boston and London: Snow Lion Publications.

Cabezón, José Ignacio. 2013. *The Buddha's Doctrine and the Nine Vehicles: Rog Bande Sherab's Lamp of the Teachings*. New York: Oxford University Press.

Cabezón, José Ignacio, and Penpa Dorjee. 2019. *Sera Monastery*. Somerville, MA: Wisdom Publications.

Callahan, Elizabeth M., trans. 2019. *Moonbeams of Mahāmudrā*. Boulder, CO: Snow Lion Publications.

Chandra, Lokesh, ed. 1981. *Sarva-tathāgata-tattva-saṅgraha: Facsimile Reproduction of Tenth Century Sanskrit Manuscript from Nepal*. Śata-Piṭaka Series 269. New Delhi: Sharada Rani.

Chang, Garma C. C. 1983. *A Treasury of Mahāyāna Sūtras: Selections from the Mahāratnakūṭa Sūtra*. University Park: Pennsylvania State University Press.

Chim Jampaiyang (ca. 1245–1325). 2018. *Ornament of Abhidharma: A Commentary on Vasubandhu's Abhidharmakośa*. Translated by Ian James Coghlan. Somerville, MA: Wisdom Publications.

Clarke, Shayne. 2009. "Monks Who Have Sex: *Pārājika* in Indian Buddhist Monasticisms." *Journal of Indian Philosophy* 37: 1–43.

Conze, Edward. 1948. "Text, Sources, and Bibliography of the *Prajñāpāramitā-hṛdaya*." *Journal of the Royal Asiatic Society of Great Britain and Ireland* 1: 33–51.

———. 1960. *Prajñā-pāramitā-ratna-guṇa-saṃcaya-gāthā: Sanskrit and Tibetan Text Edited by E. Obermiller*. Photomechanic reprint with a Sanskrit-Tibetan-English index by Edward Conze. The Hague: Mouton and Company.

———. 1973. *The Perfection of Wisdom in Eight Thousand Lines and Its Verse Summary*. Bolinas, CA: Four Seasons Foundation.

Cox, Collett. 1995. *Disputed Dharmas: Early Buddhist Theories on Existence. An Annotated Translation of the Section on Factors Dissociated from Thought from Saṅghabhadra's Nyāyānusāra*. Tokyo: International Institute for Buddhist Studies.

Crosby, Kate, and Andrew Skilton, trans. 1995. *The Bodhicaryāvatāra [of Śāntideva]*. Oxford: Oxford University Press.

Cutler, Joshua W. C., and Guy Newland, eds. 2000. *The Great Treatise on the Stages of the Path to Enlightenment [of Tsong kha pa]*, vol. 1. Ithaca, NY: Snow Lion Publications.

———. 2002. *The Great Treatise on the Stages of the Path to Enlightenment [of Tsong kha pa]*, vol. 3. Ithaca, NY: Snow Lion Publications.

Czaja, Olaf. 2013. *Medieval Rule in Tibet: The Rlangs Clan and the Political and Religious History of the Ruling House of Phag mo gru pa, with a Study of the Monastic Art of Gdan sa mthil*. Vienna: Verlag der Österreichischen Akademie der Wissenschaften.

———. 2019. "Mantras and Rituals in Tibetan Medicine." *Asian Medicine* 14: 277–312.

Dalai Lama XIV Bstan-'dzin-rgya-mtsho. 2001. *Stages of Meditation*. Root text by Kamalashila, translated by Ven. Geshe Lobsang Jordhen, Losang Choephel Ganchenpa, and Jeremy Russell. Ithaca, NY: Snow Lion Publications.

———. 2002. *Illuminating the Path to Enlightenment: A Commentary on Atisha Dipamkara Shrijnana's "A Lamp for the Path to Enlightenment" and Lama Je Tsong Khapa's "Lines of Experience."* Translated by Thupten Jinpa. Long Beach, CA: Thubten Dhargye Ling Publications.

Das, Sarat Chandra. 1893. "Bodhi Patha Pradīpa by Dīpaṅkara Śrī Jñāna." *Journal of the Buddhist Text Society* 1.1: 39–48, and 1.3: 21–26.

Davidson, Ronald M. 1981. "The Litany of Names of *Mañjuśrī*: Text and Translation of the *Mañjuśrīnāmasaṃgīti*." In *Tantric and Taoist Studies in Honor of R. A. Stein*, edited by Michel Strickmann, 1–69. Mèlanges Chinois et Bouddhiques 20. Brussels: Institut Belge des Hautes Études Chinoises.

———. 1995. "Atiśa's *A Lamp for the Path to Awakening*." In *Buddhism in Practice*, edited by Donald S. Lopez Jr., 290–301. Princeton, NJ: Princeton University Press.

Dorje, Gyurme. 1987. *Guhyagarbhatantra and Its XIVth Century Commentary Phyogs-bcu Mun-sel*. PhD dissertation, University of London.

Draszcyk, Martina. 2015 "The Indian Mahāsiddha Tīlopa's Upadeśa on Sahaja-Mahāmudrā in the Eyes of Karma pa Rang byung rdo rje." In *Sahaja, The Role of Dohā & Caryāgīti in the Cultural Indo-Tibetan Interface*, edited by Andrea Loseries-Leick, 75–92. Delhi: B. R. Publishing.

Ducher, Cécile. 2020. "Goldmine of Knowledge: The Collections of the Gnas bcu lha khang in 'Bras spungs Monastery." *Revue d'Études Tibétaines* 55 (July): 121–39.

Dutt, Nalinaksha, ed. 1966. *Bodhisattvabhūmi: Being the XVth Section of Asangapada's Yogācārabhūmi*. Patna: K. P. Jayaswal Research Institute.

Edgerton, Franklin. 1953. *Buddhist Hybrid Sanskrit Grammar and Dictionary*. New Haven, CT: Yale University Press.

Eimer, Helmut. 1978. *Bodhipathapradīpa: Ein Lehrgedict des Atiśa (Dīpaṃkaraśrījñāna) in der tibetischen Überlieferung*. Asiatische Forschungen 59. Wiesbaden: O. Harrassowitz.

———. 1982. "The Development of the Biographical Tradition Concerning Atiśa (Dīpaṃkaraśrījñāna)." *Journal of Tibet Society* 2: 41–52.

———. 1986. "Again: On Atiśa's *Bodhipathapradīpa*." *Sikkim Research Institute of Tibetology* 2: 5–15.

Eimer, Helmut, and Pema Tsering. 1994. "Legs skar / Skar bzang / Sunakṣatra." In *The*

Buddhist Forum, vol. 3, edited by Tadeusz Skorupski and Ulrich Pagel, 1–10. London: School of Oriental and African Studies.

Engle, Artemus. 2009. *The Inner Science of Buddhist Practice: Vasubandhu's Summary of the Five Heaps with Commentary by Sthiramati*. Ithaca, NY: Snow Lion Publications.

———. 2016. *The Bodhisattva Path to Unsurpassed Enlightenment: A Complete Translation of the Bodhisattvabhūmi*. Boulder, CO: Snow Lion Publications.

Everding, Karl-Heinz. 2002. "The Mongol States and Their Struggle for Dominance over Tibet in the 13th Century." In *Tibet, Past and Present*, edited by Henk Blezer, 109–28. Leiden: E. J. Brill.

Fausbøll, Viggo, ed. 1962–64. *Jātakāṭṭhakathā*. 6 vols. London: Pali Text Society. (Reprint of 1877–96.)

Fremantle, Francesca. 1971. "A Critical Study of the *Guhyasamāja Tantra*." PhD dissertation, University of London.

Frye, Stanley, trans. 1981. *The Sūtra of the Wise and the Foolish (Mdo mdzangs blun) or Ocean of Narratives (Üliger-ün dalai)*. Dharamsala: Library of Tibetan Works and Archives.

Germano, David. 1994. "Architecture and Absence in the Secret Tantric History of the Great Perfection (*rdzogs chen*)." *Journal of the International Association of Buddhist Studies* 17.2: 203–336.

Gokhale, V. V. 1955. "Der Sanskrit-Text von Nāgārjuna's Pratītyasamutpādahṛdayakārikā." In *Studia Indologica, Festschrift für Willibald Kirfel zur Vollendung seines 70. Lebensjahres*, edited by O. Spies, 101–6. Bonner Orientalische Studien 3. Bonn: Selbstverlag des Orientalischen Seminars der Universität.

Gómez, Luis O., and Jonathan A. Silk, eds. 1989. *Studies in the Literature of the Great Vehicle: Three Mahāyāna Buddhist Texts*. Ann Arbor: Collegiate Institute for the Study of Buddhist Literature and Center for South and Southeast Asian Studies, University of Michigan.

Goodman, Charles. 2016. *The Training Anthology of Śāntideva: A Translation of the Śikṣāsamuccaya*. New York: Oxford University Press.

Guenther, Herbert V. 1993. *Ecstatic Spontaneity: Saraha's Three Cycles of Dohā*. Berkeley, CA: Asian Humanities Press.

Halkias, Georgios. 2014. "Translating the Foreign into the Local: The Cultural Production and Canonization of Buddhist Texts in Imperial Tibet." In *Translation and Global Asia: Relocating Networks of Cultural Production*, edited by Uganda Sze-pui Kwan and Lawrence Wang-chi Wong, 143–66. Hong Kong: Research Centre for Translation, Chinese University Press.

Harding, Sarah. 2011. *Niguma, Lady of Illusion*. Ithaca, NY: Shambhala Publications.

Herrmann-Pfandt, Adelheid. 2008. *Die Lhan kar ma: Ein Früher Katalog der ins Tibetische Übersetzten Buddhistischen Texte*. Vienna: Verlag der Österreichischen Akademie der Wissenschaften.

Holmes, Ken, and Katia Holmes, trans. 1985. *The Changeless Nature: The Mahāyānottaratantraśāstra*. 2nd ed. By Arya Maitreya and Acarya Asanga. Eskdalemuir, Dumfriesshire, Scotland: Karma Kagyu Trust.

Hugon, Pascale. 2009. "Phya pa Chos kyi seng ge's Synopic Table of the *Pramāṇaviniścaya*." In *Sanskrit Manuscripts in China: Proceedings of a Panel at the 2008 Beijing Seminar on Tibetan Studies October 13 to 17*, 47–88. Beijing: China Tibetology Publishing House.

Iuchi, Maho. 2016. *An Early Text on the History of Rwa sgreng Monastery: The Rgyal ba'i dben gnas Rwa sgreng gi bshad pa nyi ma'i 'od zer of 'Brom Shes rab me lce*. Harvard Oriental Series 82. Cambridge, MA: Harvard Unversity Press.

Jackson, David P. 1985. "Madhyamaka Studies among the Early Sa-skya-pas." *The Tibet Journal* 10.2: 20–34.

———. 1987. *The Entrance Gate for the Wise (Section III): Sa-skya Paṇḍita on Indian and Tibetan Traditions of Pramāṇa and Philosophical Debate*. Vienna: Arbeitskreis für Tibetische und Buddhistische Studien, Universität Wien.

———. 1993. "rNgog Lo-tsā-ba's Commentary on the Ratnagotravibhāga." Foreword to *Theg chen rgyud bla ma'i don bsdus pa: Commentary on the Ratnagotravibhāga by rNgog Lotsaba Blo ldan shs rab*. Dharamsala: Library of Tibetan Works and Archives.

———. 1994. *Enlightenment by a Single Means: Tibetan Controversies on the "Self-Sufficient White Remedy" (dkar po chig thub)*. Vienna: Verlag der Österreichischen Akademie der Wissenschaften.

———. 1996. "The *bsTan rim* ('Stages of the Doctrine') and Similar Graded Expositions of the Bodhisattva's Path." In *Tibetan Literature: Studies in Genre*, edited by J. Cabezón and R. Jackson, 229–43. Ithaca, NY: Snow Lion Publications.

———. 2010. *The Nepalese Legacy in Tibetan Painting*. New York: Rubin Museum of Art.

Jackson, Roger R. 2004. *Tantric Treasures: Three Collections of Mystical Verse from Buddhist India*. New York: Oxford University Press.

———. 2019. *Mind Seeing Mind: Mahāmudrā and the Geluk Tradition of Tibetan Buddhism*. Somerville, MA: Wisdom Publications.

Jinpa, Thupten. 1999. "Tsongkhapa's Qualms about Early Tibetan Interpretations of Madhyamaka Philosophy." *The Tibet Journal* 24.2 (summer): 1–28.

———. 2002. *Self, Reality and Reason in Tibetan Philosophy: Tsongkhapa's Quest for the Middle Way*. London: Routledge Curzon.

———. 2006. *Mind Training: The Great Collection*. The Library of Tibetan Classics 1. Boston: Wisdom Publications.

———. 2008. *The Book of Kadam: The Core Texts*. The Library of Tibetan Classics 2. Boston: Wisdom Publications.

———. 2013. *Wisdom of the Kadam Masters*. Boston: Wisdom Publications.

———. 2019. *Tsongkhapa: A Buddha in the Land of Snows*. Boulder, CO: Shambhala Publications.

———. 2022. *Stages of the Path and the Oral Transmission: Selected Teachings of the Geluk School*. The Library of Tibetan Classics 6. Somerville, MA: Wisdom Publications.

Johnston, E. H., et al., trans. (1950) 1991. *The Uttaratantra of Maitreya: Containing an Introduction, E. H. Johnston's Sanskrit Text, and E. Obermiller's English Translation*. Delhi: Sri Satguru Publications.

Kano, Kazuo. 2008. "Rngog blo ldan shes rab's Topical Outline of the *Ratnagotravibhāga* Discovered at Khara Khoto." In *Contributions to Tibetan Literature: Proceedings of the Eleventh Seminar of the International Association for Tibetan Studies, Königswinter 2006*, edited by Orna Almogi, 127–94. Beiträge zur Zentralasienforschung 14. Halle, Germany: International Institute for Tibetan and Buddhist Studies.

———. 2016a. "Jñānaśrīmitra on the *Ratnagotravibhāga*." *Oriental Culture* (Institute for Advanced Studies on Asia, University of Tokyo) 96: 7–48.

———. 2016b. *Buddha-Nature and Emptiness. rNgog Blo-ldan-shes-rab and a Transmission of the Ratnagotravibhāga from India to Tibet*. Vienna: Arbeitskreis für Tibetische und Buddhistische Studien, Universität Wien.

Kapstein, Matthew. 2000. *The Tibetan Assimilation of Buddhism: Conversion, Contestation, and Memory*. Oxford: Oxford University Press.

Karmay, Samten Gyaltsen. 2007. *The Great Perfection (rDzogs chen): A Philosophical and Meditative Teaching of Tibetan Buddhism*. 2nd ed. Leiden: Brill.

Katsura, Shōryū. 2018. "Four Yoga Stages in Ratnākaraśānti's *Prajñāpāramitopadeśa*: With a New Synopsis." *Journal of Indian and Tibetan Studies* 22: 210–23.

Katsura, Shōryū, and Mark Siderits. 2013. *Nāgārjuna's Middle Way: Mūlamadhyamakakārikā*. Boston: Wisdom Publications.

Khedrup Norsang Gyatso (1423–1513). 2004. *Ornament of Stainless Light: An Exposition of the Kālacakra Tantra*. Translated by Gavin Kilty. Boston: Wisdom Publications.

Khoroche, Peter. 2006. *Once the Buddha Was a Monkey: Ārya Śūra's Jātakamālā*. Chicago: University of Chicago Press.

Kittay, David R., with Lozang Jamspal. 2020. *The Vajra Rosary Tantra (Śrī Vajramālā Tantra)*. New York and Somerville, MA: American Institute of Buddhist Studies and Wisdom Publications.

Klong-chen ye-shes-rdo-rje, trans. 2005. *Nagarjuna's Letter to a Friend: With Commentary by Kangyur Rinpoche*. Ithaca, NY: Snow Lion Publications.

Kobayashi, Mamoru. 2018. "Some Remarks on the Dharmatācalasūtra." *Bulletin of Tomakomai Komazawa University* 33: 33–95.

Kong-sprul Blo-gros-mtha'-yas. 1998. *Buddhist Ethics*. Translated by International Translation Committee. Ithaca, NY: Snow Lion Publications.

Kragh, Ulrich T. 2003. "Karmaphalasaṃbandha in Verses 17.1–20 of Candrakīrti's *Prasannapadā*." PhD dissertation, University of Copenhagen.

———. 2015. *Tibetan Yoga and Mysticism: A Textual Study of the 'Yogas' of Nāropa and 'Mahāmudrā Meditation' in the Medieval Tradition of Dags po*. Tokyo: International Institute for Buddhist Studies of the International College for Postgraduate Buddhist Studies.

Kramer, Jowita. 2012. "Descriptions of 'Feeling' (*vedanā*), 'Ideation' (*saṃjñā*), and 'the Unconditioned' (*asaṃskṛta*) in Vasubandhu's *Pañcaskandhaka* and Sthiramati's *Pañcaskandhakavibhāṣā*." *Rocznik Orientalistyczny* 65.1: 120–39.

Krobath, Florian. 2011. "Kritische Edition, Übersetzung und Interpretation des *Lta ba'i khyad par* von Ye shes sde." MA thesis, University of Vienna.

Lamotte, Étienne. 1949. *Le Traité de la Grande Vertu de Sagesse de Nāgārjuna (Mahāprajñāpāramitāśāstra)*, vol. 2. Louvain, Belgium: Bureaux du Muséon.

———. 1998. *Śūraṃgamasamādhisūtra: An Early Mahāyāna Buddhist Scripture*. Richmond, UK: Curzon.

Lang, Karen C. 2003. *Four Illusions: Candrakīrti's Advice for Travelers on the Bodhisattva Path*. New York: Oxford University Press.

La Vallée Poussin, Louis de. 1903–13. *Mūlamadhyamakakārikās (Mādhyamikasūtras) de Nāgārjuna avec la Prasannapadā Commentaire de Candrakīrti*. Bibliotheca Buddhica 4. St. Petersburg: Académie Impériale des Sciences.

———. 1907–12. *Madhyamakāvatāra par Candrakirti*. Bibliotheca Buddhica 9. St. Petersburg: Académie Impériale des Sciences.

Lessing, Ferdinand, and Alex Wayman. 1968. *Mkhas grub rje's Fundamentals of the Buddhist Tantras. Rgyud sde spyi'i rnam par gzhag pa rgyas par brjod*. The Hague: Mouton.

Lévi, Sylvain, ed. 1907. *Mahāyāna-Sūtrālaṅkāra: Exposé de la Doctrine du Grand Véhicule selon le Système Yogācāra.* Paris: Champion. Reprinted in 2 vols., Kyoto: Rinsen Book Company, 1983.

Lewis, Todd. 1995. "Story of Siṃhala, the Caravan Leader." In *Buddhism in Practice*, edited by Donald S. Lopez, 153–69. Princeton, NJ: Princeton University Press.

Liljenberg, Karen, and Ulrich Pagel, trans. 2021. *The Śrīgupta Sūtra (Śrīguptasūtra, Toh 217).* 84000: Translating the Words of the Buddha. https://read.84000.co/translation/toh217.

Lopez, Donald S. 1988. *The Heart Sūtra Explained: Indian and Tibetan Commentaries.* Albany: State University of New York Press.

MacDonald, Anne. 2015. *In Clear Words: The Prasannapadā, Chapter One.* 2 vols. Vienna: Verlag der Österreichischen Akademie der Wissenschaften.

Maitreyanātha/Asaṅga and Vasubandhu. 2004. *The Universal Vehicle Discourse Literature: Mahāyānasūtrālaṁkāra.* Translated by L. Jamspal, Robert Clark, Joe Wilson, Leonard Zwilling, Michael J. Sweet, and Robert A. F. Thurman. Treasury of Buddhist Sciences. New York: American Institute of Buddhist Studies.

Manevskaia, I. 2008. "Preliminary Observations on Compositional Methods in Haribhadra's Āloka." *Buddhist Studies: Papers of the 12th World Sanskrit Conference*, edited by R. Gombrich and C. Scherrer-Schaub, 98–117. Delhi: Motilal Banarsidass.

Martin, Dan, 1987. "Illusion Web: Locating the Guhyagarbha Tantra in Buddhist Intellectual History." In *Silver on Lapis: Tibetan Literary Culture and History*, edited by Christopher I. Beckwith, 177–220. Bloomington, IN: The Tibet Society.

———. 2020. "Pakmodrupa Dorje Gyelpo." *Treasury of Lives.* http://treasuryoflives.org/biographies/view/Pakmodrupa-Dorje-Gyelpo/2539.

Mathes, Klaus-Dieter. 2006. "Blending the Sūtras with the Tantras: The Influence of Maitrīpa and His Circle on the Formation of Sūtra Mahāmudrā in the Kagyu Schools." In *Tibetan Buddhist Literature and Praxis: Studies in Its Formative Period, 900–1400* (proceedings of the Tenth Seminar of the IATS, Oxford 2003, 10.4), edited by Ronald M. Davidson and Christian K. Wedemeyer, 201–27. Leiden: Brill.

———. 2008. *A Direct Path to the Buddha Within: Gö Lotsāwa's Mahāmudrā Interpretation of the Ratnagotravibhāga.* Studies in Indian and Tibetan Buddhism. Boston: Wisdom Publications.

———. 2015. *A Fine Blend of Mahāmudrā and Madhyamaka: Maitrīpa's Collection of Texts on Non-Conceptual Realization (Amanasikāra).* Vienna: Verlag der Österreichischen Akademie der Wissenschaften.

———. 2016. "'Gos Lo Tsā Ba Gzhon Nu Dpal's (1392–1481) Analytical and Direct Approaches to Ultimate Reality." *Journal of the International Association of Buddhist Studies* 39: 487–518.

Matsumura, Junko. 2011. "The Story of the Dīpaṃkara Buddha Prophecy in Northern Buddhist Texts: An Attempt at Classification." *Journal of Indian and Buddhist Studies* 59.3: 1137–46.

Matsunaga, Yukei. 1978. *The Guhyasamāja Tantra: A New Critical Edition.* Osaka: Toho Shuppan.

May, Timothy Michael. 2012. *The Mongol Conquests in World History.* London: Reaktion Books.

McCleary, Rachel M., and Leonard W. J. van der Kuijp. 2010. "The Market Approach to the Rise of the Geluk School, 1419–1642." *Journal of Asian Studies* 69.1: 149–80.

McGrath, William A. 2017. "Buddhism and Medicine in Tibet: Origins, Ethics, and Tradition." PhD dissertation, University of Virginia.

Mei, Ching Hsuan. 2009. "The Development of *'Pho ba* Liturgy in Medieval Tibet." PhD dissertation, University of Bonn.

Miller, Robert et al., trans. 2023. *The Chapter on Going Forth (Pravrajyāvastu, Toh 1-1)*. 84000: Translating the Words of the Buddha. https://read.84000.co/translation/toh1-1.html

Mimaki, Katsumi. 1982. *Blo gsal grub mtha': chapitres IX (Vaibhāṣika) et XI (Yogācāra) et chapitre XII (Mādhyamika)*. Kyoto: Kyoto University.

Mimaki, Katsumi, and Tōru Tomabechi. 1994. *Pañcakrama: Sanskrit and Tibetan Texts Critically Edited with Verse Index and Facsimile Edition of the Sanksrit Manuscripts*. Tokyo: Centre for East Asian Cultural Studies.

Mizuno, Kōgen, and Gaynor Sekimori. 1996. *Essentials of Buddhism: Basic Terminology and Concepts of Buddhist Philosophy and Practice*. Tokyo: Kōsei Publishers.

Nagao, Gadjin Masato. 1964. *Madhyāntavibhāga-bhaṣya: A Buddhist Philosophical Treatise Edited for the First Time from a Sanskrit Manuscript*. Tokyo: Suzuki Research Foundation.

Nance, Richard F. 2012. *Speaking for Buddhas: Scriptural Commentary in Indian Buddhism*. New York: Columbia University Press.

Nanjio, Bunyiu. 1923. *The Laṅkāvatāra Sūtra*. Bibliotheca Otaniensis Series 1. Kyoto: Otani University Press.

Napper, Elizabeth. 2001. "Ethics as the Basis of a Tantric Tradition: Tsong kha pa and the Founding of the dGe lugs Order in Tibet." In *Changing Minds*, edited by Guy Newland, 107–32. Ithaca, NY: Snow Lion Publications.

Nattier, Jan. 2005. *A Few Good Men: The Bodhisattva Path According to the Inquiry of Ugra (Ugraparipṛcchā)*. Honolulu: University of Hawai'i Press.

Nishizawa, Fumihito. 2014. "gSang phu ne'u thog: Its Contribution to the Re-Establishment and Development of Tibetan Buddhism in the Later Diffusion (phyi dar) Period." *Journal of Research Institute* 51: 343–66.

Obermiller, E. 1937. *Prajñāpāramitā-ratna-guṇa-saṃcaya-gāthā*. Bibliotheca Buddhica 29. St. Petersburg: Imperial Academy of Sciences.

Olivelle, Patrick. 1996. *Upaniṣads*. Oxford: Oxford University Press.

Orofino, Giacomella. 2022. "Empty Iridescent Spheres: Notes on the Metaphysics of Light in Indian and Tibetan Buddhist Tantric Sources." *Revue d'Études Tibétaines* 65 (October): 159–86.

Pagel, Ulrich. 1995. *The Bodhisattvapiṭaka: Its Doctrines, Practices and Their Positions in Mahāyāna Literature*. Tring: Institute of Buddhist Studies.

Pandeya, Ramchandra. 1999. *Madhyānta Vibhāga Śāstra: Containing the Kārikās of Maitreya, Bhāṣya of Vasubandhu, and Ṭīkā by Sthiramati*. Delhi: Motilal Banarsidass.

Pāsādika, Bhikkhu, trans. 1978–82. *The Sūtrasamuccaya: An English Translation from the Tibetan Version of the Sanskrit Original*. "Linh-So'n"—Publication d'études bouddhologiques 2–20. Joinvillele-Pont (Paris): Institut de recherche bouddhique Linh-So'n.

———. *Nāgārjuna's Sūtrasamuccaya: A Critical Edition of the mDo kun las btus pa*. Copenhagen: Akademisk Forlag, 1989.

———. 2015. *The Kāśyapaparivarta*. New Delhi: Aditya Prakashan.

Patt, David. 1993. "Elucidating the Path to Liberation: A Study of the Commentary on the *Abhidharmakośa* by the First Dalai Lama." PhD dissertation, University of Wisconsin–Madison.

Pradhan, Pralhad. 1950. *Abhidharma Samuccaya of Asaṅga*. Santiniketan: Visva-Bharati.

———. 1975. *Abhidharmakośabhāṣyam of Vasubandhu*. Patna: K. P. Jayaswal Research Institute.

Prasad, H. S., E. H. Johnston, and Eugéne Obermiller. 1991. *The Uttaratantra of Maitreya: Containing Introduction, E. H. Johnston's Sanskrit Text, and E. Obermiller's English Translation*. Delhi: Sri Satguru Publications.

Python, Pierre. 1973. *Vinaya-Viniścaya-Upāli-Paripṛcchā: Enquete d'Upāli pour une Exégèse de la Discipline*. Paris: Adrien-Maisonneuve.

Rāhula, Walpola. 1971. *Le Compendium de la Super-Doctrine (Philosophie) (Abhidharma-samuccaya) d'Asaṅga*. Publications de l'École Française d'Extrême-Orient 78. Paris: École Française d'Extrême-Orient.

———. 2001. *Abhidharmasamuccaya. The Compendium of the Higher Teaching (Philosophy)*. Translated from the French by Sara Boin-Webb. Fremont, CA: Asian Humanities Press.

Reat, N. Ross. 1993. *The Śālistamba Sūtra: Tibetan Original, Sanskrit Reconstruction, English Translation, Critical Notes (Including Pali Parallels, Chinese Version, and Ancient Tibetan Fragments)*. Delhi: Motilal Banarsidass.

Rhoton, Jared. 2002. *A Clear Differentiation of the Three Codes: Essential Distinctions among the Individual Liberation, Great Vehicle, and Tantric Systems: The Sdom gsum rab dbye and Six Letters*. Albany: State University of New York Press.

Roberts, Peter Alan. 2011. *Mahāmudrā and Related Instructions: Core Teachings of the Kagyü Schools*. Library of Tibetan Classics 5. Boston: Wisdom Publications.

Roberts, Peter Alan, and team, trans. 2022. *The King of Samādhis Sūtra (Samādhirājasūtra, Toh 127)*. 84000: Translating the Words of the Buddha. https://read.84000.co/translation/toh127.html

Rockhill, William Woodville. 1892. *Udânavarga: A Collection of Verses from the Buddhist Canon*. London: K. Paul, Trench, Trübner and Co.

Roerich, G., trans. 1979. *The Blue Annals [by 'Gos lo tsā ba]*. New Delhi: Motilal Banarsidass.

Roesler, Ulrike. 2009. "Once Again on the 'Three Kinds of Individuals' in Indian and Tibetan Buddhism." In *Pāsādikadānaṃ: Festschrift für Bhikkhu Pāsādika*, edited by M. Straube, R. Steiner, J. Soni, M. Hahn, and M. Demoto-Hahn, 343–57. Indica at Tibetica 52. Marburg: Indica et Tibetica.

———. 2018. "*Rgya gar skad du*—'in Sanskrit'? Indian Languages as Reflected in Tibetan Travel Accounts." In *Saddharmāmṛtam: Festschrift für Jens-Uwe Hartmann zum 65 Geburtstag*, edited by Oliver von Criegern, Gudrun Melzer, and Johannes Schneider, 352–68. Vienna: Arbeitskreis für Tibetische und Buddhistische Studien.

Roesler, Ulrike, Ken Holmes, and David P. Jackson, trans. 2015. *Stages of the Buddha's Teachings: Three Key Texts*. Library of Tibetan Classics 10. Somerville, MA: Wisdom Publications.

Rotman, Andy. 2008. *Divine Stories: Divyāvadāna, Part 1*. Boston: Wisdom Publications.

Saito, Akira. 1993. *A Study of Akṣayamati (=Śāntideva)'s Bodhisattvacaryāvatāra as Found in the Tibetan Manuscripts From Tun-Huang*. Tsu, Japan: Mie University.

Sangpo, Lodrö. 2012. *Abhidharmakośa-Bhāṣya of Vasubandhu: The Treasury of the Abhidharma and Its (Auto) Commentary*. 4 vols. Delhi: Motilal Banarsidass.

Schaeffer, Kurtis R., and Leonard W. J. van der Kuijp. 2009. *An Early Tibetan Survey of*

Buddhist Literature: The Bstan pa rgyas pa rgyan gyi nyi 'od of Bcom ldan ral gri. Cambridge, MA: Dept. of Sanskrit and Indian Studies, Harvard University.

Scherrer-Schaub, Cristina. 1991. *Yuktiṣāṣṭikāvṛtti: Commentaire à la Soixantaine sur le Raisonnement ou du Vrai Enseignement de la Causalité par le Maître Indien Candrakīrti*. Brussels: Institute Belge des Hautes Études Chinoises.

Schoening, Jeffrey Davis. 1995. *The Śālistamba Sūtra and Its Indian Commentaries*. Vienna: Arbeitskreis für Tibetische und Buddhistische Studien, Universität Wien.

———. 1996. "Sūtra Commentaries in Tibetan Translation." In *Tibetan Literature: Studies in Genre*, edited by José I. Cabezón and Roger R. Jackson, 111–24. Ithaca, NY: Snow Lion Publications.

Sferra, Francesco. 2000. *The Ṣaḍaṅgayoga by Anupamarakṣita, With Raviśrījñāna's Guṇabharaṇīnāmaṣaḍaṅgayogaṭippaṇī: Text and Annotated Translation*. Rome: Istituto Italiano per l'Africa e l'Oriente.

———. 2003. "Some Considerations on the Relationship between Hindu and Buddhist Tantras." In *Buddhist Asia 1: Papers from the First Conference of Buddhist Studies Held in Naples in May 2001*, edited by Giovanni Verardi and Silvio Vita, 57–84. Kyoto: Italian School of East Asian Studies.

Sharma, Parmananda, trans. 1997. *Bhāvanākrama of Kamalaśīla*. New Delhi: Aditya Prakashan.

Shaw, Miranda Eberle. 1994. *Passionate Enlightenment: Women in Tantric Buddhism*. Princeton, NJ: Princeton University Press.

Sherburne, Richard. 1976. "A Study of Atīśa's Commentary on His *Lamp of the Enlightenment Path* (*Byang-chub lam-gyi sgron-ma'i dka'-'grel*)." PhD dissertation, University of Washington.

———. 1983. *A Lamp for the Path and Commentary of Atiśa*. Wisdom of Tibet Series 5. London: Allen & Unwin.

———. 2000. *The Complete Works of Atīśa Śrī Dīpaṁkara Jñāna, Jo-Bo-Rje: The Lamp for the Path, the Commentary, Together with the Newly Translated Twenty-Five Key Texts (Tibetan and English)*. New Delhi: Aditya Prakashan.

Sherpa, Trungram Gyaltrul Rinpoche. 2004. "Gampopa, the Monk and the Yogi: His Life and Teachings." PhD dissertation, Harvard University.

Shirshova, Elena. 2018. "Brain, Function, Diseases, Healing." PhD dissertation, Sorig Khang International.

Shukla, H. S. 2008. "Agriculture as Revealed by the Pāli Literature." In *History of Agriculture in India, up to c. 1200 A.D. Agriculture in India*, edited by Lallanji Gopal and V. C. Srivastava, 385–409. New Delhi: Project of History of Indian Science, Philosophy and Culture, Centre for Studies in Civilizations.

Silk, Jonathan A. 1994. *The Heart Sūtra in Tibetan: A Critical Edition of the Two Recensions Contained in the Kangyur*. Vienna: Arbeitskreis für Tibetische und Buddhistische Studien, Universität Wien.

———. 2007. "Good and Evil in Indian Buddhism: The Five Sins of Immediate Retribution." *Journal of Indian Philosophy* 35.3: 253–86.

Skilling, Peter, and Saerji. 2014. "How the Buddhas of the Fortunate Aeon First Aspired to Awakening: The Pūrva-praṇidhānas of Buddhas 1–250." *Annual Report of the International Research Institute for Advanced Buddhology [ARIRIAB] at Soka University for the Academic Year 2013* 17: 245–92.

Skorupski, Tadeusz. 1996. "The *Sampuṭa-tantra*: Sanskrit and Tibetan Versions of Chapter One." In *The Buddhist Forum, Vol. IV: Seminar Papers 1994–1996*, edited by Tadeusz Skorupski, 191–244. London: School of Oriental and African Studies.

———. 2002. *Kriyāsaṃgraha Compendium of Buddhist Rituals: An Abridged Version.* Tring: Institute of Buddhist Studies.

Smith, E. Gene. 2001. *Among Tibetan Texts: History and Literature of the Himalayan Plateau.* Edited by Kurtis R. Schaeffer. Studies in Indian and Tibetan Buddhism. Boston: Wisdom Publications.

Snellgrove, David L. 2010. *The Hevajra Tantra: A Critical Study.* 2nd ed. Hong Kong: Orchid.

Sobisch, Jan-Ulrich. 2002. *Three-Vow Theories in Tibetan Buddhism: A Comparative Study of Major Traditions from the Twelfth through Nineteenth Centuries.* Wiesbaden: Ludwig Reichert Verlag.

Sonam Rinchen, Geshe. 1997. *Atisha's Lamp for the Path.* Translated and edited by Ruth Sonam. Ithaca, NY: Snow Lion Publications.

Sopa, Geshe Lhundub, with David Patt. 2004. *Steps on the Path to Enlightenment, Volume 1: The Foundation Practices.* Boston: Wisdom Publications.

———. 2005. *Steps on the Path to Enlightenment, Volume 2: Karma.* Boston: Wisdom Publications.

Sopa, Geshe Lhundub, with Dechen Rochard. 2017. *Steps on the Path to Enlightenment, Volume 5: Insight.* Boston: Wisdom Publications.

Sørensen, Per K., and Guntram Hazod, in cooperation with Tsering Gyalbo. 2007. *Rulers of the Celestial Plain: Ecclesiastic and Secular Hegemony in Medieval Tibet: A Study of Tshal Gung-thang.* Vienna: Verlag der Österreichischen Akademie der Wissenschaften.

Spiro, Melford Elliot. 1972. *Buddhism and Society.* New York: Harper & Row.

Staël-Holstein, Alexander von. (1926) 1977. *Kāçyapaparivarta: A Mahāyānasūtra of the Ratnakūṭa Class.* Shanghai: Commercial Press. Reprint, Tokyo: Meicho-fukyūkai.

Stcherbatsky, Th., and E. Obermiller, eds. (1929) 1992. *Abhisamayālaṃkāra.* Bibliotheca Buddhica 23. Delhi: Sri Satguru Publications. (Orig. pub. Leningrad: Academy of Sciences of the USSR.)

Stearns, Cyrus. 2001. *Luminous Lives: The Story of the Early Masters of the Lam 'bras Tradition in Tibet.* Studies in Indian and Tibetan Buddhism. Boston: Wisdom Publications.

Stein, Rolf A. 2010. *Rolf Stein's Tibetica Antiqua: With Additonal Materials.* Leiden: Brill.

Steinkellner, Ernst. 1989. "Who Is Byaṅ chub rdzu 'phrul? Tibetan and Non-Tibetan Commentaries on the *Saṃdhinirmocanasūtra*—A Survey of the Literature." *Berliner Indologische Studien* 4/5: 229–51.

Sur, Dominic Di Zinno. 2015. "A Study of Rongzom's *Disclosing the Great Vehicle Approach* (*theg chen tshul 'jug*) in the History of Tibet's Great Perfection Tradition." PhD dissertation, University of Virginia.

Suzuki, D. T. 1932. *The Laṅkāvatāra Sūtra.* London: Routledge and Kegan Paul.

Szántó, Péter-Dániel. 2021. *The Suhṛllekha of Nāgārjuna editio minor 2.0.* Leiden: Universiteit Leiden.

Takasaki, Jikidō. 1966. *A Study on the Ratnagotravibhāga* (*Uttaratantra*). Rome: Istituto per il Medio ed Estremo Oriente.

Tatz, Mark Joseph. 1978. "Candragomin and the Bodhisattva Vow." PhD dissertation, University of British Columbia.

———, trans. 1985. *Difficult Beginnings: Three Works on the Bodhisattva Path by Candragomin.* Boston: Shambhala Publications.

———. 1994. *The Skill in Means: Upāyakauśalya Sūtra.* Delhi: Motilal Banarsidass.

Thuken Losang Chökyi Nyima (Thu'u bkwan III Blo bzang chos kyi nyi ma, 1737–1802). 2009. *The Crystal Mirror of Philosophical Systems: A Tibetan Study of Asian Religious Thought.* Translated by Geshé Lhundub Sopa et al. Edited by Roger R. Jackson. The Library of Tibetan Classics 25. Boston: Wisdom Publications.

Thurman, Robert A. F. 2018. *The Life and Teachings of Tsongkhapa.* Somerville, MA: Wisdom Publications.

Tucci, Giuseppe. (1956) 1986. *Minor Buddhist Texts.* Delhi: Motilal Banarsidass. (Orig. pub. Rome: Istituto italiano per il Medio ed Estremo Oriente.)

Upādhyāya, Jagannātha, ed. 1986. *Śrīlaghukālacakratantrarājasya Kalkinā Śrīpuṇḍarīkeṇa Viracitā Ṭīkā Vimalaprabhā*, vol. 1. Bibliotheca Indo-Tibetica 11. Sarnath, Varanasi: Central Institute of Higher Tibetan Studies.

Vaidya, P. L., ed. 1958. *Lalita-Vistara.* Buddhist Sanskrit Texts 1. Darbhanga: Mithila Institute.

———. 1959. *Jātakamālā.* Darbhanga: The Mithila Institute.

———. 1960a. *Bodhicaryāvatāra of Śāntideva with the Commentary Pañjikā of Prajñākaramati.* Buddhist Sanskrit Texts 12. Darbhanga: The Mithila Institute.

———. 1960b. *Gaṇḍavyūhasūtra.* Darbhanga: The Mithila Institute.

van der Kuijp, Leonard W. J. 1987. "The Monastery of Gsang-phu Ne'u-Thog and Its Abbatial Succession from ca. 1073 to 1250." *Berliner Indologische Studies* 3: 103–27.

———. 2018. "The Bird-Faced Monk and the Beginnings of the New Tantric Tradition: Part Two." *Journal of Tibetology* 19: 86–127.

———. 2020. "Indo-Tibetan Tantric Buddhist Scholasticism: Bhavyakīrti and His Summary of Sāṃkhya Philosophy (part II)." *Journal of Tibetan and Himalayan Studies* 5.1: 1–62.

van der Kuijp, Leonard W. J., Arthur P. McKeown. 2013. *Bcom ldan ral gri (1227–1305) on Indian Buddhist Logic and Epistemology: His Commentary on Dignāga's Pramāṇasamuccaya.* Vienna: Arbeitskreis für Tibetische und buddhistische Studien, Universität Wien.

Verhagen, Pieter C. 2005. "Studies in Indo-Tibetan Buddhist Hermeneutics (5): The *mKhas-pa-rnams-'jug-pa'i-sgo* by Sa-skya Paṇḍita Kun-dga'-rgyal-mshan." *Journal of the International Association of Buddhist Studies* 28.1: 183–219.

Vetturini, Gianpaolo. 2007. "The bKa' gdams pa School of Tibetan Buddhism." PhD dissertation, School of Oriental and African Studies, University of London.

———. 2013. "The bKa' gdams pa School of Tibetan Buddhism." Revised unpublished PhD dissertation, School of Oriental and African Studies, University of London.

Vinītā, Bhikṣuṇī, trans. 2010. *A Unique Collection of Twenty Sūtras in a Sanskrit Manuscript from the Potala.* Vienna: Austrian Academy of Sciences Press.

Vitali, Roberto. 1996. *The Kingdoms of Gu.ge Pu.hrang: According to Mnga'.ris rgyal.rabs by Gu.ge mkhan.chen Ngag.dbang grags.pa.* Dharamsala: Tho.ling Gtsug.lag.khang Lo.gcig.stong.

———. 2004. "The Role of Clan Power in the Establishment of Religion (from the *kheng log* of the 9th–10th Century to the Instances of the dByil of La stod and gNyos of Kha rag." In *The Relationship Between Religion and State (chos srid zung 'brel) in Traditional Tibet: Proceedings of a Seminar Held in Lumbini, Nepal, March 2000*, edited by Christoph Cüppers, 159–88. Lumbini: Lumbini International Research Institute.

Vorobyova-Desyatovskaya, M. I. 2002. *The Kāśyapaparivarta: Romanized Text and Facsimiles.* In collaboration with Seishi Karashima and Noriyuki Kudo. Bibliotheca Philologica et Philosophica Buddhica 5. Tokyo: International Research Institute for Advanced Buddhology.

Wangchuk, Dorji. 2002. "An Eleventh-Century Defence of the Authenticity of the *Guhyagarbha Tantra*." In *The Many Canons of Tibetan Buddhism*, edited by Helmut Eimer and David Germano, 265–91. Leiden: Brill.

———. 2007. *The Resolve to Become a Buddha: A Study of the Bodhicitta Concept in Indo-Tibetan Buddhism*. Tokyo: International Institute for Buddhist Studies of the International College for Postgraduate Buddhist Studies.

———. 2009. "A Relativity Theory of the Purity and Validity of Perception in Indo-Tibetan Buddhism." In *Yogic Perception, Meditation, and Altered States of Consciousness*, edited by Eli Franco in collaboration with Dagmar Eigner, 215–37. Vienna: Austrian Academy of Sciences.

———. 2016. "On the Identity and Authenticity of the **Sarvadharmacaryopadeśābhisam ayatantra*: A Tantric Scripture Associated with the Vikramaśīla Tradition." In *Relationship between Tantric and Non-Tantric Doctrines in Late Indian Buddhism*, edited by Norihisa Baba, 95–106. Oriental Culture 96. Tokyo: Institute for Advanced Studies on Asia, University of Tokyo.

Wayman, Alex, and Hideko Wayman. 1990. *The Lion's Roar of Queen Śrīmālā: A Buddhist Scripture on the Tathāgatagarbha Theory*. Delhi: Motilal Banarsidass.

Wogihara, Unrai, ed. *Abhisamayālaṃkārālokā Prajñāpāramitā Vyākhyā: The Work of Haribhadra*. Tokyo: Toyo Bunko, 1932–35.

Wylie, Turrell V. 1977. "The First Mongol Conquest of Tibet Reinterpreted." *Harvard Journal of Asiatic Studies* 37.1: 103–33.

Yao, Zhihua. 2007. "Four-Dimensional Time in Dzogchen and Heidegger." *Philosophy East and West* 57.4 (Oct): 512–32.

Yuyama, Akira. 1976. *Prajñā-pāramitā-ratna-guna-samcaya-gāthā (Sanskrit Recension A)*. Cambridge: Cambridge University Press.

Zimmermann, Michael. 2013. "The Chapter on Right Conduct in the *Bodhisattvabhūmi*." In *The Foundation for Yoga Practitioners: The Buddhist Yogācārabhūmi Treatise and Its Adaptation in India, East Asia, and Tibet*, edited by U. T. Kragh, 872–83. Harvard Oriental Series 75. Cambridge, MA, and London: Harvard University Press.

Index

A

Abhidharma, 4, 34, 35, 105, 112, 136
action resembling its cause, 56, 321n144
adventitious stains, 210
afflictions/mental afflictions
  avoiding causes of, 204
  eliminating, 74, 143, 150, 155
  faults of, 234
  hitting on head, 215
  increasing, 61
  indulging, 60
  latent, 58, 215, 300
  as mind, 34, 56, 177
  mindfulness and, 173
  root of, eliminating, 220
  seminal aspects, liberation from, 66, 323n158
  subtle, 62, 65, 82
  taming, methods for, 235–36
  as unreal, 206
aggregates, five appropriated, 64, 71, 212, 257
aging, 50, 62–63, 153
agitation, 246–47
Ākāśagarbhasūtra, 123, 128, 129–30, 331n254
Akṣayamatisūtra, 105
Akṣobhya (monk), 114
Amé Jangchup Rinchen, 17
Amitābha, 274
analogies and examples
  for appearances, 76–77
  for awakening mind, 125
  bird's traceless tracks, 44, 81, 177, 202
  bird's wings, 43, 79, 174, 280
  boat of human life, 50, 321n130
  butcher with long life happy in poverty, 59
  conch and its whiteness, 78, 170
  constructing building, 31
  cowherder, skillful, 44, 81, 140, 177, 187, 202
  crystal, 42
  dreams, 44, 73, 80, 166
  drinking salty water, 61
  Druna and Kashmiri kings, 118–19
  fire at end of eon, 77
  hair pulled from butter, 63
  horses, giving a whip for, 154, 335n292
  in India and Tibet, differences in, 137–38, 157
  island of jewels, returning empty-handed from, 50
  from Kagyü tradition, 140, 187
  leather covering earth, 56, 321n146
  medicine for a sick person, 73
  merchant's son following friend, 236
  mice, black and white in Tsaphung, 144
  mother tending dying son, 82, 167, 178, 195
  nyagrodha tree, 65
  parrot's recitation, 57
  Phakmodrupa's, 22
  plantain tree, 145, 270
  reflections, 41, 58, 81, 166, 171, 172, 210
  rope seen as snake, 171, 209
  seed and sprout, 58, 322n148
  sesame oil and seeds, 43, 78, 79, 139, 170, 209
  ship's captain, 127, 129, 331n252

Siṃhala Island story (sorceress spirits), 67, 124–25, 329n229
sky, cloudless, 42, 139, 218
space, 38, 75, 78, 170
thief in empty house, 167–68, 178
three defects of vessels, 109
turtle in ocean, 50, 120, 142
udumbara flower, 117
water and waves, 78, 166
water bubble, 145
water into water, 116
wish-fulfilling jewel, 73, 117
Analysis of Realization (Atiśa), 4
analytical mediations, 42, 138–39
anger, 57, 65, 69, 70, 295, 297, 304
animals, 55, 57, 62, 149–50, 152
annihilation, 65, 177, 271. *See also* nihilism
antidotes, 34–35, 77, 205, 218, 235–36, 294
to afflictions, 114, 132, 206, 235–36
for belligerent thoughts, 68
Lamp as, 14
for oppressive conditions, 202
to sickness, 242–44
for solitude, 74
for three poisons, 105, 162
anuttarayoga class, 39
apparent objects, 81, 201
appearance aspect, 78
appearances, 71, 76–77
as allies, 44, 177, 202–3, 212
and emptiness, indivisibility of, 40, 44, 78, 80, 89, 139, 172–73, 211
as illusion, meditating on, 157–58
as lacking inherent existence, 80
and mind, integrating, 215
as naturally free, 168
as reflection, 58
unceasing, 177
as unreal, 179, 205–6, 212
Ar Jangchup Yeshé, 21
arhatship, 37, 60, 66, 67, 125, 155, 323n158
Arigh Böge, 24
ārya beings, 174
Asaṅga, 111, 113
Bodhisattva Levels, 16, 107, 126, 130, 292
Compendium of Higher Knowledge, 227–28, 258
on one-day precepts, 31
system of, 127, 128, 262
Yogācārabhūmi, 33–34, 112
aspirational awakening mind, 156
generating, 157
precepts, 294
vows, 192
aspirational awakening mind ritual
main rite, 271–72
preliminaries, 266–71
Atiśa, 1, 31, 259
birth and parents, 111–12
Commentary on the Difficult Points of the Lamp for the Path to Awakening, 29, 30–31, 32, 38, 39, 292
early teachers and instructions, 4
Entry to the Two Realities, 30
Extensive Commentary on the Root Downfalls, 39
Great Exposition of View and Meditation, 18, 22
lineages, 15, 26, 113, 185
Madhyamakopadeśa, 17
Mahāsāṃghika ordination, 32
mastery of five fields of knowledge, 112
qualities of, 113
synthesizing efforts of, 5
written works, 5–6, 16
attachment, 50
arising of, 51
cessation of, 168
eliminating, 72, 80, 160, 197
to friends, 61
as illusory, 166
as impediment to serenity, 192
influence of, 52
maturation of, 54, 60
mindfulness and, 178–79
reanimating, 205
to sentient beings, 74
Avadhūtipa, 4
Avalokiteśvara, 105, 124
aversion, 60, 61, 72, 80, 166, 197
Avīci (Relentless Agony) hell, 53, 324n165, 334n227
awakening mind, 75, 192
benefits of, 68, 269–70, 276, 294

embodiment of, 210
equivalencies, 40
examples for, 125
free from extremes, 71
generating, 74–75, 160, 199
merit of, 67
naturally occurring, 41
need for, 79–80
renunciation and, 60
three classifications of, 125
training in, 72, 89
See also aspirational awakening mind; conventional awakening mind; engaging awakening mind; ultimate awakening mind

awareness
clear, 162
comprehension of, 190
experiential, 200, 201
freshly established, 177
of increasing realizations, 81
mistaken, 66
movement and, 166
nonconceptual, 78, 251
pristine, 125
radiance of, 170, 194
unobstructed, 200

B

Barron, Richard, 31
benefiting others, 72, 73, 127, 156, 216, 298–99
Benefits of Reciting the Names of Mañjuśrī, 103
Bengal, 111
Bhandanta Vimuktisena, 113
birth, 62, 144, 153
Birth Stories of the Buddha (Āryaśūra), 16, 109–10
blessing water, 238–39
blessings
as hindrances, 253
lineage of, 13, 39, 113
need for, 190
permission blessing, 105
requesting, 250
twofold power of, 104

bliss
attachment to, 196, 206
experiencing, 194
non-tantric meaning, 138
realizing, 210
as selflessness, 257
in ultimate awakening mind, 126
unconditioned, 162
Bodhgayā, 4
Bodhibhadra, 4, 31
bodhisattva discipline, threefold, 38, 68–69, 291–92, 294
bodhisattva vows
benefits, 276
corrupted, 274
pratimokṣa as foundation, 31, 38, 69, 123–24, 126–27, 291
restoring, 294
restoring, secrecy in, 278–79
ritual, 68, 324n161
Bodhisattvapratimokṣa, 109, 127, 128
Bodhisattva's Scriptural Collection, 110
body, 51
appearance of, 172
attachment to, 66
as conditioned, 144–45
at death, 154
distracted, 73–74, 196
emptiness of, 76–77
as essenceless, 145
isolation of, 158
lack of intrinsic nature, 166
as light, contemplating, 75
mindfulness of, 155
offering, 71, 203, 212, 216, 217, 251, 255
pliability, 219, 298
relaxing, 161, 202
secret practices of, 251
serviceability of, 198
undistracted, 80–81
See also posture
Brahmā, 59
Buddha Śākyamuni, 278
contemplating, 269
hardships of, 230
merit of, 274
past lives, 304, 344n397

qualities of, 134
recollecting, 276
buddhahood, 45, 265
aspiration for, 67
attaining, 77, 80, 245
for benefitting others, 73
cause, 157, 272
as final goal, 37
as mind itself, 281–82
buddhas
arising of, 222
deeds of, 132–33
homage, directionality in, 49, 320n123
monastic vows of, 36
and sentient beings, equal nature of, 81
as without mind, 76
burial grounds, in India and Tibet, 144

C

Cakrasaṃvaratantra, 4–5, 18, 187
Candragomin, 130. See also *Twenty Verses on the Bodhisattva Vow*
Candrakīrti, 113
causally concordant result, 151
cause and effect
as congruent, 65
conviction in, 75, 206
delusion about, 60, 61
and emptiness, indivisibility of, 35, 43, 59, 79, 139, 173–74, 211, 304
indivisibility of, 78
of negative actions, 91–92
not abandoning, 79
of positive actions, 92–93
space-like, 174
subtle, 89
celibacy, 32, 259
cessation
absorption of, 167, 335n299
truth of, 155
See also nonanalytical cessation
Chakdum, Ācārya, 226, 237
Chakriwa Gongkawa Jangchup Pal, 13, 18–19, 20, 26, 113
Chan tradition, 184
Chandra Das, Sarat, 1
Chekawa Yeshé Dorjé, 22
Chengawa Tsultrim Bar, 14, 15, 22, 137, 263, 283, 334n279
China, 88
Chökyab Sangpo, 24
Cittamātra system. *See* Mind Only
clarity, 41, 196, 206, 210, 298
Clarke, Shayne, 32
clear light, 5, 187, 205, 218, 220, 337n312
Close Placements of Mindfulness Sūtra, 147
coemergence, 42, 126, 257
coemergent union, 41, 335–36n299, 335n297
cold hells, eight, 33
contemplating, 62
location, 52
suffering of, 53, 57, 149
Collected Works of the Kadampas, 2, 8
Collection of Purposeful Sayings, 16, 110–11
compassion, 208
cultivating, 71, 89
and emptiness, joining, 280
increasing, 232
instinctive, 216, 219
lacking, 214
need for, 79–80
for oneself, 50
for others with no understanding, 157, 179
protection of, 67
purifying, 174
for sentient beings, 206, 218, 233
Compendium of the Teaching Sūtra, 222
Compendium of Training (Śāntideva), 16, 38
Complete Enlightenment of Vairocana Tantra, 123
Completely Pure Discipline Sūtra, 130
concentration, 75, 125, 134, 195, 196, 206, 298
conceptual thought/conceptuality, 133
arising with no trace, 202
distraction of, 74
eliminating, 162, 196
emptiness of, 42, 71, 166, 201, 210–11
eradicating in emptiness, 77
as fault, not viewing, 167–68
mental solitude for, 191

as mind, 177
naturally dissipating, 44
not engaging with, 162
pacifying, 219
purifying, 77
taken as friends, 81
as unreal, 205
Condensed Stages of the Path, 87, 89
conditioned karmic action, suffering of, 64
conduct, 89
meaning of term, 325n185
in *Stages of the Path to Awakening*, 108
ten points of, 123
treatises on, 107
confession, 82, 123, 129, 196, 254
general, 303
for obstacles, clearing, 230
recitations for, 302–3
to Three Jewels, 69, 294
conscientiousness, 44, 52, 81, 82, 127, 128, 149, 297, 298
consciousness
conceptual, 271–72
six aggregates of, 75, 81, 216, 324n168
contentment, 134, 190
conventional awakening mind, 39, 125–26, 174. *See also* aspirational awakening mind; awakening mind; engaging awakening mind
conventional realities, two types, 322n148
creators, 133, 333n273
crossing over, 187, 194, 201, 208
cyclic existence, 36–37
as cause and effect, 322n148
causes, 94, 154–55
clearing away defects of, 196
faults of, 93–94, 151–53
faults of, contemplating, 62, 65, 89, 253
liberation from, 77, 94–95, 155
as mind, 75, 177
mode of apprehension, 78
as not established, 76
revulsion toward, 125

D

Dakpo Lhajé. *See* Gampopa Sönam Rinchen
Davidson, Ronald, 1
death, 143
averting, inability in, 146–47
certainty of, 51, 144–45
contemplating, 89, 235, 253
meditation at, 243
mindfulness of, 50–51
suffering of, 63, 153–54
time of, uncertain, 145, 265
Death Lord of Karma, 53
defeats, 128, 320n127, 323n154
definitive meaning, 107
deities, 187, 216, 232, 253, 282
delusion
Abhidharma and, 105
antidote, 235
appearances of, 171
eliminating, 197
emptiness of, 131
influence of, 52
mindfulness and, 178–79
of permanence, 61
suffering from, 152
demigods, 64, 154
Densathil Monastery, 21
dependent arising, 34, 79, 94, 218, 219, 221, 235, 271. *See also* twelve links of dependent arising
Descent into Laṅkā Sūtra, 133
desire, 124
attachment to, 65
emptiness of, 131
five objects of, 61
for food and clothing, 74
inclinations toward, 154
result of, 59
reversing tendency toward, 253
Vinaya and, 105
desire realm, 60, 196, 258
devotion, 173, 208
increasing, 73
lacking, 214
limitations of, 200
to spiritual teachers, 175, 180, 189–90, 203, 213, 217
Dharma, 250
abandoning, 170, 213, 303–4

benefits for upholders, 300
Buddhist and non-Buddhist, distinguishing, 120
greatness of, 114
realizing, 73
recognizing, 181–82
studying, 204
three classifications, 117
of words, 103–7
Dharma body, 40, 68, 78
great concentration on, 134
manifesting, 218
mind-as-such as, 41
as perfect gnosis, 75
as permanent, variant views, 134
realizing, 220
result of, 43
as source, 200
See also under spiritual teachers
Dharma teaching, 108, 109
listening to, 180, 204
purpose, 111
results of, 109–11
variations in, purpose of, 134–35
Dharma wheels, 105, 107
Dharmakīrtiśrī, 4, 113
dharmas, 59, 66. *See also* phenomena
Differentiating the Sūtras (Maitreya), 109
Dignāga; *Pramāṇasamuccaya*, 112
diligence, 57, 150, 297, 298. *See also* energetic diligence
disciples, 108, 125
discipline, eleven instructions on, 279, 342n375
Dohākoṣa, 280
Dölpa Sherab Gyatso, 15, 21
Ḍombhipa, 113
downfalls
confessing, 196
countermeasures, 302–3
eliminating, 204, 213
fetters as, 70
five divisions of, 60, 323n154
five fundamental, 283
four fundamental, 342n375
of kings, 129–30
restoring, 294
See also eighteen root downfalls; root downfalls
Drakgyab, 24
Drepa, Geshé, 19
Drepung Monastery, 2
Drigung Jikten Gönpo, 22, 26
Drigung Kagyü, 21, 22, 24, 113
Drigung Thil, 24
Drolungpa; *Great Exposition of the Stages of the Doctrine*, 24–25
Drom Sherab Meché, 14
Dromtön Gyalwai Jungné, 2, 15
disciples, 137, 334n279
lineages, 22, 26
Sanskrit name, 263, 283
Stages, request for, 4, 10, 13
drowsiness, 247–49
Drukpa Kagyü, 21

E

early dissemination period, 101
eight extremes of elaboration, 41, 76
eight inopportune moments, 33, 318n94
eight kinds of superior beings, 117
eight unfavorable conditions, 49, 120, 142
eight worldly concerns/perceptions, 35–36, 59, 323n153
abandoning, 150, 159, 298
avoiding, 198
contemplating, 65
distraction of, 143
equanimity toward, 163
leveling out, 75, 82, 197, 206, 215
as obstacle, 246
renouncing, 196, 203
test with, 169
eighteen root downfalls, 38, 69, 128, 292
eightfold path, 117
elements, 71, 246–47, 257
emanations, 156, 198, 218
embarrassment, 127, 129
emptiness, 162
abiding in, 169, 200
actualizing, 210
analytical/intellectual understanding, 77, 139
attachment to, 206

benefits of realizing, 77
bliss as, 126
deviating from, 205, 214
direct vision of, 42, 139
of ground, 170
intrinsic, 168
and lucidity, inseparability of, 170
meditating on, 61
of mind, 76–77
nonconceptual, 139
not realizing, sign of, 167
recollecting, 82
roots of virtue and, 190
stable realization of, 173
See also under appearances; cause and effect
energetic diligence, 150, 179, 195, 205. *See also* diligence
engaging awakening mind, 40, 156, 157
precepts, 294–96
vows, 192
engaging awakening mind ritual
main rite, 276–79
praise and introductory explanations, 273–74
preliminaries, 274–76
training, 273–74
Enhancing Practice and Removing Obstacles on the Path, 12
overview, 225–27
supplementary materials, 227–28, 257–58
equality of self and others, 71
equalizing and exchanging yourself and others, 68
equanimity, 71, 82, 163, 198, 282
esoteric Buddhist traditions
four activities in, 210, 338n313
pointing-out instructions in, 183–84
Vajradhara in, 39
Essence of the Bodhisattva Vow (Atiśa), 12
on benefiting beings, 298–99
on gathering virtuous qualities, 296–98
introduction, 294
overview, 291–92
supplementary material, 293
topical outline, 300–302
on vows, 294–96
Essence of the Perfection of Wisdom, 131
evil deeds, 74, 81, 82, 214
causes, 58, 148
counteragent, 59
eliminating, 75, 143, 155, 204, 244
emptiness of, 205, 215
purifying, 81
results, 64, 148–50
subtle, 150
experiences similar to cause, 321n144
Extensive Commentary on the Root Downfalls, 123
Extensive Play Sūtra, 231

F

faith, 82, 114, 116, 231, 267
faulty actions, secondary, 69–70
fear, 64
of death, 153, 154
of enemies, 154
five types, 219
obstacles from, 232
firm ascertainment, 41
five buddha bodies, 131–32, 332n265
five buddhas, 117, 320n123
five fields of knowledge, 112
five heinous acts, 69, 135, 170, 213, 295, 324n165, 334n277
five hinderances, 195, 298
five poisons, 234
five wisdoms, 45, 82, 131, 332n266
Flower Array Sūtra, 120, 143
food, 74, 191, 193, 230, 248, 251, 255
form realm, 196
formless realm, 196
Fortunate Eon Sūtra, 266–67
forty-six minor infractions, 38, 128, 292
four certainties, 263, 276, 279, 283
four daily activities, 82, 324n172
emptiness in, 205
mindfulness in, 167, 173, 178, 335n298
four immeasureables, 38, 67, 68, 127, 268, 279, 298
four opponent powers, 38, 70, 129, 296
four pairs of persons, 117, 125
four seals, 106, 114, 325n182
four times, 42, 77, 144, 324n170

four types of mindfulness, 37
four ways of gathering disciples, 68, 279, 298, 324n162
four yogas
  distinctive features of, 218–21
  Stages and, 186
  See also insight; serenity; signlessness; union (*yuganaddha*)
fourth time, 168, 335–36n299
freedom from elaborations, 44, 71, 76, 81, 140, 200, 202, 211, 254
freedoms and favorable conditions, 89, 91, 142–43, 253, 265

G

Gampopa Sönam Rinchen, 3
  collected teachings, 20–21
  Kadam training, 18, 19
  lineages, 13, 26, 113
  Ornament of Precious Liberation, 20–21
  pointing-out instructions of, 138, 184
Gangthang Karwa, 23
Gar, Geshé, 185
Garland of Birth Stories, 16
Gayāśīrṣa Hill Sūtra, 279–80
Geluk tradition, 10, 15
Gendun Drub, First Dalai Lama, 327n201
General Meaning of the Stages of the Path, 4, 12, 228
  on Atiśa, greatness of, 111–14
  Dharma, general presentation in, 103–7
  on Dharma, greatness of, 114
  on Dharma, listening and explaining, 108–11
  on downfalls, 292
  on *Essence of the Bodhisattva Vows*, 291
  lineage list, 13, 15, 17–23
  small and middling capacities in, 30
  three strands of exegesis in, 101
  on three vows, 31
  traditional scholarship style of, 101
generation stage, 233, 338n320
gnosis
  nonconceptual, 134
  perfect, 41, 75
  self-arisen, 133
  space-like, 43, 78
Gö Lotsāwa Shönu Pal
  Blue Annals, 13, 20
  on Tsongkhapa, 25
Göden, 24
gods
  abandoning, 48–49
  desire-realm, 54
  rebirth as, 59
  suffering of, 64, 154
Golden Light Sūtra, 104, 133–34
Gön Ö Jowo, 23
Gönpawa Wangchuk Gyaltsen, 13, 15
  lineages, 17–18, 26, 113, 185
  Sanskrit name, 263, 283
gradual path, 6, 21
grammar treatises, 112
Great Middle Way, 17, 35, 335–36n299
  free from conceptuality, 81
  as freedom from extremes, 17, 43, 44, 59, 79
  signlessness and, 186
Great Perfection, 184
great seal, 126, 257. *See also* mahāmudrā
Great Vehicle, 60, 174
  awakening mind in, 192
  entering, 245, 259
  mind of, generating, 68
  Vinaya as training for, 122, 123
ground
  three characteristics, 170
  union of, 42, 77–78, 139, 209
Guhyagarbhatantra, 131–32, 227, 257
Guhyasamājatantra
  controversy about, 101
  ground, path, result triad in, 139
  on meditative experiences, 337n312
  on mind, emptiness on, 40, 130, 319n114
  on ultimate awakening mind, 130–31, 262, 281
  Vajradhara in, 39
Guṇamitra, 113
guru yoga, 81
  meditative equipoise, 176–77
  sustaining, 177–78
Gya Tsöndrü Sengé, 5
Gyayön Dak, 19

H

Hālāhalalokeśvara, 119
happiness, 50
  casting aside, 146–47
  cause, 272
  of Dharma, 114
  emptiness of, 167
  as illusion, 252
  impermanence of, 152
  as mind, 35, 75, 177
  in serenity, 198
Haribhadra, 112, 113
harmful spirits, 231–32, 233, 234, 247, 248, 251
harmfulness, 54, 159, 230
hatred, 50, 52
  antidote, 235
  arising of, 154
  causes, 65
  cessation of, 168
  emptiness of, 131
  as impediment to serenity, 192
  mindfulness and, 178–79
  result of, 59
  suffering from, 64
  Sūtra collection and, 105
Heap of Jewels, 222, 273
Heart of Wisdom Sūtra, 105. See also *Essence of the Perfection of Wisdom*
hells
  adjoining, 53
  eighteen, 148, 335n291
  mind of emptiness and, 77
  as nonexistent, 200
  ten nonvirtues and, 53–54
  See also cold hells, eight; hot hells, eight
Hevajratantra
  Atiśa's early study of, 4
  on awakening mind, twofold, 126, 257, 265
  on conduct, 123
  on ultimate awakening mind, 130, 227
hot hells, eight, 33
  contemplating, 62
  location, 52
  suffering of, 52–53, 57, 148–49
Hülegü, 24
humans
  delusion of, 152
  opposing conditions for, 145
  rebirth as, 59
  sufferings of, 94
hungry ghosts
  mind of emptiness and, 77
  realm of, location, 54
  rebirth as, 41
  suffering of, 54–55, 57, 62, 149
  three types, 33–34, 321n139

I

ignorance, 170
  cyclic existence and, 62
  deluded regarded to suchness, 154
  grasping objects as real, 61
  of the imaginary, 154
  reversing, 67
  as root cause of cyclic existence, 155
  of self, 65
impermanence, 33, 60, 72, 91, 265
  contemplating, 50–51, 61, 89, 147, 235, 253
  external and internal, 144
  of mind, 66
  suffering of, 64
Inconceivable Secrets Sūtra, 132–33
Indestructible Tent Tantra, 269
Indian Buddhism
  pointing-out instructions in, 183–84
  pratimokṣa in, 32
  summary meaning in, 87
  Tibetan assimilation of, 327n201
indivisibility, four types, 293, 304
Indra, 59
Inquiry of Avalokiteśvara on the Seven Qualities, 259
Inquiry of Nārāyaṇa, 110
Inquiry of Pūrṇa, 135–36
Inquiry of Vīradatta, 38, 276
insight, 40, 164–65
  and compassion, integrating, 39
  conceptual thoughts subsequent to, 168–69
  cultivating, 41–42
  discordant factors, 298

distinctive features of, 219
enhancement, 203
increasing, 81–82
pointing-out instructions, 75–76, 139, 165–66, 186, 201–2
preliminaries, 198–99
and serenity, indivisibility of, 44, 82
signs of progress, 169, 206
stabilizing, 199–200
stages of, 200–201
subsequent practice, 203–6
sustaining, 167–68, 202–3
Instructions for Select Disciples (Atiśa), 12, 88
authorship, 137–38
on direct cognition, 139
on four times, 42
meditation instructions in, 139–40
on middling-capacity individuals, 151–56
novel features, 140
on obstructions, three types, 45
and *Pointing-Out Instructions*, differences between, 186
on small-capacity individuals, 141–51
on supreme-capacity individuals, 156–81
title, alternative, 137
interpretable meaning, 107
Introduction to the Practice of Awakening (Śāntideva), 16, 136, 143
on awakening mind, generating, 270
on awakening mind, twofold, 125–26
on boat of human life, 321n130
bodhisattva vows, 273
on hide covering the world, 321n146
on merit, 274
on mind, 272
on suffering, 244
irreversibility, 267

J

Jackson, Roger, 138–39, 184
Jangchup Ling temple, 6
Jangchup Ö, 1, 6, 7, 23
Jayulwa Shönu Ö, 19
jealousy, 197, 215, 220, 235
Jewel Torch Dhāraṇī, 267
Jitāri, 4
joy, 49, 66, 72, 119, 163, 255

K

Kadam tradition, 259
and Great Seal teachings, convergence of, 19
Milarepa and, 20
pointing-out instructions in, 183, 186–87
practice domain of, 136, 137, 181, 334n279
public and restricted teachings, distinction in, 14, 15, 260
scholasticism of, 87
six authoritative treatises for, 16
system of inclination in, 30
on ultimate awakening mind, 228
Kagyü tradition
Instructions for Select Disciples and, 139–40
Kadam influences on, 186–87
mahāmudrā in, 3, 41
pointing-out instructions in, 184
Kālacakra-based traditions, 337n312
Kalyanaśrī, 111–12
Kamalaśīla; *Bhāvanākrama*, 17
Kamawa, 15
Kapstein, Matthew, 183
karma, 34, 59, 60, 61, 71, 173
accumulated action of, 58, 59, 322n149
appearances of, 171
confidence in, 179
contemplating, 147, 235, 253, 297–98
eliminating, 143
emptiness mixed, 79
general instructions on, 93
illness and, 244
as mere deluded perception, 322n148
as nondeceptive mere conventionality, 147
not refraining from, 208
obstacles of, 230, 231
overturning stream of, 65–66
refraining from creating, 163
Stages' emphasis on, 9
suffering of, 74
trust in, 180
unaccumulated action of, 322n149
uncontaminated, 37
virtue and nonvirtue mixed in, 59
vows and, 127

Katyāyana, 119
Khamkom, 22, 23, 26, 113
Khampa Lungpa, 18
Kharak Gomchung, 21
Khön family, 22, 23, 26, 113, 316n64
Khubilai, 24
Khyungpo Naljor, 185
Kindling the Power of Faith, 120
King Beauty of Awareness, 114
Kriyāsaṃgraha, 138, 187
Kṣitigarbhasūtra. See *Ten Wheels of Kṣitigarbha Sūtra*
Kusulu the elder, 113
Kusulu the younger, 113

L

Lama Shang, 184
Lamp for the Path to Awakening (Atiśa), 1
 analytical approach of, 138–39
 audience for, 30
 authorship, 9
 awakening mind in, 39, 259
 on bodhisattva discipline, 292
 composition, 5–6, 7
 Dromtön's secret guidance on, 14
 in Gampopa's *Ornament*, 20–21
 influence of, 24–25
 manuscript, 8
 scriptural citations in, 38
 three transmission lines, 313n13
 three types of individuals in, 29
 transmission, 21
 on wisdom, 40
Langlungpa, Geshé, 22
Langri Thangpa, 18
Later Dissemination, 88
laxity, 246–47
laypersons
 abandoning life of, 60, 122–25
 conduct of, 32
 devotees, two types, 32
 five vows of, 60, 91
 offerings of, 49
 ritual for establishing, 288–89
laziness, 70, 195, 265, 295
 abandoning, 50, 89, 265, 298
 antidotes to, 205
 causes of, 247
 increasing, 297
 reversing tendency of, 35, 59, 150
Lechen Kunga Gyaltsen; *Lamp Illuminating the History of the Kadam Tradition*, 13–14, 15, 17, 18, 25, 316n53
leisure and fortune. *See* freedoms and favorable conditions
Lhodrak Namkha Gyaltsen, 24–25
Lhopa Könchok Pal, 21
Liberation of Maitreya, 270
lifespan, 265
 of animals, 55
 in hells, 54
 of hungry ghosts, 55
 Stages' unique description, 33
 in *Treasury of Higher Knowledge*, 34
 uncertain, 51, 145
Limitless Doorways Sūtra, 133
lineages, three united by Atiśa, 13, 113
Lion's Roar of Queen Śrīmālā Sūtra, 122, 123
logic and epistemology, 112
Lotus Crown, farmer's son, 114
love
 cultivating, 71, 89, 113, 233
 increasing, 232
 instinctive, 216
 meditating on, 68, 156–57, 235
 purifying, 174
Lower Vehicle, 60, 122, 192
lucidity, 42, 78, 162, 166, 170, 202
luminosity, 41, 194, 200

M

Ma Gewai Lodrö, 260
Madhyamaka tradition, 17–18
 Atiśa's approach, 19, 26, 34, 37, 322n148
 awakening mind rites in, 17, 262, 263
 doxographic distinctions, 315n38
 Indian, analysis in, 139
 Perfection of Wisdom and, 112
mahāmudrā
 clear light in, 187
 meditative experiences in, 337–38n312
 pitfalls of, 337n310
 pointing-out instructions in, 138–39

in *Stages*, similarities to, 3
Vajradhara in, 39
Mahāsāṃghika Vinaya tradition, 3, 9–10, 26, 32, 49
Mahāyāna. *See* Great Vehicle
Mahāyoga class, 39, 101
Maitreya, 13, 113. See also *Differentiating the Sūtras*; *Ornament for Clear Realization*; *Ornament of Mahāyāna Sūtras*; *Uttaratantra*
Maitrīpa, 183
Mañjuśrī, 113, 239, 294
mantras, 146, 221–22
hundred-syllable Vajrasattva, 138, 165, 187, 190, 204
medicinal, 222, 228, 239–41, 243
name-mantras, 263, 283, 343n386
protecting from incidentals, 256
taking internally, 238–39
Māra, 121, 214, 254, 270–71, 280, 300
Marvelous Array Sūtra, 269–70
Mass of Jewels Sūtra, 121–22
Mathes, Klaus-Dieter, 139, 184
maturation effect, 36, 37, 45, 148, 150–51, 181
Māyājālatantra corpus, 101
medicine, Tibetan, 226, 237
Medicine Buddha, 242
Medicine God Sūtra, 123
meditation, 180
appearances of, 171
changing residence, 212–13
channel and vital wind, 249
empty hole, 250
faulty, 248
and knowledge, relationship of, 57
and post-meditation, not differentiating, 220
rigor in, 255
three results, 150–51
without view, 75–76
meditative equipoise, 44
body and mind in, 80–81
discordant conditions, 169
emptiness ascertained in, 76
mindfulness in, 82
on mother sentient beings, 282
meditative experiences, 209, 337n312
meditative stabilization, 44, 215
arising, 166
"magical display of Samantabhadra," 267
nonconceptual, 75, 171
obstacles, 246–51
physical isolation for, 74
on selflessness, 66
Meeting of Father and Son, 103
mental afflictions. *See* afflictions/mental afflictions
mental disease, pacifying, 241
mental facets, 76, 78
mental isolation, 159, 191
mere appearances, 34, 35, 322n148
merit, 254
accumulating, 67–68, 72, 190, 196, 266–67, 274–75
appearances of, 210
of Dharma training, 120
of engaging awakening mind, 274, 276
increasing, 49
from moral discipline, 60
from pleasing teachers, 73
of seeing guru as buddha, 192
from teaching Dharma, 109, 110
middle way, 131, 134
middling-capacity individuals, 214
liberation desired by, 151
obstacles, 236
overviews, 36–37, 59
See also individual practices
Mikyö Dorjé, Eighth Karmapa, 41
Milarepa, 19, 20, 185
mind
appearances as, 34, 212
appearing through cause and effect, 58
as clarity and emptiness inseparable, 41, 75
clearing faults of, 250–51
distracted, 73–74, 196
emptiness of, 42, 66, 79, 165–66, 201, 282, 319n114
established in serenity, 176
free from elaboration, 254
free from extremes, 43, 44, 59, 71, 81, 177, 186

mindfulness of, 155
pliability of, 198, 298
primordial purity of, 43
relaxing, 161, 202
undistracted, 80–81
as unproduced, 281
See also nature of mind
Mind Only, 112, 262, 263. *See also* Yogācāra tradition
mind-as-such, 41, 76
mindfulness, 81, 215, 330n244
correct, 42
four applications of, 155
in guru yoga, 178
insight, protecting with, 204–5
of sense doors, 192
in subsequent practice, 163
sustaining, 167, 202
undistracted, 77, 212
uninterrupted, 44, 82, 179
of vows, 128, 297
Minyak, 23
Mokchok Rinchen Tsöndrü, 185
Mongké Khan, 24
Mongols, 23–24
Moon Lamp Sūtra, 119–20, 122, 124, 128
moral conduct, 74, 159, 189, 190
Mother. *See* Perfection of Wisdom scriptures
mother sentient beings, 156–57, 282, 335n294
motivation, 35, 59, 117, 148, 180, 198, 302
Mūlasarvāstivāda lineage, 10

N

Nāgārjuna, 34, 226, 237, 271
Five Stages, 116
Fundamental Verses on the Middle Way, 16
lineage of view, 13, 113
system of, 127, 128, 262
nāgas, 55
Naktso Lotsāwa Tsultrim Gyalwa, 15, 16, 291
Nālandā University, 4
Nanda's Ordination Sūtra, 120, 142
Nārāyaṇa, 138, 146
Nāropa, 20, 39, 113
nature of mind, 43, 59, 76, 173
Neusurpa Yeshé Bar, 15, 16, 18, 23
Ngok Lekpai Sherab, 15
nihilism, 205
avoiding extreme of, 35
freedom from, 43, 59, 76, 798
not grasping, 81
Nine-Ingredient Black Pill, 226, 237
nirvāṇa
attaining, 155
awakening mind as, 126, 257
of buddhas, 132
as cause and effect, 322n148
for middling-capacity, 37
as mind, 75, 177
mode of apprehension, 78
as not established, 59
and saṃsāra, equality of, 208
nonanalytical cessation, 34–35, 56
nonconceptuality, 41, 81
attachment to, 196, 206
establishing, 181–82
mastery in, 298
practicing, 80
presence of, 167
realizing, 210
remaining in, 161, 335n297
in serenity, 162, 194
nonmeditation, 76, 195, 217–18
nonmind, 76
nonreturners, 125
nonvirtue, 52
attachment to, 65
eliminating, 150
projection and completion of, 58
rebirth and, 50, 55–56
results, 147
subtle, 35, 82, 178
See also ten nonvirtuous actions
Nyangral Nyima Öser; *History of Dharma*, 18
Nyantso, 17
Nyethang, 4, 13
Nyingma tradition, 184
Nyukrumpa Tsöndrü Bar, 19

O

objects of knowledge, 103, 152, 221, 275
obstacles
from distraction, 231
to favorable conditions, 230–31
from harmful spirits, 231–32
human-made, 229–30
incidental, 256
from mental afflictions, 234–36
transforming, 233–34
See also sickness
obstructions, three types, 45, 82, 181, 190
Odantapuri, 4
omens, 221–22, 232, 233, 253, 278
once-returners, 125
One Hundred Salutations Repairing Breaches, 227, 257
one taste, 176, 208, 215
one-day precepts (*upavāsa*), 9, 90, 264, 314n19, 318n90
Atiśa's view of, 31
eight constituents to abandon, 49, 320n126
for lay community, 32
ritual for, 286–87
one-pointedness, 41, 298
Open Basket of Jewels (Atiśa), 39
awakening mind in, 259
on bodhisattva discipline, 292
composition, 5
on vows, 31
oral teachings, 104, 137, 185
Ordination Rite, 122
Ornament for Clear Realization (Maitreya), 107
Atiśa's study of, 4
examples from, 125
as source for *Lamp*, 14
Ornament of Mahāyāna Sūtras (Maitreya), 16
on altruistic thought, 125
on Dharma and enjoyment bodies, 134
practice sequences in, 30
on spiritual friend, 108

P

Paramapurṣa (buddha), 114
Paramasena, 113
path
characteristic of, 171
distractions from, 205
emptiness and clarity of, 170–71
straying from, 174, 208
union of, 42–43, 77–78, 209–10
path integration, 236, 244–45, 255, 335–36n299
path of application, single-session, 66, 323n157
path of preparation, 117, 323n157
path of vision, 117, 322n148, 323n157
path with result (*lam 'bras*), 21
patience, 54, 235
Perfection of Wisdom, two systems of, 112
Perfection of Wisdom scriptures, 131
permanence, 76, 81
avoiding extreme of, 35
delusion about, 152
fixation on, 51
freedom from, 43, 59, 65, 79, 177
view of, 61
Phakdru Kagyü, 24
Phakmodrupa Dorjé Gyalpo, 13
lineages, 21, 26, 113
written works, 21–22
phenomena
emptiness of, 174
mindfulness of, 155
unborn nature, 40
See also dharmas
phenomenal marks, 82
Phenyul Gyal Lhakhang, 24
Phuchungwa Shönu Gyaltsen, 137, 334n279
Piled Up Stūpas Tantra, 116, 280
pointing-out instructions
for insight, 75–76, 139, 165–66, 186, 201–2
in *Instructions for Select Disciples*, 138
meaning of, 183
for serenity, 75, 161–62, 186, 194–95
for signlessness yoga, 216–18
for union, 77–78, 139, 169–72, 186, 208–11

Pointing-Out Instructions in Sets of Five (Atiśa), 12, 22
authorship, 185
circulation, 184–85
on four yogas, distinctive features, 218–21
on insight, 198–206
novel features, 187–88
as oral tradition, 183
overview, 185–87
preliminaries, general, 189–90
on serenity, 191–98
on signlessness yoga, 216–18
supplementary material, 221–22
on union, 207–16
post-meditation, 44, 217, 220
posture
of Amitābha, five-point, 140, 160, 176, 187, 193, 335n296
changing, 213
effort and, 167
not needed, 178
for pacifying sickness, 241–42
while not meditating, 204
Potala Palace, 2
potential, two aspects, 283
Potowa Rinchen Sel, 15, 23
Blue Compendium, 16, 317n75
Dharma Exemplified, 16
disciples of, 18
holder of textual tradition, 137, 334n279
praise for, 25
Sanskrit name, 263, 283
tradition of, 17
pratimokṣa vows
eight types, 258
losing, 126
maintaining, 297
seven types, 30, 38, 69, 123, 126, 279, 318n87
shared for all Buddhists, 122–23
pratyekabuddhas, 117, 303
precious human rebirth, 32–33, 50, 230–31, 265. *See also* freedoms and favorable conditions
pride, 64, 222
abandoning, 108, 197
antidote, 147
Atiśa's, 112
obstacles from, 232, 253, 254, 256
of self, 203
pristine cognition, 278
Prophecy of Mount Gośṛṅga, 122, 124
prostrations, 274
methods and purpose, 116, 328n204
recitation during, 116–17
protection circle, 226, 228
protector deities, 146
provisional goals, 37
purification, 42, 178, 196
of afflictions, 44
of evil deeds, 81
forceful, 245
of misdeeds, 254
obstacles from, 242
through devotion, 175, 178
through mindfulness, 82
Vajrasattva mantra for, 138, 187, 190

Q

Question of the Devaputra Sūtra, 103
Questions of Upāli Sūtra, 120, 140, 181–82
Quintessential Instructions on All Dharma Practices Tantra, 101, 108

R

Radiant Light (monk), 114
Radreng Gomchen, 22
Radreng Monastery, 14, 17, 23, 24
Rahulaguptavajra, 4
Ratnabhadra, 113
Ratnagotravibhāgavyākhyā, 16–17
Ratnākaraśānti; *Prajñāpāramitopadeśa*, 186
Ratnakūṭa. See *Heap of Jewels*
Ratnasena, 113
realization
elevated, 174
enhancement for, 254–55
as obstacle, 253–54
prerequisites, 168
of union, 210–11
as unreal, 206
realm of reality (*dharmadhātu*), 42, 166, 210

investigating, 126, 257
as mind, 78
never moving from, 218
one's own mind in, 170
pointing out, 138
ultimate mind of awakening and, 39
reasoning, 12, 40, 42, 138–39, 145, 165, 242
rebirth, 196, 265
in higher realms, 59, 80
karma and, 147
in lower realms, 52
from nonvirtue, 50, 55–56
Reciting the Names of Mañjuśrī, 131
red instructions, 137
refuge, 90
benefits of, 49, 320n125
as cultivating one's own mind, 282
never relinquishing, 48–49, 118–19
rituals for, 267–68, 280–81, 284–85
supreme-capacity person's, 68, 71
reification, 67, 82, 298
renunciation, 60, 120–21, 122, 232, 245
result
illusion-like, 174
nature, essence, and characteristic, 172
union of, 77–78
reversal of tendencies, three aspects, 150
Rinchen Sangpo, 5, 11, 18
Ritual for Generating the Awakening Mind, 227, 265
overview, 259, 260–63
purpose, 12
supplementary material, 263–64, 283
See also aspirational awakening mind ritual; engaging awakening mind ritual; ultimate awakening mind ritual
ritual of the ācārya, 48
Rongpa Chaksorpa, 15
root downfalls, 164, 295
four, 49, 320n127
in Mahāsāṃghika Vinaya, 49
mistaken systems, refuting, 129–30
numbers of, variance on, 292
voiding, 126–27
root infractions, 69
roots of virtue, 182, 267
affliction and, 182
cutting off/destroying, 126, 129–30
dedicating, 45, 83, 213, 262, 272, 283
four immeasurables and, 268
incomplete, 190
superior, 208

S

Sachen Kunga Nyingpo, 21
Sāgaramatisūtra, 135, 140, 182, 274, 293, 300
Sakya Paṇḍita Kunga Gyaltsen, 23, 26, 262–63
Sakya Throneholder, 23
Sakya tradition, 24
Salu Sprout, 114
Samādhi of Heroic Progress, 270–71
Samādhi That Gathers All Merit Sūtra, 110
Saṃcayagāthā, 279
Saṃvarāṇavatantra, 116, 280
Saṅgha, three classes, 117
Sangyé Öntön, 14
Sanskrit, purpose of titles in, 115, 291, 327n201
Śāntarakṣita, 129
Śāntideva. See *Compendium of Training*; *Introduction to the Practice of Awakening*
Śāntipa, 112
Saraha, 183
Śāriputra, 105
Sarvāstivāda tradition, 335–36n299
Sarvatathāgatatattvasaṃgraha, 138, 187
scripture
divisions, 104–6
nature, 104
six ways of comprising, 105
twelve branches, 117, 325n181
Seal for Ridding and Restoring, 130
seclusion, 21, 41, 74, 75, 82, 165
Secret Night Sūtra, 265
Secret Tathāgata Sūtra, 128
self (*ātman*)
delusion about, 65, 77
grasping, 36–37, 154, 254
mistaken apprehension of, 66, 76
as not established, 245
reversing clinging to, 155, 203, 252

self-cherishing, 203, 255, 297
self-cognizant wakefulness, 43, 78, 201, 236
self-grasping, 61, 66, 212
  abandoning, 76, 77, 169, 245, 255, 297
  reversing, 67
  subtle, 217
selflessness, 60, 66, 89, 126, 257, 297
sensations, mindfulness of, 155
sense desires, 61, 152–53, 155
sense faculties, 80
  not binding, 216
  restraining, 44, 75, 160, 192, 196, 204
  wrongdoing due to, 60
sense objects, 82, 163, 192, 213
sense pleasures, 67, 197, 206
sensory spheres, 71, 257
sentient beings
  acting on behalf of, 279
  emptiness of, 174
  not abandoning, 273–74
  regarding equally, 61
  See also benefiting others; mother sentient beings
separation effect, 36, 37, 45, 181
separation result, 150–51
serenity, 40, 41, 66
  characteristics, 138
  distinctive features of, 219
  enhancement, 196
  hindrances to, 164, 195, 298
  increasing, 81–82
  and insight, indivisibility of, 44, 82
  meditative equipoise, 193
  nourishing, 204
  pointing-out instructions on, 75, 161–62, 186, 194–95
  preliminaries, 159–61, 191–92
  as preliminary to insight, 165
  signs of progress, 163
  stages of, 193–94
  subsequent practices, 196–98
  undegenerated practice, 162–63
Serlingpa, 31
Seven Treatises on Valid Cognition (Dharmakīrti), 106–7, 112
seven-limbed prayer, 127, 267, 274, 340nn353–54
sexual desire, 53–54
shame, 70, 127, 129, 296
Shang Ö Jowo, 23
Sharawa Yönten Drak, 15, 16, 18, 25. See also *Stages of the Path of the Three Types of Individuals*
Shawo Gangpa, 18
Shenyen Balpo, 18
sickness
  antidotes, 242–44
  clearing bodily, 249–50
  integrating into path, 244–45
  lack of intrinsic nature, 245
  mantras for guarding against, 222, 238, 240–41
  medicine for, 236–37
  pacifying with body training, 241–42
  suffering of, 63, 153
siddha culture, 183–84, 230
signless emptiness, 186
signlessness, 139, 186, 187
  distinctive features of, 220–21
  practice, 217–18
  preliminaries, 216–17
  signs of success, 218
  in *Stages*, 81
signs of progress
  in insight, 169, 206
  meditation and, 147
  as obstacles, 253–54
  in serenity, 163
  in union, 179
  on unmistaken path, 82
single-pointedness, 194–95, 199
single vehicle (*ekayāna*), 37
six collections of Madhyamaka reasoning, 107, 112
six perfections, 68–69, 127, 157, 279, 296–98, 304, 324n163
six realms, 50, 72, 152, 153, 171, 196, 209
skillful means, 40
  meditating on, 156–58
  and wisdom, inseparability of, 43, 80, 139, 173, 174, 211, 304
Skillful Means of the Great Secret Sūtra, 127, 128, 129, 130
small-capacity individuals, 214

interest in future lifetimes, 141
outline, 90–93
overviews, 31–36, 48
See also individual practices
Smith, E. Gene, 316n64
solitude, 60, 89, 169, 195
in insight, 204
physical and mental, 81–82, 158–59
places for, 191
remaining in, 163, 215
renouncing activities, 178
serenity and, 191
Sönam Lhai Wangpo, 14, 18
Sopa, Geshe, 320n123
special insight, 66
Special Instructions on Coemergent Union, 39
speech
blessing through, 105
distractions of, 196
nonvirtuous, results of, 54
secret practices of, 251
spiritual teachers, 77, 111, 174
above one's head, meditating on, 161, 192, 199
as buddha/Dharma body, perceiving, 39, 68, 71, 73, 175, 187, 217
characteristics of, four, 189
contempt for, 213
denigrating, 73, 230
despising body of, 170
duplicity toward, 52
inseparability from, 200
kindness of, 254
offerings to, 203, 216, 269
pleasing, 73
qualities of, 108, 109
relying on, 158
role of, 40–41
as root of all qualities, 190
supplicating, 165
supporting, 267
as supreme refuge, 280
as three buddha bodies, 213
See also under devotion
spontaneous accomplishment, 45
spontaneous practice, 251
spontaneous presence, 41, 44, 75, 81, 166, 211
śrāvakas, 68, 174, 295
Śrāvastī, female servant of, 49, 119
stages of the path (*lam [gyi] rim*)
Atiśa's system, 8
earliest use of term, 4
four cycles of, 90
in Kagyü tradition, 20
lineages of, variant, 15
pratimokṣa as foundation, 31
prototype, *Lamp* as, 1
public discourses and personal instruction, distinctions between, 137
and stages of the doctrine (*bstan rim*), distinction between, 14–15, 313n4
synonyms, 14
Tsongkhapa's system, dominance of, 24–25
Stages of the Path of the Three Types of Individuals (Sharawa), 16–17, 262
Stages of the Path to Awakening (Atiśa), 1–2
accompany texts, 2, 12–13
Atiśa's other works and, 4–6
authorship, 9–10, 32
awakening mind in, 259–60
composition, 4
composition oath, 117–18
as endpoint of scripture, 108
Essence of the Bodhisattva Vows and, 291
format, 7, 9
hidden tradition of, 3
homage, 29, 48
introductory material, outline, 90
and *Lamp*, comparisons of, 7, 9, 12, 15, 26, 41
lineage, 26
manuscript, 8
one-day precepts in, 31
overview (table), 46–47
pointing-out instructions in, 184
structure and content, 10–12
sūtra and tantra integration in, 3
title, 115
transmission, active, 13–15, 18
transmission, diminishing, 20, 23–24, 26
stream enterers, 37, 67, 125

Structural Analysis of the Stages of the Path to Awakening
authorship, 87
on middling capacity path, 93–95
overview, 88
pointing-out instructions in, 138, 186
on small capacity path, 90–93
on supreme individuals, 95–99
Subhūti, 105
suchness
as emptiness, 173
ignorance of, 154
meditating on, 242, 243
of mind, 36–37, 65
and pristine wisdom, indivisibility of, 293, 304
realization of, 189, 218
reminders, 236
suffering, 56, 60
casting aside, 146–47
causes of, engaging, 61
as dissatisfaction, 152–53
eight types, 62–64, 153–54, 323n155
emptiness of, 167
as illusion, 252
of lower realms, 55, 76, 94
as mere mistaken appearances, 72–73
as mind, 35, 75, 80, 177
from nonvirtue, 52
as not established, 272
protection from, 67
separation from, 155–56
temporary and ultimate, 68
three types, 64, 323n155
unpredictable, 152
as unreal, 206
wishing to avoid, 50
Sukhāvatī, 274
Sumatra, 4
Sunakṣatra, 40–41, 73
supersensory knowledge/power, 113, 125, 156, 198, 216, 219, 232
Supreme Splendor, 114
supreme-capacity individuals, 138
foundation of path, 125
obstacles, 236
overviews, 37–45, 67
results, 181
reversals of, 180
vows for, 291
See also individual practices
Sūtra collection, 105, 107
Sūtra Gathering All Fragments, 303–4
Sūtra Illuminating Appearance of All Things Distinctly without Their Departing from Their Essential Nature, Emptiness, 134–35
Sūtra on the Fully Pure Monastic Code, 227, 257
Sūtra on the Householder Śrīgupta, 147
Sūtra the Unifies the Intentions of the Buddha, 280
Suvarṇaprabhāsasūtra, 101

T

Taklung Kagyü, 21, 22, 24, 113
Taklung Thangpa Tashi Pal, 22, 26
Tangut, 23–24
Tārā, 113
Teaching of the Armor Array, 168
Teaching of the Great Magical Display, 120–21, 122
Teaching on the Four Qualities Sūtra, 129
Teaching on the Inconceivable Properties of the Buddhas, 131
tempering metal, 168
ten freedoms and endowments, 49–50, 142
Ten Levels Sūtra, 104–5
ten nonvirtuous actions, 34, 294
concordant effects of, 55–56
general dominant result, 56
hell rebirth and, 53–54
three poisons and, 154
ten virtues, 56–57, 150, 279
Ten Wheels of Kṣitigarbha Sūtra, 30, 125, 128–29, 279
Tengyur, 9, 260, 291
textual exegesis
general meaning commentaries, 101
purpose connection (four-point framework), 101, 117–18, 324n174
summary technique in, 87
topical outlines, 88

Thirty-Three Gods, Heaven of the, 114
Tholing, 7, 259
Three Baskets, 105, 136
three bodies of a buddha, 45, 78, 82, 117, 131–33
  aspiration for, 283
  permanence or impermanence of, variant views, 133–34
  protection of, 67
  as result, 71
three doors, 57
three equalizations, 276
Three Jewels
  faith in, 123
  homage, 29
  meaning of, 117
  never relinquishing, 268
  offerings to, 49, 212, 216, 295
  precepts on, 284–85
  refuge in, 116
  as spiritual teacher, 280
  worshiping, 254, 277
three marks, 155
three poisonous afflictions, 105, 154
three realms, 67, 155, 323n160
three spheres, 297, 298
three trainings, 73, 114, 327n200
three types of individuals
  in Atiśa's compositions, 2, 3, 5
  Atiśa's personal guidance on, 13–14
  Chakriwa's awareness of, 19
  as complete teaching, 114
  distinctions between, 30, 48
  four qualities of each, 89, 118, 138, 324n173
  four types of indivisibility for, 293, 304
  in *Lamp*, 7
  overview (table), 46–47
  pointing-out ultimate awakening mind for, 281
  in Sharawa's *Stages*, 16–17, 315n37
  sources for, 29–30
  summary, 89
  supplementary instructions, 221
  in Tsongkhapa's tradition, 25, 317n80
  vows suitable for each, 291
threefold purity, 294, 299
Tibet, 1, 6, 23, 24
Tilopa, 13, 39, 113, 183, 335n297
training, five topics of, 261, 340n346
treatises
  divisions, 106–7
  nature and etymology, 106
  purpose, 107
Trisamayavyūharāja, 113
Tsalpa Kagyü, 24
Tsalpa Kunga Dorjé, 15
Tsongkhapa
  Great Treatise on the Stages of the Path to Enlightenment, 3, 4, 15, 320n123
  Songs of Experience, 25
  stages of the path tradition, 15, 24–25, 317n79
Tuṣita heaven, 113
twelve links of dependent arising, 65–66, 322n148
Twenty Verses on the Bodhisattva Vow (Candragomin), 129, 274, 278
two collections, 78, 116, 297
two realities, 103, 152, 304
Twofold Armor, 185
twofold purity, 172

U

ultimate awakening mind, 39–40, 156
  desiring, 70–71
  generating, 126, 130–31
  generating, controversy on, 228, 257, 262–63
ultimate awakening mind ritual, 279–80
  main rite, 281–82
  preliminaries, 280–81
  preparations, 265
  subsequent practices, 282–83
ultimate reality, 30, 166, 208, 262, 281, 293, 304
union (*yuganaddha*), 40
  benefits, 216
  distinctive features of, 219–20
  enhancement, 212–13
  hindrances in, 179–80
  intellectual understanding, 78–79
  meditations for supreme-capacity individuals, 42–43, 77–78

meditative equipoise, 176
of mind, appearances, emptiness, 43–44
pointing-out instructions, 77–78, 139, 169–72, 186, 208–11
preliminaries, 175, 207
signs of success, 179, 215
stabilizing, 207–8
stages, 208
subsequent practice, 213–15
uncorrupted method, 178–79
vision of, 43, 79–80, 172–74
Upāli, 140
Utpala Ornament, 114
Uttaratantra (Maitreya), 263, 283

V

Vaibhāṣika tradition, 34, 107, 112, 335–36n299
Vairocanabhadra, 113
Vairocanābhisaṃbodhitantra, 128, 130
Vaiśravaṇa, 269
Vajra Pinnacle Tantra, 123
Vajra Rosary, 269
Vajraḍākatantra, 4, 123
Vajradhara, 39–40, 71, 116, 324n166
Vajrasattva, 119, 269, 328n208. *See also under* mantras
van der Kuijp, Leonard, 23, 26
Vasubandhu
lineage, 113
Treasury of Higher Knowledge, 33, 34, 126
Treasury of Higher Knowledge Autocommentary, 17, 29–30, 37, 323n158
Verses That Summarize the Perfection of Wisdom, 131, 190
Vidyākokila, 4, 113
views
correct, 56, 57, 60, 110
free from extremes, 78–79
of perishable aggregates, 76
wrong, 54, 71, 282
Vikramaśīla Monastery, 1, 4, 5, 13, 102, 113
Vimalamaṇiprabha (Stainless Jewel), 119
Vimukisena, 113
Vinaya, 107
as antidote, 105
Atiśa's study of, 4, 112
on causality, 272
on root downfalls, voiding, 126
Viniyatasena, 113
virtue, 61, 214
accumulating, 178
applying oneself to, 65
becoming accustomed to, 57
causes and effects, 150
diligence in, 35, 89
eleven types, 127
emptiness and, 71, 205, 215
gathering, 296–98, 301
obstacles to, 252–54
projection and completion of, 58
results of, 67, 147
subtle, 163
three thoughts while listening to Dharma, 109, 110
See also ten virtues
virtue creation (*dge ba chos sdud*), 127, 279
Viṣṇu, 138
vows, 258
contradictory factors, 148
damaging, 164
five lay, 60, 123, 151
four points on, 127
holders, qualities of, 128
keeping, 128
monastic, 36, 60, 151
protecting, 141, 150, 204
purpose of, 52
repairing, 128–29
ritual, 69, 127–28
three, 123, 279
See also bodhisattva vows; pratimokṣa vows

W

wealth, 51, 64, 74, 153, 212
winds, vital
five elemental, 247–48
karmic, 61
meditations with, 249, 250
wisdom
all-knowing, 218, 221
five types, 45, 82, 131, 332n266
mantra for, 256

nondual, 81
pristine, 117, 172, 245, 281, 293, 304
supreme-capacity person's cultivation, 40
three types, 66, 155, 298
See also under skillful means
wisdom realizing emptiness, 77, 79
wrathful approach, 233, 338n320
wrongdoing, 34, 54, 56, 61, 71, 89

X

Xixia, 24

Y

Yaśomitra, 323n158
Yeshé Dé, 101
Yogācāra tradition, 17, 34, 262, 263, 322n148, 335–36n299. *See also* Mind Only

About the Author

James B. Apple is a professor of Buddhist studies at the University of Calgary. He has published over seventy-five articles on the study of Buddhism. His books include *Stairway to Nirvāṇa* (2008), *A Stairway Taken by the Lucid* (2013), *Jewels of the Middle Way* (2018), *Atiśa Dīpaṃkara: Illuminator of the Awakened Mind* (2019), and *The Old Tibetan Avaivartikacakrasūtra* (2021).

What to Read Next from Wisdom Publications

Jewels of the Middle Way
The Madhyamaka Legacy of Atisa and His Early Tibetan Followers
James B. Apple

This book presents a detailed contextualization of the Madhyamaka (Middle Way) school in India and Tibet, along with translations of several texts in the *Bka' gdams gsung 'bum* (*Collected Works of the Kadampas*), recently recovered Tibetan manuscripts that are attributed to Atiśa and Kadampa commentators.

Saraha's Spontaneous Songs
With the Commentaries by Advayavajra and Mokṣākaragupta
Klaus-Dieter Mathes and Péter-Dániel Szántó

"For the first time, the most important work of spiritual poetry from late Buddhist India is now available together with its only existing Sanskrit commentary as well as the defining commentary for the reception of Saraha's poetry in Tibet. Together these three major works illuminate a rich and dynamic period of Buddhist thought and practice. A magnificent achievement."
—Kurtis Schaeffer, author of *Dreaming the Great Brahmin*

Stages of the Path and the Oral Transmission
Selected Teachings of the Geluk School
Translated by Thupten Jinpa

"Expertly curated and lucidly translated, *Stages of the Path and the Oral Transmission* is a magnificent collection of practice-oriented texts from the Geluk school of Tibetan Buddhism."
—José Ignacio Cabezón, Dalai Lama Professor of Tibetan Buddhism and Cultural Studies, University of California Santa Barbara

The Book of Kadam
The Core Texts
Translated by Thupten Jinpa

"This volume brings key classical Tibetan texts to the Western world."
—*Eastern Horizon*

Essential Mind Training
Tibetan Classics, Volume 1
Thupten Jinpa

"Anyone intrigued by the potential to bend our minds in the direction of greater clarity and kindness will find great satisfaction in *Essential Mind Training*."—Daniel Goleman, author of *Emotional Intelligence*

About Wisdom Publications

Wisdom Publications is the leading publisher of classic and contemporary Buddhist books and practical works on mindfulness. To learn more about us or to explore our other books, please visit our website at wisdom.org or contact us at the address below.

Wisdom Publications
132 Perry Street
New York, NY 10014 USA

We are a 501(c)(3) organization, and donations in support of our mission are tax deductible.

Wisdom Publications is affiliated with the Foundation for the Preservation of the Mahayana Tradition (FPMT).